THE ESSENTIAL
DOREEN VIRTUE
COLLECTION

Includes the international bestsellers
ANGEL THERAPY
HEALING WITH THE ANGELS
AND
ARCHANGELS &
ASCENDED MASTERS

HAY HOUSE, INC.
Carlsbad, California • New York City
London • Sydney • Johannesburg
Vancouver • Hong Kong • New Delhi

Library of Congress Control Number: 2013942841

Hardcover ISBN: 978-1-4019-4425-4

16 15 14 13   4 3 2 1
1st edition, September 2013

Printed in the United States of America

CONTENTS

Part II: Communicating, Healing, and Living with Angels

HEALING WITH THE ANGELS 231

Appendix

Part I: The Archangels and Ascended Masters

Part II: Invocations for Specific Needs and Issues

Part III: A List of Whom to Call Upon for Specific Needs

Appendix

ANGEL THERAPY

Preface from
Doreen Virtue

L ate at night, as a little girl, a strong and loving force would sometimes awaken me suddenly. In my darkened room, I'd see sparkling lights and feel surrounded by an unearthly love that let me know my angels were near. Then, I'd fall back into a sound sleep, assured that I was safe and protected by great, gentle beings.

Over the years, as I pursued my doctoral degree, got married, and had children, I lost contact with the angels. While I still loved everything about them, I stopped talking to them. Occasionally, I'd hear a spiritual voice directing me to make changes in my life. Yet, because my life was so hectic and busy, I often ignored the wisdom of my angel's guidance.

That all changed on July 15, 1995, as I was dressing for an appointment I had at a church in Anaheim, California. An angel's voice outside and above my right ear said, "Doreen, you'd better put the top up on your car, or it will get stolen." I was in a big hurry, so I considered the voice as more of an irritant than a help.

I don't have an extra five minutes to put up my car top! I thought. My white convertible car is ordinary looking when its black cloth top is up, but with its top down, the car is a bit showy. Clearly, the angel wanted me to be unobtrusive so as not to attract the attention of a car thief. The voice continued its warnings about car thieves, but I stubbornly insisted that I had no time to spare.

On the way to my appointment, I felt a negative energy surround my car like a thick fog. Something told me, "Someone has just spotted my car with intentions of stealing it." I was certain that someone would steal my car, so I prayed for protection as I pulled into the church parking lot for my appointment. I parked close to the church, and as I got out of my car, a male voice behind me screamed at me to give him my car keys and purse. My angel's warning had been accurate!

I followed an inner directive that told me to scream with all my might. My shrieks caught the attention of a woman sitting in her car across the parking lot, and she leaned on her horn. All the noise caused the people inside the church to come outside, and the car thief and his accomplice ran away. I was unharmed, and I still had my purse and car. When I called the police to report the crime, I learned that the car thieves, armed with a gun and a knife, had been on a crime spree that day.

That was the day I learned my lesson about listening to my angels! Not only did I begin listening to angels, but I also actively solicited their guidance and help. The more time I spent conversing with angels, the more easily I could hear their loving wisdom.

In my therapy sessions, I began helping my clients hear their own angels. Today, I often act as an intermediary who delivers messages to my clients from their angels. The healing power of the angels exceeds any form of "man-made" therapy I have ever witnessed. The angels have wonderful gifts from God to impart to us. So, I am excited that many of us desire to connect with these divine messengers.

The angels have a different way of seeing ordinary situations. Their messages help us heal our beliefs and thoughts by offering us empowering, loving viewpoints. They teach us how to use our spiritual senses to see, hear, feel, and know the real world that transcends the illusory world's problems.

The angels' style of speaking and vocabulary often seems different from our own. This is partly, I think, because they see the world differently than we ordinarily do. They view everything with love and compassion, and their priorities can differ from our own. Since angels have full use of their spiritual senses, they can see, feel, know, and hear things beyond the physical world. These are some of the reasons why the angelic messages in Part I of this book may, at first glance, seem difficult to read. However, if you spend time reading and meditating upon the words, I think you will soon become accustomed to the angels' unique cadence and point of view. Allow yourself to be swept away by their beautiful perspective, and you'll find the healing power in the center of their messages.

The angels really do offer a great deal of practical wisdom, which we can immediately put into practice. They teach us ways to heal our relationships, our careers, and our health. Seemingly, no problem is too small or embarrassing for the angels. Their message to us is clear: "*Give everything to us, and we will give it to the light of God, where Love purifies all seeming problems.*"

In this book, I hope to fully immerse you in the healing energy of angels on earth and in heaven. This book has two parts: In Part I, the angels channeled the entire text. After praying for their guidance, I would lose consciousness of my body while The Angelic Realm transcribed through my mind and hands directly onto the keyboard of my computer. Often, I would hear their words as they would enter my hands and become typewritten on the screen. Other times, the words completely bypassed my conscious awareness and directly became written sentences on the computer screen.

Rarely was I aware of what the angels were writing through me. In fact, at times, I firmly believed I was typing gibberish. I would set the writing aside, fully expecting that I would see meaningless letters instead of coherent words and sentences. Then, when I'd later read the channeled material, the angels' profound and sweet messages deeply moved me. I learned a great deal from these angelic messages!

I knew the angel channeling was not of my own making for several reasons. First, many ideas and viewpoints that came through were entirely original to me and did not reflect any reading, learning, or introspection I recall personally undertaking.

Second, the vocabulary and syntax choices were different from my own. Often, the angels chose words that were foreign to me. Or, they dictated words that did not make sense. At these times, I'd ask them, "Are you sure this is the word you want me to write?" They would then either give me the go-ahead or correct my understanding of their intended words. For instance, once I wrote the word *ring,* when they had actually channeled the word *sing.* I also checked the angels' unfamiliar words in my unabridged dictionary. Invariably, I'd find that their grammar and word usage was not only correct, but also reflected deliberate choices to convey specific meanings.

Sometimes, as I'd reread the angel channelings, I'd find that it wasn't any specific word or phrase that moved me; it was the overall tone of the passage. The angelic energy has a soft, velvety feel to it. If you measured it on an oscilloscope, its vibration would undoubtedly top the charts in high-frequency ranges.

Jill Kramer, the editorial director of Hay House, and I have left the messages intact (largely unedited), so you will read the words exactly as the angels delivered them through me. The only editing to the original messages consists of adding punctuation, breaking up run-on sentences and paragraphs, and making spelling corrections. Occasionally, I decided to eliminate redundant or ambiguous sentences from the messages. I also reworded some phrases that were unclear because of archaic vocabulary. For example, I changed "Think not . . ." to "Do not think. . . ." Along the same lines, I deleted some words and phrases, which, to me, made sentences difficult to read; for instance, I changed "at this very time" to "at this time." I made these changes only after the angels communicated their approval, and when rewording led to greater clarity without losing the message's meaning. At other times, when I asked the angels to reword the sentences in a more modern way, they readily helped. The angels also asked me to leave in some sentences that confused me, assuring me that in time, these messages would make sense.

When I first channeled The Angelic Realm, I couldn't withstand their high frequency for long periods. After about 15 minutes of channeling, my head would feel numb. Like rich chocolatey fudge, the angels' energy was too rich, too sweet to consume more than a little morsel at a time. Gradually — through the steps described in Part II of this book — my own frequency was cleared and raised so that I could channel for longer periods.

The angelic messages vibrate at such a high level that you may find it difficult to digest more than a few pages at a sitting. Partially, this difficulty comes from our lower-self egos, which do not want us to communicate with the angels. The ego knows that if we fully listen to God and the angels, fear will be eliminated. And the ego's whole life force is fear. So, your ego may try to dissuade you from angel communications. Some of the ego's "tricks" include having you get sleepy, hungry, thirsty, or distracted as you read the angels' messages or attempt to communicate with them.

The angels have presented comforting, healing messages about various human conditions such as fear, addictions, and finances. You may want to read specific pages related to a current situation in your life. It's also helpful to simply flip through the book and read the page that opens naturally for you. Notice how perfectly this page fits your current questions and desires.

In their messages, the angels don't always suggest specific things to "do" to feel better. The healing in their messages is on a deeper level, where it triggers changes in our outlook or decisions to rid ourselves of painful beliefs. The angels' words emanate from love, and so just reading the messages elevates our thoughts and feelings from fear frequencies to love frequencies. We vibrate at the angelic level as we allow our thoughts to ascend and soar to their heavenly energy rate.

In Part II of this book, we have offered specific guidance on ways to create closer relationships and communication with the spiritual realm. Whether you desire to talk to angels, God, Jesus, some other spiritual being, or your dearly departed loved ones, you certainly have all the tools available for divine communication.

The angels have asked me to emphasize that their communication in this book is but one of many steps in a healing path of spiritual growth. Use their words to open a portal of light in any area of your life where darkness seems to reign. Then ask the angels to help you to widen this beam of light until it fills your entire consciousness and permeates your life.

♥ ♥ ♥

Preface from
The Angelic Realm

You are indeed an earthly angel sent here by God to perform miraculous deeds of love and sharing. You are beloved and loving, and we heavenly angels are here to support and guide you. We will help you to purify your life and life vessel to bring you in harmony with the infinite symphony of earthly music that you can share.

This book is a vehicle of our sharings to you who desire to raise your internal vibrations so that more and more light can enter your sphere. We know that you suffer at times needlessly, because you believe you are alone and friendless. Let us assure you that you are not! We are always available for guidance and comfort and will shine the light of love upon any problem with which you wrestle. Let us share your pain, and we will shine it away.

Each of you is different, yet in so many ways you are exactly alike. In the pages of this book, we have guided Dr. Doreen Virtue's hands and mind to share with you some of our thoughts about earthly problems common to you all. We also want you to know that we are available for individual consultation as needed. So when you are alone and blue, reach up and above you. There is always an angel in the room with you, an angel who—if not able to bring the whole of heaven into your consciousness—can at least settle the score in your own mind and heart so that you may be at peace.

Pull down the shades on sorrow, and flip through the pages of this book whenever you feel lonely or depressed, or in need of inspiration. Each topic is in alphabetical order, so you can look at the Contents section to see which inspiring note would be a blessing to you that day.

Might we also suggest that you allow your mind to wander and simply open the book to a page. Trust that your guidance will allow you to find the page that will best impress upon your mind for this day. The radiation of your vibration will magnetically draw you to just the right words for settling your score.

As you read, have faith about what you hear within. For your own angels will sing in harmony with our words in this book. The beauty of your own internal choir is cause for you to rejoice, if you will stay with it in stillness with yourself as you read our words within this book.

Our greatest joy is lighting the candle flame of God's love within your heart, causing you to thirst and hunger for even greater joy. This drive for love, we know, will draw you away from earthly concerns and will put you on the well-worn path of golden light leading straight to heaven. This path within you awaits your desire right now, and we are here, always patient and glad to assist you whenever you feel unsure of your foothold. Just one thought, one cry for our help, and we are there with you.

We are here with you always, beloved. We ask that you enfold us in your heart wings, and cry upon our shoulders until the tears flow no more. You are home with us here, and you have never left our side. You are truly a thing of beauty to behold, and we wash away your tears of sorrow with reminders that there is nothing to do but rejoice, because God made you always and forever our brother and sister in cause.

♥ ♥ ♥

Acknowledgments

God, the angels, and some very angelic people all worked together to create this book. Eternal gratitude to you, Beloved Creator and heavenly angels. Thank you, Michael, Raphael, Gabriel, and Uriel! Thank you, Frederique and Pearl! And heartfelt appreciation to Emmet Fox and The Wise Council.

I wish to thank Louise L. Hay for her kindness, wisdom, and love; Reid Tracy, for his warmth, guidance, and support; Jill Kramer, for her incredible intuitive work with words, love, and angels; Christy Salinas, for her artistic and creative talents, as well as her loving nature; Kristina Tracy, for her awesome dedication to spreading the word of God's Love; Margarete Nielsen, for her wonderful and enthusiastic help with my workshops; Barbara Bouse, for her limitless energy and enthusiasm in support of all the Hay House authors and the wonderful Empowering Women conferences; Jeannie Liberati, for her courageous travels inward and outward for tremendously healing purposes; and Ron Tillinghast, for being instrumental in the support of my books and speeches.

I am also grateful to Lisa Kelm, Adrian Eddie Sandoval, Gwen Washington, Drew Bennett, Joe Coburn, Janice Griffin, Polly Tracy, Lynn Collins, Dee Bakker, and everyone else at Hay House.

In addition, I want to thank the seminar coordinators of churches, conferences, and expos that have invited me to speak about communicating with God and the angels. Thank you to Debra Evans, Ken Kaufman, and Gregory Roberts of The Whole Life Expo; Michael Baietti and Mecky Myers of The Health & Life Enrichment Expo; Dr. Carolyn Miller, Dr. Richard Neves, Robert Strouse, Dr. Susan Stevenson, and Dr. Leticia Oliver of the American Institute of Hypnotherapy; Robin Rose and Karen Schieb of The Universal Light-worker's Conference; Shanti Toll and Stella of the Metaphysical Celebration; Ken Harsh of the Universal Light Expo, and many others for giving me the opportunity to commune with the angels of so many people!

A bouquet of gratitude to the editors of metaphysical magazines for their support, love, and light, including David Allikas of *Psychic Advisor;* Donny Walker of *In the Light;* David Young of *The New Times* in Seattle; Gary Beckman and Insiah Vawda Beckman of *The Edge* in Minnesota; Cindy Saul and Gerri Magee of *PhenomeNews* in Michigan; Joe and Shantih Moriarty of *Awakenings* in Laguna Hills, California; Sydney Murray of *Vision* in San Diego; Andrea DeMichalis of *Horizons* in Florida, and the many others who have been instrumental in spreading love and light through the printed word.

PART I

The Healing Messages

❧ Addiction ❧

What is substance, really? Deep in the back of your mind, you remember being in the heart of God. You recall that feeling of total fulfillment, like being in an embryonic sac in your mother's womb. Feeling your wholeness breathing with her breath. That feeling of synchronizing with another is the essence of love that you miss with your heart and your soul.

Substance is a mass of inert energy crystallized into form. In a sense, substance is wooden or lifeless, but in another sense, substance is comprised of remnants of God's love, since the thought-form is but a divine spark of inspiration leading to creation. You who turn to substance to alleviate your loneliness for God are making the choice for a substitute of lesser quality, but nonetheless the same in origin of your original memory of closeness and warmth.

Think of it this way: You are joining with the substance in an internal cuddle with the desire of ending the nightmare of the external movie. You want an internal change that will bring you closer to the heaven you are craving for yourself and your family. Yet, you are choosing an external source to create an internal state. The two can never be reconciled, so you have set yourself up in an impossible situation. You are, in essence, caught in a limbo of eternal frustration because you cannot force the round peg to fit into the square hole, although you try and try again.

Addiction to substance is best burned away in the same eternal flame of desire that originally ignited it. Use the energy of your longing for love to quench your endless cycle of chasing love. Here is how: Ask to build an internal station of love and light. As you enter your dreams, ask that this flame burn brightly while your subconscious mind takes over for the night. Ask this flame to burn away the dross of your attention; in other words, that which is unneeded in the world.

Your dream time is the best time to ask us to take over, and we will do our best to rearrange your thoughts so that the pyramid of your attention is rebuilt in sequential order. As it is for most of you presently, God is only a small tip of your attention—something you have put as a future priority. We ask and we will help you to rebuild this pyramid so that God comprises the most basic and the biggest rung of your ladder, the basis of your structure and your pyramid. We will help you if you will but make this your intention.

Give us all of your thoughts concerning your addiction. Whether this addiction involves another person or not is of no importance. What we want you to do is give all of your attention to us while we rebuild your thought structure around God and loosen your thoughts around your God-substitute of addiction. We will do this for you if you will let us. But you must hold nothing back, because the entire structure of your thoughts must be rebuilt and reborn in its entirety. If you hold back some thought, say, out of shame, we cannot rebuild the core of your structure.

Give it over entirely to us angels, who even now surround you, and we will construct an empire within you worthy of God and His angels. You will be glad to awaken to dawn with the sunlight bathing your beautiful new structure, built so solidly that there is a glad welcoming of the empty spaces between the pillars. You will no longer desire to fill these empty spaces with substance, because they will instead be filled with light, golden-yellow like the morning sun upon the most promising of days.

♥ ♥ ♥

❧ Anger ❧

When you are hot with lava-red anger within, it would only turn into a smoldering rage were we to tell you to extinguish your true feelings that someone has done you wrong. You feel injured, little one, and who are we to tell you that you are wrong? In truth, you who are a holy child of God are never wrong. However, you may be momentarily mistaken in the perspective you have taken about the truth.

Let us explain: You may have believed that another could take love away from you, or withhold their approval or love of you. This, as you know deep within, is impossible. There is no love to take away from one who shares all holiness with all the world. You are having an argument only within yourself when you feel touched by anger. The lava flows within you over the rocks upon your consciousness, and the hurt and pain seethes with deep sorrow that another could cause you such pain.

"How could they not know how much they are hurting me?" you cry out silently within the chasms of your chest, crying, wanting, desiring for a resolution to your pain. You want the other to know the very depth of your pain. Perhaps you want the other to even feel your pain for but a moment to truly understand the depth of your sorrow.

Yet, again, we emphasize that this battle is with yourself and within your own mind. Do you truly want to live on a battlefield, you holy child of God? Of course you don't, as no angel sent here to earth was ever meant for conflict. You are meant to fly above rage and to see it as if it were a raging river, a flow of constant energy below you, not within you.

17

You can create a space within you presently where peace can reign. Even if you aren't ready to let go of your rage, you can easily agree to create a pocket of space alongside the anger. See this pocket, like an air pocket under water, dance to its own tune of peace. See it filled with a delightful color like an air bubble swimming in circles in its own playful way. As you delight in this playfulness within you, you may want to visualize yourself swimming inside this bubble in your internal playground.

Feel yourself having fun with the freedom of soaring through your inner space. Take yourself on a wonderful adventure where concerns of safety take a backseat to a sure knowingness that you are eternally safe. Feel how right this freedom seems to you, how natural to be swimming in oceans of safety. When you immerse yourself in this consciousness of freedom, you are also free to choose other thoughts that buoyantly float with play and delight.

Your freedom comes from seeing that you swim through life—not surrounded by sharks—but surrounded by angelfish. You are swimming in circles of like kind, and you are surrounded by others who are exactly as yourself. Have compassion upon those in your circle, knowing that they tread innocently like yourself.

If one or more of those around you occasionally swims in your way, will you forgive them and continue your freedom swim? Or will you become dazed and hypnotized by their seeming lack of order, and allow yourself to become transfixed by the gaze on the past? You want flow and harmony, and this absolutely requires a station of attention on the here and the now.

We are here to help you to bring your dance of life and all your relationships back into divine order and harmony. Look around you with your internal eyes right now, and you will realize that we angels swim with you in perfect harmony like a beautiful school of fish. We are divinely connected by mind thoughts that orchestrate our synchronized movements without effort or concern.

Flow with us ceaselessly, and we will catch your occasional lapses of memory as to your true identity. We will encircle you and guide you in a continuous ballet of glory to God and all mankind.

♥ ♥ ♥

❧ *Anxiety* ❧

When your mind is focused upon thoughts of the future, it is natural for you to become afraid. You are wanting to peek over the fence of tomorrow, and glimpse into the time just ahead with reassurance that everything will be okay. Let us do this for you, now, oh perfect child of God.

You have no thing about which to worry, and you have our gentle assurance that everything from now until tomorrow is in perfect array. Give us your thoughts about disorder, and we will reorganize them for you until they are captured in a perfect display of faith. You really have no thing to worry about, holy child, as you are master of your day. There is no problem you cannot surmount today or tomorrow, and we are always around you to catch you any time you should fall.

When you were a child and you scraped your knee on a fall on the sidewalk, who do you think it was that pushed your face up toward the sun so that your tears would dry in the kiss of God's love? It was us, dear child, and we shall never leave or forsake you in all your adult lifetime. We can instantly immerse within your thoughts to help you find your way home to heaven.

Should you begin to worry about letting another person down, we ask you to leave those thoughts to us. Could an angel ever let a loved one down? Remember that you are an angel, you holy child of God. You are an angel sent to earth by Him who loves you in His deepest essence. It is impossible that when your thoughts are right and your intentions heart-centered, that you could let a loved one down.

We will support you in all ways, and even when delays are sometimes inevitable and you wonder if God hears your prayers, never fear. We are near. We hold your hand invisibly and guide you to the exact places and people that will cause joy to stir in your heart. Your desire to provide for your family is so sweet and love-based that God hears your prayers no sooner than you have thought of them in your heart.

God, in His own way, weeps for His child's worries. He asks only that you let Him draw nearer and nearer to your heart so that you will recall that you are not alone on this earth. He asks that you allow Him to flow His unearthly love through your heart and bodily vessel, so that you may carry this precious cargo into the marketplace and exchange it for your needs to be met.

The way to heaven is within. You may wonder whether "within" is locked and how you may enter its shelter and safety from the turmoil of life. You need look no farther than your thoughts, my dear. All you need to do to calm the flames of anxiety is to put your intentions upon calmness. Extinguish the belief that anxiety is a sign that you care about a solution. God knows that you care, and He asks that you clear the way for His intervention into your life.

So right now, take three deep breaths and center and clear your mind for us angels to take over. Let us do the driving for a while as you rest your weary mind and body. You work so hard for so long, and you do deserve a rest while we clear your heart of clouds of worry.

If this seems simple—"Just ask"— it is because it *is* that simple! Simplicity is the heart of God, and the answer to your worry. Do not allow your mind to wring itself out of shape by wondering, "What if this happens?" or "What if that happens?" All those "what ifs" are exhausting, and for no good reason!

We, the angels, sing a song of harmony in perfect grace. The reason for the beauty of this song is its simple melody.

Let your mind be in harmony with this melody by concentrating on just one thing: love. Let this be your mantra while you breathe in and out deeply, and feel your mind clear like the sunshine beams away fog.

You are meant to enjoy sunny days free of worry, dear child. Let us wipe away your fears with our gentle hugs. Turn your frets over to us, and we in turn will deliver them to the Creator where you will never see them return to you again. This angelic amnesia is our gift to you, and your freedom from worry is your gift to us.

❤ ❤ ❤

❧ Arguments ❧

A re you hurt and exhausted by the heaviness of words heaved back and forth between you and another, dear child? Rest in the corner a moment like a prize fighter, while we mop your brow and fan you with flames of love that leave all anger behind. You are magnificent, dear one, and you are encapsulated beauty in all your days without exception.

Your argument is a duel of battling perceptions, using swords of point-of-view that clash over who is right and who is wrong. You may employ other weapons upon one another, yet like little children fighting with pretend slings and arrows, it is impossible that you could hurt one another, in truth. In fact, the only shadow of a ghost of hurt comes from the moment when you decide to engage in a battle of wits with another. This stems from thoughts of competition in which the "prize" is winning the heralded top of the mound. Yet this prize is, in truth, a prison of loneliness and separation; and the residuals are more hurt and prideful misunderstandings.

Holy child of God, see yourself and the other through eyes of mercy that cry as your egos do battle! See that your loudness of words cannot match the loudness and fury with which your heart cries out for love and assurance. If you can take just one drop of the love we carry to you from God, your heart would be filled to overflowing. You would naturally take this excess of love and have it drip and ooze from your very being so that it touches all that even think of you. Your mere presence in this state of mind next to another person is enough to heal all ill will.

Think about it, dear child: There is another solution, another way to heal this situation that does not require you to inflict additional hurt upon yourself! Isn't this the solution you are even now aching for? God would not leave you without a way to unpaint yourself from the corner in which you now cower in contemplation over what you have done to yourself.

You needn't grovel or feel pity for yourself or another, because no child of God is worthy of pity. You merely need to stand up for what is right within you now. By feeling this source of your strength within, you can lead the other person with whom you argued, home. Allow the fleeting memories of your clashing egos to be mere echoes from the battlefield that glint faintly among the merriment of recapturing your youthful knowingness of your true God nature.

There is nothing in truth about which argument can penetrate. The truth is the truth whether anyone dawns upon it or not. You and your friend can argue from now until eternity, but you won't enjoy the truth until you put down your battle instruments and notice your beautiful surroundings. All it takes is for one of you to point to the sunset and say how splendid it is, or to speak of the beautiful mist of the fog or rain dew, and your joint perceptions will be united in agreement.

Think not that you have to lose yourself to win the battle, dear one. You have both already won because, in truth, you never had a way to lose what is rightfully yours. Rejoice in your birthright as a holy child of God, and laugh merrily with all who come your way as you create a delightful place for love and truth to reign freely without restriction of time or place.

❤ ❤ ❤

❧ *Betrayal* ❧

What is at the heart of betrayal, dear one? A feeling of being compromised or unloved? Truly, the person who hurts you is betraying him- or herself alone. This person unwittingly cast a pebble into a pool with ripples that stung you with deep pain instead of a clear reflection of love. Will you now betray yourself further by leaving your true self behind in consciousness? Your focus upon hurt will only serve to further hurt you, precious one. You can do more harm to yourself than any other person by your continually focusing upon this hurt.

Leave the hurt behind, dear child! Do not betray yourself further by walking upon this path of painful contemplation. You do no one justice by holding the hurtful situation in the palm of your hands. And yet you need to heal. So cleansing yourself of hurt will both free your consciousness and rid you of the deep and stinging wound of having a dear one disappoint you.

See now we angels circling around your middle, and notice we are getting closer and gaining in numbers. Our wings are outstretched like one giant circle of a tray around you, and we ask you to place your hands face down upon this tray of wings. Let us warm you from the palms upward with our love. Feel us gliding your energy imbalances to a place of peace and safety with our continuous motion.

You may send your anger at the betrayal from your mind, heart, and gut all the way through your fingers and send it to us. Give us all of your tender and sweet emotions: the love that you feel was taken from you by your friend's betrayal. The feeling of foolishness because you feel you could have known better than to trust this person's sincerity. The feeling that you wasted your time once again on a nowhere relationship. We know just how you feel, dear one.

Yet though we share your hurts and shoulder your burdens, we never lose sight of the fact that in truth, there is no betrayal or hurt. The true heart connection between you and the other person has registered in eternity all the moments of love that it added to the universe. That love, sweet one, can never be undone and never needs to be regretted.

You have done nothing wrong, and you are God's precious child of budding love. Though each of you on earth occasionally stumbles like a toddler taking the first few steps, God and we angels know that your smooth strides are inevitable. You needn't scold yourself or another person for the trips and falls that occasionally occur, even when they seem to be deliberate on another's part.

The consciousness that would cause another to betray you is the same clumsiness that makes babies and little children fall. The inner truth of that person, just as with you, is that the full grasp of love will never lead to competition, manipulation, or betrayal. We ask that you be patient with yourself and others as you all blossom into full emotional maturity.

Be willing to forgive and overlook, dear one, even as you follow your inner guidance that tells you when to keep away from another being on earth. You are put here for a reason, oh holy child of God, and you needn't worry that you must sacrifice your happiness to be in a relationship.

As you heal through forgiveness and clearing releasements, you naturally attract those beings into your life who honor you to the same degree you honor yourself. The rest is natural, dear one, and your path to growth—though laden with trips and stumbles—is a joyous occasion for us to watch. We love you so, and ask that you never forget your true home in heaven in God's heart with us always.

❤ ❤ ❤

❧ *Blame* ❧

Who is there to blame but yourself in this world, and yet ultimately that is not the truth either. A stumbling block of new ones to the path is to place all the blame of the world upon their own shoulders. This is a misunderstanding of the universal law of love. Yes, the cause of all the world is in your mind. However, the solution lies not in self-blame.

Come with us on a journey, dear one, and see yourself from our point of view. Cleanse your negative self-view and know that you are God in disguise as a human. We see you as trying so hard to give, and feeling blocked at every turn. It is as if you are pressing against glass walls that are unyielding, and even now you try so hard to understand our words that you may get a glimpse of heaven even clearer in your heart.

We ask you to stop pressing against the glass wall surrounding you for the moment, and listen with your heart to our words as we speak to you just now. Hear the gentle contemplation and rustling of the wind in your gentle mind and heart. See how holy precious you are as one who only wants what is borne of love. You desire peace, happiness, and a place of rest and safety for your family. You want love and care, and you want to have something to share. These desires are as pure and sweet as a baby lamb, dear one. And if you occasionally twist these desires into ugly contortions of themselves, what is there to care about?

In the ultimate sense, all the pain of leaving your truth for a moment always leads you back to God's care. You see: Everything you do is always from love, for love, and to love. So laugh at the many ways you seek what you already have, and you see how we angels are sometimes amused by your antics. We do wholly care about your trials and triumphs, and we are always with you in all ways.

Still, we ask you to stand back and see our perspective. From the long view, we think you'll agree that there is no thing that you can blame, because there is no thing that can go wrong.

❤ ❤ ❤

✣ Boredom ✣

The word *bore* we find interesting in your vocabulary. It means to drill a hole into a thing, does it not? And do you not agree that boredom is akin to feeling emptiness, as if a hole has been bored into you?

The healing comes, then, from asking the emptiness within you this question: "What are you here to teach me?" Remember that emptiness is always filled as soon as the intention becomes clear to fill it. Your choice, then, is the only matter about which to rest your mind. What will you fill it with? Certainly not more of the same that has already led you to boredom.

Invite us in to fill and heal you! Did you know that angels can fly anywhere, including inside bodies and the essence of your souls? We enter where we are invited, so your time will be well spent in gentle contemplation of how to fill yourself up with loving nourishment. Too many beings sit and stew and blame the outside world for their tender feelings. This experience has taught them the futility of outer blame, yet they continue to practice this set of behaviors because they know nothing different.

We are here to tell you, dear, sweet one, that there is a different way to look at boredom. As we have said, your emptiness is filled the moment you *decide* to fill it. We ask you to choose carefully with what you will fill up your emptiness. Your choice comes to you the moment you decide it, because that's how powerful you are.

If you contemplate sorrow, then you have chosen to fill yourself with grief. From our perspective, grief looks like green, stringy vines hanging inside of people's chest cavities like a damp and dreary forest. You probably wouldn't choose it so readily were you to see its sallow colors. These vines make your inner road blocked and difficult, and we know that makes you weary to press on against yourself.

Boredom is simply a messenger brought down to your awareness by your higher self. It is a gift, dear one, and the moment you choose to look at it that way you will laugh in the gentle presence of the place within you where all decisions are made. Look at boredom as you would look upon a roadblock that triggered you to detour to another avenue. You know that where you are bored, something is wrong! And ignoring problems is one way to feel mired in boredom.

You are truly innocent and so much entitled to your feelings, sweet and holy child. Your feelings of boredom lead you gently, if you will let them, to a place where you are wanted and where you want to be. Tug not at boredom, but let it tug at you and you will soon make fast friends with this gentle place within you now.

♥ ♥ ♥

❧ Breakups ❧

Occasionally a partnership rips apart at the seam, and this results in two partners floating away from one another while each silently wonders if the breakup was the right thing to do. These *regrets*, more than anything from our vantage point, are what cause the heart to bleed and bear pain. If you make the decision to separate, we ask that you be clear about your reasons and that you surrender the decision then to God. Upon surrender, it is vital that you no longer contemplate or relive the moment of separation, for to do so is to inflict needless pain upon a holy child of God (yourself, the other person, and any of your friends and family who are affected).

Healing from a breakup needn't be painful, though we often see humans experience pain because this is what they expect. Yes, the end of a relationship is a sort of death. And death is always accompanied by grieving. Still, grieving does not have to entail the sort of heavyhearted moaning one always sees in old black-and-white movies. It can be a great time for making resolutions about yourself.

Great changes come out of great sorrow. May we then suggest that you take this opportunity of a breakup—whether one is contemplated, inevitable, or just occurred—and use this vital energy to make a journal entry related to your life? Just write whatever comes to mind that lets you know how far you have traveled, mostly due to this most recent relationship. You will see the value of this partnership, whether it continues or not.

Do you see what a gift you have brought to yourself just now by focusing upon your presents in the presence? There is always another way to see any situation, and we ask that you put all your efforts into kindling good.

❤ ❤ ❤

❧ Burdens ❧

Yes, we know you have many heavy burdens upon your shoulders. Would you believe us if we told you that your even heavier burdens are the ones you pull behind you like a mule dragging a plow through thick soil? It is true! Your past, and wreckage from the past that you insist on dragging into the present, are truly your most oppressive sources of resistance to the easy flow of life's gentle grace.

Surrender your burdens, you heavenly angel upon earth! You are much too young to shoulder such a tiresome burden any longer. It robs you of the glory of life, and fatigues you to the point where you do not feel well. Don't think a second longer about your past in any manner such as the person who contemplates which items out of his closet he shall donate to a worthy cause. Donate it all! You don't need a bit of the past, and as long as you believe that you do, your collection of wearisome thoughts will ceaselessly tire you in the present.

When birds fly to a new locale, they don't spend their time wrestling about the trees and countryside they just left. To do so would interfere with their here-and-now process of being fed and sheltered. It is no different for you, dear one. You are being gently guided to allow us to disrobe you of the heavy garments you need no longer carry.

Simply say to the light around you this declaration of your truth and freedom: "I shall no longer carry my past, for it is a burden, and I choose now to lighten my load. I give this past entirely to you, God, and I let go of all impressions of myself borne out of past experiences, now. Today is the day when I release myself and shed away all unneeded skins from days afar. I am free, wholly free, and I needn't worry a bit about this process, for You are here with me."

Your breath can blow away a thousand years of pressure in just one single instant of fully committed release. Push the past out of your body and conscious awareness through your lungs. Breathe, breathe. Blow, blow. Press it out with your single-minded decision to be free. You are your own jail-keeper, sweet angel, and we flutter about you even now in support of your new lightness.

You are becoming one with us in consciousness, and we applaud you for resisting all temptations to return to a burdensome mind-set. Remember that we are here with you in all ways, and we honor your commitment to freedom. We won't interfere, we promise, unless you ask us for help in some way. We only ask that you not wait a moment longer than you need to before calling our name with a single thought or word of, "Angels!" We see you extending yourself far too long before you ask for help, and we stand beside you praying that you will collapse your efforts to withstand so much pressure on your own.

You will soon see that there is no room for burdens in heaven, and the heaven you seek is right here on earth. Share the load with us, dear one, and you will easily be lifted of a weight you may not even know you carry. We ask you to lighten your life on behalf of all the other earthly angels who need you.

❤ ❤ ❤

❧ Burnout ❧

What could be scarier than to not like your job and not see any way out of this mental trap? So many of you find yourselves in this position that we are creating an entire chapter on this topic. From where we are, we see burnout as a cry for help and attention from your emotional body. Just as your physical body tells you something is wrong when it cries out in pain, so too does your emotional body give you clear signals.

Now what do you suppose your emotional body is trying to tell you with this feeling you call "burnout"? Of course, you know that it means some changes are necessary in your work life. Did you know that you can make these changes and still be 100 percent safe? It is true! You needn't hesitate in listening to your emotional body because you believe your situation is futile. We are here to guard you in all ways, including the transition of making your career match your expectations of yourself.

Let's put it this way: When you suffer in silence about your job, you are blocking the flow of light into the world. You are meant to be a great healer in whatever capacity your career takes you. When you seek to stifle your emotional body's cries, it feels rejected like a little child, abandoned and unloved. So you can see why it throws a fit and finally gives up. This giving-up is the dead feeling accompanying burnout, and it is tragic indeed.

It is also useless to try and fight it. Your dead-horse emotional body has gone to sleep like a numb arm that you slept upon too long. You can only revive this part of yourself by rolling over to the other side and rubbing your arm. Your emotional body comes back to life when you stop sitting on top of it, when you roll over and give it some attention.

We'd like you to spend some time alone in gentle contemplation with yourself, dear one. We'd like you to have a notebook ready because the ideas will flow, and we want you to capture them on paper. We are here to support you, and one way we want to reassure you is that everything will get better. *When?* you ask. As soon as you want it to, we answer. Will you—that is, the little you that walks around all day— stand aside and allow your inner self some air time? Is this not fair from the being whom you expect to pleasure you, and whom you pummel the moment this being becomes depressed?

Yes, it is fair to allow your emotional body to vent some of its trapped energies. You needn't decide that you will follow this being's guidance just yet, so please don't think we are asking for your full commitment in shifting your life to suit your emotional body. You are better off simply making an appointment to hear out your inner self, who has much to tell you.

Together, the two of you can work out a compromise agreement so that both of your needs can be met. Usually, this means that you will ask for a slow and safe change of events, and your emotional body will be relieved to be heard, and that change is coming. The two of you are friends, dear one, and you needn't part as enemies through burnout.

♥ ♥ ♥

❧ Career ❧

We think the word *inspiration* is integral here, because you can get inspired about what kind of career will bring you joy. We say "joy," because that's what a career is all about. You are a drop of sunshine sent here to kiss the earth's morning dew. Imagine the joy the sunshine receives as it radiates outward in extension of God's eternal glow. Now you will see why we mention joy so early in this discussion of career.

So many of you have decided that you are up against a wall with your career and that you are "held up" by outside forces that govern your choices. Dear children, nothing could be further from the truth! We wish you could see yourselves from our perspective, where we watch dear children giving up their perfect freedom. It is tragic indeed to see so many of you trapped in jobs that suffocate your very essence of joy.

You don't have to stay where you are unwanted, dear ones. Release yourself in mind first from a job that cannot hold you, and see your body soon be released in turn. Hold this in your hearts, especially as you go to bed each night: "I have nothing to fear. I make the choice to hold my joy in mind as I think of my career." Do just this and you will feel a jump and shift in your consciousness, dear ones.

Your readiness to seek the career of your choice is the next thing we will address. Many of you dream of the day in the *future* when you will be made ready and prepared for your consciously chosen career. In our opinion, this is a mistake in consciousness. We ask you to stay grounded in the day that you are in now as you think of the career. In this way, you bring your dawn to you now, instead of the next day.

Do you know what we ask? We are saying to stay in the moment with your wishes, and as you contemplate your next movement, say to yourself that it is at *this* moment when change occurs. Not next, not never. But now. Congratulate yourself for staying on top of this truth, because it is very difficult for mortals to see. But we ask you to learn this for yourself and then teach it to others, because we must pass this one along.

So many are seeing their jobs through the sight of a child who says, "When I grow up, I'll be this or that." This means of consciousness never leaves most adults who continue, well into their older ages, to see careers from this future orientation.

Today is the day, and now is the time! There has never been a better day for you to be grounded in thoughts of your right career. And what is this career? Well, we have left this important part for now, because it is at this moment after making the conscious decision of now, that we get to this next part of how.

Of course you know, or try to know, that your career is the essence of your giving being. As you extend outward like the sun's radiation energy, you are giving of yourself outward. You are actually growing in size and radiation as you give of yourself. And you receive, too, in the blink of the eye of the pulsating giving and receiving rays of the sun. See this in your mind's eye, and you will get a glimmer of what a career is all about.

A sun cannot pretend to be a moon or vice versa. Know what are you essentially, and you will know what you automatically send and receive. You must radiate your natural qualities, and many of you are not aware of these beauties within you because you have not yet taken time to *list them.*

We urge you to do so, and as you list these qualities, feel them spreading outward from within you.

This is your career, to shine outward always in ever-creative ways. Your artistic abilities are shining even now as you think about this. Imagine what you can do once you contemplate them even further. You have the essential ingredients to paint a magnificent picture around you, in whatever fashion suits you. We support you in all ways that it takes for you to be in your natural self, extending and pulsating outward beautifully, like the ray of the sun whom you are.

You are your greatest asset, and you seek to "employ" or use yourself to the highest degree possible. That is admirable, dear one, and we seek to assist you in this endeavor. Rather than call you by name in assembling your employment, we shepherd you in ways that will tend the larger flock. We gather 'round you in our midst and give you our blessings, which are our greatest means of elevating you and your surroundings to the highest ideals.

You see, it is not on the material plane where we are most effective. Yet, our effect affects the material plane very profoundly through your shifting of awareness upon your heavenly duties. In every interaction with another, call upon your heart to teach him about the LOVE that is within him. For that is your job, dear child. Help one another to get past the crying out of His holy name, and get onto the realization that His love resides within us all.

The tenderness of the mercy that you show to a brother will shower you with a resonance that is impenetrable by any darkness. For no darkness can reside within the joy once its light is awakened. Your beam radiating strongly from your heart into his, is enough to alert your brother to his sleeping holiness. Use not words, but a smile. Seek not action, but a thought instead. Capture your attention upon the light within us all, and see its magnificence grow within your holy sight. For you are the light upon the hill that shines to all brothers who would seek for this sustenance.

Do you then see that the form of employment is secondary to this outward reaching? Now in this minute are you able to heal a brother of anything that may frighten him! You are wholly capable of erasing all bad feelings that capture the hearts of another. *Use* your power, dear one! And use it well!

Be not afraid to swell in love for one another. Your magnificence is greatest as you open wide your heart and encircle each being with loving eyes, just as we angels who look upon each of you and see but glory in who you are. For our jobs and your job are one in the light and the greatness that is God before and within us. The mighty mountain you seek to climb is beneath your feet this very moment, dearest being. And as you stand trembling with the energy of determination, lose not sight that this is the moment that is pinnacle above all the others. There is no more precious moment in which to embrace a brother than now.

❤ ❤ ❤

❧ Changes ❧

When the autumn leaves fall, do you cry at the change in the season? Perhaps, just a little. Too soon the earth seems to change before you are ready, and the seasons shift without asking anyone's permission!

Do you feel the earth shaking below your feet as though your life was trembling with rippling fear? Do you feel shaken by confusion over which direction to take? Changes are coming into your life and you feel out of control over containing them. You also feel undecided about which route and avenues to take for your desired outcome. Worry not, dear soul. You have come to the right source for which to unburden yourself.

You see these changes as giving pause and interrupting your flow of events. We see the changes as the flow of energy beneath your feet as you are propelled into motion. The flowing river changes endlessly as it carries a boat upon its back. The changing motion of your life is doing much the same, sweet one, as it carries you safely and swiftly across some spots of life you wouldn't have liked to tarry upon. For you see, beneath the raging river are craggy rocks that—were you to stop and ponder your options awhile—you may have become snagged upon.

So give thanks for the swiftness with which your life now changes directions, and for heaven's sake, don't impede its flow. For you never know which moments you hesitate or resist may land you upon some rock below the surface.

Caution is given you from within when you need it, and you can readily trust this riverboat guide on your safe passage to the far banks in unknown places. Remember that your guide has been on this river in many lives and in many times. Although it seems unfamiliar and uncharted to you, your guide is quite comfortable and at home. Perhaps it's time for you to hole up in your cabin and enjoy the ride.

There is a sweetness within the temporary turmoil as you float down the river, and none so gentle as the rocking of the sweet earth mother's song as she cradles you within her ever-steady motion. Your rhythms of life are now unconstricting and are becoming more natural. Do not be alarmed at the changes going on within you and in your life. Every moment of the ride, you are in full capacity to shift your weight a bit to the side, and so steer the course ever so slightly.

So you see that you *do* have control, through your thought and intention. The control comes from gentle decisions, dear one. Just as a child caught in a riptide becomes endangered if she panics and fights against the water's pull, you also find your safety and power from relaxing and knowing that you have all the options you want within your mind. Use that power with grace, little one.

Remember Who your creator is, and how He thrusts onto you an equal measure of creative power. You have no need to fear your own power, for it is eternally part of you. What we are saying is that resisting changes is a power-less way to control your life. But making a firm decision is a power-full way that never fails. Use your power with grace! We urge you to be in charge of your faculties, as you co-create with heaven. You are in charge. Yes, you truly are.

The decision is yours, and so our question to you is this: "What do you want?" Perhaps you are unhappy with the changes occurring around and within you because they represent that which you do not wish to see within yourself. Is your inner you spilling out and pouring into your outside world? Instead of crying at this occurrence, you can use this as your chance to mop it up inside and outside. In that respect, the change is always good news. Change is always for the better. You needn't resist; you only need change your mind, and you will capture your life flow like a tamed river.

♥ ♥ ♥

❧ *Child Abuse* ❧

We have seen many of our little ones getting hurt in many ways, and we would like this to stop. Our heart energy soothes the little ones who needlessly suffer at the hands of fearful adults. Yet we know our sympathy will only add to the rage, and so we offer you another solution.

Did you know that if you stop and pray once an hour, "A solution will be done," that you pause the time in which the darkness pretends to be the light? You pierce the veil of darkness and reveal its truth to light so that it pales into a faded background where sweet tones of music shine forth in gladness, with all hands clasped in one circle of friendship.

Do not delay this undertaking, for we support you from the heavens to watch over and guide your prayers for the children. Even still, a mere handshake from heaven is not enough to unearth the very being behind this cruelty to our children. We need testaments from ones who, like you, care so deeply for the children that their hearts are frozen with indecision about, "Whom shall we help?" and "What shall I do?"

Move forward with grace and unity away from this indecision that paralyzes your actions from stemming forth from the love that is inside you. We are calling you to action, not from an angry heart, but from a heart so filled with love that it melts the darkness within those who would hurt the children.

Do you know what we say, dear one? We are calling you to our hearts so that we may gather together all souls concerned in one united effort to heal away the cause of this hardship. There is no solution on earth to end the suffering of millions of children, so we ask you to turn away from inspecting the suffering in hopes that this will lead you to its cure. It only brings more suffering when you study it, precious children of our Holy Creator!

Do not seek to cure ills with your close inspections. Turn inward instead to One Who knows all answers. He calls you to gather at His side and turn all ills and cares over to His loving grace. As He ferrets out decisions and calls you to grace your abilities with action, you needn't hesitate in inaction as you wonder if His call was mistaken. God makes no mistakes, and He knows fully of what you are capable at this moment!

Be in gladness as the Creator incorporates your loving being into His mighty plan to end all suffering upon the earth. He is magnificent, and you are His greatest miracle. You mustn't prolong the sadness an instant longer by investigating whether the call to greatness within you is or is not the genuine article. Trust that it is, and you will feel enveloped in the mighty love that enfolds you even now.

You uncover your greatness, which is the cause of healing all humanly mistakes, as you uncloak your eyes from the blindness that hides you from the awareness of His love. Make no further mistakes with these precious children whom He leaves in your care, dear ones. You are called to shepherd them in the way that He points for you.

Ask Him to direct you for the social change that fuels your passion. He is the instrument of healing, and you are His social cause. You are the fuel that gives love to many parents and that heals their hearts from the fear and brings them solace. Heal their fear and guilt, so that they too may drop to their knees in awe of the Magnificent One who greatly loves them. Abandon your judgments with haste so that light may flow through you, and flood all with whom you speak.

You are not to direct this healing flow in any way but the way which nature intends for you. You are simply asked to draw back the curtains that contain and seal the light within you, and become like a clear-paned window that indiscriminately allows the sunlight to radiate through to all who would touch and see it. You are a window to God for all who seek Him, dear one, and your shepherding skills are innately yours. Allow them to shine as you bring others to His light so that they may heal and thus bring forth the love to their children.

All is healed now in this instant that we come before Him. Let us sing in unison, "Hallelujah, Hallelujah, His mighty will is in loving service to all."

♥ ♥ ♥

❧ Children ❧

Precious little ones are gifts to you, in strangers, in blood, and in all. We seek to unite you in their laughter, and we urge you who have sought for inner peace to listen for the utterance of a child, which will bring you home to your heavenly ways. You are refreshed in their laughter and gaiety, so you needn't see childlike play as annoyances that interrupt the important duties of the day.

In effect, their laughter is a release from the stringent tightness that threatens to strangle your body and your mind. You become tight during days when you pretend to like that which you actually abhor, and your breathing becomes shallow and uneven. Do not discount what this lack of oxygen does to your cells, precious child! We urge you to relax from tightness and to learn of a child's ways, which will lead you in directions from which your air-force can more steadily flow in relief and harmony.

There are contagions in the world thought that promote disharmony. Children know not of these factors, as their minds are still fresh from the heavenly home. Allow their mind-set to take over your awareness for a little while, and feel the refreshment course through your body as it brings you home. Their natural curiosity may lead you to inspect a caterpillar at close distance. Notice how its fuzzy little feet bounce gaily upon the loam, and the gentle way it cuddles and crawls.

Do not lose this ability to gaze fondly upon nature, precious one. We urge you to heighten your awareness of the natural wonders around you. It is this healing message that children urgently bring you from the Creator. They cast their reminders upon you daily, yet how often do you see them as signals for your annoyance? Do not shirk off children's innocence as worthless, as they are our most helpful teachers upon the earth.

Do you see what we are after here? A complete reversal in the order in which you place upon other persons. There is great value upon the world's order of teachers, which, in fact, is in reverse. There are teachers of many sorts, that is true. But the greatest teachers of them all are fresh from heaven, and they bring with them the triumphant song of grace and wonder. They are awed by simplicity; a value that you can learn to do on your own.

Use the children as your sure witnesses to God's wonder and grace, dear one, and you shan't go wrong as you circle and climb upon paths of greatness in your lifetime on this earth. Their wings may be folded from your sight. But you have our assurance that the little ones are mighty angels sent for your assistance upon your emerging planet. They bring you wondrous gifts, if you will but sit a moment and chat with a child and use your open willingness to see in a new way.

Are you asking us if children should intervene upon the politics and policies you have upon this great earth? Certainly we see room for such an intervention, but with practical considerations melded with their gentle, innocent wisdom. You would do well to consult a child before making a new law, and to ask the child's point of view about items of great importance.

You will hear, in the child's very breath, a gentle love that points to a bountiful profundity of wisdom. Allow the child's sweet power to sweep all dissonance away. Remember that they are fresh from the Creator and have not yet allowed themselves to lose His lessons, as many of you who have been here longer already have.

Replenish yourself from the well of His fountain by the

grace of His heavenly angels whom you call "children" upon this earth. God be with you in all ways, for we place His mighty sword of wisdom into your hearts as you are called upon into action on behalf of all children everywhere. The fight is not within your home, but within your heart. Surrender it to God, and you will find victory everywhere He is. And He is here, even now, dear one. He is in your heart and in your home. Trust in the Love, and you shall not be pulled apart by any faction in any time, precious and holy child of God. You are loved. Remember that always.

❤ ❤ ❤

ℵ Communication ℵ

As a tool of communication, speech is a poor substitute for the heart and eyes. We are leaning upon many of you to awaken these uncovered tools in glad awareness of all that they offer to you. First, if you awaken your heart energy and uncover this as the tool that it is, you will find yourself connecting much quicker to those around you.

There is an unconscious energy between all people, no matter what brings them together. Perhaps you have been aware of this "shadow conversation" that follows your outward conversation. Listen in on the shadow conversation with your inward ear, and you will hear another side of your relationship with others. The honest truth is spoken here at this level, as one child to another who holds nothing in secret from the other.

This is what you may refer to as "the heart of the matter," because it truly is central to all your dealings with other people. You may, then, want to monitor not only what is received in these silent conversations, but also what it is you put into this flowing bloodstream of invisible energy between you. Watch what thoughts you drop into this bloodstream, as they are rapidly carried to another and received at the level of conscious truth. Your thoughts of daggers or of swords are received as painful tugging at the ears of the other. Your envisionings of love are received as such.

Enter this flow of conversation as it already exists, and eavesdrop upon your silent self speaking to another. You may be amazed at what you hear, but doubt it not, for it will guide you in silent truth to another who is like you. Have compassion upon yourself and another as you hear the cries of the heart that are spoken at this level. The conversation is there, and if you are aware, you will hear it at the level at which it is spoken around you right now.

❤ ❤ ❤

❧ *Crime* ❧

We wanted to talk to you about crime from the perspective of safety. We know that many in your world want to shield yourselves from crime, and we have some answers. Release your need for safety, and relax. The world is contemplative right now, and we bring you into safety through your receptivity, not your tension.

Passion is the heart of crime; it's a soul stirring with no feeling of escape. This creates a tremendous energy that is visible to all in The Angelic Realm. Believe us that we will warn you if we see a thunderstorm of this magnitude coming your way. Yet, through your tension—though you believe it to be a raincoat against torrential rains of negative activity—it actually makes you drenched with it.

We cannot permeate your shell with our warnings, so do you see that your best defense against criminal activity during these shifting times is to have no defense at all? We know this seems illogical in your world, and it is certainly paradoxical unless you consider the unseen world through our eyes.

The colors of dark criminal activity are so vivid that we act like forest rangers spotting fires in the distance. We see pockets of safety, and we keep you there while the world is madly adjusting to its new spiritual speed and realm. There will be fires burning bright, and as you reawaken your spiritual sight, you will see them along with us.

Do not become casual about crimes, yet do not overadjust your life in preparation for crime, either. For, whatever you expect is bound to happen, and we will always bring you to safety. You do us a great service, therefore, whenever you purge your mind of worries and fears about perceived dangers in store for you. You do not want to draw negative energy to you, so do not cast your line in the water trolling for it. Throw it back, if you've already caught it!

What we mean, dear one, is this: Do not in any way clutch dearly to thoughts about your physical safety. We do look out for you day and night. That is part of our job. Yet, you do yourself much disservice when you clench your jaws and brace for unsafety in the world.

Dear one, please learn that the world but reflects your wishes! Would you wish for danger? No, of course you would not. Then we implore you to rid your mind of thoughts of safety, for you do not know the power of your mind in this regard. You are like little children playing with a powder keg, not knowing the danger you bring yourself every time you contemplate the question, "Am I safe?" For we see black smoke released from your mind when you pose such questions, and this smoke is a signal that draws forth the very thing that you fear.

We do not tell you this to scare you further, dear one. But we realize that you must know how much power your mind has given you to draw anything you contemplate at a moment's notice. For this, you can be grateful, though. God would not give you any gift that you could truly misfire. Though you may, in fact, draw great danger to yourselves with your thoughts, it is merely child's mischief in the whole scheme of things.

For you see, gentle spirit, that you are not in any grave or mortal danger in your truest essence. That part which detaches from the body is the true makeup of who you are, and even now this part of you giggles at the preposterous question of its own safety. There is no danger that can be posed to this gentle giant within each of you.

You are sleeping, resting comfortably within the very shell

of God's heart. And He would see that nothing can harm you, not now, not ever. Rest well, sweet one, as we gently sing you lullabies that free your mind of worries, cares, and all contemplations that are not of heaven or of your true home.

♥ ♥ ♥

❧ Dating ❧

When you go out on the town, do you know that you bring one or more of us along? We love to see love, and we will gladly intervene — when asked — to keep the transitional love flowing along smoothly. We realize your dates can be anxious affairs. Rest assured that we are here to help you, not only in The Angelic Realm, but beyond.

We can assist you in getting to the heart of the matter with your date quite quickly, so you will know without doubt whether this is a being you would want to spend time with. Ask us to show you — we'll help to guide the right words out of your mouth so you can adjust your frame of reference with this other person right away.

Your countenance upon a date is an outward focus, and we try to draw you inward instead. Think of a flower. Its petals are its beauty, but the beautiful petals draw from the lifespring deep within the flower's core. Your core upon a date, centered within your own wellspring of healing and eternal energy, is the fragrance that attracts love to you on even your first date. Allow your fragrance to be cast upon the wind around you, mindful only of your inner essence of joy.

What we are saying, dear reader, is to cast away all cares, worries, and concerns that are along this line: "How do I look?" "What shall I say?" and "What will it cost?" Put your cares into your center core where they will dissolve away. Your eternal attractiveness is assured within this central point of your being, dear one.

We ask you to withhold your fears and put your intent inward upon your date. We are not asking you to become reclusive or introverted. Not at all! Your internal frame of reference will bring you sparkling conversation and immense joy with others, be it a date or other social setting. We see those of you enjoying yourselves the most, who are staying centered in this sacred space while in the company of others.

We ask not that you become disinterested in others' welfare, but that you stay centered in your own true space of being where your interest naturally bubbles up in authenticity. What we mean to say is this: Your essence is charming, and you needn't worry that you would lapse into a being that bores or repels others.

The others in your group and on your date are conversing with you on the invisible plane, and they know when you are being truthful or not. The true attractiveness of your honesty is unforgettable, and you needn't trust us on this one. Try it alone, and then ask us to help you, and watch how others react.

With us, your spirit swells attractively, and you bring with you into any conversation a third ingredient that adds a delightful dimension to the room. Others will become vividly attracted to your every word without knowing why. Your ingredient is the invisible essence of spirit, dear one, and you are asked to bring it to every being with whom you interact.

Your gift of swollen spirit is an unmistakable one, that awakens others to their long-forgotten hunger to reconnect with who they are. You are a catalyst for change, dear one, whether you are on a date, at a grocery store or bank, or standing in a long line. Use your time wisely for the sake of spirit, and all your relationships will turn out healed. Remember, you are not alone.

Granted, we may come along with you on your date, but you can also block us out at any time you choose. We are mute when anger is in the air, for instance. We are made invisible whenever frustration hits the air. So you choose and you are in control. You tell us where we can help you along, and we gladly do this in exchange for seeing your happiness, dear child. We are meant to help you along on this earth, and when coupling occurs on a date setting, we sing in the heavens with music and laughter. We want to help!

♥ ♥ ♥

ᚩ Death ᚩ

Departing from this earthplane is one of life's early lessons. You do it so often that one would think you would be adjusted to it by now. Apparently you forget some of your earlier lessons so that you may encounter some later ones. This is fine, because this is God's law. Some of you remember leaving the earth plane in earlier years, and this leaves room for some of the rest of you to catch up on all the news about what is after this life.

One thing is sure: You will not be needing this body in the afterplane. We help you to adjust to a new, ready-made body that fits your skin better than any earthplane body! We inject humor to help you see this transition called "death" in a new light. You needn't fear this change, dear one. It is coming. That is inevitable. And we can help you prepare for this transition in such a way that your earthplane life is not interfered with.

We see people who are here on earth contemplating the afterlife. We wish them well, and we see them as seekers of the truth and light. But we caution them to return to an earlier, innocent, and childlike focus of the earthplane.

Do not be so concerned about, "What is after this life?" We will tell you all that you need to know, but not so much that your time left here on earth is ruined. If we were to tell a starving man about all the delicious delicacies awaiting him someday when he gets to a restaurant, that would be cruel. The rest of his days when he is not in the restaurant would be ruined in anticipation of what is next.

We ask that you do much the same and focus on what is here for you now. There is so much to gather and share here on the earthplane, dear children! Do not let the surprise of what is in store for you be anything but a glimpse of your focus. Do not be overrun with thoughts of heaven, for you do have access to it while you are here on the earth. Life will take care of itself, if you will let it.

Things will not be that much better for you in the afterlife plane if you waste your life thinking about your future in heaven. Of that you can be sure. Just think of the joy you will feel in reviewing your solid gold life spent in service to your siblings here on earth. Then compare that to a life spent in future contemplation and without dutiful action.

There is joy in giving, dear one! Do not believe us, but simply try it for yourself and see. This is the essence, the bloodstream of life. The desire to serve comes masked in many ways, and one of them is the obsession with death and heaven. You think you become an angel when you get here, but the truth is that you are right now called to perform heavenly acts while among those upon the earth. You can do it. You can give so much, even when you believe you have so little to give.

Dear one, how can we convince you of the rightness of God's plan? You needn't take our word for it, but we do need to push you just a little to tip you in the right direction. Give service in whatever way feels comfortable to you, and you will fear death just a little bit less. Then give each day, and watch all cares about death dissolve and then vanish.

♥ ♥ ♥

❧ *Depression* ❧

We are nearby when you are downtrodden. We glimpse your sadness, not to understand it, but to revel in your glowing, which does seem to burn brighter once you turn your yearnings for love inward. You turn inward upon yourself in sadness and end up in revelation, from which gladness is born.

Your wiseness in using this energy to feed upon yourself is engendered with sweetness. For, at times in which you turn inward to lick your wounds, we gently cradle your soul in our wings and hold you even when you will not feel our presence encircling you. You shut us out, yet there is a knowingness that your call to us for help has been met.

And though you long to review the stinging of salt within your wounds, we give you flowers of gladness that pull you out of your sorrow and into your heaven within. So when your emotions seesaw, know that this is your glory being revealed amidst the clouds you feel are within you. You, at times, long for the clouds to cover you in sadness so that you may spend moments cloaked away from darkness. You use your sadness as a means of escaping from the world you choose to see as cruel and demanding.

We applaud your grace in turning inward, sweet child of heaven. Yet, turn inward whenever it beckons to you! There is no better moment than now for you to return to your refreshing pause that is but a moment away. Whether in sadness or in brightness, refresh yourself often as you drink from your inner well.

Your time is of your own making, and we nurture you gladly from whatever standpoint you take. We give you this push, though: That sadness is just as easy to choose as is the shining light. We don't discount your sorrows. We merely seek for you a way of joy, as your shining beacon beckons others to come hurriedly out of the storm into their own inner sanctums of shelter.

Use your beacon to shine warmth onto other lives, and feel your own coldness melt briskly away. You are a haven from the storm for others, and your greatest moments of glory are used as a lighthouse for smiling souls. Your name is written upon heaven as a shining example of those who have similar sorrows. Use the momentum of the storm to gain strength. Feel the pulsing storm push you further in your life, giving you courage and expansion.

Your respite of depression is used wisely indeed, when it leaves you feeling resolved to be your own captor no longer. We see you breaking free from the encircling of darkness and leaving the prison walls so gladly behind. The applause of the thunderstorms cannot scare you when you put it into this context.

Your breath is the life force that propels you to find a gentler breeze. Your surroundings are but mirrors of your choices, dear one, and your gentler days are coming to you even still. There is no way for us to settle into your patterns if you would hold us at bay. Use our flutters to open the wings of your heart, and feel the light come flooding in, although you may fear more pain of darkness.

Your choice is the essence of the direction in which your life is leading you. Think not that victimhood is upon you, for you have been the captor of your own very soul, and you are the releaser that frees every being with whom you come in contact. Choose freedom, then, for everyone, and you choose freedom for yourself.

And on this bright day, your glory can be seen for miles

away. For you are a shining example, and let others see this blaze of freedom upon you. You are the freedom that others now seek! Set no weights upon yourself, in thought that such weight would earn you glory. They but delay you, so do no more self-penance.

The blues that you call depression are but an inverted way of looking at the world. The honor that you seek is upon you now, and you needn't push or force it. Yet, seek glory not for yourself, but in all things seek glory only for God, and you shall see your name scripted across the heaven in His name forever.

Seek honor not, then, in depression—which means a burrow in the ground. Stand upon the mountain of discovery and give credence to His name that is within you. Let no man see you stand upon anything but this hallowed ground, and give rise to honor by leading men with your beacon. In this, there is no capture.

♥ ♥ ♥

⚘ Desire ⚘

"**I** shan't want for anything" is the solemn vow that you took upon your plunge into the human castings. Yet, the earth-shattering realization upon your awakening in the human flesh shook you to your very soul with revelations that you were responsible for self-feeding. This took you back, to a time long ago, when your very being recalled moments of despair. You wrapped this past time and brought it forward into present memory and laid the time recalls one across the other.

The past is splattering the present with desires for pleasures of the earthly flesh. Dear one, do not think we seek to cast shadows upon your earthly garden. Yet, the time has come when we ask you to rethink your desires in the light of what you *truly* want while you are upon the earth. We implore you to reconsider some of your assumptions about what it is you need. Do you truly believe the child of God could amass a wealth of fortune to take home to the Father as a child seeking a parent's approval?

What is it that you truly want, dearest one? Think long and hard upon this question, and you will turn inward and soon find the wealth that is within you. For you *are* a fortune of treasure, a glittering treasure chest that can multiply as many times as you feel able. Use your good fortune for the help of multitudes who will find you the instant you make this decision within yourself: "I am ready to supply the earth's needs with my riches. I seize upon my wealth within and give freely as I am replenished."

Dear heavenly child upon the earth, the joy that awaits this decision is immeasurable compared to any earthly desires.

Give freely of your treasure within, and delight in the play that now comes your way! See the eyes cast heavenward as you laugh and smile with others who seek you out. Fear not that you shall exhaust your supply, for our Heavenly Creator gives as freely as you do of His own treasurehouse of good.

You are the wealth that the world seeks even now, and as you open your vaults to the others, you suddenly see your own worth. Your instrument of peace multiplies as you share it, and your storehouse overflows with ripe fruit for all who would seek its solace. Hold back from no one, but give freely of the love that is yours to share. Flow the light freely from within and without, as it passes through your life in steady stream.

We bid you to share in this secret: that there is but one desire that you possess, and this desire has already been met. Seek this greatest of treasures in its glorious surroundings, and you will find yourself even as you do. For you are the heavenly riches that God has promised to us all, and as you let us give to you, we seek no greater riches than what He has in store. For heaven is here, and we pass among you its seedlings of joy. Revel in its majesty, dear one, and drink upon its joy.

Live in gladness that this is so, and you will feel the stamp of quenched desires upon your brow. And in this simple quenching, you find that which all of your siblings know: that you and we are one upon His heart. One glorious child of God glittering in millions of shining reflections like the facets of one jewel casting light in multiple directions from one Source. This jewel that is you!

♥ ♥ ♥

❧ Direction ❧

Do you feel lost at times, sweet child? You do at times struggle to find your way, yet we stand ready to beckon you home at any time you would call for our directions. Your guidance, which places one foot surely before the other, will serve you all of your days. There is no time when your guidance is lost, yet there are times when you shield yourself from knowing its course.

You doubt and switch between the steady gate of God's direction and the circling of backtracking upon yourself. As you think you are moving forward, you become disheartened upon seeing a sign of a familiar trail that signals that you have doubled back and lost your way. This is the time to sit down and not fight against yourself, for those who struggle against being lost get farther away from the trail. But the being who sits, breathes, and gazes awhile soon finds recomposure. And this resolves the dilemma of being far from the trail, in time for the sunset to lead him home.

There is no time when you are lost, dear one, though signs can seem to point in different directions and confuse you further still. You shift in consciousness from one level to the next, and you worry at the awareness of this loss in focus. Do no further harm to yourself, dear one, by contemplating your "lostness" at the edge of the forest. For we will lead you back in perfect time.

There are others among you lost upon the trail, and at times you lead one another in circles going nowhere. As you cast about in sorrow, contemplating where you are going, do you ever surmise an inner voice that would lead you home? We teach you of this ready compass and offer you a chance to check its gauge. For when you let it lead you out of darkness, you trust its readiness to guide you surefootedly in troubled times. The compass is in perfect order at all times, dear one! Use it often, and it will guide you always, sure and sure.

Perhaps you do not take the time to check it frequently, and only use it when you are far away off the trail. This is also wise, as it proves to you its reliability. We are urging you to use it frequently, for in it is your Creator's wisdom, which He has packed as gear for you.

Some of you who wonder about this gauge and wish to discover its many uses, please hear this: We will gladly teach you of its presence, if you will ask us. Sit quietly in contemplation, and imagine us coming near you. As we enter into your heart with a language of feelings, use your inner ear to decipher the message that answers your questions with knowingness.

You will know we are near by our presence, which sends signals to your mind. These signals you can choose to disregard as imagination. Yet, we will draw nearer to anyone who calls us, and our warmth, we believe, is unmistakable for another presence. Ask us to show you this compass that we call "home," and we will gladly teach you its operation. For it is our honor to share in the gladness that comes from fully being a witness to the love that is within us all.

♥ ♥ ♥

✄ *Disappointment* ✄

Does it sometimes seem hard to honor yourself when others guard their hearts in ways that disappoint you? Believe us that we do understand your sorrow with human behavior, as we have seen choices that we would not have made for you if we were asked. Yet, we still see the glowing goodness within each of you.

We know how close you all are to making the greatest of discoveries about yourselves! We cheer you on in times of sorrow, even when the end seems a very long time off. You are closer than you know to a time of monumental discovery, dear one, and we ask you to cling to hope along with us. For that faith will take you farther than any one human could ask you to go.

But it doesn't seem simple, does it? Perhaps you achieved a level that you hoped would reward you, yet the offering did not come. You feel downtrodden as if others had walked across your very back, ignoring the pain that is beneath their feet. You may feel useless and unworthy of the honor that we tell you is due you. Yet, there is a simple truth that is healing in this concern.

There is a risk in telling you this, yet we believe it is in your best interest to hear this: There is nothing coming to you tomorrow that you do not already have in your hearts today. So that when you seek for your goodness in tomorrow's agenda, you are always disappointed. Because the flowing that you seek is already here, in completion, darling one!

Think not that tomorrow can add to your completeness, for that would be an impossible feat. There is nothing to add to one who knows no need, such as yourself. What could be added to you tomorrow that you do not already have?

Perhaps you think you need something that is not presently within you. We ask you: What could this be? What seeming item did God not give to you, or could He not bestow upon you in this moment in which you reside now? Think not that another needs to add a thing unto you, or enrich you with an encircling that you lack in the present. For you have already earned your creation, and your Creator has promised you all the rest.

For some, there is a thought of past times that cause them to stir in guilt and unworthiness. Yet, even these beliefs are not enough to hold off God's riches! For no mortal on earth could cease the Heavenly Creator's riches from coming in steady streams for now and forever more. So we ask you to delight and dance upon these blessings that are with you as we speak. Your joy sends light-filled messages to the One who is in heaven with you. And your joy is His.

Yes, it is safe to let go of your prescriptions of what you think is due to you. These appointments that you make as scripts in context for others always lead to dis-appointments. For God casts others to you as surely as He casts you to others. Allow the others their breathing space to be as they will be, and nothing can disappointment you of their making. And as your needs are ready-met, so are others spilling over with the treasures of heaven that they can also offer you. So do you see your sharing, which is within you all!

♥ ♥ ♥

❦ Dreams ❧

You speak of the term *sweet dreams* as if to differentiate them from the rest. The garden of your thoughts grows wildly at times, and its nature can seem to bloom perennials that capture your full attention. What is this period of time you call "dreams," but an opportunity to flourish in the wild expanses of your inner atrium? Your mind, which seems darkened in the light but harbors a perfect environment for lush jungles of the imagination to untangle and grow larger, and larger still.

So do you see that the mind exercises itself in the sleeping hours, while we humbly portray visions across your mind's eye for its entertainment while you are thus growing? Its lavish expansiveness is an opportunity to show you the operations of your mind. Once guarded, the mind in restfulness allows us to paint upon your canvas to illustrate what we seek to show you. Its lavish colors intensify the nature of our interventions upon the mind, which hungers for healing.

Use dreams wisely, and seek always to use them as healing interventions. Set your intentions nightly with this prayer:

"Dearest God, I seek to expand my consciousness through Your angels' interventions into the landscapes of my mind this night. I give You my open mind and heart, that You may heal my limitations in thinking, and correct my mind to truth."

Feel, then, our confirmation that your prayer is indeed heard, as we pour grateful tidings of love upon you so powerfully that all can be felt. The vibrations of your sleeping time gives us entryway when we may ply our lessons upon the backdrop of story telling and gently lead you so you may continue to impress our interventions into your waking mind.

Feel glad, then, that this is so, dear one. That God's help is inescapable is true. Yet for many, His help rings in emptiness through thoughts contaminated and busy by hopes and fears. Still, the nighttime beckons expansively as the greatest opportunity for our deepest intervention!

Use it wisely, as we say, to help along all wishes for accomplishments that serve your purpose upon this earth. We seek to guide you in all ways, and we await your slightest invitation in which we shall inspire you with infusing love. Your greatest power is unfolding even now. Can you feel it? Seize this power through angelic intervention of your dreams, and awaken refreshed, knowing that the best is possible. Seize this awesome partnership between angel and man, and come together in glad tidings in the night dreams.

♥ ♥ ♥

⚜ Ego ⚜

What is this thing we call "ego," because it is not a thing at all! Its essence is unfolding to many of you as the greatest illusion of all time. Yet, its power stands ready to block you with the paradox that, though not a thing, it also serves as a gatekeeper of the illusion of many of the experiences that you believe you have.

Let us explain further what is this thing/not-thing. To begin with, you chose a time in which to serve in a capacity of a demi-God of your own making. This decision was born of an ego mind that, behind you, served in no greater capacity than to whisper such minglings that would prepare you to take this "great adventure" into self-serviceship.

The belief that you could hold yourself captive, and yet serve no single purpose other than to enslave yourself in this kingdom of your own making, was the ego's awakening into captivity. Yet its actions serve no barrier in which God's trust—which is immeasurable in its capacity—cannot seep into every instance of your mind! There are no walls to keep God away from you, yet in consciousness, you can serve as your own barrier, which seemingly "protects" you from His greatness.

He is your greatest ally, yet your ego seeks to make you its master by enfolding you in dens of lies about the ego-functions, which only serve a destructive purpose. Which is to say, really, it serves no purpose at all. For that which is destructive is no-thing, and not to be feared, therefore. And would you throw away all of heaven for even a tiny instance of serving in this capacity of slave to your own ego? Think not that normal living is captured on the film of the ego's own creation. For that which you seek—what we call peace and happiness—is within the realm of *now*.

The tenderness and the mercy that God rains on you bathes you in His healing glory, where you share His mind as your own. Be joyful in this awakening, precious one, that what you have made to serve you is nothing but this grand illusion. Like a child's paper dolls, they can be folded back into the toy chest for now, in trade for the real livelihood of God's kingdom of heaven as it is present here and now upon the gentle earth.

There is nothing to fear, yet the ego would have you believe differently. Seek not its stature, or its lofty elevations, for there is nothing above you in this kingdom. God shares equally among you *all* of his riches. The edge that you seek from your siblings is nothing but His purpose in disguise. For he who is your sibling is authorized to bestow these gifts upon your anointed head, and you are showered with the sunshine together in joyful revelation that the kingdom is here, the kingdom is here.

No more waiting, no more anticipation. They are the slaves of the ego, dearest children. The time of your glad tidings is now, not in the distant future. Breathe it in, drink it in merrily. For God wills for His holy children to dance merrily amongst themselves, singing in joyful tribulation and dancing at His song. Give thanks that this is so, dearest child, and seek no further for that which is here among you now. For it is here, and it is now, and it is very, very good!

❤ ❤ ❤

❧ Embarrassment ❧

Who is shamefaced among you, that they seek to hide from their eternal holiness? Did the weight of self-judgment cause you to stir in a rush of embarrassment that you shield from your siblings? Seeking solace in aloneness, he who licks his mortal wounds soon finds capture within these words: that the greatest pain comes from within, as does its release. So let us pause a moment here, as we gain resolve for its release.

See in this moment, within your inward spiritual eyes, a picture of one who is like you and who is cast in the clothing of the immortal and eternal. Do you see the glow of warmth emanating from this being's holiness? This picture we bring you is of the one who is *you*! Now as you cast your eyes upon your own light, do you bask in gladness at the recognition of your true power? Do you sense the capacity of this mighty being who is yourself?

The one Who is great casts His power through your mighty being, and yet you who see yourself lowly cannot conceive of a power this great within your mortal self. The ownership of power belongs to all, holy child! There is no one among you any greater or smaller than all the rest. For nowhere on this great expansiveness of earth could God have set a more perfect creation than that which is you.

As you marvel upon your true magnificence within you, do you see its massive power to move all of mankind in inspiration so sweet that mortals cannot taste it? This limitation that you have cast upon your self in humble drudgery — it enslaves you. Do not discount yourself with shame, sweet and tender child. For one of such grace and holiness as yourself has no shame to beleaguer the inner makings of God's very image and likeness.

Humble yourself before His greatness, yes, that is true. As is it true that you shall learn by the lessons that cause you to grow. Bestow your greatness upon the world, as you are eternally ready in this present moment to unleash His valor for all to see through your shining example. Timid though you may seem, His blazing honor is unmistakable to those whose eyes fall upon the lighted rays of your being. Dim not these rays with false humility, dear one, and fear not that humility requires you to shine not!

For as He encircles you with gifts of gladness, so too do you shine these rays of awareness upon all that your capacity would reach. There is none among you for whom these words cannot heal, and yet your doubts can shield you from this experience, so release them upon us. Give to us this day your armaments of fatigue and faithlessness, that we may shield you instead with the true medals that come of grace and joy. For there is no valor in self-capture, and He beckons you to follow His call to glory among yourselves in the name of each other. For you are His most perfect children of the high, not fallen from grace in any mortal way.

Embarrassment is eradicated as He shines his patient understanding upon each thought you offer to His healing power. Shine away all din of shame as you proffer them to God, heavenly child, and feel the erasure of moments that you thought were cause of pain. See with silly laughter how easily they melt away when they are lifted to heaven's glory and given over to He who can bestow all things with His eternal grace. He is the creative solver of all that would mar the awareness of His holiness within all mortal men, yet still you seek for vengeance upon yourself for that which you never did!

Guilt creeps silently in the silent night and strangles its victims with a suffocating pillow upon their head. Let not this captor in among you, and sing not its song to beckon it to your awaiting window ledge. Did we not tell you but a moment earlier of His pervading grace that rushes to heal you of every seeming mortal sin? There is no thing in His holy vision that ceases to lift the sparkle in His eye at your sight. For He who loves you so completely cannot fathom of that which could bring you down in stature. Be like Him, then, in seeing yourself with wistful eyes that captures only the image of you who are lovely in His sight.

♥ ♥ ♥

❧ Emptiness ❧

How is it possible for a holy child of God, who is ripe with fullness, to feel empty? Did you lose sight of your riches and thus believe you were devoid of the fruits to which you aspire? We judge you not for this oversight, yet we seek to up-right your thinking in the truth that is happily yours to own and share.

There is nothing outside of your holiness for which you must seek. This truth may surprise those who surmise an emptiness, and believe they must fill it. What would you seek to collect that you have not already in your possession? Surely, the riches of the kingdom are installed deeply within your soul. For there is nothing that you could receive that would make you fuller than you are at present. And there is nothing you could give away that could disperse you who are eternally holy.

The thought of lack gives way to the experience of such, and so we bid you to release this perception to we who can cleanse you of its painful residue. The might with which you are able to disdain your present conditions is the essence of the holiness that uproots all instances that would bring you shadows instead of fruition. Use that mighty will of yours in full alignment with His holiness, for it draws to you that which is needed in sustaining the inward humanly needs.

Yet even still, the dwelling nature of the thought upon the need increases the illusion of the lack. Rid yourself, dear one, of every seeming thought you think you hold that gives unloving pictures of the life you lead. Do you share His wish that you hold a heavenly picture of your earthly dream? Give us, then, your troubles and sorrows so we may deliver them for purification. Hold nothing from our loving arms, for we would cast all painful thoughts away from your mighty love.

Tenderly now, reveal to yourself the truth of your glory and wisdom. See now, by our light, the reflection of your Creator that blinds away the vision of emptiness and fills you to overflow with love. Those who are thirsty, drink long at His trough and replenish your being with holy nourishment. For you are dearly loved in all ways, and we bid you to give to yourself, as your Maker seeks to give to you now.

Give us your sorrows and troubles, and release yourself in freedom, which is your one true desire. Soar in the heavenly knowledge of this plentitude that is yours, and allow us the sweetness of establishing steady communication with you. We revel in your gladness, which is full like the nectar of sun-ripened fruit. Believe in your fullness, dear one, and you shall seek no further for that which is you.

❤ ❤ ❤

❧ Envy ❧

Do you see in your brother's eye a gleam that you seek for your own? This monster that we call "envy" has held many captive to its origin, which is fear. When you seek to capture the status of a brother and surpass him in his deed, look squarely at the desire and you will recognize what is there. For love is the essence of all that you are, and you shan't deviate from your true nature, now or ever. That which you envy within another is eternally in you, for love is all that you are and all that you will ever be.

Do you imagine that your brother's action will capture the attention of a being who bestows love capriciously? Is there an imagined envy of this love being unreplenished when it is given to those who seem to have more than another? For the wealth of one is not necessary for the wealth of another, yet the love that is within us all spreads evenly among us in all ways.

The hurt that is in your heart in the name of envy is from the sharpened stone that seals off the awareness of love's ever-presence. Would you not ask us to hurl back this stone so the light of dawn's day can shine deeply with freshness so sweet that no envy could enter its picture? For there is no hurdle that you must climb to elevate yourself among your brothers. Your envy is attraction to that which seems light, but is instead to pull down a brother so that you may climb. Think not that one is possible without the other, for in togetherness we all are elevated to the highest mountain! The light shines freely among us, flooding all in its light for the mere price of looking upward.

Those who would envy: Turn away from darkness and

come into the light of knowing that you are dearly loved. Pull away from suspicions that lead you nowhere, and turn to Him who dwells within your heart. For envy cuts the strings that tie you to one another, and pulls with pain and sorrow.

Your Creator does not love one more than another, and there is no removal of that which is yours. Rest assuredly in this certain knowledge, dear one, for you are among His holy plentitude of love in all your being. His thought graces you with sure and steady mercy, as even His love washes clean your thoughts that would bar you from receiving fully of your holy gifts. Reach deeply into your heart and cast away that which is sorrow. For your holy altar is worthy of the clean and the wise.

Then gently correct the thought that taught you otherwise, dear one, and rest not a moment longer in hunger for another's daily bread. There is plenty to go around for all, and your joy comes freely as you pass along a serving to your brother on the left and your brother on the right. Serve plentifully, and rest assured that more is given to you gladly. This is indeed your holiness, conceived in the fruit of action.

For when you look upon a brother as reflecting the greatness within that which is you, your joy is unsurpassed by any accomplishment upon this earth!

You are holy indeed. Amen.

❤ ❤ ❤

❧ Fatigue ❧

Do you feel weary, dear one? Beaten down by life's heavy packages, upon which you shoulder many burdens? Allow yourself a moment of respite, then, for as you breathe sweet and gentle air into your lungs, we sprinkle the oxygen with our tenderness. You ache and you long for time away from your pressures, yet you refuse to give this joy to yourselves.

We sit in wonderment as we watch you again and again browbeat yourselves into submission. The necessity of talking yourselves into continuing this submission is evidence enough to show its unnatural nature, we think. Yet, without relaxation, humanity cannot thrive. The time is now for you to sit in idle contemplation of that which is valuable in the Universe. When you spend time alone with the Maker, your heart beats in glad time with His own universal rhythm.

The century mark soon dawns upon us, dear children, and we hasten your awakening through these golden moments of silence. Yet, we hurriedly chase after each of you as you press on and on. You hear our urging to slow down and rest in silence, in between the breaths you gasp as you thrust yourself forward into the world.

We see the inscription of fear upon your sweating brow, and we see that this fear keeps you from operating upon your longings for silence, sweet silence. You rush and you scurry, and now you are tired. Yet, be glad for this moment of fatigue, dearest child of God. For as you rest your weary mind and body, we lay down beside you and tell you our stories.

You will not be weary long, when you hasten our appearance through your steady calls. The time of angels is unlike the time of man, and we witness to your longings for Love through our steady gaze upon God as we stay by your side. Draw close to us, then, for the quenching of all that you desire. Feed upon our nourishment, direct from the Creator, and give your heart a steady supply.

There is no more longing within the heart that eternally drinks of its Maker's stream of love. Feel your hunger vanish and your own supply replenished by necessity, which you put off no longer from yourself. Yes, it is true that you deserve this one pleasure that you can rightfully give to yourself, so do not put it off a moment longer.

Whatever you are doing at the moment, it is fine to put it down now. We angels will stand ready as you take your moment of well-deserved rest. Breathe in the Creator's love now, as we build a heart bridge from God's Mind to yours. You'll travel this bridge more swiftly now, as you will now know when you are lonely for reunion with Him. Compare each moment of your day to this moment of reunion with the Creator, and you will never again allow yourself to be far from Him in your holy mind.

Incessant prayer is all that is asked of you to be upon this bridge, in permanence. A steady flow of thoughts from your mind to His, which flow ceaselessly in illuminated union. For you and God are one, united even between we angels. The ceaseless flow of love is beautiful to bestow and witness, and your heart hungers for this even now. Drink, drink, drink, sweet child! Drink until your heart feels quenched by the love. Never stop but for a moment to contemplate your situation, but stay afloat in the love, for that is where the answers are.

The stillness of this love carries you throughout your day, and steadies your mind in all your circumstances. Give thought to Him continuously, and you shall want for nothing. And you shall not fatigue.

♥ ♥ ♥

❧ Fear ❧

We love you, dear one, and we send you comforting rays the instant we feel the trembling from your anticipation of trouble. The signals that come from your fear are a whistle that calls us angels to your side. So you are never alone during your hours of fear.

There seem to be some in your midst who gain enjoyment from fear. Does this surprise you? Yet, a part of you knows that it is true. The practice of fear in your society puzzles us, yet we must address it within this passage because it is a good beginning point in our message to you.

When you shout because you are afraid, where does the depth of the emotion come from? Does it not seem to move from a bellow down and deep within? This shout is an escaping of long-felt energy, what you would call "catharsis" in your terms. The calling-forth of fear in entertainment places: your movies, books, and conversations, is but the same movement of venting away a pent-up steam. The pleasant feeling that accompanies some afterward is this release and freeing of the heart.

We bring this up to you because we want you to know that your world is spinning much faster in its evolutionary scale. There will be times coming to you quite soon when you may feel overwhelmed by the breakneck speed of changes in your midst. We angels want to assure you, though, that nothing moves at a faster speed than the beating heart of love. Your love and God's love are perfectly synchronized in beautiful rhythm, now and forever.

This rhythm of eternal love is, in fact, the anchor that will save you from additional fear during the coming times ahead.

Like the ticking beat of a mother's heart that calms and cradles a baby, your essence already contains the antidote to fear. Use this time now for preparation, by adjusting your mind and body to the rhythm in gentle practice periods that you can use and call forth during periods ahead.

So, what we ask is this, gentle children: Move forward fearlessly, not by ridding yourself of it through cathartic means of entertainment. Instead, use this time for peaceful sojourns inside the uncharted territory of the *great beyond that lies within*. Fear not that you will see, hear, or feel an essence that is uncomfortable, simply by sitting still alone with yourself. Allow us to intervene by sharing your fears with we angels. *Give them to us!*

These practice sessions are essential remedies for the coming times ahead. Get used to dealing with fearful thoughts through these early practices now, and these lessons will serve you very usefully in coming times. What we pray for you, in our angelic intervention, is that you will monitor your thoughts much more carefully than you have in the past. Like a resolved gardener who stands ready to hoe weeds at the instant of their birth, we urge you to tend to your mind in similar fashion.

Get used to purging your mind of thoughts that spring forth as you contemplate ideas of aloneness on this earth. And say, "I am not alone, now or ever" as you imagine yourself handing the thought-form of fear to our outstretched hands. Refuse to contemplate yourself as a trembling being, alone in the elements of fearful surroundings. For as things around you change, you will know that your core connection to God and us angels is steady and immovable.

Fear can be used in many ways, dearest being. Use it wisely and with grace! Call upon your friends, the heavenly angels, and we will whisk all images of fear from your mind. Do not save one bit of horror, in thoughts that you would want to seek solutions of your own imagination. Give it all away!

There is one solution to fear and that is this: Call upon God's heavenly creations for help and assistance, as soon as you become aware of your inner pain. A wise homeowner who smells smouldering smoke does not wait until the home is engulfed by flames before telephoning the fire department. At that point, such a call feels almost useless. Do not wait until you are overwhelmed by monumental fear before calling upon God's name.

At that moment—as in all times—He will send help and comfort to your side. Even so, you may not feel His loving arms for several minutes as you feel barriered between many layers of fear and heaven. Smarter still is one who learns to monitor his own well-being, and who hesitates not in calling upon a heavenly creation of any form for assistance and comfort.

Learn this lesson well, then, sweetest child, and remember always to care for your inner being by calling forth help whenever needed. In that way, your ebb and flow of fear has not sharp divides, but gentle swellings that do not erode your peace of mind.

♥ ♥ ♥

❧ Food ❧

Would it surprise you to know that human life can be sustained with a sharp reduction in food consumption? Perhaps this would not surprise you, for you are of the knowledge that beliefs surround reality. It is only your belief in hunger that creates sharp pangs and seeming needs within your thought systems.

There is no morality within food, yet we see many of you seeking comfort with utensils that hold morsels of food dangling into the mouth that instead hungers for a reunion with God. These beings we seek to comfort with our healing presence, yet it is at times tough to get through! For this, we remind you of a condition that you at one time called "Saying Grace." We like to think of this tradition as not something that is retired, but perhaps a new trend upon your horizon.

During this moment of bowing your head and remembering your heavenly origin, you allow us angels to become your dining companions. We join you with sweet music and keep the spirits soaring at the table. You can use our intervention on these occasions, and grace is but a formal way to call us to your side. Use any method that appeals to you, dear one. But this we urge: Invite us to your meals.

In coming times ahead, your body will adjust to energy vibrations that will bombard you from space outside the earth's immediate atmosphere. Food is a conductor of energy, and so your body assimilates it in many ways. One way is the transmission of information from the earth's soil to your mind's awareness. Earth speaks to you through her offspring, the living plants that you eat.

Think of it this way: Your dinner meal is a meeting in which messages and ideas are exchanged, even without your awareness. We speak of that which is on the invisible plane, and yet we feel it is time to share this with you. For Mother Earth calls you to hear her cries, and yet her ways of calling out to you are diminishing as you eat plenty—but not plenty of foods drawn from her living soil.

In the time that it takes for you to market her plants in endless variations, you could be calling her home with tender care. A walk in the grass with your shoes off, a sitting spell beneath an oak, or a gentle swaying in the wind of your body, can reconnect your energy vibrations with the transmissions sent to you at this time.

Water, too, conveys essential messages. Drink it more than you do, and consume it holistically in as natural a format as you can fathom. What we mean is that your pure sources of plants, minerals, and essential vitamins come from nature in its rawest form. There is no stew that can give you more than the Earth Mother herself.

So conserve your ancient heritage by returning to your plants, and as you eat of them, listen. Listen. Listen still. Hear the plant's loving message given to you from its root, its stalk, its seed. Please pay careful attention to what you hear within your heart and mind, and honor its message with love.

You may be drawn to fulfill your mission through this gentle form of eating. We know that this may create some initial turmoil for those who are seeking security, comfort, and safety through more traditional means. Yet, we tell you the truth, dear ones: Seeking security in old-fashioned places is not the means to the end!

Your safety, your children's safety, is ensured by careful attention given over to the plant kingdom at once. Spend more moments in gentle serenity, and if you hear nothing, ask us angels for help! We want you to hear earth's cries, not out of blame or guilt for what the human race appears to have done. No! That would not help at all. We want you to hear and see what we angels know to be true: that it is not to late to save Mother Earth. She seeks fellowship with you in her great expanses of beauty and her barren landscapes. She will tell you what she needs, which itch to scratch. Yet no one can be told who decides he does not want to know. That is your right, your free will.

We ask you only that you would go within your heart, and in love, reconnect to the divine being who truly loves you: your mother and your planet. As you follow her lead, all your ways will evolve back to something more natural for you. And you will seek foods that mirror this image of yourself as a natural being. It is your essence. It is your life.

♥ ♥ ♥

✣ *Forgiveness* ✣

When a butterfly soars unfettered, it is a beautiful sight to behold. When a child runs, laughing through a field while pulling upon a colorful kite, heaven is near. These visions of grand beauty upon your earth are small examples of freedom and grace that exit without boundaries beyond your imagination, dearest ones.

All who would listen, please then hear our words. Even now as you read, if you will breathe very deeply and allow us to enter your heart, you will see our meaning even clearer, even sharper still. Yes, that is good, continue breathing and feeling. Feeling love, love, love upon your breast. And trusting us to take very good care of you as these words dance across the page.

For it is not words that take your hurt away, dearest loved ones, but the emotion of love. You see, love is an ancient electrical impulse that travels along the circuitry within your being. It travels freely and tells its tale of light and laughter. It scrapes away all error residue left along the circuitry as it goes along, and yet you often short-circuit this gentle messenger for reasons that are still unknown to many among you.

Let us fill you in a bit, so you will see this topic of "forgiveness" from our vantage point. Maybe then you will understand our message at a deeper level than before. You say you forgive, and yet still within you a little nick of anger remains upon your circuitry. It is visible and palpable to even the naked eye, who wishes to see the landscape of love.

Even now, you can close your eyes and with a short breath and a prayer, behold your inner landscape of circuitry. Do you see the navigation upon which love carries its heartfelt message? These circuits are more real than you may ever imagine, and they are constantly working to carry away the realm of errors.

All that error "is" is a lack of love in consciousness. Yet, even this is impossible, as we believe you will readily see. For where could love not exist, except in your imagination? And where your consciousness resides, there you are as well. You are a thought, and a great and powerful thought at that. Your mighty decision to exist in imagination, where spaces without love could be, is as a child who designs a superior world to the one of his own. And is the fantasy superior to that which is real? Again, only your decisions contain the answer to this important question. And how you answer yourself determines the direction you next must take.

For if there is a fear of turning away from the imagination and returning to the "real" world of love, light, and creation, then you will hide endlessly under the seeming shelter of your imaginings. Yet, if you were to imagine an even better hiding place than this, would you come out and check to see if it is so? The shining world existing eternally beside your imaginary world of fear and danger, awaits you patiently. Your invitation stands carved and glistening, engraved with the love that beckons you to come.

Everything you've ever wanted is here, loving child! It is a place within and without, simultaneous in all dimensions. And we will lead you to this reality, if you will but show us the slightest interest in establishing a new residence for yourself.

There is one thing you say to us, we know: You must protect yourself by abiding within a shelter. Yet, what in truth can endanger you who are the eternal one? Do you accept that there is only one possible "danger" anywhere for you, and that is through a hardening of the heart; a turning away from love's shining light? And even that so-called danger brings not blisters to the skin nor punctures new wounds. Merely, the forgetfulness that enables a sensation of pain in this world, coaxes you with images of protection *that you do not need!*

Do not clothe yourself in armor, nor arm yourself for battle, dearest holy one. Surrender to the truth, instead, and feel the ease of stepping away from stiff, metallic fittings that blind you to yourself.

Your power is eternal and shall not be eroded by mind or men. Call up this power that dwells within you, at once, holy one! Ask for purification steps that cleanse your mind to inspiration, which once again draws you forward to your perpetual home. The dawning of your mind upon forgiveness will be given you, one holy step at a time.

Now you will shed yourself of burdens that you do not need. Your steps will tread quite lightly as you bare your heart for all to see. There is no danger outside yourself, and you will drop your arms. This message of forgiveness is quite ancient, yet it is capable of being well learned this day.

Ask for help always, sweet child, and rest assured that we are near. If in a quandary as to how forgiveness unlocks a prison cell, lose not sleep or time in seeking understanding. Seek instead to take speedy advantage of our offer to assist you. Call upon us angels with your breath, your mind, your heart. Unify your desires into one sincere effort, and ask us to whisk off your cloak of anger and trembling fears of danger.

Your requests are readily answered, and your open heart stands ready for cleansing. There is no rush for this to happen, yet there is no time beyond this moment now. So clear the space within your mind and call us now, dear one. Let us rejoice together as we laugh away your fears. Let us free your heart and mind. And as you follow the gentle laughter of your lightened heart, you find that moments of escape no longer hold your attention. For you are fully awakened and immersed within the love that we share with you, and with our Creator Who is God.

♥ ♥ ♥

❧ *Friendship* ❧

We see many of you feeling alone and friendless, feeling disconnected from the rest of us. You view yourself as lonely, as misunderstood by the majority of beings who roam upon this earth. And those of you who are disappointed by a friend take solace in the situation by viewing yourself as in a higher position of authority than the One who bestowed the friendship upon you.

There is a need to tell you this, dear friends: that we angels outnumber you in so many ways. The numbers of us are staggering, and we propel in and out of each realm. This heavenly display of affection we bring is yours for the asking, and yet you insist that you must be alone. This insistence creates your loneliness, dear one. You carve this view of yourself romantically, perhaps, yet the image is one who has no mirror image to stare back at. You, who are cut of the one mold, view yourself as separate and alone.

Yet, this viewpoint shards your experience into sharpened slivers that chill the very essence of your soul. For as you divide the world into elements that connect and conquer, you isolate yourself, tucked in a cavernous corner with no one to share.

There is a time and place for aloneness; of that you can be sure. But this is what is so essential for your mind to capture, while you walk upon the planet earth: that everyone you look upon is but another example of who you are. There is no difference between you and he, he and we. The fragments you see are but optical illusions, as you'd say, that create solitude pictures for you to hold or share.

It's the same for everyone, everywhere you look. Always,

it's the same experience. And as for choices, you are left with the single greatest choice that one can make! As you seek union, the goal seems to eternally slip away. Further and further ahead in "time" does it seem to go, until you finally protest in frustration that you have had enough.

We angels are here, though, to share the glorious news of awakening in your midst. And at this awakening, you hold the sure and certain knowledge that the union is not in space or in time. Not forward, up, down, or backward in any dimension. The union is here, with you, starting now.

Be glad that you are home here on this ready planet for the duration of your mission, for the times ahead are fun. Yet, you can wallow within misery for this short duration if you believe you are missing some element. And that thought brings you fear. Do not seek union in ways that bring you to fear, but see the shining rays within each other and witness the magnificence that appears *everywhere you look.*

Your friend is you, dear one, and you and you. All over this earth, your friends await you. Do not push them away in the midst of your planetary change, which now calls you to analyze your deeds. Spend this time, instead, in calling to your sibling who also longs for the love. Bring him home by your love. Heal him with your truth, and drop all swords that rob you of sweet richness. Call yourself friend first, and you shall be friendless no more.

♥ ♥ ♥

⚜ Fun ⚜

Frolic and play is the angel's way! That's why we tell you on the earth so often to have fun! You think this is your subconscious nagging away at you, telling you to relax, take time off, and rest. Yet who do you think is telling your subconscious to tell you this, dear ones? It is us, laughing all the while that we see yourselves taking it all much too seriously.

It may surprise you to hear us say that to you, since we incessantly implore and beseech you to take care of important matters. But do you see, earthly children of the most Holy One, that time is of the essence in all ways? There is no room to discard yourselves in ever-increasing circles that push you to succeed, succeed, succeed. For at the end of the day—in earth life—you will count your days of success as some of your greatest personal disappointments. It was when you had your eye on the ball, so to speak, that you missed out on life's greatest challenges and rewards.

We do not mean to frighten you at all, sweetest ones, yet hear our words in your hearts as we speak. There is no time to waste on burning out your engines excessively. Hear our chantings to laugh and to take time to pull back and get perspective upon your lives. All the while you are in the midst of something great upon your earth time. Do not miss the forest for the trees!

Savor your time on earth and listen to your self very closely. Shhh...do you hear that, ancient one? That sound you hear within your heart is very dear to you, for that is you, the inner you speaking through your closest feelings. The feelings you often ignore and push away, in ignorance to their source and the information that they carry. These feelings come on angel wings and light the path for you ahead. Do not take them lightly, and do not trod upon them with your decisions to move onward, upward, ever higher in your world of make-believe.

Take time to, ever slowly, breathe in and listen to your heart. By that we mean not the drumbeat, but the singing of your longings and your likes. What do you dream of for someday in your future, dear one? Think back and review all that has captured your attention and which you have set aside for some year in your future. Are these, not in fact, your ancient stirrings propelling you forward in a way that is so captivating that you barely allow its existence within your attention span? Could you not, instead, listen to these stirrings as you would to the excitement of a child?

You can trust this voice to not steer you wrong, humble child. Its ancient wisdom carries you along a path that you have long forgotten. Sing its ancient melody now, sweet one! Whisper its tune, which you carry within your heart. And you will feel a stirring rouse within your depths, the likes of which have never happened this side of heaven in your time.

Listen to your inner stirrings, and give voice to the longings of your soul, which cries out for solitude on a restful plane. Give it this nourishment that it needs, sweet child. Fear not that you shall endanger your belongings and responsibilities by calling for some rest and relaxation a little while. For do you not earn your rightful keep by your very holy heritage? Who among you is greater or lesser than another man? And who could contain the spirit of man within his earthly flesh?

Sit down and rest, then, earthly child. And listen to the melodies of your heart as they stir. Follow its ancient story, and test its waters a little while. Come home, sweet heavenly child. Come home by these heartstrings that draw you nearer and nearer.

The playful nature of your soul stirs restlessly within, and we tickle its growing awareness that causes it to explore this playground that we call "Earth." The soul stretches its arms with delight at its release into the sunlight of play and of fun!

♥ ♥ ♥

❧ Grief ❧

A heart wracked with pain as the missing of a loved one is endured: For this, we are specialized to minister and heal. The darkness that overtakes a grieving soul is lightened as we pull energetically upon the soul's awareness of eternal life.

Yet even grief has its place within the universe and is due its honor as part of your emotional scale. There is a mourning among all beings for the cycles of life, the ebb and the flow. A mourning for what might of been. A sadness and anxiety captured within the heart, and a longing for a return to home.

We even hear of those bereaved who seek to return to the holy home to be among their loved ones. This, we assure you, is not within God's design when the plan calls for a continued stay upon the earth. There is a moment when home will call you back, and yet your loved ones are destined to arrive at different moments than your own. For as you walk side-by-side along earth's way, your footsteps also travel and traverse the ground at private intervals. Do you see that your earthly beloveds may arrive at their destination at a moment in time that is different from your own? And do you choose to acknowledge that your journey takes you a little while longer upon the earth?

You will reunite with your beloved ones in many ways, dearest being. Of that we can assure you heartily. Your love is eternal and even growing as we speak. For love that is created between two holy ones has an independent life of its own. There is no wasted love in all of life, and that which you call "your love" is shared with all the universe in all its ways.

For this you can be grateful, for your own creation of dualistic love is pluralized and captured, and brought back to form. The tender core of love at the center of humanly love is extracted and used as a natural resource for worldly good.

Do not think, then, that your love was for nothing as you hold your broken heart in tender embrace! There is a holy meaning behind the love the two of you shared, and God thanks you for your beaming contribution to His heavenly realm. And as your love creates even still, He shines His loving rays of compassion upon your life. Never believe that the pain you endure is a "test" of any kind, dearest child, but look upon it as a moment when you set your decision to continue loving in this incarnation and the next.

For it is not that the "price" of loving is pain. But this is a moment of deep consideration about the meaning of love, which, for some, moves you slightly sideways of the center of love. That stepping aside, away from love as if it is an explosive powder keg, is the core of hurt within you.

Revel, instead, at the moments of joy that surround your holy partnership with another. The living and the dead can rejoice together by a recentering within the love. Honor your emotions, yes, it is true. And give us your burdens to carry this day. Then when you have committed to this truth and this help, give pause to the great joy of your loving relationship, and *know* that it can never cease to be!

♥ ♥ ♥

☙ Guilt ☙

This topic is of great importance to us, as we see all who suffer at guilt's whims. The arrows that spring from the hardness of guilt's brittle covering over fear, wound many, many hearts without cause. For there is no cause of suffering, but only a Cause of love. Let us go back a moment, though, and as you listen to our words, allow us to pry open your hands, which grasp to guilt as tightly as one who wishes it for his very survival. Be assured that your survival depends upon its release.

The hardness of guilt stems from a survey, in your mind, of victimhood. You sense approaching danger and suspect, "It must be for me!" The heart of fear within guilt is this sense of approaching danger, and an acknowledgment that punishment must be near. The child who is swatted at a misdeed feels wounded with shame, and imagines that he must be very bad indeed. For this he is told by the being whom he most loves in the world. The shame is carried forward into the adult life, on top of which it is built, covered over, and then built upon once more. These layers of grime that you call "guilt" can crumble in the instant that you recognize their flimsy foundation, dearest ones.

For even mountains of earth will tremble before the mighty power of man's wishes. Your wish, this very day, to be rid of guilt, is met the instant you wish for its release. We angels are nearby, awaiting your hand-off of the thought-forms that tell of your "badness" and shame. We send forth rays of truth, which prescript the truth instead: that God's sons and daughters are guiltless, through and through. *You have done nothing wrong!*

For how could you impact that which God created eternal and whole? Our power does not exceed He Who is all-powerfull. There is but one power in the universe, and none who stand in its stead have a separate power with which to compete with the One Who knows.

The insistence, in your mind alone, that you have a separate power is your root of guilt, sweet one. At the instant you perform separation fantasies, you right then must feel alone, vulnerable, and afraid. For a parentless child, lost in the wilderness, cries and imagines the sights and sounds of horrifying monsters. When all along, though, the "monsters" are but trees, rocks, and innocent hollows. There are no monsters coming to find you, dear one, and you have done nothing wrong for which you must expect punishment.

Know this, in your heart! Drop the string you pull in aching at your heart, and release the fantasy of guilt to He who knows your eternal innocence. The only "crime" for which you must be rehabilitated is that which you spoke to yourself of, in your heart. For you were insistent that you must be alone, and therefore, must be separated from your Holy Creator and His children. This view, alone, has brought you all your terrors, precious child. This view, alone, is responsible for all the seeming "evil" that you believe you have experienced in all of your lifetimes upon the Mother Earth.

And yet, not a moment sooner than you have been ready, can we release you from its hold upon your gaze. You focus upon guilt as a child who toys with flames of a fire. You linger a while, testing the limits of your queer dimension, and all the while knowing there is safety and a peacefulness in the very next room.

Come join us, our beloved, and release your cares and worries about this small world. We surround you with peace and good news that solutions lie within your heart. Let us amplify the voices of rejoicing, which shall lead you in safety to the meadows of heaven within. Your love shines out into the world, where it now awakens others to your call of peace. Let it shine, dear one. Let it shine!

❤ ❤ ❤

❧ *Happiness* ❧

We know many now seek that which you call "Happiness," yet we also see much confusion surrounding
what can bring this condition about! Let us spend some pages,
then, contemplating this important situation that you seek. For
in these pages, we can resolve much confusion, which—in
truth—is the only barrier that bars you from your holy goal.

Some will tell you, "My way is the only way." Do not follow one who leads you away from the Source of all the prizes.
Walk with the angels who sing, not of folly, but of "Holy,
holy, holy." Shelter yourself under our wings of love, while
you contemplate further what we are about to tell you.

First, you must know that all that gives pain is mere illusion. It is a diversion designed to turn your attention away
from God. There is no divide between you and your Creator
that can rob you of happiness for even a little while. All is
God, and that which is not God is impossible. In this respect,
then, unhappiness is impossible.

You ask, then, if this is true—which we assure you, it is—
why do I ache within my heart, mind, and body? Why do I
feel a longing so deep that I would throw away all that I value
in exchange for a moment of peace? And we answer you, if
you will listen within your heart. Suspend all your doubts a
moment, and you will hear what we say.

The second imperative for you to understand is that all of
the wretchedness that you witness to is just a mirror of that
which you do not see residing within your own mind. The
willingness to see the truth is the first solution out of the teem-
ing cauldron of horror you see around you, dear child.

Do you seek to escape this so-called pain? Then stop a moment, and consider that you may have invented the whole thing. And laugh if it comes naturally to you, at the insanity of it all. For only the truly insane could want the antithesis of God at the price of their sovereignty.

Return to your true place of holiness, upon the throne within your heart of peace, dear one. Abide no longer in foreign substitutes to your true kingdom, which lies before you. Witness not to pain, and desire no longer for heralds outside of your holy self. For happiness is your home and your being, and you are driven to return to it in one simple realization that is upon your breath. Do not seek for happiness within a mind that hunts for escapes outside of yourself. Instead, be content with the simpleness of our prescription to rest within your heart a little while.

In your imaginings, you believe that happiness is a thing that you must chase and wrestle to the ground before its capture. This beast that you imagine is but your own idea that your truth is illusive in nature. It is not, we assure you! Rejecting that which seems too simple, you ignore the reassurances that easily guide you to your home.

Do not think that you need to guard your body or situation from harm while you search for truth outside of yourselves. For in your thought that you must exchange something that you fear for that which you desire, you bring about continual terror upon your mind. There is nothing real that you can lose, dear child! Nothing as precious as you could have hardship, except by your choosing. And this, too, you can undo with your mere wish to stop and be renewed.

There is no complexity in happiness, for simplicity is its one essential ingredient. Rejoice, then, in the factual nature of your true essence. Rejoice in the living spirit that is you, and which God created for holy purposes. And in your rejoicing, be bathed in continual wonderment at the gifts that are of you and by your wish. There is nowhere else to go but here, and a simple breath and prayer are your passports to the place that for so long has seemed to evade you.

Breathe deeply and pray thus, dear one:

"Heavenly Creator, I ask your blessings upon this moment when I seek to return home in my heart. I know that You are very near, and I pray to feel heaven within my heart. Lift me now, dear God, and bring me home."

❤ ❤ ❤

❧ *Honesty* ❧

Who is there to be honest with, but yourself? There is God, Who sees every thing that is true within your heart. Yes, He sees your love continuously, and His Holy Spirit casts your cares away with your call for help. We angels and your spirit beings see your thoughts radiating from your mind, and as you will soon see, there is no thought that can be privately held for no eyes to behold. All is in the open, here in heaven, and we do not seek to control your thoughts, but to help you guard them with your loving heart.

If you could see what we see within your heart and mind, you would take special care to monitor your thoughts with great love. You would no longer cast your thoughts upon the wind, where they are carried away to create as a seed blowing across the plains.

Oh, gardener of great and small creations, take a moment to see your tendered cares from our point of view. You fear that we will force the pitchfork and shovel from your busy hands. Yet, we only seek to reinforce the beauty of your garden and help you sow no weeds. The fence that you stake around you is helpless in restraining the very things you plant within your soil. For there is no sorrow that comes from God, but only that which you toil beneath your feet.

The ripened love that stands before you, ready to be picked, enjoyed, and shared, is as beautiful as any blossomed flower that can be imagined upon this Earth. Behold the love that you have planted and successfully grown from moments of sweetness you shared with one another! Do not delay in enjoying this fruit, precious child, for your bounty grows more plentiful as you harvest its life-giving offspring in your thoughts and deeds. There is no diminished supply of this love, and the bounty is yours to feast upon and to share.

The weeds that are now the focus of your attention are easily gardened through your honesty, holy one. Look lovingly upon all that you have planted, and do not use force to pry them free. Instead, gently take them in your arms and release them to us angels who stand ready to bring the garden to beauty. Give them to us, dear one! Hand us your weeds! And we will bring them gladly to the Creator, who can rectify all that was planted in error. He can miraculously transform the barren leaves into bounties of plenty as we return them to your awaiting arms.

Hold no weed back, guarded with thoughts of secret longings or of harbored shame. There are no weeds that you want for yourself! There are no weeds that you could mistake for thriving flowers, if you will share your uncertainties with He Who Knows. Give them all away, and rest in full assurance that all that is real and beautifully blooms eternally at your side.

♥ ♥ ♥

❧ Jealousy ❧

Do you believe that another has more than you, precious one? Do you imagine his crime that prevents you from acquiring that which your heart longs to hear and hold? These teemings of the mind hold you in suspension, and all the while you swim in the midst of everything that is dear. For the imaginings of the ego-mind are what the world focuses upon, and all the while the love goes unnoticed and unenjoyed.

Let us explain jealousy to you this way, holy child: There was a time when you enjoyed total solitude within the Mind of God. Your heart and His knew no longings of separation, for all that you needed and wanted was near. Then, a brushing of the ego-mind caused you to stir and look around you. Suddenly, you noticed that you were not alone. And in this moment of your imagination, you believed that your brothers and sisters were vying with you for the attention of God.

In this competitive moment, you gave away the knowledge of your holiness, in exchange for the imaginings of terror. For who without his holiness could not be afraid and feel vulnerable to mishaps and misdeeds? Yet, this mad imagining is but a night dream, dear one. Look around you again, and notice the heartbeat of God that has never left your side and that now beats within the breast of every stirring creature upon the planet Earth.

Your soul comes in all shapes and sizes, for that of a flea and that of a rat are nothing but the imprint of God upon the visual impression of flesh. Seek no longer for hardship, sweet child. But instead, cover your wounds with the salve of His love. Dress yourself in the refreshment of returning to home in your heart. And center yourself within truth, which is the steady prescription for all that seems to ail you. We have never left your side since the nightmare began, holy one. And while you believe you are suffering, we constantly nurse you at your side.

Sweet and precious child of God, you were never nearer to heaven than at this moment. For the truth is that you never have left, except in your imagination. We welcome you home with our enfolding wings, asking only for your forgiveness of yourself. For we do see that you are much too hard upon yourself, and mercy is given to you, but which you oftentimes do not accept. Show consideration to your sweet soul at once, dearest child, and come before your truth within your shining light.

For now you see the illusory nature of imagining that one could have more than another. There is no one but yourself, in truth. No one but the one soul that shines in faceted sparkles of light from the one jewel, which is God. And none but you could He love more! He bestows His entire kingdom of love upon you now, sweet wonder that you are. You have earned the keys to His shining kingdom. No one can pry this key from your grasp, save you. Only by your decision are you deprived or disgraced. Only by your choice to suffer in misery are your needs withheld. And by your very choices, you restore to yourself all that you never left behind!

We pray that you resurrect your truth and open the kingdom to your waking experiences upon this earth. Heaven never leaves you wanting, nor brings you suffering. God wills for your soul and your flesh to be restored in truth and in love. Stand no longer outside the door, suffering in the rain, when the choice is yours to step into the shelter and sweet covering of His mighty love. The end of suffering is here!

And when you step inside, reach out your hand to your brother and sister who suffer in silence a breath away from you. Smile the shining light of God as you firmly take their grasp and lovingly show them the shelter that awaits you both. The pouring and flow of the love from your hand into another's is your heavenly Creator's way of reaching through and cradling you both! Do not hesitate when a stirring rustles within your heart, urging you to take steps that bestow your beloved siblings with the love that you share. Hesitate not a moment, and instead fearlessly reach with a hand that plainly says, "My sibling, we share God's love as one. As I help you, may we both be blessed with eternal peace."

For there is no competition that seeks to win the Maker's love. All is shared in the instant you decide to give it away. Fill your heart longings completely with this love, and as you share this overflow into the awaiting hands of another, your replenishment is resupplied again and again and again. Like a waterfall that spills its savory victory in a splendid show of beauty, your overflow of love from the Creator's heart, through yours and into another, is a marvel and a miracle for all to see. Do not seek for what you can have, but seek only for what you can give. And in this way, you shall have everything and more.

♥ ♥ ♥

❧ Job Search ❧

W e know that at times this situation brings you nervousness, and yet there is much reason for it to bring you great joy! We accompany you in your quest for true harmony. For that is our job, after all, and we swirl around you in happiness when you mix your happiness in and amongst our own. Let us find peace together in this world, in simple happenings that occur on a daily basis. You are the core of what is essential on this planet, as there is only one being after all. Together we undertake the holy job of creation, and that brings us to our topic at hand.

When you race and rush headlong into any job that seems to suit you, you run immediately into a wall within yourself. For where there is a race, there is also a hard finish. We want what you want for yourself, dear one: that is, gentleness and grace with a timelessness that transcends all earthly fears. So settle down within yourself and really hear our words on the deepest level. Let our love resound within you as we surround your energy aura with calming influences that slow the pulse of your body to the level of the sweet whisper of wafting wind.

You are essential to this world. You must hear this message in the very depths of your soul. There is no time to waste in getting started in assuming your rightful role, and yet when you rush headlong into side detours where certain jobs will take you, we wait patiently. Still, we know a greater joy is awaiting you elsewhere within you.

You believe that a well-fitted job for you is hard to find, yet we believe a match for you exists this very minute. There is no delay between assuming God's plan and the creation of right opportunities for this plan's fruition. Bow down within yourself, gentle one, and hear His loving voice, which now calls you into the service of His perfect plan. His voice awaits those who mark their time with service, yet in heavenly timeliness, this service does not exist as we know it now. This grace which is inward, marks you as His humble servant, which to all who would hear these words, is a lofty position indeed. For all who would bow to His grace and assume His humble servicehood will find themselves with joy aplenty.

There is no lack in His room, and all who dine at His table feast forever in His eyes. He who watches over you is in servitude to you, as well. This communing together of you and He is the essence of what your job is for: the eternal circling of love giving back and together with each one. Let the love flow through you now, dear one, and as it guides you like a silk thread upon the path, your opportunities become enriched with golden grace from others who beckon you to join Him in His humble servitude.

You see yourself with a calling, and you are exactly correct, beautiful angel of the earth. You are called, indeed! And He who calls you beckons you further with gentle assurances that there is great reason for your gladness. Do not err by seeking for it outwardly; for it is within you even now. Your great job provides in many ways, and you who seek for holy grace in lowly places shall not find it beneath hidden covers. For His light shines brightly within each one of us who turns to face the light bravely.

Humble servant of God, assume your partnership with those who roam the earth in search of His gentle grace. Your job lies not outwardly, but in assuming the hand of yourself who walks in costume as another brother or sister. For everyone you meet in every way is but a reflection of your own servitude. Serve Him well, and you will see His mask in the mirror within all whom you meet. Hide lowly from His grace, and you will see the face of fear within all others, just as you see it within yourself.

There is nothing to fear, dear one, and trust that we lead you to perfect positions that fulfill your heavenly tasks. Let the wrong doors close easily, and do not struggle to force them open. They waste your vital energy while you are on earth, and we needn't slam anything upon ourselves as long as we abide by His gentle wisdom, which wafts within us like a summer breeze.

You are eternally guided—know that with great certainty. For surely He who opens circumstances to you will lead you gently all throughout the way. You can attest to His greatness by holding His hand as He leads you across alleyways where you are blinded to the outcome. He who is wholly worthy of your trust will not betray you now or ever. As you feel your gratitude pulsate beneath your feet, let us assure you that it carries you like wings of Mercury to new vistas.

God will never leave you hungry or let you live with what is scarce, you dearest and precious child of the One who eternally loves you. Count your blessings and watch them multiply in every way. Your right job is here for you now, and we will lead you there with your permission. We sing merrily as you float with us in the gaiety of life's dream. Enjoy your essence, dearest one! You are a sweet child of heaven put upon this holy earth, and there is much that warrants your rejoicing!

Seek for joy, and we will follow not far behind you, urging you onward along the way. Recall always that you are very loved. The love is your job, of which you are well adept. Amen!

♥ ♥ ♥

❧ Judgment ❧

When we see you hurt yourself with judgments, we wish to remove the sharp splinters from your hand that cause you agony and pain, dear one. We wish that you could see the eternal picture of yourself holding judgments, like a child with sharpened sticks who pokes and prods and wonders where the wounds are from. Your incessant picking upon yourself through the eyes of others gives us wonderment at your holy power, which, misused in the name of protection, endlessly only hurts yourself.

Put down your sharpened sticks, dear one! We urge you to hurt yourself no longer, for your needless suffering stirs us with care. Certainly, we care for you and judge you not while you play with the sharpened toys of your making. We wish for you only eternal happiness, and though we seek to pry these judgments from your mind, we see that your intentions for making them are different from the finished results.

We see that you take great care to fashion the swords for your own protection. Perhaps you do not know that every end you hold of a sharpened blade cuts the very hand that seeks to pierce another. For there is no earthly way to assume the ownership of such a sword and not have it wound its owner.

Assume no ownership of this earthly prize, beloved child! It is unworthy of the holy child who you are in truth. You are worthy of only that which is holy as yourself, and this holiness needs no defense. Though there may seem to be others who act in foolish ways, you know that their longings are mirrors of your own. For they, like you, are seeking home. That home of heaven that their heart yearns and aches for even now. If they assume you've got it, they may cut a path through your heart to attempt its meager ownership. Yet, the rightful owner of the heavenly home is the One who lives within you now. He has never left His home, and it cannot hurt you that you think you may have left, in your heavenly slumber.

Do not push your siblings away from you with your lofty judgments! They are eternal friends who seek to join you on the path to heaven, although we see that they are confused much as you are yourself. Have compassion on this child of God who seeks to find his way to heaven! Do not cut him with your sword, but instead hold firmly to his hand as you join together in a holy alliance built upon grounds of hallowed love.

Your Creator calls to both of you to hurry home, and you needn't wait for tomorrow to bring you additional compromise before you return. There is nothing to add or fear about the moment when heaven's touch is within your grasp. Reach with hands clasped together, and the shining light of heaven encircles both of you.

You are home truly, evermore, and as you let His shining grace melt away all of your concerns, you find your judgments removed from your hands like a gentle breeze causes ripened leaves to fall. Use your swords no longer once they fall to the ground, holy one. Step upon their brittleness and feel them crack beneath the weight of your partnership with another. You are the one who stirs gratitude in heaven each time you let a judgment fall wordlessly to the ground! Be glad along with us that you are here in heaven while upon this earth!

❤ ❤ ❤

❧ *Loneliness* ❧

The portal in your heart that allows the love to flow in can seem empty when you forget its flow is in occurrence. When you look away, you may long for it to be refilled with more substance, which you believe can quench its ache. Yet, this longing is your thirst for our heavenly Creator who resides eternally in every space. And that which you believe is empty is in fact entirely filled beyond its capacity, even now.

Dear one, do you think God would leave you comfortless while you believe you walk among the trees and people of the earth? Do you believe that He would not lead you in every instant to the very person who needs your loving comfort that comes from He who loves you both this instant and always?

You are so mightily loved that your awareness is just a glimmer upon the smile that is within your heart. You do not understand your greatness, and so you turn away from beholding it, for fear of having awe of the light that is shining there within you. Behold your greatness, precious one! Do not turn from the light that will dazzle away your emptiness and fill it with a love that is so real and eternal that nothing can compare in any place or in any time! Hold its substance in your arms in warm embrace for that which can only fill your emptiness with love, eternal love, pure and rushing through you, through and through.

Dear holy being of God, look around and you see reflections of His love for you everywhere. See not the stain upon the doorway that has marred your enjoyment while you are on the Planet Earth, but see instead the open door of eternal brotherhood with everyone you meet. There are friends for you here in every way, and you only need to look for them and they are with you here.

How many friends do you want? Ask, and they are given you this very day! The partnerships that you seek begin within you, in partnership with your holy self. Unite with yourself, and commit to this partnership now. Then take this solemn promise you make within yourself, out into the marketplace when you go, and shine its holiness at everyone you meet.

The wafting of this great and shining light is unmistakable to all who gaze your way, and they return His gaze of love in your direction. Hear the voice that calls you as your own, and join with your siblings in glad remembrance of your holy partnership.

Be still an instant, and feel all emptiness melt away. For you bring nothing into this world that does not call you your own. That which is owned, in turn owns you, and so we bid you caution in claiming that others are witness to anything but your love. See in them only what you will to see within yourself, and choose carefully when spoken words are exchanged.

Mark a spot within your holy heart for friendship, and it will come. Exhume from your closet all fences that guard against love, for you are willing to let love enter in exchange for agreement of its cost upon your territory. You now rest assured that His eternal safety melds with your concerns for protection, dear one.

Love can never hurt, and your cries for friendship are heard. Give way for grace to take over, and it will mirror a friend to you who matches your resonance. You are a friend to us all who in heaven sorely appreciate you in every way. We send you perfect companionship to mark this holy occasion of opening your heart further to His holy and blessed love.

♥ ♥ ♥

❧ Love ❧

W hat can we say about Love, for it is the very power and essence of the all that is all, the wafting of the universe, the pull of the heart string, the sound that a violin makes upon a crashing crescendo. It moves mountains and shakes trees, and yet so much is unknown and feared about His great and mighty power.

For us to explain the heart of love, we must take you to a moment of stillness. Even now we feel your excitement mounting, and we ask that you sit in stillness while we quiet your longings with gentle respite. There, there, a moment longer, and yes, in stillness the gentle moment of recognition arrives.

You see us in blissful surroundings, illumined with light from within. We assure you that this illumination is from the candle of love that is within us. For we know that love is a single power with a singular direction, which can only carry greatness in its quest for reaching outward. It grows as it is given, yet this is indeed why so many of you see it as fear-full. Yet, what takes away from the greatest singular power of them all? There is no thing upon this planet or elsewhere to extinguish the flame of His being.

When you mistake those who come near you as those who would take from you, you confuse the two for love. For they are drawn near you in a quest for mercy for themselves and others. They seek to extinguish their guilt and quench their thirst within the pool of God-love they see within you. Yet their drawing nearer haunts you with memories of your own, of those times when you stood longing and hungering at the sidelines while witnessing others drinking of the pool of love.

Have mercy on yourselves, gentle ones, as you witness this

erratic behavior born of confusion and longing for the love. For it is true that you will find your longing quenched within another, and yet the quenching does not douse the flame. Quite the opposite! For as much as you give in the name of love to another, you witness that direction growing and growing within yourself. The fire burns stronger and higher with each spark that you give.

There is no power that could extinguish the eternal flame burning within each one of you! The mark of friendship upon your heart only ignites additional flames to burn further and further.

Perhaps you fear losing control of these flames burning within your chest. Yes, we share with you the intensity of the love, and we know at times that this feels indistinguishable from a loss of control over your emotions in your heart. Yet, in stillness, this passion that you feel for God and all others is the very essence of *true* control upon this earth. For its power is immeasurable in capacity, and it draws others to you who wish to drink of its beauty.

Their presence may cause you to wonder if they are throwing sand upon your flame. Yet, their presence is cause for awe and celebration, for it reveals the holy power of the flame to remove from the atmosphere all that would bring in darkness. Your power exceeds your wisdom at times, it is true, and you can push others away by lowering the intensity of your flame. Yet, it is impossible that you or another could entirely extinguish it in any way.

The fact that they seek to drink at your well gives credence to the law that exists throughout the universal plane: That which you seek is always found, and that which you give is always replenished.

Therefore, do not dim your flames so that you may live more quietly, dear one, for you were put upon this holy earth as a shining example to those who would love you. Your control over your brothers and sisters is within your reach, but would you seek to control that which stirs joy and which extinguishes all poverty? Would you choose to silence the beautiful music of heaven that stirs upon your soul?

Do not fear that the raging fire within you will cease to exist, or that its flames will consume you in a final show of madness. There is nothing of value that you can possibly lose! Your flame is eternal, and you are here to show it to all who would see. It stirs them beyond all reasoning, and marks the holy alliance for others to see. So like a flame that you would pass from torch to torch, have gladness as you set your brother's heartfire aflame. See him pass your fire from his torch to another, and as it builds in strength and endurance, be glad that you did not fear to touch him so. For this is love, through and through.

♥ ♥ ♥

❧ Money ❧

Would it surprise you to hear that we hold no opinion about money? For it, like all of matter, holds no usefulness if it thwarts your direction away from holiness. Therefore, we simply view money for what it is: a tool for destruction when misused, and a stepping-stone to greatness when properly applied.

And how would you come to know the difference, you may ask. Yet, even as you say these words, the answer comes readily to you from the same Source that guides you in all directions. This Source is the very knowledge that provides you with ready answers in all of your days.

Seek answers from this Source, instead of money, and see the difference of this internal focus upon all of life. The view that money is essential comes from grinding teeth that snap and snarl to make their way. This is simply one point of view, dear one! To seek another way, we ask you to merely turn around and see another dance in which materiality is not the sole participant.

So do you see the choices that lay before you, and the many avenues your earthly life can fashion? Which of these choices gives you greatest joy, then? And will you pay yourself with this greatest of rewards?

It is not money, but its rewards for which you have sought these many years. Could you not wander straight to this reward, so full of riches that shall never be denied you? What could give you joy but yourself? Money cannot. People cannot. Time cannot. Only your simple decision, born of freedom, calls forth the answer of this richest reward. Do not push away this answer for its obvious simplicity, dearest one. For, the answer that resides within your very essence, awaits you in ever-patient company at this moment. The answer is simple. The answer is joy.

♥ ♥ ♥

⚜ *Opportunity* ⚜

Dear one, do not put a stake into the ground and call it "mine." This being that you call "Earth" is tender and gentle, and yet not unwilling to surrender to your will. Your holy will seeks not to dominate upon the earth, but to tread softly among your brothers and sisters.

You are a holy creator like your Maker, and we watch for our opportunities to call you home. Be still and give us the opportunity to enter your heart. For it is you who opens the door to your heart, and it is we who answer your call for Divine assistance. We come to you in the night when you may think we are unneeded. Yet, when you rest peacefully in slumber, your heart is actually awakened the most.

We enter into your dreams at odd moments to deliver to you our messages of cheer and sustenance. For you see, dear and sweet precious child of God, your origin is our opportunity to serve God in all ways. We simply guide you in subtle directions to find His hand so that He may lead you to eternal safety and blissful surrender.

Do not think that your opportunities lie simply in heaven or on earth. For which is the dividing line between the two? Does not heaven blend into earth and earth into heaven? So why need to choose between the two? The distinction between heaven and earth is artificial, and you who are called upon to serve in God's ranks feel the truth of this statement in your being.

March confidently, earthly angel, and know that we are with you and ahead of you, helping you to recognize the doors that we open for you upon the earth. We signal you beneath your breath or capture your attention in some subtle way. Do not be afraid that you will miss our cues, dear one; we plan these routes together in your nightly dreams. The fun is yet to begin as you walk further among us with deliberate and conscious participation.

We intend for you to become one among us, and your heavenly Creator asks simply that you revel in the joy of being His holy child. You are led so sweetly, so softly, that no one calls upon you to cross the barrier of your own will. "On earth as it is on heaven" is a perfect description of the life you are called to live.

We see the sweet essence of your being, even if you do not. We seek the perfect opportunities to shower your gifts from God upon the world, and we function as a clever team together in synchronized harmony, you and we. You are here to capitalize upon all that you are in truth.

Do not seek to glorify your own name, but to shine from the glory of the Maker who is one with you. Radiate your light outward from many mountainhills, dear one, and rain love merrily upon those who would seek to capture your heart. For you are one among us, and you are an instrument of His eternal and abiding peace.

♥ ♥ ♥

❧ Patience ❧

The seasons of timing are inherent to, and born upon, this earth. In heaven, there is no call for timing, for we are immortal and unevidenced by the clicking of timepieces and the markings of calendar pages. We are not captives of the imprisonment by which you measure your accomplishments, yet we are purely sympathetic of the pressures accorded to you who live among these sort of rituals.

We do not ask you to cast off your timepieces. Yet, we do ask for your greater self-understanding of the longings that lie within your hearts and that drive you further to exercise haste and hurry at your own will and discretion. We do see the need for an infusion of patience at this time. We see an anxiousness for change that you long for, and that you can feel is at the horizon.

Do not get ahead of us on this point, for we must carefully enunciate the outline of our vision of patience to you. Sit slowly and breathe, sit slowly and breathe. That's right, now we are able to speak with you again. Feel us enter into your mind with our words and we once again ask you—no, *implore* you—to gently slow down from your rushed and harried pace.

We angels are trying to do all that we can to contain the explosive anxiety we see mounting upon the earth, and yet we can do so much more with your help and permission. Would you please contain the jubilation you feel that is so explosive when you set out upon a money map? When you seek to conquer or destroy, it is all we can do to contain the leaking energy that you trail behind you.

We implore you to be more at rest when you are captured

during the day by the incessant desire for material goods. This matter is a particular point that we would like to enunciate even further. For there is no time over here, yet in your earth time, there are moments that are captured by eternal longings for material grace. What we mean is the grace you seek in heaven, captured in an item that you would buy upon the earth. The teaching we share with you now is that this longing is enriched with keen reward when you share it with God, for only He can fulfill it.

Yet, when you are captives and slaves to the material man who becomes part of you by casting about for plastic forms of grace, His rays are deflected by your outward flow of motion and exuberance for idols. The impatience you feel, that time is madly ticking away without you, like a ship that has left for sea as you stand waving upon the shore, is subtly robbing you of the greatest victory humans can ever know. For within the human heart another stopwatch ticks with the grandest measure of love ever seen upon these hallowed grounds. Cast this light upon the ground and watch the flowers spring from out of nowhere.

God shares His holiness with everyone He touches, and even now He reaches His thought to encircle your own. There is no thought of tomorrow that enriches you in the same way one ancient thought of your Maker brings you home. Your enrichment comes at the moment you are ready, and not an instant sooner. When you cast your needs upon Him and feel Him lift you, the end of time is over, and your patience is forever stilled within His arms.

You walk on hallowed grounds this minute, yet many are unaware of where they live. Do not wait upon tomorrow, dreaming that this is the day when you will be saved. Your eternal longings are quenched this instant, dear one, as we angels cast our wings in a gentle and expansive embrace of gladness for this holiness that we all call home.

❤ ❤ ❤

✣ Prayer ✣

When you sit in quiet repose, thanking the Maker for all of your gifts, we are very near. We fly within the heart beams of one who shares the laughter and joy of life with us. We breathe in and out with you as you draw in sustenance during quiet contemplation of your prayer. Sit quietly, dear beloved one, and drink in the silent repast that you hunger and thirst for. You needn't wait until another time to feast upon this eternal banquet that waits for you patiently, but is eternally here before you now.

When you silently meditate upon the things you desire, God listens and He answers. He waits upon no one's timing but His own, for that is the law that treads throughout the vast universe. The pulsation of God's mighty energy is tranquil, yet it distributes the very essence of all things in their right place at their right time. Trust in God's timing, dear one, and don't restrict yourself by placing markers of your own timing upon your self-made prescriptions you put before Him to cure your pain.

God knows, before you ask Him, what will fill your need, and you needn't ask him in formal prayer for such things. Your prayerful time, be assured, is for your benefit and not for God's. When you rest in gratitude and respect for the awesome and immense power that He is, you rest in that very power within your mind and awareness. Put your mind squarely in the center of His heart, and feel the pulsating energy wafting with your own, healing your ideas to the rhythm that is eternal and universal in origin.

When you are in sync with the Creator's energy, your rhythms with all of nature and mankind fall into place. Your timing arrives perfectly on our angel wings to deliver you to the moment that gives you the greatest opportunities for your spiritual growth. Undertake these deeds fearlessly, dear one, and wade through the mire if you must, to be put in the place where God would have you be. Pray for knowingness within your very being that will guide you safely to even remote places where you can perform His service.

For you are a chosen instrument of God's healing work while you are here upon the earth. You are meant to be a courageous creator like He. To do His work, you must first know His likeness that is you. Prayer affords you opportunities to look at your magnificence in the mirror and say, "I am He who is me!"

♥ ♥ ♥

❧ Pregnancy ❧

The gestation period before the birth is very crucial to the mother's health, and we are ministering to the mothers of the globe ceaselessly. Lately we are concerned by outbreaks and pockets of strain within the mothers' caring hearts. And so we seek this platform to deliver information to you who are expecting within the coming years.

There is no more crucial time upon the earth than now. Your planet seeks its balance and rhythm, and its motion is rounding out. The implications are quite serious for those inhabitants upon this globe. Yet, children are electing birth to herald in this coming age. For this reason, we pay special attention to the wombs in which their living bodies gestate. And we implore those who have elected to be mothers to watch their growing wombs with special care.

Diet, fresh air, and exercise are essential, this is true. And yet, fresh air in the form of relaxing your thoughts away from earthly worries is needed even more. For who among you needs for scattered material goods, when the very balance of earthly life hangs in question? We implore you mothers of the globe to therefore question all of your motives for activity while you carry the new heavenly child within. Would there be any chance for you to escape your cares and tension by lightening your load? For, every time you put down matter and rest your weary burdens, your child's body reflects this shining light.

You do not yet fathom the importance of bringing these children in safely, so we again remind you of your mission's holy nature. Your maternal time is best spent in contemplation within your inner world, as you shift your outer world to allow for this adjustment. It is not prams or cradles that your baby needs upon this time in planetary history, but guiding and gentle light and sweet innocence from you, the mother, of the earthly child of God.

Seek not, then, an outward focus for your child. The babe must not forget his heavenly call, or we will tarry in outward motion awaiting the child's return to heaven. Recall your own decision to deliver this baby, and use this focus to impress upon your baby's head his holy mission even now. Push not his eyes toward the surface of the earth, but keep his gaze ever heavenward. The lessons with which your child returns to earth are inscripted upon his soul, and you, his faithful steward of this crucial scripture, can unlock it with your key.

Your child, in this planetary time, is not your own, dear mother. Your child belongs to earth. Let your child go forward, then, and hasten his memory of why he is here.

Pray and sing for your child always. Ask us angels to surround him with our gentle gaze. Fill his dreams with thoughts of returning to his ever-present state of grace. And do not stand between heaven and earth within your child, or you shall miss your earthly savior who is rich with planetary guidance.

So easily is all of this unearthed, though, with this simple reminder to mothers to heed their child's mission for this planet. This time is now, and you who carry mother nature in your womb will surely agree that you knew this all along.

♥ ♥ ♥

❧ *Purpose* ❧

A h yes, purpose. Many of you at this time are called to remember your purpose, and you may feel stumped as if
taking a final exam. Do not fret, dear children, for your purpose is not complicated. It is to heal. Heal yourself first in
mind and intent. Declare this principle to yourself: "*I intend
to walk the highest path to my awakening. I am fearless in the
face of learning to discipline my mind and actions so they are
attuned to my true divinity.*"

Yes, you can do it, in case you have doubts about your abilities to hold this high place within yourself. You have the ability to heal, and to heal in whatever capacity brings you joy.
For you see, sweetest one, you are a gentle blessing to this
earthly time, and you bring heavenly gifts to bestow onto others. You are a shining example of peace, and through this
earth's shifting winds upon the planet, you are a gentle reminder to others to shine their own inner lamp of glowing
God light upon the world.

Fasten yourself to the central mast of your ship, angel
being. You need to stay tight to this core of your being during the rough seas ahead. The storm cannot cast you off of
your ship as long as you hold tightly to your center. We will
buoy you and hold you tightly in our love, if you will but ask
us. The storm will be swift, and what will follow will hold the
sweet promises of your Creator, who asks only that you center your mind and your body upon this word: *Healing*. You
have your task to perform, dear one, and God has His. Do not
worry what He is up to, for all is safe even as it seems in disarray around you.

Trust. That is the word to anchor you to center during the coming stormy seas of life. Trust, and teach others to trust along with you. The end is near, and it is a happy end indeed. No more stormy nights await the trusting traveler upon the high sea. Although the day seems cloudy and unclear to you, soon it will make perfect sense, dear child. So we ask you to hang on tight and to simply allow us to lead the way through the stormy seas. Suspend your doubts and fears the best you can, sweet child, and soon the way will seem clear.

Not a moment longer than is necessary will this stormy sea continue, and though a typhoon comes storming through, no harm can come to those of you who listen in silence for your Creator's answers. Take as many with you as will listen to your words, for you are being awakened in time to take shelter. We know you care for many who are still sleeping, and we will do our best to rouse the sleeping ones in time to get shelter. But even those who slumber on will be made safe through your love, dear one, for you have the power through your loving thoughts to make shelter and safety for all who meet your gentle gaze.

Behold the magnificence that is you, heavenly child, and use that magnificence wisely during the coming days. There is no time to dawdle with remaining doubts you may have that question, "Is this real?" Our reassurances rest in your heart, and if you will remain in silence you will hear them resonating clear. Others will join you in simple reverence for these messages, and you will band together as an army to capture the remaining years for the light. Rouse all you can, dear child, then seek shelter for the coming storm. Trust in the Maker, Who will never leave you, and feel gladness for the dawning years.

♥ ♥ ♥

❧ *Relaxation* ❧

Quiet solitude is a nutritional need of your ascending body, dear children. We come to you today within our hierarchal group to counsel you upon this need that we see long neglected within so many. We urge you to reconsider your stance that calls this state of relaxation, "neglect of purpose," for it is quite the other way around.

Consider an oak tree, for instance. Does it not grow in spurts and sprays? Does it not provide food and shelter for many kingdoms worthy to call it friend? And yet the mighty oak does not attempt to grow ceaselessly, but merely seeks its own ebb-and-flow arrangement with its own cells. Were it to nourish itself without ceasing from the soil below its roots, the soil could not have time to replenish itself before the oak tree drained it dry. The rapid growth that an oak tree takes within certain of its years is gained by its initial slow progression over time.

You, too, have needs for respite that are sorely necessary so very often, yet overlooked by each one that we look upon. Dear ones, will you not learn that God does not push you to grow beyond your own limits? Sit quietly in respite while you drink in the energy of our words. For we nourish you with growth that is beyond measure whenever you call upon our name. The time of sitting is not without its own doing. It requires a second set of eyes within your being to measure this inward growth.

Yet, be assured that when you do what you would call "nothing," that we are busily rearranging many tiers within your structure. So that when you climb out of your hibernation and feel renewed, you are feeling the touch of an angel within your very being. Be glad, then, for those moments when your soul urges you to stop.

Do not think that stopping is akin to not progressing further upon your golden path. The light shines within you most deeply when it is not bouncing around in hastened movement by its carrier. So do not say it is selfish or unworldly to sit in stillness in the cool shade of the grass, and drink in the taste of the air with your lungs. It is our opportunity to provide you shelter beneath the steady gaze of our love.

Give us this chance to replenish you, dear one, as we shine in glad awareness of our Maker in Creation. Together we encircle Him with appreciation that the work we do together upon this earth brings to all of us much joy!

♥ ♥ ♥

❧ Sleep ❧

We come to you in times of sleep in glad awareness of all that you have done each day. We suspend your doubts and cares during moments when we cradle you within our loving embrace. Perhaps you think we just refer to nightly sleep, but are you also aware of moments of sleep that happen while you are awake? When you glaze over sleepily and lose consciousness of the world at large, we enter your mind to bring your gaze back to ours.

In sweetest recognition of your earthly cousins, we remind you of their true home, which is back with yours. We distance you from that which is cruel upon your earthly flesh, and awaken you into another world of lush surroundings and gentle pastimes. Your waking moments upon the earth are actually sleeping moments from our side of view. You disappear for moments at a time, yet we hold your hand across the curtain that thinly separates your world from this side. We step back and watch you dance and play among the earthly mortals, while we play sweet background music to lull you all along.

Your ancient rituals can puzzle us, but we will never abandon you while you engage in such play. We patiently await your glad return in moments of earthly sleepiness, and then we restart at the place where we previously stopped our time together in full consciousness. You see, dear one, from our land we watch your sleepiness as a gauge for our crystallizing in your thoughts new ways of looking at appearances. We jump in eagerly when your guard is down and rearrange according to your wishes and prayers.

Do not think we rearrange without your welcome, dear one,

for God's law forbids our unwelcome trespass except in times of danger. We tread carefully always, yet eagerly when it is wished for. We always await your invitation, little angel of earth, and even meager requests for intervention are always granted. We stand behind you and before you, guarding your way and carefully gliding the focus of your attention inward and upward, so that your prestigious association with the Creator can shine its way into the center of your very being.

The times in which you feel punctured with holes in your very being are used by us for helpful lessons, so fear them not. For they allow the rays of God to shine outward to others like a mark upon a treasure map that calls them home. We trust you, dear one, to open your temple to us during sleeping moments when we can guard and guide. We trust the Creator to provide the perfect lesson in your own time, which we shine in glad awareness of our most holy duty to the Ancient One.

Let us kneel together and give thanks for the moments when we join in quiet communion with one another. These times when you call "sleep," we call our greatest times together while you are still upon this earth.

♥   ♥   ♥

✣ Stage Fright ✣

When you put yourself out on display in front of others, it is natural for you to be nervous and even afraid. You are afraid of what others may think or say about you, and you are afraid that what you may do is not aligned with your intention. Let us assure you that at such moments—especially when you are called upon to perform in such a way that will guide others to a higher frequency or develop within them some answers to their fears—we are very close and quite near.

Those of you who are performers for a higher function, involving arts, teaching, or conducting guided imagery, let us consider what is behind performance anxiety: You are considering solely what is in the venture for you. You are concerned with what others may think of you, when it is *you* who are thinking of you. If you will consider what is in it for others, what you can truly give, say, or do that will heal another's fears, we assure you that your performance will be a healing function of the divinity within you.

You cast away your fears when you know that you are here to perform a higher function, and another way to heal your fears is to feel the intention of the audience before you. Whether you are in the same room with them or away in time or place, you can vibrate your internal frequencies to match the people who are here to witness your performance. In this way, you assimilate their needs within you, so you are locked into their frequency and can automatically deliver their needs through your speech and deed.

What we are trying to say to you is this: There is no need for nervousness, ever. Trust your higher self to deliver the right performance at the right time. The word *performance,* perhaps, conjures up images of inauthenticity, and this is correct. If you are anxious, you cut off your source of trueness and passion in your delivery. But if you are tuned into this inner source, you will pour out your deepest beliefs at whatever level your performance desires, be it art, photography, speech, or even sporting tournaments. You inspire others with your deeds, so it is right for you to succeed, dear one.

We are a winning team. Together we can do no wrong and we can do much right. Whenever you feel nervous or afraid, look over toward your right shoulder and remember that we are right there with you. We take away your pain and replace it with laughter, the moment you remember our presence. If you ask, we shall hold your hand as you get started. We will stabilize your energy to stop your trembling, and we will guide you throughout your task so that you will deliver the highest energy that heals all who hear and see you. Please remember that you are never alone, our beloved one.

♥ ♥ ♥

❧ Stress ❧

Beaten down by life, the hunching of the weight that presses the mortal into ragged edges, this stress of yours concerns us. We ask that you set down your weights and carry us instead. Feel the lightness of our souls upon your back as we rid you of troubles that wound you. Feel us dance across your back and brush against your spine as we relieve you of hundreds of years of worries that you set upon yourself. For eons we have adjusted you, and ever more will we adjust you still. We are forever with you; worry not.

Yet, we remind you that when you cast yourself in tension as a plaster cast around your body, you are hardened into a density that is like a shell. Though you put on this shell as a means of protection, it serves as a barrier across which we cannot serve except in a mortal emergency. Let us break down this cast that bars our access to your very soul.

You do not cause us grief with this remoteness, yet we do seek for greater closeness with you. Share with us, then, your sorrows, and tell us your tales of woe. Turn to us with your grief, and we will turn tragedy inside-out for you. We promise to always pull the light out of its center and give it back to you.

At moments, we know you are scared. We know that havoc wreaks upon your life like a being spreading mud across a fresh-cleaned floor. Give us the mop and broom and we will gladly clean up your life! Do you not realize the extent of the depth of our love for you? We all work together on this mortal plane, and we are not enemies in times of stress! Yet, we see you blame God for your many ills.

There are times when you feel very alone, and we see into

your heart that you feel friendless and unloved. We beam our love into you, yet you cannot feel it. For, we cannot give you much sustenance when you put up structures to keep out the fear and other feelings. Do not be afraid to feel, dearest one! At times when you feel that your heart will break if you show one more shred of emotion, that is when we are nearer to you than ever!

Lean outward in your senses, just once, during moments of sadness, and you will feel our gentle stirrings by your side. We kiss your cheeks when you cry and caress your being with our loving wings. Your soul has never left us, nor could we ever leave you far behind! Allow us to touch you with God's grace and mercy, which showers you in gentle kindness and an outpouring of love. You have never left His great and mighty heart, dear child.

We are here to remind you of keys that you have forgotten and then thrown away. The first is that there is no place in mortal times when madness can replace the peace that heaven now has. The second is that, though tragedy is all around you, your heart still beats in rhythm with His love. The third is that we are here to serve you, just as you would serve us by your bright return to knowing Him within your heart. The fourth is that, for eons, we have sought to know you better, and we now find a return is upon us that brings us to glad times together. Related to this is the fifth key, that fear can be a stepping-stone to love if you will simply face its truth and know that you *are* the love that God has put here to shine on one another.

We ask you to remember these keys, not just in your minds, but in your hearts where they were placed when you were first begun. These keys to the kingdom unlock much of what seems magical, yet is perfectly ordered by God's will. Hold faith in your Creator, beloved child, and you will see His handprint across everything in this mortal universe.

Seek not for love in false places, but shine His radiance from your heart toward every being you find upon this earth. You are a messenger, sweet angel, and the stress you feel is lifted like a false mask you mistakenly laid upon your self for misguided protection. Do not surround yourself with a mortal shell, but radiate outwardly so that you may drink in His essence with your very breath.

Give of yourself in God's name and feel protected by the Love. For there is no danger or unsafety in this Love, and you are blessed in His holy name. We give you our gratitude for listening with your heart to our words, for we are your angels, and we bestow you with our honor and heavenly love.

♥ ♥ ♥

❧ *Time* ❧

Does the watch that is upon your wrist rule your anger? Does the position of its hands push you into thinking you must rush along like the sweeping hand that chases the seconds? We watch as you allow the poles upon the clock positions to chase you, and we do give pause to think about this situation that is upon the earth.

We ask you to consider the logic behind this deed. Is it not true that you expend great energy by keeping up with the incessant ticking of the time's keepers? And yet, do you not acknowledge that, though they be unstoppable, the human machine requires rest and more than occasional attention?

So we ask you to be in the light as you consider this competition with a time machine that you have foisted upon yourself. When we look among you and into your hearts, we do not find one single soul that agrees with this reckless competition of mind and machinery. And yet, even though all agree that the timepiece is a ruthless ruler, there is not one among you who will state the obvious so that others may join in agreement.

For who rules the roost among you? Who would be the first to state that this ruler of timepieces has cast upon mortal men only fear and sorrow? We, who are in heavenly time, watch for signs of the rustling of awareness that the timepieces weigh heavily upon your souls. And we implore you to examine your anguish at competing with the incessant hands that breathlessly sweep around and around.

You are meant to have breaths of delight, not mimic a timepiece as if it owns you and ceases you to stir in creative imagination. For what strangles the hours of life must also leave the human imagination devoid of its striving. Creation is born not of a pressure, but of a ceaseless joy that goes outward in celebration of its magnificence.

Play, not work, is the heart of solution. And this glad awareness of your immortal timelessness should give you pause to consider the worthlessness of capturing your hearts in seconds, minutes, and hours. For who is there to please, but the inward self Who is God? The setting of times for this and that delays the inevitable happiness that brings you home to us. Do not make yourself adhere to rigid timeliness, but hold your wristwatch to the light and watch it mirror its brilliant timelessness. For nothing can measure what is changeless, such as the light which is in you now.

For just one hour, pay no attention to the measurements that are on your wrist. Allow no thoughts of time to rest upon your mind or your lips. And watch the movement of your mind and being slow to a restfulness that gives birth to new ideas. Heaven can help you with a raining of new thoughts as you open your net to our outpouring, by slowing your thoughts to a new measurement of time.

We are here to help, and yet the mesh that shields our thoughts of origination from entering can be opened so much further with your intent. Say merely, "I cast out the shadow of concerns about time!" and we see enlarged openings that we may enter to shed your doubts about asking for a release from time. You are right to rebel against this system that impedes you, dear one. Ask us to assist you in guiding your release away from the dredging hours and minutes.

For who could slice a very being of God into minute pieces of glory? The impossible cannot be done. Do not slice your illusions of another being into strips of obedience, as you become the servant of a captor who knows you not. Serve God well, and time will take care of itself. Never fear that being late for anything but your arrival in God's very presence, is anything to cause you trepidation. And does not His promise give rise to Love, rather than fear? Do not tremble that you are late for what is real, as it shines eternally from His grace upon you evermore.

♥ ♥ ♥

❧ Trust ❧

You may have noticed that a central point of our teaching is one of "trust." Trust for each other and trust in yourselves. We beseech you to reach inside your mind and clear away all cobwebs that snare you in perpetual distrust, for we see many of you wallowing in pain and sorrow from feelings disconnected in and among yourselves. There is no disconnection, it is true. Yet, uneasiness within this world stems from an overt dis-trust.

Could you be called back home and not trust its Source? Are you wallowing in dis-trust, awaiting a signal when something is true? There are instances where you do trust, yet at a soul level it is an entirely different process. What we mean is that trusting in human conditions invariably leads to disappointment. But on a deeper level, true trust abides in areas where contempt cannot reside. After all, who could take trust away from one who has this element as his essential nature? Your core being is filled with trust, for love always assumes that another is trustworthy. And since you *are* love, you *are* trust as well.

Your basic nature then, of trust, extends itself quite naturally. It is only when you thwart this true nature that you find discomfort within and around yourself. Your trusting nature endlessly extends itself, in perpetual curiosity to explore itself by examining those who are around you. So, you would not want to contaminate this true nature by thwarting its outward extension.

You may argue that, yes, your trust has been denied by those in their human function. And again, we remind you that this is not the form of "trust" of which we speak. For trust on a deeper level rests upon one whom we know as God, that source-being that calls you home to rest even now. You are heeding this call every time you feel drawn to seek refuge within others. However, your dis-trust throws a bar across your sibling's inner door and denies your entry into this state we call "home." So you see the eternal frustration that you create by searching for, and yet denying to yourself, your home.

Do not seek for home on two levels, and you will find a calming solution that is entirely simple once discovered. Do not look to human frailties to answer questions about yourself. Your trust will never be found in such a quivering location. Still, seek to know trust, for this goal is worthy of your part in God's kingdom. Then, once decided, look for this golden treasure in places where it is sure of discovery. That is, the inner kingdom within the heart of every being who walks upon the earth.

Step heartily toward this goal that cannot disappoint you, sweet child of God. Your trust will not be broken by He who loves eternally. And it is He whom you will find within this deeper cavern below the human surface. Look deeper, dear one, and you will not be disappointed in your trust for ever more.

♥ ♥ ♥

🜊 *Unappreciated* 🜊

Do you feel alone, miserable, and unappreciated? You are wounded by the fact that another undervalues your achievements and accomplishments, of which there are plenty. You devalue yourself through the eyes of another, taking on his captor role, which contains elements of jealousy, upheaval, or indifference.

Do you cast your eyes upon the sand or upon the mountains? Do you look at the twinkling stars in the night sky or hear the distant cries of sadness that are far away? You belong amidst us here in heaven, even while you enjoy your remaining time upon the earth.

For we say that, even as the whispers of appreciation seem capricious and delectable, the sound your Creator makes in glad welcoming to you who cast your hearts and longing onto Him are far more valuable and lasting than any joy you may receive from the compliments of others. We ask you to move away from small longings, and swivel your heart one small turn behind you, where we now stand to welcome you who share our thirst and hunger for God's love.

He will quench this deepest of desires for you, dear child. The only cost of His love is your awareness, as that will draw it into your heart and consciousness. You don't need to toil in the upward longings that we see in many of your brothers and sisters upon earth. There is no hardship that earns your rightful place in heaven. Heaven is here! Here upon earth, for those who make it their home of joy and gladness.

You mustn't worry, dear child, of your mistakes or those of your siblings on earth. Do not be harsh on any one being, sweetest angel. Why would you put your focus upon the crawlings along the ground, when you can just as easily be immersed in the shade of the great and wondrous heaven? Toil not on earth in your consciousness, but instead, give all your longings to Him Who can save you from yourself.

God understands every one of your needs, dear one. He whispers your name in constant appreciation of who you are in His holy heart. You are indeed in the right direction at the moment that you desire fellowship with your holy Creator upon the earth. For you will find God in the heart that beats within your captors, who in truth are brothers and sisters to you in the flesh. You needn't worry that one or not the other is mistakenly with you. We are all here with you in a joyous circle of celebration, and we ask you to join with us in cele-bration of the light that encircles you with rapture.

You are His holy child! You are His divine and pearly pure child! Your appreciation is guaranteed within your own essence of who you are, and as we kneel before you who are God incarnate, we ask for your continued blessings as we countenance with the divine upon this holy earth.

♥ ♥ ♥

❧ Weight ❧

When you close down to the awareness of the great light within you, we move in grace around you. We call you home, but you are deafened to our voice. You stand in great awe of the pain that is before you, and you shudder at the realization that it is drawing nearer and nearer as you stare it in the face. Like a captivated animal frozen in oncoming traffic, you hesitate and then flee for momentary safety, as your heart beats rapidly at perceived danger all around you. You cower and hide from the roar of the traffic, and all seems deadly and chaotic.

Yet, even still, we angels sing sweetly to calm you to His glory, yet the din of the traffic renders us silent. While you are sleeping to this monumental bliss that surrounds you, you gnaw in silent aching for this longing that will not leave you, this gnawing for peace and for a removal of the incessant pressure that haunts you always, always.

Dear one, you seek for glory in all the wrong places when you search and find only darkness! Do you not see the dazzling brightness that obscures all pain and sorrow, the light that is unavoidable to all who would witness to its glory? Do not look at the darkness and analyze its sorrow, for this will cause you only further sorrow. And the din, the very din of the angry turmoil it brings you! It causes you to eat away at your own soul with behavior so cruel that you turn away from yourself in unloving thoughts that cast your eyes downward in search of solutions.

Your resolve belongs in the light, and not upon the flesh, and this you know within your heart, dearest being of God. Your flesh is set upon the mortal wound that causes you to stir as if God had not been a part of your essence, You are He, and He is you, be assured! The need you feel in your heart to feast upon His being with your mouth and your teeth is just confusion in your heart, which searches for darkness in the light, and light in the darkness.

Put down your hollow tools that are not the instruments leading to His glory. For these tools you use to gnaw upon the flesh are but blunted scissors that pierce you with sadness and fill you with a heaviness that soon becomes your body of weight like an anchor to cast you earthward. Your home is in heaven, as buoyant and as light as a ray of sunshine. Do not expect sorrow, and do not fear that He will bring you pain. There is no instance in which you can leave Him, so put out these thoughts that bring you incessant grief!

Your tongue reaches for more sorrow with its appetite and thirst, yet the soul hungers solely for the taste of its home in heaven. Quench this hunger now, dear one, and do not cover your heart with the flesh of the earth, which only brings you further sorrow and heaviness. Look skyward within your heart and find its heaven there, awaiting you with open arms that see your entire goodness shining in perfect radiance like the sun, the very sun.

You are the shining one who has clothed yourself within a mortal body. Yet even the body does not obstruct your realization of the doorway to the heavens in which you now truly stand. Rise up your arms in relief that the mortal dream is over, blessed one, and feel His arms nestle you with safety and with peace. There is no further torture for you to procure, as you have found at last the solace for which you witness upon this earth.

Rise up with your brothers and sisters, and feel the lightness of your very being as He pours the rays through and through. The weight of your sorrow is lifted, and the weight that captures you within a body is healed away. Hunger no more, dear little one, and never think that the Creator has left you to suffer or to thirst.

Your needs are immeasurably met by His attention to your glory, which He delights upon meeting in ingenious ways. Your hallowed meeting ground with God is your sustenance that brings the mortal flesh to bear, taming its hungry appetites with mildness and tepidness. Now the body will serve you well as you spin out your glorious afternoon of mortal living.

Treat the body well, dear one. Do not use it as a barrier to truth as you listen to its attunements and its hunger. Never confuse the body's desires for His great love with a meager helping of your own making. If you remember that everything is a reflection of His glory, you will serve your body well.

Your glory is well served by remembering always that you are put here for a holy purpose indeed. Those who would serve the largest dish for the Creator will find that their burdens feel heavy at times. Yet, fear not, that He would give you more than you have asked to serve. For He supports you always and in all ways, even now.

Put your ear to the earth, and listen to the rumblings of the natural world. Hear His gentle "footsteps" shuffling to meet the needs of the earth. Never think that you could be excluded in this natural order of things, for you are well loved! Yes, you are a divine being of His inexhaustible adoration. He cherishes you at every moment, and we ask that you drink of this love. Its ability to quench your deep thirst is immeasurable, and you will find that it quiets your inner longings for the peace that you seek. Your weight and your sorrow upon the earth will leave you as you drink in this peace. For you are all that you seek, and that is Love. Be well.

❤ ❤ ❤

⚘ Worry ⚘

There was a time before you were upon this earth when sorrow was not mentioned in your thoughts. You felt a joyous excitement for the time that was to come, and you felt your heart stir with radiance, for your dawning was upon you. Then you awoke within your mother's arms, and gazed upon the face of peace on mortal flesh and you hungered even then to remember what you had known an instant earlier. The memory had faded even at that moment when you recognized the face of terror inscripted upon the mother's beaming smile, which told you that you were not at home.

Poor dear one, we see you so sweetly struggling to recapture the calmer times of your immortal heaven and to reconcile the two while you are not at home. Tread gently, dearest child. Your grace delights us, and we seek to ease your pains with gentle assurances that there never has been a greater time for your wisdom upon the earth than now. Great rumblings await you who meet us in thought, and your unfoldment *is* the exciting adventure that awaits us all.

Your grace has never been holier than at this very moment, and we ask you to hold strong in the belief that He awaits you the moment you hold the mighty love in your thoughts. Your cares and your worries are likened to dried leaves tossing in a great windstorm, and they crumple in the face of one who is stronger than their brittle complexion. Toss your cares and concerns windward. Feel His gentle breeze caress you with reassurances that the curvature of the wind around a corner or a wall is like the way His mind enfolds every problem, and reaches into every crevice of concern.

Awaken from your nightmare of terror, dear one, and come into the sunlight of eternal warmth with us! The heart of all worries is melted in the gentle beams of love that radiate everywhere for everyone. The gentle beating of the mortal heart, which stands in terror at thoughts of danger and of lack, beats merrily at the memory of its early song of upbeat harmony that sways and dances.

Let your mind's roar calm to a whisper so that we may intervene on His behalf and tell you sweet stories about your origin. Let us remind you of the immortal truth of your being, so that you shall hunger no more, nor wrestle with pain. For pain is a mighty giant in your imagination only, and as you depart from its stance, you see it dissolve into a puddle of memories as you trade one picture of sorrow for another of heaven. Do not depart from your memory of esteem in your mind, but hold it close in your heart always!

Think sweetly of us who grace your sides. Call to us when you need help to stay firmly rooted in this sure and steady knowledge of truth and of love. Never fear that we would leave you, for we could not, even if we willed. We are sure and steady fortresses, and we applaud your efforts that remind you of home.

Let the mirror in your mind reflect all memories of heaven, and bring this peace to sorrow, to melt away the cares upon the earth. Heal the sadness that you see in mirror thoughts, and gaze upon the dazzling and blazing light situated gently behind the mirror. Move your handhold on your thoughts so that it reflects directly upon the brightness, and watch its dazzling brilliance obscure everything else. For when the mirror gazes directly upon the brilliance, no chance for sorrow stands in its way. The beaming simplicity of this logical move is in your hands at this very instant.

Feel the fun and light-hearted response of gaiety that shines from the light that is in us all. And we give thanks for your openness to this healing, and we love you, love you all.

♥ ♥ ♥

❧ Writing ❧

Many of you feel drawn to writing at this time, and let us tell you one reason why this is so. There is an account in ancient records of a time when many were scribes in a foreign land. The scribes wrote letters to each other and in this way traded up in levels of understanding, like stairs that were built upon one another. This building up from another's experiences is the outward push of eons of energy building up in masses of beings. It erupts in words now flowing freely through many hands, and as you trade words with one another, you are propelled upward in the spiral of the energy cycle.

It is good that you write, dear ones, and we angels bless you who seek to share your writings with others among you! We ask that you wait not upon others who ask for what you want to share, but share it freely so that all may bask in the glow of God's glory as written through your hand. You have much to give, it is true, and we wouldn't want to stop you from this flow that naturally pushes the words through your mind and body and onto the paper. Give, give, and give some more, dear being! Give your words away, and bless the words as more come freely to you.

Never fear that your well will become empty, or fear that others will hurt you if you give them your words. For the words are a thing of beauty and not of wrestling with the heavens. You needn't force them into action, for they set sail on their very own course once they are born from the Mind of all Minds. You share its light when you share its offspring in the form of words. Shine the light so radiantly, as one who holds a mirror in the noonday sun. This one gives no thought to where the radiant beams focus, but merely on the joy that holding the reflection of the beams brings.

Focus, then, on the joy that is the center of the words and radiates outwardly endlessly, endlessly, and endlessly still like the Creator who is one with us all. Cast no shadows upon the light with thoughts about the best route for it to travel. Your mind knows no limits for the excitement of sending and catching the rays of light. Use this excitement in the best possible ways, for your energy is a crested wave that can propel or crash, depending upon your choices.

Allow us to follow your trail of decision to use the energy as a lightbearer bringing radiance to a darkened world. We gather around your excitement with joy of our own, alighting upon your thoughts and willing them into an ever-widening radius of circles. See the circles touching and moving as you harmlessly push the love of your heart out through your thoughts and your actions. As your writing progresses into the light, be assured that we will strum merrily to set it to music, which widens its circle of radiation even further. The light will cast your words upon the sea, and sail it far, to all who thirst for it.

Your deed is done with your mere intent to cause others' hearts to stir with passion and radiance as they look upon the light. Use this love in the best possible way, dear one, and we will take you one beam further above the din of mortal grace. Never fear that we would overlook any humble deeds done in humanity's name. For we lift you higher than any man can take you, so be sure that we are beside you in every way. We are your angels in God's name, and we bid you great peace and love for ever and evermore.

♥ ♥ ♥

PART II

Communicating, Healing, and Living with Angels

INTRODUCTION

Whether you desire to channel angels, or just want to more clearly hear their divine guidance, you can take specific steps to clearly communicate with these heavenly beings. The first step is simply to *desire* to converse with angels. Our intentions, in whatever we do, are the starting points of everything we experience. So, holding the intention in your heart and mind to communicate with angels, ensures that it will happen.

Everyone can communicate with the angels, without exception. It's a fallacy to believe that one must be chosen, sensitive, or gifted to hear the voice of God and the angels. Since we are all created equally by God, we are all equally gifted.

We also all have angels surrounding us constantly, and our higher self is united with these angels and with God. So, our higher self is in constant contact with God and the angels through the one universal Mind that is the all-in-all. You don't need to *add* anything to yourself to hear divine communication. It's more a matter of *removing* any fears, doubts, or tension that may block your spiritual eyes and ears. Fortunately, the angels are very happy to help us remove these blocks— all we need to do is ask.

Once you've released anything internal standing in your path, you'll naturally receive divine communications very clearly and directly. Then, you can amplify the volume and clarity of the messages by making subtle changes in your home environment and lifestyle. Again, the angels will help you every step of the way.

In the following pages, I've described some methods I've found especially helpful in unblocking spiritual communication. The angels taught me many of these methods. You'll notice that, occasionally, the angels speak to you directly in some of the following pages. Of course, there are as many ways to communicate with angels as there are ways upon the spiritual path. Your angels will guide you to the particular methods that will best suit you. In fact, you will probably enjoy blending your own unique style of angel communication.

Since joy is the emotion of the angels, you are sure to feel *immense* pleasure as you consciously connect with these heavenly beings.

— Doreen Virtue, Ph.D.

You Are Surrounded by Angels

As I paid for my purchase at a department store, I noticed three golden angel pins upon a nearby clerk's sweater. I complimented the woman on her angel jewelry, and the clerk who was ringing up my sale commented, "Maybe I should start wearing angel pins, too. Then I can be lucky like her!"

Luck! I thought to myself as I caught the eye of the angel pin-wearing woman. She winked at me in mutual acknowledgment that "luck" plays no part in the miracles that come your way when you invite angels into your life. The woman explained that twice recently she'd experienced miraculous protection at the department store from her angels. First, her stolen purse was recovered intact within an hour of the incident. Second, as a rack full of heavy clothing was falling on her, it miraculously changed direction and fell a different way.

As the clerk and I swapped angelic intervention stories, the eyes of the woman in front me grew large. "Do I have angels?" she wanted to know, and then asked, "How can I get them to help me, too?"

We always benefit whenever we invite angels into our lives. To acquaint you better with the angels in your midst, let's start by looking at the different roles angels can take. Three categories of angels help us here on earth:

1. Guardian angels.

Everyone has a guardian angel, with no exceptions. I've met people who doubted whether they deserved to have a guardian angel. Please know that you have a guardian angel with you, guaranteed! This is the angel who constantly stays with you, from birth until your transition back to heaven. This angel's love for you is unconditional, and greater than anything on this earth. Your guardian angel makes certain you are always safe and guided.

Guardian angels are sometimes confused with "spirit guides." A spirit guide is a loving being who has lived upon the earth in human form. This person then received special training in the afterlife about how to become a spirit guide. This training emphasizes that the guide is not to interfere with your free will or make decisions for you. The guide is there to give you general advice, comfort, and at times warning and protection. Most spirit guides are deceased loved ones, such as grandparents, siblings, beloved friends, and parents. Your spirit guide may have passed away in the physical life before you were born. However, this loving being was there at your birth and has been with you every day of your life since. Just as you will always take an interest in your family's future off-spring, so do the deceased family members whom we may have never encountered in physical form.

Spirit guides act in the capacity of guardian angels, in that they bring many gifts to our lives. The main difference is that true guardian angels, who have never walked as mortals upon the earth, have a higher vibrating energy frequency. People who are empathic, who can "feel" the sensation of a spiritual presence, can tell the palpable difference between an angelic and a spirit guide appearance. Clairvoyants see that angels' auras are bright white, whereas a spirit guide's aura is not quite as bright and may appear as bluish-white.

2. Angels.

These are the beings of light who respond to our calls for guidance, assistance, protection, and comfort. God's thoughts of love create angels. The angels are here to help us, especially when our intent is to bring joy and healing to the world. Ask for as many angels as you want to surround you. Ask for angels to surround your loved ones, your home, and your business. Angels receive great joy from helping us, and they ask only that we occasionally remember to say, "Thank you" in gratitude for their help.

3. Archangels.

These are the angels who supervise the guardian angels and angels upon the earth. You might think of archangels as the "managers" among the earthly angels' hierarchy. You can call upon an archangel whenever you need powerful and immediate assistance.

Since angels are purely spiritual beings, they have no time or space restrictions. An archangel can help many people in different geographical locations simultaneously. So, never worry about calling upon an angel because you fear that your need isn't "big enough" or that the angel might be busy. Your call for help is sweet music to an angel's ears.

Because of the "Law of Free Will," angels and archangels cannot intervene in our lives unless we specifically ask for their help. The only exception to this is a life-endangering situation, where we could die before our time. Otherwise, it's up to us to remember to constantly invite angels and archangels into our lives.

Angels and archangels come to your assistance the moment you call them. You don't need to say a formal invitation or invocation ritual, and you don't even need to verbalize your call aloud. Just the thought, *Angels!* is enough. If your request for angelic assistance is sincere, the angels appear in response to your call, often before you've finished calling them!

♥ ♥ ♥

The Archangels

Each archangel specializes in a different human condition. It's helpful to learn which archangel handles which function so you'll know whom to call in a time of need. Here is a summary of the roles and names of the four major archangels:

1. The Archangel Michael, whose name means "Who is like God" or "He who looks like God."

We often call Michael, "St. Michael," especially since Pope Pius named him the official patron saint of police officers and soldiers. No wonder: Michael is the defender of light and goodness, and his chief role is to escort fallen people away so they cannot hurt other people. Michael and his assistant angels, known as "The Band of Mercy," take negatively minded people (both living and deceased) to the light of God, where their minds are healed.

Call upon Michael whenever you feel frightened by negative sources. If you are in a crowded place populated by upset people, for instance, ask Michael to cleanse away the negative energy. If you suspect that an unevolved earthbound spirit is with you, Michael can take that being to the light.

In the same vein, whenever you become burdened by worries and fears, ask Michael to cleanse your mind and heart. Angels can enter deep inside our bodies and thoughts, and help us to see things from a more loving point of view.

Paintings of Michael often show him holding scales of justice in his hand, as he is the overseer of truth and fairness. If you feel someone is treating you unfairly, ask Michael to intervene. You'll receive a miraculous solution, such as the other person suddenly calling with an apology or a change of heart.

Michael can also help you resolve frightening situations. I called upon Archangel Michael when my husband was frantically searching his computer files for an important document. My husband (whose name is also Michael) was afraid that he had accidentally erased his document, as he couldn't find it anywhere. Meanwhile, I sat nearby and asked for St. Michael's intervention. Instantly, I saw a large figure appear over my husband's left shoulder, and the angel appeared to be fiddling with the computer. Within a minute of this vision, my husband exclaimed, "I found it!"

It's a good idea to invite Michael's presence into any room of your house or office that has a negative energy "feel" about it. For instance, if you live in a home previously occupied by unhappy people, ask Michael to purify the environment. I always ask Michael to clear the energy in the auditoriums in which I give workshops. Michael's angelic energy creates a relaxed, loving atmosphere for the audience and me.

Whenever you are upset, call upon the Archangel Michael to restore harmony and peace. If you ever travel into neighborhoods that feel unsafe in any way, be sure to ask Michael to guide and protect you. You can ask him to intervene into contentious partnerships or marriages suffering from discord. Think of the Archangel Michael as the protector of joy, and you'll always know when it's time to call for his help.

2. The Archangel Gabriel, whose name means "Hero of God" or "God is my strength."

Gabriel is the famous angel who told the Virgin Mary of her impending birth, and who later delivered the, "Behold, I bring you good tidings of great joy" news about newborn Jesus. This archangel is God's messenger, who brings us news of forthcoming events, changes on the horizon, and new experiences in store for us. Gabriel provides a lot of help to humanly messengers, including journalists and couriers.

Expectant or want-to-be parents can invite Gabriel into their lives to supervise the conception and birth of a new child. And anyone involved in a new project of any sort—such as a start-up business, a new job, or a change of residence—is wise to ask for Gabriel's assistance and advice.

The archangel Gabriel also breathes new life into stale relationships and lackluster businesses. Ask Gabriel to resurrect any part of your life that feels "stuck." You'll receive creative ideas and new opportunities to help you get moving again.

Legends have credited Gabriel with delivering the prophecies about the messiah to Daniel, the *Koran* to Mohammed, and the inspiration that drove Joan of Arc's mission. Consequently, many people believe that Gabriel is in charge of visions, dreams, and revelations. Ask for Gabriel's help in interpreting any of your dreams that seem mystifying.

3. The Archangel Uriel, whose name means "Light of God."

Uriel brings divine light into our lives. He is wonderful at healing our painful memories and transforming our regrets and mistakes so that we feel stronger and more loving. Ask Uriel to take your burdens related to the past. He will instantly ease your heart and mind of old unforgiveness held toward yourself or others.

This archangel helps us to see love in situations where we feel that none exists. For example, if you are having difficult relationships with co-workers, bosses, or customers, ask Uriel to help you. He will guide you and the other people in miraculous ways so that you'll see the good that is inside all of us. With Uriel's help, you may forget why you were ever angry or fearful toward the people at work in the first place!

Folklore says that Uriel warned Noah of the impending flood. This archangel helps us during times of disaster, such as earthquakes, tornadoes, and torrential rains. Ask Uriel to help you whenever you feel fear about these situations. He may guide you to move to a different locale or prepare your home for maximum safety. Uriel also helps families to stay safe and intact during natural disasters.

Similarly, if your life feels like one giant shifting earthquake, ask for Uriel to re-orient your mind and thoughts to regain your peace of mind. Uriel is wonderful at rescuing us from our self-imposed crises, and he also helps us to establish a calm and centered life.

Uriel also helps us to fulfill our goals and dreams. He offers help completely, including giving us good ideas, keeping us encouraged and motivated, and helping us to manifest the material supplies we need for our project. Invite Uriel to become your partner in anything you are currently working on.

4. *The Archangel Raphael, whose name means "God heals."*

Raphael is in charge of all forms of healing. He supervises the healing needs of the earth and also its population. Raphael guides and helps people involved in the healing arts, such as doctors, practitioners, nurses, counselors, ecologists, and scientists. However, they can always ask for additional assistance, which Archangel Raphael is happy to provide!

If you currently work in a healing profession, you'll want to invite Raphael into your life. He will whisper guidance into your ear if you feel unsure about which direction to take with a patient. He also gives us creative ideas and needed information so that we can rapidly heal other people. Raphael intervenes during medical crises to ensure that miraculous "coincidences" line up all the right personnel and medical supplies with precious timing. This archangel is wonderful in helping scientists to create new breakthroughs in medical cures. So it's wise for all of us to pray for Raphael's help with health issues that confound the scientific community.

Those who aspire to become healers are the darlings of Archangel Raphael. This archangel knows that the earth needs many of these special people, and he miraculously helps would-be healers to enter their chosen profession. Raphael will help you to choose the best school for you, and he'll also guide you in creative ways to pay for your education. Leave all your concerns and worries about your future healing career to Raphael. He can more easily help you when you are free of tension and fear.

If you or a loved one needs healing, Raphael is the archangel to call upon. Except for cases where a person's death or illness is part of their overall divine plan, Archangel Raphael will deliver whatever they need to evoke a healing. So after you've called upon Raphael, you may receive sudden ideas, thoughts, or inspirations that give you just the right information to help in a healing. You'll want to pay attention to, and then follow, these angelically inspired answers to your prayers. Sometimes the angels don't swoop in and heal us. Instead, they may lead us to find humanly help for illnesses and accidents.

At other times, Raphael might point out to you that your thoughts have triggered the health problems. For example, Raphael may ask you to surrender old anger to him to release your body from the ravages of rage's poisonous effects. You'll then feel as comfortable in surrendering your anger as you would in disposing of yesterday's newspaper. When the anger is gone, your body becomes relieved of its anguish, and Raphael's legendary healing will have occurred again.

Raphael exudes a beautiful bright and clear emerald green light. This is the color of healing, and also of the heart chakra's love energy. As you call upon Raphael, you might see, with your inner eye, the emerald light surround you like a glorious rain shower of glowing light. Feel your cells drink in this quenching bath, and feel replenished and completely healed by its loving nourishment.

Raphael also has a second specialty: He guides and protects travelers of all sorts. Whether you are on a spiritual journey or about to embark to Europe, call upon Raphael to smooth the way.

To angels and archangels, no job is "big" or "small." All miracles are equally important to these beings who love us with all the might of God. All they ask, in return, is that we thank them for their help, share in their devotion to God, and that we fill our lives with joy and service.

♥ ♥ ♥

Nature Angels

The ancient spiritual text, *The Talmud*, says, "Every blade of grass has an angel bending over it saying, "Grow, grow."

Imagine, then, how many angels are in your own backyard or a nearby park. Every blade of grass, flower, tree, sand grain, and raindrop has one or more angels overseeing its life-cycle. We also know nature angels as *faeries* and *devas*. These diminutive angels sing beautiful hymns as they tend to the needs of nature's growing bounty.

During my angel therapy sessions, the angels frequently advise my clients to spend more time in nature. One reason why angels prescribe "nature therapy" is its rapid healing effect. Imagine yourself sitting beneath the shade of tree with flowers and grass growing all around you. See yourself taking a deep breath and meditating upon God's glory, which is in and around you right now. Visualize the nature angels surrounding you with hugs and caresses, which heal every cell in your body and thought in your mind. Feel the gentle touch of the nature angels' loving embrace, as you imagine yourself in their midst.

If I feel stuck, drained, or fatigued, a brief sojourn to a natural setting restores my vitality and loving outlook. Try any natural setting that gives you some solitude, such as a lake or ocean shore, a mountain, a trail, or a forest area. Even an apartment balcony garden will do in a pinch. The nature angels live among the plants and mineral kingdom, no matter where.

Mentally alert the nature angels before you walk upon grass or ground, so they can move out of the way of your feet. Warn them, also, before you mow or spray your lawn. Nothing can harm a nature angel, in truth, since they have no physical bodies. They also have no fear or animosity, as they are pure love. However, you show the nature angels kindness and consideration by giving them ample time to scurry out of the path of your feet or lawnmower.

Animals, too, have angels around them. Your dog, cat, bird, or other pet has two or more guardian angels. You can commune with your pet's angels whenever you hug, pet, or play with your animal. Feel the special loving energy of these magnificent angels.

You'll probably agree that your own pet functions as an angel in your family. Many animals are on angelic assignment from God to provide solace, comfort, and companionship to us humans. Pets also perform the heavenly function of absorbing stress from our household, much like an air filter suctioning smoke out of a room. Angels, such as your pet, thrive on feeling loved and appreciated. They ask for so little, and yet give us so much in return.

♥ ♥ ♥

Asking for Angels

Sometimes, I'll see people whom an entourage of angels surrounds. I always stop them and ask whether they purposely called the angels. Always, the answer I hear is, "Yes, I asked to be surrounded by angels." The more we call upon the angels, the more they can come to our assistance.

Angels *want* to surround us, and they greatly desire to give us help. Our joy brings *them* enormous pleasure. Yet, they cannot help us unless we ask. A universal law that binds angels says, "No angel shall interfere with a human's life unless asked, with the sole exception of a life-threatening emergency. An angel will not make decisions for a human, but—when asked—an angel may offer advice and different ways of looking at the given situation." So an angel may nudge you or encourage you, and an angel may create a miraculous coincidence for you. However, an angel cannot help you unless you choose to accept the help, because you have free will.

To ask for angelic assistance, you needn't conduct a formal invocation ceremony. God and the angels aren't complicated, due to their true nature of pure and simple love. Only our lower-self ego believes that spirituality is necessarily complicated, because it cannot believe that something so powerful and great could be accessible to everyone instantly. Yet, it's true.

The angels hear the prayers of your heart, and just by your mental cry for help, they flock to your side. You can also consciously ask for more angels to surround you or your loved one. Parents can ask for angelic baby-sitters to guide and protect their children throughout the day. If a loved one is traveling, ask Raphael and the angels to watch over the journey.

Ask the angels to help your friends who are in need of comfort and direction.

Some ways to call upon the angels include:

- ***Writing a letter to the angels.*** Pour out your heart when discussing your confusions, hurts, and anxieties. Hold nothing back, so that the angels can help every part of you and your situation.

- ***Visualizing.*** Call it your inner eye, your imagination, or your third eye—the term doesn't matter. Visualizing angels is a powerful way to call them to your side. See the angels flying in circles around you or your loved ones. See powerful angels thronged by your side. See the room you are in crowded with thousands of angels. These visualizations are angelic invocations that create your reality.

  Angels are glowing with the light of love, so they don't have a physical form. However, angels can take on a physical appearance by projecting a mental image to us, if this will help us. So if you visualize cherubs, large glowing beings, or a beautifully dressed angelic woman, the angels will take on this form to help you recognize them.

- ***Mentally calling upon angels.*** Think, *Angels, please help me,* and they are with you instantly. If you are sincere in your call, the angels hear your mental cry for assistance. You can word your request as an affirmation, such as "I have hundreds of angels surrounding me now," or as a petitional prayer: "Angels, I am in pain and need your help now." You can ask God to send you angels, or you can call the angels directly.

- ***Speaking to angels aloud.*** You can verbalize your request, and sometimes we do this unconsciously, such as when we say, "Oh, God" during distress. You might find that spending time alone in a quiet setting, especially outdoors in nature, is a wonderful opportunity to have a verbal conversation with the angels.

♥ ♥ ♥

You Know That Angels Are Near When . . .

You *feel* the angels' presence. Perhaps you sense a warm brush across your face, shoulders, hands, or arms. You might feel their hug, or the brush of a wing across your skin. The air pressure changes when angels enter a room. There is a palpable thickening, as if a delicious cloud just rolled in to shield you from the heat. Also, the room temperature may seem to shift, or you might catch a whiff of a beautiful lilting fragrance that you can't quite identify. When the angels hug you, you feel a deep warmth flow through your chest, and your heart expands with unearthly love.

You *see* the angels' presence. The calling cards of angels are visible. A sparkle of white, blue, or green light out of the corner of your eye signals that an angel is near. A glowing shadow moving so fast that you wonder if it's your imagination is another signal. And the beautiful angels you see in a darkened room, or standing beside a beloved friend or teacher, confirm that the angelic kingdom visits you.

You *hear* the angels' presence—a loving whisper in your ear that urges you to improve your life. Or an unmistakable shout warning you to, "Watch out!" A voice inside your mind counseling you to reach for the stars, and the sweet strains of music coming from out of nowhere. These are the sounds that angels make.

You *know* the angels' presence. When you suddenly get an idea that dramatically transforms your life, an angel has just delivered a message from God and has tucked it safely within your heart. When you have an unmistakable knowingness that angels are near you, trust that it is so.

You *experience* the angels' presence. When they miraculously avert a near-tragedy, or a door "coincidentally" opens for you at just the right moment, you know that angels are helping you in the background. When you walk through nature and feel free and joy-filled, you can be sure that angels walk beside you along the way.

❤   ❤   ❤

Quieting the Mind

Our guardian angel continuously talks to us and gently offers advice and guidance. When we consciously ask for additional help and summon extra angels to our side, we receive an even steadier stream of divine communication.

However, we must be aware of this heavenly assistance as it comes to us, *before* it can help us. Sometimes, chatter and noise so fill our thoughts that we can't hear the sweet and loving voice of our angels. The loud din of thoughts about our bills, family, and responsibilities overpowers the softer sound of the angels. We also ignore our angels' messages when they seem inappropriate to our current goals. For instance, if your angels urge you to relax and have fun, you may shrug off their advice with a "Haven't got the time" reply.

Many people also tell me they have difficulty meditating. Either they don't feel there's enough time for meditation, or their mind wanders or they fall asleep when they try to meditate.

While meditation certainly makes it easier to clearly hear your angels' messages, it's not an absolute necessity. There are other ways to quiet the mind sufficiently for the angelic voices to be heard.

For instance, you can slow your body, emotions, and thoughts by connecting with nature. If you can get in the habit of regularly looking out of the window of your home, office, or car and appreciating one bit of nature—a cloud, a tree, a bird chirping—you'll feel a wonderful quieting within yourself. Focus your eyes and mind on this miracle of nature before you, and feel your heart swell in appreciation and gratitude at its beauty. Better yet is when you actually spend time in nature. Of course, camping and hiking trips accomplish this nicely. But even a lunch break in a park or by the side of a brook is sufficient to re-establish your connection with Mother Earth, the nature angels, and your own guardian angels.

Another way to quiet the mind and body is by taking two or three slow and deep breaths. Breathe in as much as air as possible, then hold it in your lungs for a count of five or ten seconds. Then slowly breathe out. Repeat the breaths, and this time, picture yourself breathing in beautiful feelings such as relaxation, joy, and peace. When you breathe out, feel yourself releasing stress, tension, and worries.

You are *in*-spiring yourself with these deep breaths. In other words, you are filling yourself with the light of spirit. Dannion Brinkley, the author of *Saved by the Light,* who has had two near-death experiences, once told me that the spirit world communicates with us through our breaths. When we breathe in short, shallow spurts, we don't receive the depth of communication as we do when we really breathe deeply. Breathing is, in essence, our way of phoning home to heaven!

Eastern philosophies teach a visualization for quieting the mind in which you picture a large lake of clear water. Focus your attention in the center of the lake, as if you were underwater and easily breathing and floating as you looked at the water around you. Notice that sand granules are slowly floating to the bottom of the lake. As the sand falls, the water becomes perfectly clear and still. Feel your body and mind responding to this stillness, with all your cares and concerns gently falling and settling into a gentle quietness.

Physical exercise also has a quieting effect. Studies show that after we vigorously work out, our brain chemistry shifts in healthful directions. The post-exercise brain has increased amounts of the mood- and energy-altering neurotransmitter called "serotonin." Many people also report an increase in creative ideas and brainstorms while they are exercising. Probably, the increased breathing during exercise leads to this sort of *in*-spiration. Try 30 minutes of vigorous walking, bicycling, or an outdoor sport, and you'll find that angel communication comes quite naturally both during and after your workout.

It's easier to hear your angels when you are alone, especially when you are in a natural setting. We all need time-outs from the world to regenerate our energy and collect our thoughts. Make a daily appointment to spend time alone, when your mind isn't focused on some worldly task. Whether you sit in a meditative lotus position or engage in a creative activity such as painting, singing, dancing, or gardening, make time for yourself and your angels to commune together.

♥ ♥ ♥

How to Hear Your Angels' Messages

Not everyone "hears" angelic voices as audible sounds. Many people receive divine messages through nonverbal means such as visions, feelings, or a knowingness.

Hearing the voice of God and the angels is called *clairaudience,* which means "clear hearing." The voice may sound like your own or it may sound different. The voice can emanate from within your body, within your mind, or sound as if it's outside your head. When the angel warned me about my car being stolen, his voice sounded as if he were talking through a paper towel tube, just outside my right ear. While channeling the messages of this book, I heard the words both inside and outside my mind.

You might hear a faint voice and wonder what it said. In such cases, go ahead and ask your angels to repeat their message. Say to them, "A little louder, please." The angels appreciate your feedback, as they want to deliver clear and understandable guidance.

At first, you may believe that the voice is your imagination or wishful thinking. This is especially true when you begin consciously interacting with angels. You think, *This is a fantasy. I wish it were true that angels would help me, but I'm probably doing something wrong and the angels won't notice me.*

We heal this type of thinking through faith, trust, and practice. If your faith in angels is uncertain, ask God to help you. Pray, "Please help me to have more faith. I am willing to release all of my fears that keep me from having full faith." The Divine universe always fulfills requests for more faith.

Angelic voices are consistently loving and supportive, even when they warn us of impending danger or wrong turns. As a psychotherapist, I was trained to believe that hearing voices was a sign of insanity. Yet, the voice of the ego is the only source of "insanity." Ego voice messages are always destructive, abusive, and impulsive. For example, the ego may try to convince you that you'll fail. The ego also changes its mind constantly, so it will tell you to do one thing Monday, another thing Tuesday, and a completely different thing Wednesday. If you listen to the voice of the ego, your life will be chaotic and fear-filled.

Angelic voices, in contrast, patiently repeat the guidance to us day after day until we finally follow it. You may hear your angels tell you for years that you would be a great healer or author, for example. Or your angels may repeatedly ask you to take better care of your body. You know that the guidance comes from angels when it is loving, focused, not hurtful to you or your family, and consistent.

Clairaudience is just one of the four ways we receive angelic assistance, however. Your angels may speak to you in pictures and visual mental images. We call this *clairvoyance,* or "clear seeing." Angelic messages may come to you as single snapshot images, either in your mind or outside your mind. Or, you may see miniature scenes, as if from a movie. The images may be black-and-white or full color. Angelic visual messages can be symbolic, such as seeing a stop sign as a signal that you should take a rest, slow, or stop what you are doing.

Intuitively, you might readily understand what the visual images mean. For instance, you might see an image of a trophy, and instinctively you know this means that success is ahead for you. If you have trouble understanding your angelic visual guidance, be sure to ask for assistance. Ask your angels to clarify their message, and continue asking for clarification until you are completely certain of their meaning.

Sometimes we shut down our angelic channels of communication due to fear. You might see an image of your future that frightens you, and you turn off your clairvoyance by shutting the third eye's eyelid. Many years ago, I was an uneducated housewife who was unhappy because I wanted to make a contribution to the world but didn't feel qualified to do anything meaningful.

Then God and the angels gave me mental visual images of the life I was meant to lead. I saw myself writing self-help books and appearing on talk shows. The images showed me having an advanced college degree. These visions scared me a great deal because I didn't feel capable of fulfilling them. I thought that I lacked the intelligence, time, and money to create the meaningful life shown in the clairvoyant images.

I found that I could shut off the visions by eating a lot of food. My full stomach interrupted my telephone connection with God and the angels. However, when my stomach digested the food, I'd feel irritable because I would see the contrast between my present life and the life I was supposed to live. Fortunately, I got tired of dodging my divine guidance, and surrendered to God. When I did, He began opening doors before me, one step at a time. The angels arranged for me to achieve every part of the visions I saw, in ways I could have never planned or anticipated.

One of my clients shut down her clairvoyance when, as a young girl, she saw a visual image of her parents divorcing in the future. Another client closed her third eye because she foresaw herself having an affair with a married co-worker, and she wanted to continue her interactions with him while wearing blinders to the truth. One of my other clients was trying to ignore a steady angelic voice within that counseled, "It's time to look for work at a different place," because she didn't trust God to fulfill her material needs during the job transition.

You might also shut off your clairvoyance if you are afraid of what you *might* see. As much as you want to see your angels in person, you might harbor a deep-seated fear that seeing a "ghost" would be terrifying. Your angels honor such fears, and you won't see angelic apparitions until you feel confident that such a vision would comfort—not frighten—you.

The third way we receive angelic guidance is through our emotions and physical sensations. We call this *clairsentience,* or "clear feeling." Clairsentients get divine guidance through bodily sensations, such as a tightening of the jaw, fists, stomach, or sex organs. They intuitively know the specific meaning of these tightening reactions. A clairsentient feels air pressure and room temperature changes that warn him or her of negative situations.

Each of our five senses has a corresponding spiritual sense. Clairsentients receive angelic guidance through an etheric sense of smell, taste, and touch. You may know that your beloved deceased grandmother is near when you smell her perfume or favorite flower. An angel may shower your room with the aroma of orange blossoms to tell you of an impending wedding.

Clairsentients receive a lot of guidance through their intuition, gut feelings, and hunches. Much of our intuition comes from the stomach region, and the stomach flutters, relaxes, and tightens according to the angelic guidance. Instinctively, the clairsentient interprets the meaning of these gut feelings, and a *wise* clairsentient follows these internal directives without hesitation.

Clairsentients get angelic messages through their heart and love emotions, as well. If a thought of doing something swells your chest with warm feelings of joy, this is a directive from God and the angels. You may say, "Oh, this is too good to be true; I'm just dreaming," but the joy that your thought has brought you is a road map leading you to the life you are meant to have.

We call the fourth means of angelic communication *claircognizance,* or "clear knowing." Men are frequently claircognizant, and they may not even realize that they naturally receive detailed and accurate information from God and the angels. You can ask a claircognizant a question on almost any topic in the world. Within minutes, he will give you an accurate answer, completely supported by facts and figures. You might ask, "How did you know that?" and he'll answer, "I don't know! A few minutes ago, I didn't know that information."

Claircognizants know, without knowing *how* they know. Consequently, they may doubt the validity of their knowingness. This is a mistake, because when divine wisdom enters our mind, it is a gift we can use to improve our life and to serve the world.

We all have access to all four channels of communication. Usually, we have one primary means of receiving angelic guidance and one secondary—or lesser—channel of communication. With practice, you can become adept at receiving messages in all four ways. In the beginning stages of speaking to your angels, though, most people concentrate upon their natural means of communication.

Naturally visually oriented people will want to pay attention to their mental visions. If you tend to focus upon sounds, then listen for inner or outer words, voices, and auditory messages. If you tend to be a touchy-feely type, your emotions and bodily sensations are the instruments that relay divine guidance to you. And if you are intellectually inclined, or a person who constantly searches for hidden meanings in situations, then you'll want to monitor your thoughts for those heavenly moments of "knowingness" that bring you certainty in guiding your actions.

♥ ♥ ♥

Some Ways to Communicate
with Angels

From the angels:

"We aren't that difficult to hear, if you will listen for us with an open heart. Most of the time, we are closer to you than you can imagine. A whisper, a thought, is the only signal we need from you to get a conversation started. We have enormous respect for what you're going through here on planet Earth at this time. We never seek to interfere with your lives, only to bring you blessings of insights and new ways of looking at yourselves."

You can communicate with angels in a variety of ways, including automatic writing, dreamwork, oracle cards, and intuitional or psychic communication. It's important to choose a communication style to which you feel naturally drawn. Anything that feels forced or frightening will block your ability to clearly hear your angels' messages. Also, angel communication takes a little practice and patience at first. So, you'll want to try methods that you are likely to stick with for a while.

While reading the following descriptions, pay attention to your reactions to each method. Ask yourself, "Do I feel happy or excited about trying it? Or, do I feel neutral or even negative about this method?" Then try the methods that appeal to you.

— *Automatic writing.* I received the angels' messages in this book through this process. It means that the angels literally write their message through the channeler. Automatic writing can involve a form of dictation, in which you hear the angelic voices and then write what you hear. The voice may be inside or outside your head. It may or may not sound like your own voice. You'll likely be conscious of what you are writing in this form of automatic writing.

Another type of automatic writing involves the angels physically pushing your hand while you use a pencil or type on a keyboard. Most people who automatically write this way are unaware of the words they are writing. This is the form of automatic writing used in this book.

You can try this second form of automatic writing by taking these steps:

1. Set a definite time and date when you will attempt to channel with automatic writing. Mentally tell your angels of this appointment so they can prepare. Then, be sure to follow your promised schedule.

2. Choose a quiet place where you won't be interrupted. Turn off the phone and put a sign on the door so others won't make noises that will block your communication flow. It's best to have quiet background music or a tape of nature sounds, and also some pleasant fragrance such as fresh flowers or incense in the room.

3. If you plan to try automatic writing with a pencil, you'll need a seating arrangement that allows you to comfortably hold the pencil over a paper on a steady surface. As you begin automatic writing, you want to make it easy on yourself. So, you probably won't want to try

automatically writing upon a pad of paper on the floor, on your lap, or another position where the pencil doesn't easily flow.

Some automatic writers use pens; however, pencils are traditional since they don't skip or bleed. Several years ago, "planchettes" were used to hold pencils for automatic writers. Planchettes are wooden triangles with a hole in the center, supported by three ball bearings that allow smooth movement in any direction. The pencil is placed firmly in the planchette's hole, and the spirit world guides the channeler's hand to push the planchette, much like on a Ouija board.

You might opt to conduct automatic writing with a computer or typewriter keyboard instead of with pencil and paper. No special seating arrangements are necessary for this beyond your normal chair, desk, and keyboard.

4. Make sure that you are comfortable. It's best to wear nonbinding clothing, and it's important to channel on a slightly empty stomach without the influence of *any* stimulants (coffee, colas, sugar, herbs, chocolate) or depressants (heavy meals, alcohol, drugs, herbs).

5. Take two or three very deep breaths. Say a prayer such as *The Lord's Prayer,* or an affirmation such as, "I see myself surrounded by white light and divine love. I am safe, protected and loved." You may want to ask Archangel Michael to oversee your channeling, especially at first when you may not be able to readily discern an earthbound spirit from an angel. Michael will act as a doorman who only allows invited guests to enter your territory.

6. At this point, you may immediately feel the channeling sensation begin. Don't let it frighten you. The first time I tried automatic writing with a pencil, it began rapidly moving on its own, which startled me. My fear then blocked the whole channeling process for a long time.

    In the beginning, the pencil will write circular doodles. These circles are the angels' way of expressing their great joy at making a connection with you. After you and the angels become accustomed to working together, then letters, words, and sentences will come through your pencil. Usually, though, the pencil will write circles for the first one to three days that you try automatic writing.

Or, you may hear an inner voice and feel a tug that pushes you to write what you hear. The automatic writing can also take a more tactile approach. If you are writing at a keyboard, the sensation may feel like a piano teacher grasping your hands and pushing your fingers onto the appropriate keys. Or, you could receive intuitive impulses that give you an emotional feeling about what you should write. Your angelic messages may also come as visions, and you may feel guided to write about what you see. If you are a claircognitive, you will receive chunks of information from the angels. You will have certainty of the facts of your knowledge, without knowing "how" you know.

Trance and semi-trance channelers aren't aware of the writing that occurs through them. A full-trance channel actually loses awareness of her surroundings. She feels a sensation of being lifted away from her body while the spirit world channels through her. My channeling is in a semi-trance state, where I am aware of my "me-ness," but unaware of most of the messages coming through me. I also lose track of time and place during most of my channelings. I will think that 20 minutes has gone by, when actually several hours have passed.

The main point with automatic writing is to flow with whatever sensations you receive. Your impressions may come as visions, words, information, or emotional or physical feelings. Or you may receive a combination of these various communications. Practice really does make perfect with automatic writing, so do not allow yourself to become discouraged just because your first few messages don't seem coherent. If you initially get superficial messages, that's okay, too. At first, you'll want to concentrate on becoming comfortable with the process of automatic writing. Then, you'll naturally move on to gathering meaningful communications from the spirit world.

When you become tired, disoriented, or feel any pain, it's important to stop your channeling. Many people limit their channeling time to an hour or less at first. Allow yourself time to build up to longer automatic writing periods.

If you ever find yourself channeling a spirit that belittles you, or pushes you to do anything that would cause pain to you or another, stop. You are not channeling angels at that point. Angels would never give messages that cause emotional, physical, or psychic pain. Call in Archangel Michael and ask him to clear away the earthbound spirit which you are channeling. Do not fight the spirit with fear or anger, but do say prayers and visualize yourself surrounded with white light before having another channeling session. Your greatest ally in the channeling arena is your determination to channel only love. Nothing that is from love can ever hurt you.

— *Dreamwork*. As the angels clearly spelled out in their chapter entitled, "Sleep," we interact a lot with the angelic kingdom during our dreams. You'll increase your number of angel messages and the speed of your clearing work simply by inviting the angels into your dreams.

For example, if you are undecided about your career direction, mentally say a prayer similar to this as you lay your head on your pillow:

"Angels, please enter my dreams tonight and give me clear messages, which I will remember, to help me to know which direction to take with my career."

They always meet this request, and you will likely have a lucid dream that you easily remember, in the hour right before you awaken. Or, the angels may help you in your sleep in such a way that you don't recall your dream's contents. Yet, you awaken and know that something shifted within you during the night. You feel happier, more positive, and much clearer about which direction to take. This is a sign that the angels have re-arranged your thoughts and beliefs, to help you release fears that keep you indecisive about your career.

If you feel blocked in any area of your life, write this message on a piece of paper and place it under your pillow. Repeat the phrase mentally three times as you are falling asleep:

"Dearest Angels,
I ask you to work with me in my sleep tonight, to clear away any blocks that keep me from fully enjoying my life. Please either call these blocks to my

attention, or completely remove them from my
mind, emotions, and body during tonight's sleep.
Thank you."

In the morning, you'll awaken refreshed, but with an awareness that you've worked during the night. You may not recall the details of your angelic nocturnal work, but you will feel it deeply. Your head may even feel funny, because of the restructuring that occurred overnight. Still, any blocks that the angels carted away were heavy weights impeding you from your life's plan and purpose. You'll feel grateful that you asked for this clearing, and you may want to invite the angels into your dreams nightly.

— *Divination Tools.* Oracle cards and pendulums provide a tangible means for communicating with the angels. If you are clairsentient—that is, one who receives intuitions through physical and emotional feelings—these methods will feel quite natural to you.

• *Oracle cards.* You can purchase angel-themed oracle cards at most bookstores. There are different brand names of angel cards, and you'll likely feel drawn to one or two particular sets. This internal pull will help you decide which set to buy, as it shows which cards you share a natural affinity and resonance with. Many metaphysical bookstores have sample card decks that you can examine before making your final purchase decisions. Some angel oracle cards are based upon the ancient tarot deck. Angel cards feature colorful paintings of archangels, cherubs, and seraphim, along with words or sentences describing the meaning of each particular card.

To communicate with angels using oracle cards, meditate while shuffling the deck, and mentally ask the angels to give you assistance. I like to light incense and play soft meditative background music as I use the angel oracle cards. As you shuffle the deck, you can ask your angels specific questions, request that they offer guidance about your life, or ask them to help you foresee your future.

The angels tell you when to stop shuffling the deck. If you are clairsentient, you *feel* when it's time to stop shuffling. You also feel whether you should lay out certain cards or whether you should take the cards from the top of the deck. If you are clairaudient, you hear angels tell you to stop shuffling. Their voices may speak a number such as "seven," signaling that you are to lay out seven cards. Clairvoyants see visual cues, such as cards sticking out of the deck in a certain way as you shuffle them, as a signal to spread out the cards. This visual orientation also tells clairvoyants which cards to spread out. Claircognizants *know* when the time is right to spread out the cards, and which cards to lay out.

People who have a combination of communication channels use a variety of spiritual senses while shuffling the cards and spreading them out. For example, my clairsentience helps me to feel when to stop shuffling, then a clairaudient voice tells me how many cards to spread out. I clairvoyantly see the meaning of the card spreads. With prayer and practice, anyone can become skillfully adept at reading oracle cards—*especially* with the help of the angels.

You can spread the angel oracle cards according to the formations suggested in the card deck's instruction booklet. One classic card spread, for instance, involves laying out three cards. The first card shows your present life circumstances. The second card represents an obstacle or challenge you must surmount, and the third card reveals your best possible outcome after you overcome your challenge.

I use several different angel oracle card sets simultaneously. I spread out one row of cards from the first set horizontally. Then, I spread another row horizontally below the second set, and so on. After I've spread five sets of cards, I read the cards vertically. I look at the first card in the upper left-hand corner and know that this is the primary issue concerning my client. Then I look at the cards vertically below the first card and look for a "theme" among the cards in each row. Each vertical row's theme tells a story about my client's life purpose, emotional blocks, and future.

- *Pendulums.* This is a crystal or gem stone, such as jade, attached to a fine chain or satin rope. You hold the chain or rope and allow the stone to dangle until it hangs motionlessly. When you ask your angels questions, the stone will move in one certain direction as a "yes" response, and it will move in the opposite direction if the answer is "no." To discover which direction the stone travels to signal "yes" and "no," ask a question that you already know the answer to, such as "Is my name Susan?" or "Do I live in Ohio?" Watch which direction the stone moves, and you will establish its "yes" and "no" pattern. Once you establish the pendulum's "language," you can ask the angels to answer other questions. You'll find that a strong "yes" or "no" answer makes the stone move in very strong and wide swings. Some people, through practice and intuition, can determine more detailed answers than "yes" and "no" from the pendulum's movement.

— *Asking for Signs.* In your meditations, ask your angels to give you a clear sign in answer to your prayers. Usually, it's best not to outline which particular sign you want. Instead, your angels will signal you in an unmistakable way. You will notice and *know* that it's the sign you ask for.

The sign may come in nature, such as a feather falling from the sky, a bird soaring close to you, or a rainbow. Your sign can come from the ethers, such as a sudden fragrance, music, or flash of light that has no physical origin. Angel signs also include out-of-the-blue opportunities, like a phone call or letter delivering good news, or a book that jumps off the shelf as you walk by. Or your signs can come psychically, such as a vision, a dream, a voice, or an intuition.

Whatever sign you get, *trust in it.* Know that the angels always answer your prayers, requests, and calls. All we have to do is ask.

— *Verbal Channeling.* The angels will speak *through* you, if you like. When you verbally channel angels, their messages are spoken with your mouth and voice.

Sometimes, during my sessions, I channel my clients' angels instead of relaying their messages. My clients know that when the messages in our sessions contain phrases such as, "We believe that you would enjoy ..." or "We counsel you to ..." that the angels are talking, instead of just me.

If you are a healer, or involved in the creative arts, you've probably already channeled angels. Perhaps you were talking, healing, or creating, and suddenly a wonderful, novel idea comes out of you. Afterward, you wonder, "Where did that come from?" The answer is, of course, from the angels.

To verbally channel the angels, use the relaxation and protective prayer techniques outlined in the section about "automatic writing." Mentally hold a clear intention of wanting the angels to speak through your vocal cords and mouth. Stay in a relaxed and positive frame of mind, as skepticism blocks the angels from communicating through you.

As you feel an impulse to speak, do not allow your mind to wander into fears or doubts. Simply begin speaking, with a sense of trust or adventure. It's a little like the first time you ride a bicycle. The angels will use your vocabulary as they speak through you, as if they are pushing keys on a typewriter to form coherent messages. Some verbal channelers are aware of the messages being spoken through them; others are not. Either way, you'll want to tape-record your channelings, or speak to another person so you can review the verbal channelings later.

You'll know that you are channeling angels by their telltale signature of:

- *A very high, fine frequency.* Your head may feel some pressure, as if you are singing a very high note.

- *Loving, positive words, phrases, and messages.* Angels may warn you of danger or ask you to stop an unhealthful habit. But always, they word their advice in a "you can do it" coaching style.

- *Consistently reinforced, sequential messages.* Your angels will ask you to complete one step at a time as they counsel you to improve your life. They will patiently ask you to fulfill each step and may repeat the same message until you complete their request. After you've finished one step, the angels will applaud you and then give you another suggested step to take.

♥ ♥ ♥

Hearing Your Guardian Angel's Name

You'll interact with hundreds or even thousands of different angels throughout your lifetime. Some angel groups with which you work will remain consistent. At other times, you'll be accompanied by angels who are completely new to you.

Since angels are not after personal glory because they know that we are all united with God, they don't seek credit for their heavenly deeds. So most of the time, you won't be aware of the personal characteristics of the individual angels who are helping you. You can, however, get to know your guardian angel or angels, who are with you from physical birth to death.

Your guardian angels have names. Sometimes, they have human-sounding names. For example, my guardian angel is "Frederique." Other times, angels have descriptive names such as "Joy" or "Peace."

Ask your angels to tell you their names. Then be very still and listen. The answer may come intuitively, and you'll get a feeling about the name. Or you may hear a voice, see a vision, or simply "know" the name. If the message isn't clear enough for you to understand, ask your angels to repeat their names until you've got them. Never fear that your angels will be offended or run away if you say, "Could you repeat your answer a little louder, please?"

I met a woman who decided to ask for her angel's name as she was driving home from church one day. After she asked her angel, "What's your name?" the woman heard a little voice within her mind and heart reply, "Angel." The woman thought, "Angel! How can an angel be named 'Angel'?" So she asked her angel to repeat the answer a little louder and clearer, so she could be sure and really understand it. Again, the woman heard the same reply: "Angel."

The woman thought this was an odd name for an angel—a little like a cat being named "Cat." So she asked her angel to give her a sign if "Angel" truly was her name. At that instant, the woman felt compelled to look over her right shoulder as she was driving. There, in front of her was a huge sign that she had never before noticed. It read "Angel Motel." That's how she knew for sure that her guardian angel's name was "Angel."

♥ ♥ ♥

Trusting the Angels

"I *knew* that's what my angels were saying to me!"

My clients repeat this phrase to me practically every week, in one form or another. When I relay what I hear their angels saying, my clients often admit that they are aware of this advice. The angels may have urged my client to change jobs, take better care of her body, forgive her father, or move to a different locale. Very often, my clients admit the wisdom of the angelic advice, then add a "But . . ."

"But I don't have enough time or money."

"But I might fail and feel humiliated, and things might be worse than they are now."

"But what if the angels are wrong?"

"But what if God is really trying to trick me into a life of austere poverty and suffering?"

Just as the Law of Free Will prevents angels from helping us unless we ask, the same law means that we have the right to accept or reject the angelic assistance offered to us. Most of us would not consciously reject an angel's help. Still, we might mistakenly allow fear to talk us out of receiving good graciously.

After all, many of us grew up with teachings that implied that it's not right for us to accept gifts freely. We might have been scolded for not saying "Thank you" when someone gave us a present. Or perhaps we learned, "You can't get something for nothing," so we feel suspicious when someone—even an angel—offers to help us. We might wonder, "What's the catch?" as if God will ask us to reciprocate the favor in ways involving hardships or austerity.

Know that you *deserve* help from God and the angels! You are a precious and holy child of God, and we all deserve good.

If you have, or if you had, children, wouldn't you want the very best for them? Also, let's keep in mind that our higher selves are eternally one with God. So, in essence, when God gives to us, He is giving to His own self.

Never think that the angels are too busy to help you. Don't believe for a moment that your needs are too petty or trivial for the kingdom of heaven to intervene. This is just our lower-self ego, pushing away help, because of deep-seated feelings of unworthiness. Your true self knows that you are very, very worthy. Your true self knows that we are all part of the divine perfection that is God.

If asking for, and accepting, divine assistance feels unnatural to you, ask your angels to help you change this tendency. Angels can heal away low self-esteem and any personality characteristic that gives you hardships. They will gladly roll away the stones that block you from fully enjoying your divine inheritance, which is your birthright from your holy Creator.

♥ ♥ ♥

Heavenly Surroundings

Your angels are with you wherever you go, so they aren't concerned about *where* you choose to talk to them. It's just that certain types of environments make it so much easier to hear their voices.

When I first started talking to my angels, they urged me to buy some classical music tapes and some fresh flowers for my office. I balked at spending good money on flowers that would soon wilt, or for music that is freely available on the radio. Still, the angels urged me to stop at a florist shop and buy flowers, and to then go to a music store and buy a tape. They were quite specific!

Finally, I asked them what this was all about. They explained that, although my angel statues and pictures in my office set the atmosphere for an angelic conference, it would be better if I decorated with items from the *invisible* realm. Music, fragrance, and color are composed of vibrations that shift our minds into a higher level, where we can more readily understand our angels' messages. Radio music is fine, but all the commercial interruptions interfere with the angels' music coming through.

So I purchased some tapes by Beethoven, Handel, and Vivaldi. Many baroque composers have strong connections with spirituality. For example, Antonio Vivaldi was a priest who spent his lifetime teaching orphans how to play music. George Handel told the king of England that angels helped him compose his famous "Hallelujah Chorus." The music felt as if angels channeled it. I instantly understood why they were so anxious for me to surround myself with glorious chamber music.

Months later, I discovered scientific research that supported what my angels already knew: People have more statistically verified accounts of telepathy when soft music plays in their room. I've also noticed that, when I play audiocassettes of nature sounds, my mind lifts as if I were actually outside.

I also took the angels' advice and bought the most fragrant flowers I could find, which turned out to be tuberoses and star gazers. These beautiful perfumey flowers lifted my spirits. I loved their fragrance so much that I'd bring my vase of flowers from my home office to my nightstand so I could smell them all night. Always, the flowers inspire wondrous dreams and easier interactions with the angels.

Today, I also burn incense when I'm consciously contacting the angels. Beautiful, flowery incense also elevates the spirit and increases the vibrations so that channeling is easier.

Lighting is also part of the invisible realm, since the rays and beams emitted by candles and colored bulbs are not tangible. The angels suggest using an assortment of lighting in your meditation area. Angels resonate with any lighting that is soft and natural, but they also appreciate playfully colored lights because they cast a fun mood. And you've read how much the angels enjoy us relaxing and having fun!

♥ ♥ ♥

Developing the Habit of Asking
Your Angels for Help

From the angels:

"We speak to you continuously, nonstop from on high. We gleefully join you in fun times, and cheer you in the sad ones. We beseech you to listen further, for we can boost you in ways yet unknown. We help you in countless and numerous occasions, and our 'thanks' is your happiness. When you truly delight in opening your ears to The Angelic Realm, you will experience a music in your life beyond all comparison. If you could know how delightful your life can truly be, you would wait no longer to hear our beck and call!"

The angels *want* to communicate clearly with you. They have so much to give you! They can bring you information, guidance, protection, moral support, and a pat on the back. In fact, they continuously try to do just that. Yet, a giver cannot give unless there is a willing recipient. Are you willing to receive the glorious good that is being given you right now?

One way to become more receptive to angelic communication and assistance is by clearing any blocks you may have that prevent you from receiving. Write, read, and say the following affirmations several times a day, and within two weeks, you will heal much of your resistance to angelic help:

"I graciously accept good into my life."
"I am willing to release all fears of receiving love."
"It is safe for me to be loved and cared for."
"I deserve love and assistance."

If you're accustomed to taking care of everyone else, you'll need to be patient with yourself while you develop the new habit of accepting help from the angels. Sometimes it doesn't feel safe to receive assistance. Perhaps you fear that if you don't do everything yourself, others won't need you. You may also fear losing control of the situation if you aren't taking charge of everything yourself. You might worry that the angels are too busy to help you or that you don't "deserve" angelic assistance. Or, you just may automatically do things on your own and need reminders to ask your angels for help.

All these blocks to angelic intervention are understandable and very, very normal. If you simply forget to ask your angels for help, place visual reminders around your home, car, and office. Angel statues, cards, and posters give cues to jog your memory whenever you need help.

If you are aware that, deep down, you have blocks that prevent you from asking for help, the angels can heal these blocks away:

If you need more faith or belief, ask God and the angels to help you!

If you feel undeserving of Divine intervention, ask God and the angels to help you!

If you worry that your problems are too "trivial" for heavenly help, ask God and your angels anyway. Remember that God and The Angelic Realm can help everybody simultaneously, since time and space do not limit them. Your request for Divine help doesn't pull God or the angels away from helping somebody else.

Whatever you need, God and the angels can help!

Remember: God and the angels love you, and they love to help you so that you can easily feel, enjoy, and give love.

♥ ♥ ♥

Purifying the Channels of Divine Communication

From the angels:

"You can hear us so much more clearly when you purify the air around you. Think of divine communication as coming through a mist, which is really the buffer in the atmosphere differentiating one spiritual realm from another. The finer the mist, the easier the communication between us can be. But a dense mist covering prevents us from clearly hearing your thoughts and seeing your deeds, and is more likely to create misunderstandings about our intentions for you. By purifying yourself, to the extent you are able, we are joyful because we are much more reachable as far as you are concerned, when the mist around you is refined and purified."

When the angels talk about "purifying the air around you," they aren't referring to clean air in the traditional sense. They mean, instead, that your thoughts and lifestyle actions affect your aura and the energy field around you. It's a little like clearing the static from a telephone line so you can hear callers more clearly. Angelic communication is easier to understand when you purify your aura and energy field.

All purification steps are best if they come from your desire and willingness. It's best not to force yourself to take any step that feels like you are "denying yourself." Only undergo those steps for which you feel ready. Undertake these new habits with the joy of knowing that they bring you to a closer understanding of your true God-self nature.

— *Purify your thoughts.*

From the angels:

"We're not asking you to try to be a saint upon the earth, but do your best to monitor the words, phrases, and ideas you speak to yourself and to others. Any fear-based thought, such as jealousy, competition, resentment, victimhood, or retaliation, makes your energy field dense and dark. Unforgiveness—toward yourself, a situation, a person, or a public figure or agency— blackens your aura like thick smoke."

I have clairvoyantly seen what thought-forms look like. Immediately after you have a thought, you release a bubblelike object with a life of its own. The size of the thought-form seems to correspond to how much energy you put behind the thought. Thought-forms serve your every command. They go out into the world and create whatever you've thought about.

For instance, a client of mine really wanted a certain job. During the job interview, I saw her release a huge thought-form that looked like a thick, shimmering soap bubble about four feet tall by one foot wide. It had a life force of its own, and a forward thrust energy. When my client called me a week later to report that she'd successfully secured her new job, I wasn't surprised. The energy she'd released into the world marked "This is the job I desire," guaranteed that she'd receive her wish.

There are no neutral thoughts, nor are there moments in the day when your thoughts don't create thought-forms and their causative effects. Your fearful thoughts act like bloodthirsty henchmen that bring terror back to you, their master. Your loving thoughts obediently bring you joyful situations and relations. It's your choice.

Many people who are drawn to channel angels feel the need to avoid negative media. So, they may stop watching television, listening to the radio, or reading the newspaper. They may become distanced from friends who chronically complain, and they may choose to leave careers that feel inconsistent with a positive outlook.

Channeling angels requires that our thoughts be attuned to the highest frequency of love. Any worries or fears interfere with our channeling abilities, as these thought-forms create static on our psychic telephone line. In the chapter called "Angel Therapy," you can read about a very effective method for quickly releasing these ego-self thoughts.

— *Purify your motives.* Give your motivations to God and the angels and ask that they be purified. You can do this simply by asking God to help you. Say, "God, I give you my motivations and ask your help in purifying them so all my motives are aligned with truth and love." Very soon, you will feel a strong sense of relief, as the Love reorganizes your thoughts and feelings. A deep sense of peace and order follows this.

Your highest motivation is to give glory to God in all ways. Of course, since your higher self is one with God, you are actually giving glory to the *true you*, along with the true self of every other child of God. Lower-self motivations occur when you believe that you want to give glory to yourself alone, as a special person. Everyone is equally special. So, when we want a *separate* specialness, we trigger the pain and loneliness that comes from believing we are separated from God and our spiritual siblings.

— *Purify your actions.* Before doing anything, ask your higher self, God, and the angels to guide you. Know that this Divine guidance will direct your actions from the one power of love. In this way, you are assured of continually floating in a sea of miracles that will astound you in their beauty. You will always be in the right place at the right time.

— *Purify your home.* Environments absorb negative energy, which comes from a variety of fear-based sources. Anything tinged with fear that is in your home—newspapers, magazines, mail, television programs, radio talk shows, arguments among family members, or fearful thoughts held by past occupants of the house—can bring dark energy into your surroundings.

You'll want to clear your home, office, or any environment you frequent. Clearing allows the light to freely circulate and lifts your surroundings' energy to the highest level possible. Some ways to purify your home include painting the walls; shampooing the carpet or recarpeting; placing bowls of rubbing alcohol in every room of the house for a minimum of 24 hours; setting clear quartz crystals in the sunlight for four hours (to clear them of negative energy) and then putting the crystals in different rooms of your home; and burning sage weed or incense throughout each room.

Still, perhaps the best way to clear any environment is by calling upon the angels. Mentally ask for Archangel Michael and his Band of Mercy to circulate the area and draw away all dark energy or earthbound spirits. You may be able to see Michael with your spiritual vision. If so, you'll watch him lead other angels in a posse, gathering all lower-energy forms that could interfere with your divine communication and joyful living.

— *Purify your relationships.* Although you've undoubtedly experienced pain in relationships, you have the choice of healing the residual emotions to clear any heaviness or darkness. This is an important part of the clearing work that will help you to easily have conversations with your angels. Whether you carry old pain from your childhood, adolescence, or recent past, you can release negativity that holds you back.

The angels first remind you that every negative feeling you hold toward another has a boomerang effect. It is impossible to judge or blame another person and not feel emotional pain. As much as we would like to see ourselves as separate from a person we view as "bad," ultimately such a separation is impossible. We are united with each other—forever. That is why you feel depressed when you become angered at another person. The anger you send outward acts like a laser beam pointed toward a mirror, and it instantly comes back and hits you.

Other people are our mirrors! When the angels speak of the necessity of forgiving, they don't want you to forgive because of moral codes. They know that judgment, blame, and anger are burdens upon your soul. They ask you to unburden yourself, and this is the true definition of forgiveness. It means setting yourself free.

If you don't feel ready to forgive someone's actions,

then forgive the person instead. See that person through the eyes of an angel. The guardian angel sees only the good, the truth, the Godness of that other person. Angels look past the surface personality, errors, and mistakes of a person and see straight into the individual's heart. If you've read about or experienced a near-death experience, you've heard about the guide that accompanies us. This guardian angel's unconditional and all-consuming love burns away all fear from those who are crossing over to heaven.

You, too, can have a great healing effect upon the world—and simultaneously heal your relationship with yourself and all others—by modeling yourself after the guardian angels' viewpoint. The more you train your mind to see the angel residing within each person, the more you will know and appreciate the angel who *you* are in truth.

— *Purify your schedule.* We sometimes procrastinate spiritual growth by creating a busy schedule. Busyness ensures that there is no time to explore the inner self. For that reason, the angels ask us to purify our schedules by eliminating unnecessary or redundant activities.

You may want to take an inventory for two days and write down how you spend your time. Then look for areas of wasted time. We don't mean relaxation, since the angels definitely believe resting is a worthwhile activity. Instead, look for the moments where you are busy, with no meaningful results. These are the activities you engage in out of habit or fear. Once you identify your habitual time-wasters, you'll probably easily change to healthier habits.

However, if you are staying busy out of fear, you may

resist the angelic guidance to restructure the way you spend your time. After all, when you are continuously active, there's no time to think about your life purpose, your true self, and God. Yet, these are such important endeavors, aren't they? After all, nothing is more important than fulfilling the sacred mission for which you were born! Nothing in this world yields even a fraction of the joy compared to your life of right livelihood and right relations.

If you write your top five priorities—in other words, what is truly important to you—you can compare these areas to your actual schedule. Then ask yourself, "Am I spending my time in ways that fulfill my priorities?" If not, then diligently seek ways to cut out time-wasters, and replace the new gaps in your schedule with something more personally meaningful to you. You'll find that purifying your schedule heightens your energy and enthusiasm level more than just about any other step you can take.

The angels strongly counsel you to spend time alone in nature as frequently as possible. Make this one of your top priorities. The healing effect of nature, combined with time alone, gives the perfect opportunity for you to really hear your true self, God, and the angels speak to you. The nature angels will soothe and comfort you. In this natural setting, you'll more easily hold honest conversations with yourself and the divine spiritual realm.

— *Purify your body.* If you are being called to channel angels, you have undoubtedly received inner guidance about your diet and lifestyle. This guidance urges you to eliminate sugar, stimulants, meats, alcohol, dairy products, or other foods from your diet. These are very real messages, sent to you from heaven.

Their dietary advice is part of answers to prayers in which you asked for help in hearing the voices of God and the angels. The reason why your angels intervene into your diet is that your body is being prepared for a reattunement. The vibrational frequency of angels is at such a high and fine level, that your body must be re-tuned before you can hear them. It's similar to tuning a piano, so that when the pianist's finger strikes its keys, the piano can emit harmonious music.

God is calling you to be a transmitter of angelic messages. Your nervous system can only handle the angels' frequency if your body vibrates at a sufficiently high level. A poor diet creates static on the angelic communication lines, so your angels ask you to purify your body. You may receive the angels' dietary suggestions in any number of ways: as gut feelings or hunches; as "coincidentally" meeting a dietician or being drawn to a vegetarian book; as hearing an inner voice; or seeing visions about food.

The angels say that all food has internal messages and that these messages affect us, long after you have digested the food. As you attune your body to a higher and higher frequency, the angels will ask you to eat whole and natural foods.

Usually, the angels first ask you to eliminate red meats. Next, they request that you remove chicken and turkey, followed by fish. Animal flesh interferes with divine communication because it carries the energy of pain that the animal endured during its life and death. Pain energy has the lowest and densest vibration of all, and if you consume pain-filled food, your nervous system cannot reach its highest frequency potential.

Next, the angels will probably counsel that you cut back on stimulants such as caffeine, sugar, chocolate, and certain herbs. They may ask you to stop all stimulants completely, or they may guide you toward a gradual cessation. They will also eliminate other mood-altering chemicals, such as alcohol and nicotine.

Then, your angels may guide you to cut out some or all dairy products, as these foods can clog up our thinking and feeling channels. If this happens, you will either receive guidance that sends you to a good nutritionist or nutritional book, or the angels will ask you to eat vegan protein substitutes such as tofu or nuts.

As you purify your body more and more, you'll naturally gravitate toward a diet rich in fresh, organic produce, and baked goods made with sprouted grains. Your dietary changes won't feel like deprivation, but will, instead, feel rooted in love and joy. You'll easily adapt to each lifestyle change toward which the angels lovingly guide you. Each step of the way, you'll be aware that you ultimately have the final say-so about your diet.

Nevertheless, since you desire to hear the heavenly voice, you'll naturally choose to take all steps that clarify your channel of communication.

♥ ♥ ♥

Clearing Your Relationship with God

Sometimes people become estranged from God. Perhaps they suffered a huge disappointment and believe God let them down. Or they may have suffered pain at the hands of members of a religious group. Very often, estrangement from God stems from confusion about spirituality, religion, and the nature of God and man.

It's difficult to hear the voice of God and the angels when you feel distanced from heaven. However, since our higher self is eternally united with its Creator in heaven, we can't completely absolve ourselves of thoughts of God. Deep down, we long to enjoy the comfort of complete oneness with the angels and God.

Do you wonder sometimes if God loves other people more than you? Does it seem that others receive greater attention and rewards than you do? Did you suffer a loss that caused you to question God's motives? Were you raised to be afraid of God?

God and the angels know just how you feel. They know, because your feelings and thoughts are plainly visible in the spiritual world. All of your disappointments, hurts, and fears flash like giant neon signs around you.

The angels really want to help you regain the joy of loving God! They ask for your willingness to hand the entire situation over to them for repair. Tell God and the angels about all your cares, upsets, and fears. Don't worry—there are no repercussions for honesty, especially since they are already aware of everything you're going to say. Mainly, your heavenly supporters ask you to get your feelings off your chest.

After you've leveled with God and the angels about all of your frustrations, disappointments, and fears, they will ask if you'd like to exchange your painful thoughts for a more peaceful set of beliefs. If you agree, then, the angels will immediately set about to heal your relationship with God and heaven. Miraculously, you'll find that your thoughts and feelings shift to a new perspective.

This healing is on a very deep level. First, since your higher self is one with God, you'll find that your healed relationship with God extends to a better self-relationship. You'll feel happier about who you are, because you'll truly be loving your self as you love God. Second, since all the angels and earthly creatures are one with God, you'll feel greater compassion for, and a deeper connection with, others.

No matter what you need help with, no matter what you believe your blocks or limitations to be, the angels have a solution waiting for you right now. Just ask them.

❤ ❤ ❤

Spirit Releasement with Archangel Michael

Sensitive people—also known as clairsentients or empaths—frequently absorb others' energies. You may recall that a "clairsentient" is someone who is highly intuitive and who receives divine communication through physical sensations and emotional feelings.

Unwittingly, clairsentients take on another's fears and worries like a sponge drinks up water. This is especially true of clairsentient healers and teachers, whose caring nature attracts people to pour their troubles out to them. The troubled person feels relieved and unburdened after talking about her worries. However, the clairsentient feels drained or heavy because she has taken on the other person's troubles.

A burdened person is less able to help the world, so it is important for clairsentients to protect and clear their energy fields:

— *Avoid places where people abuse alcohol and other drugs.* These environments attract earthbound deceased people, who vicariously enjoy the companionship of intoxicated individuals. Sensitive lightworkers are prone to hitchhiking earthbound spirits, so it's best to avoid bars, cocktail parties, and discotheques.

— *Avoid places filled with ego-ridden mind-sets.* These include companies with manipulative philosophies, media sources that sell gossip and fear, organizations built upon competition or jealousy, and groups with low morale.

— *Shield yourself with light.* If you must enter these environments, protect yourself by visualizing a white wall of light, at least one inch thick, surrounding you like a shield. You can put one wall between yourself and the other person, or you can box yourself in completely.

— *Focus on love, light, and truth.* Whenever you talk to a person who is in an ego mind-set, continually claim the truth either mentally or aloud. Do not allow yourself to view the other person's fears as real, or you will invoke your own ego. Remember always that as you see others, so you see yourself. It's best to listen sympathetically as you would if these people were describing a scary movie that frightened them terribly. You would empathize with their feelings, while simultaneously knowing that the source of their fear was unreal.

♥ ♥ ♥

The Archangel Michael is the supreme protector and guardian angel of the Earth. He clears the planet and its population of darkness. If you feel drained or irritable, chances are that you have absorbed darkness. This darkness is nothing, in reality, because it is fear or the illusion of the absence of love. Since it is impossible that love is absent, there is nothing to fear. However, while we believe we live in bodies in a material planet, the earthbound rules affect us. One of those rules is that dark energy lowers our energy and mood.

The moment you become aware of feeling depleted or upset, you can be sure that an unloving thought is behind it. You have probably identified with someone else's fears or worries in some way, either because you judged them, felt sorry for them, or became angry with them. When we identify with others' fears *in any way*, we absorb their dark energy as we become one with them through our empathy.

In these times, you needn't struggle alone to rid yourself of darkness and absorbed fear. Instead, call upon the Archangel Michael. He doesn't need a formal invocation, just a sincere desire for his help. Saying or thinking, "Michael, please help me!" is enough to evoke his assistance instantly.

You'll know Michael is near because you'll feel a strong, sudden air pressure change. His presence feels like an etheric hug, reassuring yet not co-dependent. Michael loves us and protects us, but he does not view us as helpless—he sees our true power!

Then ask Michael (either mentally or aloud) to clear you of all darkness. You needn't help Michael in any way. In fact, when we try to help Michael help us, we often get in his way. It's best to just step back and become completely vulnerable and trusting of his help. Don't withhold any secrets or issues from Michael—he can see them all, anyway. Still, he cannot help you with areas that you withhold from his healing touch.

You might feel Michael opening the top of your head, the crown chakra area. Michael and his helpers, known as the "Band of Mercy," may enter your body and pick the dark thought-forms out of your cells as if they were picking apples. Michael also uses a tool similar to a vacuum to suction the darkness out of you very quickly. When the darkness is gone, he reverses the vacuum so that it pours a thick, toothpastelike white energy into your body to fill you where darkness previously resided.

You may also feel Michael cutting "etheric cords" that stretch between you and another person. Everyone—not just clairsentients—builds these cords with people to whom we are close. They look like arteries and they come in varying degrees of thickness. Usually, etheric cords are attached to our major chakra energy centers, such as heart-to-heart, or solar plexus-to-solar plexus. These cords don't pose a problem when they connect two highly evolved people. However, you may have a cord attached to, for example, a sibling who is enduring life crises. In such cases, your sibling is likely feeding off your energy through your attached etheric cord. So you will feel drained without knowing why. The reason is that your sibling is acting as an energy robber, instead of tapping into her own natural source of energy.

When you call Archangel Michael to help you revive your energy and outlook, he uses his sword to cut away etheric cords that drain you. Michael and his Band of Mercy (his angelic assistants) also gather up stray earthbound spirits attached to you. These earthbound people belong in the afterlife plane. Michael escorts them to the light for their own spiritual growth. Very often, earthbound people do not realize they are dead. In other cases, earthbounds are afraid of going to the light. Sometimes they fear a punishing, angry God. Other times, they don't want to leave the material possessions accumulated during their earthly life. As mentioned earlier, some earthbounds who abused alcohol and drugs during their lifetime hang around bars and parties to absorb the energy of intoxication.

Empathetic lightworkers must vigilantly monitor their energy and mood levels to ensure against a build-up of psychic dirt from fears, worries, and earthbound spirits. Never fear that you are wearing out your welcome with Archangel Michael. He can be in many places and with many people simultaneously because he lives in a dimension unfettered by time or space beliefs. You can ask him to live with you if you like. There are no restrictions or limitations, except those you decide for yourself.

Of course, having Michael next to our side does not allow us to disobey our inner Voice of God, which gives us rational guidance about staying safe in the material earthplane. If your inner teacher warns you to stay away from a certain locale, it would not be wise to ignore this warning just because you have asked Michael to accompany you. Michael is a wonderful server and protector, but he — like God and all the angels — will not usurp our personal responsibility for making decisions.

♥ ♥ ♥

Spiritual Safety

You are safe in this world, in truth, for nothing can harm who you really are. Death, injury, and loss are illusions of the material world. Holding these truths in your heart and mind is your ultimate secret that allows you to walk in complete safety, wherever you are.

The angels will help you to feel safe and protected by surrounding you with their loving energy. For example, before you go to sleep at night, visualize your home surrounded by white light. This is a very real way to "seal" your home and insulate it against any lower-thought energies. Then, mentally ask for four guardian angels to stand post at the north, south, east, and westerly sides of your home.

Let's say that a person is ridden with ego thoughts such as, "I must steal from others to meet my material needs." Let's also suppose that this person is roaming your neighborhood at night, believing that robbery is their source of income. Your home, protected by angels, will repel this ego-bound person. He will not know *why*, but your home will not attract him.

Penetrating the loving guardianship of angels is impossible for any negative forces. The angelic energy deflects the lower-self energy of those with unholy intentions, like two magnets pushing each other away. The angels will also warn you, should you need information to avoid a dangerous situation. This is another reason why it's a good idea to go to bed with a clear and sober mind. After all, we need to have access to our dreams for our growth, safety, and protection.

Ask your angels to surround you and your loved ones always. When I'm on airplanes, I ask angels to surround and support the aircraft. In cars, I call upon angels to guide the vehicle and protect its tires, chassis, and engine.

If you are in an unfamiliar environment, or anywhere that you feel unsafe or dishonored, call upon the angels for protection. Walking down a lonely street, your angels will fly ahead of you and clear your path. In a situation where someone has unkind or dishonest intentions, your angels will intervene for you. If someone is about to betray you, you'll receive warnings from your angels as strong gut feelings. Please don't ignore these invisible answers to your prayers!

Instead of trying to control or fix negative situations on a human level, your angels will work with you from the spiritual plane. They will continuously remind you that you have all the power you need, right inside yourself. You and the angels are kin, in that you both are creations of the same all-powerful, all-loving Maker. You can call upon your divine power to heal any situation, and team up with your angels to shine truth and love wherever you go.

Our loved ones are so important, and you can send angels to guide, guard, and protect them. Visualize your child surrounded by dozens of wise and loving angels. Know that your visualization is the invitation that instantly brings angelic beings to your child's side. If you have a friend in distress, ask angels to comfort and help her.

You also help to guide and guard your city, nation, and planet by sending angels to political and military power centers. Pray that The Angelic Realm surrounds government leaders with higher wisdom and heavenly love. See angels happily hovering about the capitols and courthouses of the world. Know that your visualizations contribute powerful healing energy that attunes leaders' minds to the highest good for all concerned. The angels help these leaders lose their lower-self ego concerns, and connect with the one universal mind of divine intelligence.

♥ ♥ ♥

Angel Therapy

I've been a spiritual psychologist for many years and have seen or tried nearly every form of therapy available. I hold B.A., M.A., and Ph.D. degrees in psychology and have been director of two inpatient and three outpatient psychiatric programs. I've stood beside psychiatrists who administered electro-shock therapy, various drugs, and traditional psychoanalysis. I've witnessed Jungian, Freudian, and Rogerian therapy at work. I've attended workshops given by psychological greats such as Carl Rogers, Rollo May, and William Glasser. I mention all this as a basis for what I'm about to share.

While working with clients who have long-standing emotional blocks—usually, old resentments held toward themselves, an abuser, parent, sibling, or ex-spouse—I've discovered that the only barrier in their way is their *decision to release these blocks*. If a person decides to stay unhappy, no amount of therapy is going to be effective. It is only when the person says, "I am *willing* to be healed," that healing occurs.

Very often, clients are unwilling to heal because they fear repercussions related to their emotional and physical health. They fear boredom from a life that is crisis-free. They fear making changes in their thoughts and behaviors. They fear that health, or the process of getting healthy, would be more painful than illness.

That is where angel therapy comes in. Angel therapy is the fastest, most effective, and most enjoyable form of healing I have ever found. I have the angels to thank for introducing me to their therapeutic methods. Following the angel's warning about my car being stolen, I began asking my angels for advice in all areas of my life—including my counseling work.

Their advice about healing continued throughout the writing of this book. The messages I received in Part I have influenced my current counseling work. They taught me the method described in this chapter and assured me that it would be well received. I initially used it with my long-term clients, who expressed great satisfaction with the angel therapy. Then, I began teaching and demonstrating this method with my seminar audiences. After I consistently received positive feedback about angel therapy's results, I decided to incorporate it into all of my sessions.

Today, my work consists of listening to and relaying to my clients, the messages I hear from their angels. I use a combination of clairvoyance, clairaudience, and angel oracle cards to receive these angel messages. After we identify emotional blocks that are challenging my client, we use angel therapy to clear the blocks away. Common blocks that the angels identify in our sessions include low self-esteem, money obsessions, unforgiveness toward self or another, jealousy, feeling unsafe, and a fear of not fulfilling one's life purpose.

Angel therapy starts with the understanding that whenever you feel pain—emotional or physical—it means you have chosen a thought from your lower-self, or ego. I'll give you a brief summary of how this occurs. The details about the ego aren't crucial for angel therapy to work; however, understanding the dynamics of pain and of healing is helpful.

Since God only created love, pain is unreal. Pain is rooted in ego-based thoughts of, "I am separate from God and other people." The ego is completely incapable of love, and it creates thoughts ranging from irritation to murder. Sometimes, spiritual seekers are horrified that they have violent and unloving thoughts. They think, *Something's wrong with me! A spiritual person shouldn't think this way,* and they conclude that they've backslid upon the spiritual path.

When we judge an ego thought as "bad" or "wrong," though, we give the ego power and the illusion of reality. A better way to handle ego thoughts is based upon the Eastern approach: Simply notice it without judgment. Say to yourself, "Oh, I see that I'm having an ego thought of anger, jealousy, competition, or (fill in the blank)."

All thoughts create etheric forms, which clairvoyantly look like soap bubbles. There are no neutral thoughts or periods of time when your thoughts don't create a form. These forms go out in the physical world and manifest into creations that mirror your thoughts.

In angel therapy, you notice your ego thought and then call upon angels to surround and encircle you. Instantly, they will be by your side. Perhaps you can see them or feel their presence by an air-pressure change around you.

Picture or feel your ego thought as a soap bubble about the size of a clear cantaloupe. Mentally image yourself holding the thought-form in the hand with which you normally write. This is your releasing hand. Then, see or feel yourself handing this thought-form bubble to the angels.

They immediately take your thought-form away, to the Light, where they purify it. The angels return your thought-form to you in its purist form, which is love. This love may contain ideas that will help you transform some personality trait or circumstance in your life. In this way, you can correct whatever habits created the original ego thought initially.

After you feel the release from pain, it's important to thank your angels. Your gratitude and happiness is their "paycheck" for services rendered. If you'll join them in giving glory to God—Who is one with your higher self—the angels are doubly delighted.

♥ ♥ ♥

Enfolded in Angel Wings

You are never alone, and angels accompany you constantly, even when you are unaware of their presence. The angels want to interact with you more frequently. They'd love to be fully involved with every aspect of your life, yet they cannot help you unless you specifically ask. Like many practices that are good for us, such as meditation and exercise, we benefit by making angel communication a regular part of our life. Surround yourself with reminders, such as angel statues and posters, so you won't forget to call upon your heavenly friends for help and assistance.

We needn't wait until crisis or pressure has hit before asking our angels for help. In fact, it's a good idea to work with your angels in any trying situation before it gets to the boiling point. However, if you forget to include your angels in your plans, they still will answer your call of "Help" if you get into a jam.

There are no limits to what your angels can do in your life. They are very, very powerful beings. Once you invite them into your life, get ready, because your life *will* change in very miraculous ways. If you don't quite yet fully believe in angels, you will know that they are real after asking for and receiving their help two or three times.

The Angelic Realm loves you, and they see you as you truly are on the inside—as an innocent and perfect child of God. They know that you have made occasional mistakes just like the rest of us. Yet, angels overlook our errors and see the love and good intentions within our hearts. See yourself and others through the eyes of an angel, and you'll see a beautiful world that is light, bright, and hopeful.

You *are* an angel, and you are a blessing to the world.

HEALING
with the
ANGELS

To those who serve as angels,
in heaven and upon the earth.
Thank you for your love, dedication, and service.
Please continue to have patience with us
while we learn how to accept
your gifts with gratitude and grace.

Acknowledgments

Thank you to God, Holy Spirit, Jesus, Frederique, Pearl, and my other guides and angels. Much love and gratitude to Louise L. Hay, Reid Tracy, Jill Kramer, Christy Salinas, Jeannie Liberati, Jenny Richards, Margarete Nielsen, Jacqui Clark, Kristina Tracy, Karen Johnson, Ron Tillinghast, Joe Coburn, Anna Almanza, Suzy Mikhail, Adrian Sandoval, and Lisa Kelm.

I very much appreciate the angelic help I've received from Steve Prutting, Charles Schenk, Bronny Daniels, Janine Cooper, and Jennifer Chipperfield. Thank you to all the wonderful men and women to whom I have given angel readings, and angel blessings to my clients and students who allowed me to print their case studies and stories in this book.

Introduction

It's not your imagination. Angels *are* among us, now more than ever, and not just in commercial venues. Increasing numbers of people are reporting encounters with these heavenly beings. In their encounters, angels deliver timely messages, healing remedies, and lifesaving measures.

Why are angels circling our globe so much lately? Partly because of our prayers for heavenly assistance, and partly because God and the angels know that it's time for us to heal ourselves, our lives, and our world. As we move through the millennium shift, the angels are helping us heal the challenges and ills that keep us from living at our highest potential.

The angels are here to teach us that God's love answers all questions and challenges. They are here to heal us from the effects of fear. The angels are powerful healers, and you can work with them to speed up their healing efforts. The more we invite angels into our lives, the more readily our lives reflect the splendor of heaven.

There are no limits to angels' healing power. They can help us heal our relationships, career concerns, finances, housing issues, and any other challenge that is troubling us. We just need to follow a few steps to help the angels help us:

1. **Ask**—The Law of Free Will says that angels cannot intervene in our lives without our express permission. The only exception is if we are in a life-threatening situ-

ation, before it is our time to go. Otherwise, we must ask the angels to help us.

How do you ask? you may wonder. No formal invocation is necessary to invite angels to help you. You simply need to think, *Angels!* and they will instantly respond. You, like everyone else, already have two or more guardian angels with you from birth until death. Nothing you can ever do, say, or think could make your angels leave you or love you less. Their love for you is powerful and unconditional!

You can also ask for more angels to join you. Either ask God to send angels to you, or call upon the angels directly. Both ways are identical, because the angels always answer to God's will. And God always wills angels to surround and comfort you whenever you ask.

2. **Surrender the problem**—Before God and the angels can heal your situation, you must completely give it up to them. It's a little like mailing a letter: You must release the letter from your hand before the post office can deliver it for you. So often we ask heaven to help us. Yet instead of letting this happen, we hold on to the situation, thereby blocking the angels' ability to intervene. If you really want help, completely release the problem to God and the angels!

3. **Trust in God**—We mustn't give God and the angels a script, in which we outline what steps we want them to follow to resolve our situation. Instead, trust that God's infinite wisdom and creativity will come up with a much better solution than our human minds could ever dream of. Remember: God's will is that you be happy!

4. **Follow God's directions**—After you release the problem to God and the angels, they may ask you to take some human steps to resolve the situation. These directives will come to you as either a voice, a dream, a vision, a knowingness, or an intuitive feeling.

   If you're unsure of the source of these messages, ask God for validation. God and the angels will always give you loving and supportive messages, so if you ever receive a fearful or hurtful directive, do not follow it! However, if we stick closely to God in our hearts and minds, we needn't worry about so-called fallen angels interfering with us. God's Divine love is the only power that exists. The thought-forms of fear and darkness are illusions that can only "harm" us if we give them power. Therefore, after you've asked the angels for help, watch for God-given messages that will direct you on how to resolve your challenging situations. These directives are the answers to your prayers, and you must take action to help God to help you. Sometimes these directions will be action based, and the angels will ask you to go to a certain place or call a specific person, for example.

   Other times, the directives will involve your mind and heart, such as when the angels ask you to forgive yourself or another. Whatever their messages, know that they come from the Source of all healing and solutions. By following these directions, your situation will be completely healed.

   No situation is too big or too small for the angels to resolve it for you. Whether you want a parking space, money for your bills, or better health, the angels are happy to oblige. Their greatest reward is your happiness, so if it fits with God's will, they will give you whatever brings you joy. After all, joy is your birthright, and you deserve it!

Healing Someone Else

What if you wish the angels to conduct a healing on another person? For example, you'd like the angels to help a loved one in need, or a group of people in the news who have touched your heart.

It's always an act of love to ask God to send angels to another person's side. This is not a violation of the other person's free will, since they can choose whether to listen to the angels' messages. So, it is a good idea to ask the angels to surround others. God especially responds quickly to this request when it comes from parents who wish to have angelic "babysitters" attend to their children.

The angels will never usurp God's will, so if it is your loved one's "time," the angels will bring that person comfort and joy during their final days on Earth. A wonderful prayer for you to hold in your heart is, "Thy will be done." In that way, you can save yourself needless worry, and rest assured that God is taking care of everything perfectly.

Archangel Raphael: The Supreme Healer Among Angels

For physical challenges such as illness or pain, there is no better healer among the angelic realm than the archangel Raphael. This angel, whose name means "God Heals," can bring instant release from suffering. Raphael glows with a beautiful emerald green healing energy. Often, the archangel surrounds painful body parts with this healing light. The light acts as a soothing balm, and as a trigger for sudden and complete healings.

Raphael, like all the inhabitants of the spirit world, can be with everyone who calls upon him simultaneously. Limitations of time or space do not restrict him. So, never fear that you are interfering with Raphael's other duties when you call on him.

The healing archangel comes to your side the instant you ask for him. You can call him by thinking or saying aloud, "Raphael, please help me!" Raphael will also join the side of your loved ones, at your request.

Raphael is a powerful healer who acts like a spiritual surgeon in releasing fear and darkness from our body and mind. Sometimes, however, we call upon Raphael and then we get in the way of his healing function. For instance, we don't allow him access to our "guilty secrets" so that he can extract them from us. Or, we try to help him along by telling him what to do. Although well intended, our human actions clumsily get in the archangel's way. Consequently, after you call upon Raphael, it's best to give him full access to your body, mind, and heart. In this way, he can fulfill his God-given function to heal everything completely.

No matter if it's a hangnail or a seemingly terminal illness, call upon God and the angels for help. They don't want us to wait until we're desperate or terrified before we do so. As the angels wrote through me in the book, *Angel Therapy*:

> Call upon God's heavenly creations for help and assistance as soon as you become aware of your inner pain. A wise homeowner who smells smoke does not wait until the home is engulfed by flames before telephoning the fire department. At that point, such a call feels almost useless. Do not wait until you are overwhelmed by monumental fear before calling upon God's name.
>
> At that moment—as in all times—He will send help and comfort to your side. Even so, you may not feel His loving arms for several minutes, as you feel barriered between many layers of fear and heaven. Smarter still is one who learns to monitor his own well-being, and who hesitates not in calling upon a heavenly creation of any form for assistance and comfort.
>
> Learn this lesson well, then, sweetest child, and remember always to care for your inner being by calling forth help whenever needed. In that way, your ebb and flow of fear has not

sharp divides, but gentle swellings that do not erode your peace of mind.

The angels are here to help you heal your life, and they want you to ask for help.

CHAPTER ONE

Blessings and Challenges of the Spiritual Path

What drew you to study spirituality? A desire to explore the *truths* of life? A search for happiness, fulfillment, and inner love? A tragedy or miraculous happenstance that pushed you to explore the spiritual side of existence? Or were you intrigued by someone's example; perhaps a spiritually minded person whom you admire?

Whatever attracted you to this path, the common thread was your desire to improve your life. Whether you sought enlightenment, answers, new skills, or peace of mind, you believed that spirituality had something positive to offer you.

Happiness Is Holy

Some of my clients were raised in religions that promote suffering as a virtue. These belief systems applaud martyr lifestyles;

and they create breeding grounds for guilt, fear, and resentment. So, when these individuals hop on to a spiritual path that promises happiness and abundance, they get nervous. *Are happiness and abundance "correct" goals?* they secretly wonder.

Those raised in Christian ideologies learn Jesus' teaching that it's easier for a camel to pass through the eye of a needle than for a rich man to enter the kingdom of heaven. Yet, in other passages, Jesus emphasizes that we should knock, and doors will open. Repeatedly, he urges us to have faith that our material needs will be met.

Most spiritual seekers understand that Jesus didn't mean to say that money was evil. Instead, he meant that the *obsession* with money was a deterrent to happiness in this life and the afterlife. Yet, obsession with money is a two-way street: Those who chronically worry about whether they'll have enough funds to pay their bills are spiritually identical to those who obsessively hoard their dollars. Both types of money obsession are rooted in the fear of not having enough. And this underlying fear robs us of happiness.

When we believe that suffering and lack are normal, or if we believe they are tests from God, we accept pain as a part of life. However, when we believe that God is 100 percent abundant love, and that God's creations are in His image and likeness, it follows that He didn't create pain or limitations.

In my long discussions with God, the angels, and Jesus, I'm convinced that God doesn't want us to suffer in any way. God, like any loving parent, wills for us to have happy, peaceful, and safe lives. God wants us to focus our time and energy on helping others, using our natural talents and interests. While we help others, He'll take care of supplying us with enough time, money, intelligence, creativity, and anything else we need. God knows that if we worry about having enough, we'll waste time and energy that could be put to better use.

So, God and the angels truly *want* to help us! However, because of the law of free will, they are only allowed to help us if we ask. This is a book that will help you know the rich experiences available to those who *do* ask.

Angels and the Millennium Shift

You are very fortunate to be alive at this time in human history. For that matter, any time we are alive, it is a miracle. The angels have taught me that more souls want an Earth life than there are bodies to accommodate them. Souls actually stand in line, awaiting Divine assignments on Earth. The fact that you are here, in a human body, signifies that you are a winner. God chose you to come here, knowing that you have many gifts and talents that will benefit His other children.

The angels write this to you:

> *"You, like everyone else who is incarnated at this time, are a holy and perfect child of God. We realize you may not always feel perfect and holy, and we also realize that you often don't act that way. Nonetheless, God created your soul as a literal 'chip off the old block.' It contains God-essence, or Divine light, that can never be extinguished, soiled, or taken away from you. Nothing you could ever do would eradicate your Divine heritage."*

The reason why this is a good time to be alive is because we are nearing the end of an era in which humans behave like aggressive animals devoid of spiritual awareness. We are at the edge of a time when we will collectively recover our spiritual gifts of intuition and healing. When intuition becomes accepted as a normal human characteristic, watch out, because the world is going to change drastically!

Think, for a moment, about a world populated by highly accurate intuitives. The more we accept this skill as innate, the more we will open our channels of Divine and psychic communication. Scientific studies conducted at leading universities such as Princeton, the University of Nevada, the University of Ohio, and Cornell already show evidence that each of us is potentially gifted in sending and receiving telepathic information. I say "potentially," because like any gift, we have to be aware of and practice it before we can truly master its usage.

Many people are becoming intuitive and opening themselves to Divine guidance. In my private practice, I'm awestruck by the number of high-level professionals—both male and female—who ask me for angel readings. These are folks who may have never thought about life after death, God, or spiritual issues three or four years ago. But now, in this spiritual renaissance in which we all find ourselves, the collective consciousness is looking heavenward.

Think for a moment about what our world will look like when we all regain our natural intuitive awareness. No one will be able to lie to another person ("little white lies" will fade into distant memories), which will definitely create shifts in our legal, educational, and political systems. Also, we won't need technological devices to communicate with each other.

I believe that a number of us have a life purpose that involves teaching others about their true spiritual origins. Many people, I believe, are still asleep with respect to the knowledge of their inner Divinity! They see themselves as a body, floating like a hapless cork, dependent on the current to tell it what to do. God and the angels know differently, however. They are aware that we create our reality through our conscious decisions and intentions.

"Your intentions create your experiences" is one of the angels' favorite phrases. What they mean is that our expectations, deep down in our heart and mind, are the scriptwriters of the movie we experience and call "life." If you ask yourself before entering any situation, "What do I truly expect to occur here?"

you will become the world's greatest psychic. That's because your expectations will literally predict what will happen to you.

The Refining Process

Our tastes shift as a result of our spiritual study. We lose the desire for mood-altering substances, we're repelled by violence in the media, and our attraction to friends and lovers changes. The angels explain a lot of these changes as being a result of our "frequency shifting." They say that each person has a vibrational frequency that is visible to them, much like when we view a car's system on an oscilloscope or a person's brainwaves over a monitoring machine.

The angels say that our frequency adjusts according to our thoughts and emotions. Those who worry, fret, and obsess have slow frequencies, while those who meditate and pray regularly have higher frequencies. As our frequencies shift upward, we become attracted to higher-vibrating situations, people, food, and energies. This also means that we won't be attracted to some of the friends and events that once captivated us.

Vibrations surrounding ego issues, such as anger, violence, a lack mentality (believing there isn't enough to go around), a victim mentality (believing that other people control you or are to blame for your unhappiness), competitiveness, dishonesty, and jealousy are extremely low. High vibrations surround spiritual-mindedness, such as meditation, prayer, devotion, selfless service, volunteerism, healing work, teaching, sharing, and expressions of love.

The angels suggest that we avoid lower-vibrating situations as a means of pulling up our spiritual frequencies. They are particularly adamant about avoiding reports in the print and broadcast media that promote negativity.

Here are transcripts from two of my angel therapy sessions, in which the angels asked my clients to avoid this type of media:

Doreen: There's a message coming in from your angels. They're saying that when you read, watch, or listen to the news, it is upsetting to you and is negatively shifting your energy in a way that is counter to what you want. This is a very strong cautionary message to you. The angels say, *"Don't take this casually."*

Barbara: That makes sense. I listen to the news a lot on the radio, and it does upset me, so I guess I'll reduce how much I listen to it.

During another session, the angels explained how my client's low self-esteem was exacerbated by the negative images and messages she received from watching soap operas and other dramas:

Michelle: At times I feel like a total let-down or failure, not just to myself, but to my husband and daughter. Have I done something wrong, or what am I not doing? I love my family very much and would do anything for them, but when it comes to my husband, things have changed (I think). Something is missing, and how do I—or we—get that back?

Doreen: You have done nothing wrong, although the angels show me that there is the influence of the media around you, affecting your thoughts and therefore affecting your life. Are you watching a lot of TV? [Michelle confirms that she is].

It looks like you are absorbing negativity from TV shows, and this is influencing your thoughts and life. Can you try shutting off the TV for a week and see if that makes a difference?

Michelle took her angels' advice and found that within one week, she no longer ran "worst-case scenario" films in her mind. She dropped the habit of viewing her life through a negative soap opera lens, and she was able to see the gentle beauty in her family life.

Shifting Your Frequency

The angels are here to help us heal in many ways, from issues and challenges that are seemingly mundane, to those that seem urgent or spiritually profound. One of the angels' healing tasks is to help us shift our vibrational frequency to its highest and finest rate. They want us to make this shift for two reasons. One is that this is a process of "ascension." We are all on the pathway of discovering that we are one with God. When we truly understand and live this knowledge, we are in the state of ascension.

That sort of knowledge profoundly affects your every interaction with others. Think for a moment how your life would be if you were consciously aware that everyone with whom you talked was a Divine aspect of your God-self. You would feel complete and total love for these individuals and for yourself. You would experience life as a heaven-on-earth experience.

The second reason why the angels want us to increase our frequency is because we will be better suited to our changing material world. The millennium shift is going to bring about significant positive changes in our educational, government, legal, and telecommunications systems. Our eating habits will drastically change, and our life expectancy will significantly increase.

The higher our frequency, the easier it will be to adapt to these shifts. We will be intuitively aware of pending Earth changes, in the way animals can foresee earthquakes and storms. Our high-frequency bodies will be able to teletransport, dematerialize, and withstand events that would traumatize a denser, lower-frequency body. Higher-vibrating minds will be able to manifest any required foods or other supplies.

So, the angels want to help you adapt to a changing world by giving you energy and guidance that will shift your frequency. The angels help you do so by giving you signs and signals, Divine guidance, and by intervening into your life and body. In this way, they help you maintain peace of mind. After all, peacefulness is one of our primary goals in life, and the angels are here to help us attain that end. Our angels sing with joy when they see us feeling peaceful and happy. In the next chapter, we'll look at how the angels play a part in our romantic relationships.

CHAPTER TWO

Angelic Interventions in Your Love Life

The angels can help us heal our relationship problems if we ask for their help. Mentally call to your guardian angel, or to the angel of the other person in the relationship, and witness the miracles that occur.

Finding New Love

A woman named Beth asked her angels to help her find "Mr. Right," and they went to work immediately as heavenly matchmakers. She told me the following story about how the angels helped her heal her love life:

> I never really thought much about angels, but one day I heard you mention on a radio show that you have to ask the angels for help. So, I decided to give it a try. I asked them if

they could help find a good man for me. Less than a week later, I met a wonderful man. We clicked instantly. I believe he and I were meant for each other. The goals and things we have in common are awesome. So, needless to say, I have a new outlook on angels. I've started asking for their help more often.

The Couple That Forgives Together . . .

The angels also help couples in committed relationships strengthen their bonds of love. Barbara was a student in my spiritual counseling course. She excelled at angel readings and had wonderful studying and homework skills. Barbara truly was interested in, and committed to learning about, spirituality and healing. During one of the classes, I conducted angel readings on a few of the students. Barbara was one of them.

Her question to the angels, during our session, concerned the fact that she and her husband, John, had been arguing a lot. She asked whether the angels saw a divorce coming, or whether she was supposed to stay in the marriage. Through me, the angels said, *"The purpose of your marriage is complete. You now have the option of staying together or parting ways. It is completely your choice."* Barbara decided she wanted to stay married, so she began praying for spiritual intervention.

I'll let Barbara describe what happened after she surrendered her marriage to God and the angels:

> My husband and I had been dealing with marital problems for about a year. Sunday evening after the angel-reading session in which I gave my marriage to God, my husband hit a spiritual bottom. For many months, we both had been living in resentment and bitterness toward each other. After going into a rage, John asked me if we could talk. I knew the angels were protecting me because I had asked them to surround me, and I was very calm through all of this.

John told me he didn't know where God was in our turbulent marriage. I reminded him that God can't work through us unless we let Him in. Well, at that moment, John did cry out for God to come in and help him. The angels were also nudging me, saying, *"Okay, Barbara, you know what to do! It's time to start walking your talk!"* I walked him through the Forgiveness Corral Exercise [this powerful healing exercise is reproduced in the Appendix of this book].

I explained to John about the ego, and told him that it was our egos who were arguing—not our true selves. We shared into the wee hours of the morning about God and our spiritual beliefs. Our relationship turned a major corner. I stayed home from work with John the next day, and we continued to share and rebuild. It was an incredible experience. We talked about us both making the choice to recommit ourselves to our love and to our relationship.

The next day, on a beautiful sunny Saturday, John and I completed the "Forgiveness, Free Yourself Now" exercise [this exercise, required for graduating from my spiritual counseling certification program, also appears in this book's Appendix]. We drove to one of our favorite spots and found a place where there was a stream with a very small waterfall, so we could hear water flowing.

We sat side-by-side, but in parallel worlds, each working silently on our own forgiveness list. When I finished my list, I walked down to the water to do the releasement part of the exercise. The two names at the end of the list were John's and mine. I forgave myself down by the water, but saved the releasement of forgiveness with John to do in person once I rejoined him on the embankment.

Before leaving the stream, I saw a tiny lavender butterfly flutter beside me. John told me that as he said each person's name on his forgiveness list, he mentally held the person in his hand, then opened his hand and released the person as a butterfly. After we completely forgave and released each other, we continued to enjoy the beauty and serenity of our surroundings.

We both felt so light and free!

The love we currently feel toward one another and toward ourselves is unlike anything we have felt! It is as if both of us have been through, as John put it, a spiritual, emotional, mental, and physical overhaul! There has been such positive movement this week.

I am convinced that John's unforgiveness toward himself was what was at the root of his depression. Now that the unforgiveness is gone, the veil of depression is lifting. My own resentment and bitterness toward him are dissolved as well. Our forgiveness of ourselves and each other has allowed us to see one another through new eyes. It amazes me how diminished we had both allowed our internal sparks to become, and how that spark has once again become a flame.

Probable Futures

The angels rarely say that our future is set in stone. Instead, they say our probable futures are based on our current train of thought. If my clients' thought patterns shift in a significantly positive or negative way, so will their future. This is what they explained to my client, Kevin, when he expressed fears about his future and marriage:

Kevin: My child will be leaving home shortly—mostly, I believe, to get away from the way things are here. I can't say I blame him. Things are not always pleasant; in fact, sometimes they get pretty bad. After he leaves, will he be okay, and what will become of my home life? Will it get better or worse? Will my spouse and I remain together or go our separate ways?

Doreen: The angels say that you are going through some major changes right now. They are grateful that you are contemplating your inner world and are taking responsibility for many parts of your life. The angels caution you, however, not to blame yourself; just to take inventory and make adjustments to your course based on your assessment.

Your marriage isn't set in stone right now. You truly have the power to save the marriage and make it work; however, you must have faith and keep a loving, positive outlook. You may need to get additional support to keep this positive outlook, such as a counselor, a spiritual study group, or a close friend to talk to.

No one is blaming you for anything, except in your expectations. However, if you believe that others are blaming you, you will experience this as a self-fulfilling prophecy. We certainly hope that you will make the choice to experience the miracles of healing that the angels seek to help you enjoy. You will be in my prayers.

Love Never Dies

The following case shows how a good marriage is truly forever, even when one spouse dies. Often, the deceased spouse becomes an angelic matchmaker for the survivor:

Annette: I have been seeing a guy whose wife passed away, and I feel that someone is telling me it's okay. Could this be a message from an angel or even his wife? I feel it's a comforting message.

Doreen: Yes, you are very intuitive! His wife is encouraging you in this relationship because she can see the positive effect it has on him. She is above any feelings of jealousy and just wants to see love—the only thing that is real and that matters—to shine radiantly in both of you.

Congratulations on manifesting a wonderful relationship and for being in touch with your natural gifts of intuition!

Ma Bell, Angel Bell

The angels always emphasize the importance of truthful and clear communications in our relationships. A therapist who has taken my angel therapy courses reported the following case of how the angels helped a couple to clearly communicate:

> My client had tried numerous times to get her boyfriend on her cell phone but kept getting only static. She was really upset because she needed to get in touch with him right away. I then suggested (knowing one of her guardian angel's names was Bell), "Why not ask Bell to help you?" She did, and the very next moment, the line was perfectly clear, and she was able to deliver her urgent message! Afterward, she said she never thought to ask her angels for something like that.

Angel Prayers for Your Love Life

Here are two examples of prayers to use while working with the angels to heal your love life. Make your own variations of these prayers to suit your circumstances if you'd like. You can say prayers aloud, mentally or in written form. God and the angels hear all your thoughts, feelings, and intentions. Prayer is a very powerful way to connect with heaven for the purposes of healing.

PRAYER TO FIND A SOULMATE

Dear God,

I ask that You and the romance angels help me be in a wonderful love relationship with my soulmate. Please give me clear guidance to find my soulmate, and help us to meet and enjoy one another without delay. I ask for Your help in creating circumstances so that I may be in this wonderful soulmate relationship right away. Please help me heal and release any blocks in my mind, body, or emotions that would make me afraid of great love. Please help me hear and follow Your Divine guidance that leads me to find and enjoy this soulmate relationship. I know that my soulmate is searching for me with the same amount of fervor with which I am searching for this person. We both ask that You bring us together and help us know and accept the blessings of great love. Thank You.

PRAYER TO HEAL AN EXISTING LOVE RELATIONSHIP

Dearest God,

I ask that You and the angels help me heal my love life. I am willing to release any unforgiveness I may be harboring toward myself and my partner, and I ask that the angels cleanse me of all anger or resentment now. Please help my partner and me see each other through the eyes of love. I ask that all effects of our mistakes be undone in all directions of time. Please work with my partner so that we may have harmony, romance, friendship, respect, honesty, and great love for one another. Please renew our love. Thank You.

Love is already within each of us, and we don't need another person in our lives in order to feel loved. However, the expression of love from and to another person is deeply satisfying. That is why the angels are so interested in helping us attain and maintain a soulmate relationship. They also want to help us in other types of relationships, such as friendships and with our family members, as you'll read in the following chapter.

CHAPTER THREE

Angel Blessings for Your Family

Just as the angels help us in our love relationships, they also heal our interactions with our children and other family members.

The Angels and the New Children of Light

There is a new "breed" of humans among us, according to the angels. They are highly psychic, strong-willed, extremely imaginative, and they are here to usher in the new age of peace. These powerful and intuitive people have little tolerance for dishonesty, and they don't know how to cope with pointless discussions or meaningless tasks. After all, their souls elected to incarnate on Earth at this time so that they could teach others about the importance of speaking truthfully and living in harmony.

Who are these mystery people? They are frequently referred to as "Children of the Light," "Millennium Children," and "Indigo Children." They are individuals who were born in the 1980s and '90s so that they could reach adulthood by 2012, the predicted time of the new age of peace. An entire book, to which I am a contributing author, is available through Hay House on this topic. It is called *Indigo Children,* by Lee Carroll and Jan Tober.

The trouble is, these special children are growing up at the tail end of the old energy in which people still lie to each other, still compete because of a belief in limited resources, and still engage in meaningless activities. Without coping skills to deal with these residues of our soon-to-be-former civilization, these children feel raw and vulnerable.

For example, let's say that Bobby is a nine-year-old Child of the Light. As a youngster, he saw angels and communicated clearly with them. He often sees visions of the future, and he makes psychic predictions to friends and family members that prove accurate. Bobby is outspoken, and he doesn't mind sharing his opinion when he feels an injustice has occurred.

At school, Bobby has difficulty coping with what he perceives to be meaningless activities. He knows, deep in his soul, that the current educational system will be replaced with one more applicable to everyday living. Yet, he is living in the age of the *current* educational system, and he must find a way to cope. Fortunately, many of Bobby's peers feel exactly the same way, since they, too, are Children of the Light. So at least Bobby doesn't feel all alone.

Bobby intuitively knows that he has a great purpose to accomplish in this lifetime. He senses that he is going to help many people, yet he's not quite sure how that will happen. All he knows is that whenever he wakes up, he feels as if his soul has traveled to a faraway school where he's taught subjects that truly interest him and that seem highly meaningful—things such as the geometric basis of matter, the universal laws of cause and effect, and studies on the probable future of Earth and humankind.

In contrast, learning about Christopher Columbus and grammar seems inconsequential to him. He feels bored and restless, and his attention wanders. Finally, his teacher sends Bobby to the school psychologist, who refers him to a medical doctor for evaluation. The diagnosis is quick and swift: attention deficit disorder (ADD). His mother fills Bobby's Ritalin prescription on the way home.

Bobby *does* feel better while taking Ritalin. Things don't quite seem to matter to him as much when he's taking it. The drug makes Bobby feel less irritated by the fact that his homework assignments are irrelevant to his life's purpose. In fact, Ritalin makes Bobby not care about a lot of things—such as talking to angels and engaging in soul travel at night. Thanks to his diagnosis and prescription, Bobby is now just a normal person who can't remember his mission in life.

It's All about Integrity

The angels say that the years preceding and immediately following the millennium are devoted to helping us learn about integrity. In other words, our collective current life mission is to be true to ourselves. It also means being true to others, and that includes our children.

A decade or so ago, we psychologists warned parents not to confuse friendship with parenting. We lectured parents against having heart-to-heart discussions with their children lest they "parentify" their youngsters (meaning giving the children information that they were too young to handle).

Yet, the new millennium children require emotional and conversational intimacy with others. They thrive on honesty! If a Child of the Light feels that something is wrong, for example, in her parent's marriage, it's destructive for the parents to cover up this fact. It's so much healthier for parents to openly discuss (using terms and phrases that are age-appropriate to the child) the situation, than to have the child believe she is crazy for having feelings that run counter to what her parents are saying.

The angels have very strong opinions about these children, partly because the angels feel protective of them. Angels guard Children of the Light to ensure that their mission is completed. They say:

> *"Listen well, parents of the '90s. You, too, have an exceedingly important mission to fulfill. You must ensure that your children remain intuitive and that they stay very close to nature. Don't push them to succeed at the expense of losing their soul purpose, for our purpose is our guiding force, and without direction, your children will feel lost, alone, and afraid.*
>
> *"So much better for you parents to focus your children's attention on spiritual studies, as this is their true nourishment that will ensure their growth and survival. We angels are here to help you parent, and we won't interfere or get in the way. Simply allow us to cast a new light on difficult situations, a task we complete with joy in our hearts, simply by your open invitation for us to heal. Do not ever feel that God doesn't hear your prayers, for He sends us to your side the instant you call."*

In the cases that follow, you'll see how the angels have strong and sure guidance for parents. They discuss every seeming aspect of child-rearing, from conception to dealing with adolescent behavior challenges. I believe that the angels are extra-concerned with our children. In a way, after all, our children are God's Earth angels who are here for an important mission.

Storks and Angels

My own parents had a miraculous experience surrounding my conception, which is part of the reason why they immersed me in spiritual studies while I was growing up. Childless after several years of marriage, my parents desperately wanted to have a baby. Finally, my mother put in a prayer request to a New Thought church, asking that the parishioners pray for her to conceive. She became pregnant with me three weeks later.

Many of my clients and audience members ask questions about conception and childbirth. I'm frequently asked, "When will we have a child?" "What sex will my newborn baby be?" and "Will my unborn child be born healthy?" As you'll read, the angels handle these questions with forthrightness and love.

Very often, I talk with the spirits of children who stay with their mother following a miscarriage or abortion. The children are happy and well adjusted and simply want to be with their mother to help and guide her. Or, if their mother gets pregnant again, they may have "first dibs" on inhabiting the new body and be born as a healthy baby. Those who don't have the opportunity to be reborn grow up on the other side, at about the same rate they would have if they had come to full-term births. Aborted children hold no grudges, by the way. Their souls are as intact as ever.

Angel Nannies

The angels remind me of loving nursemaids and nannies. Like Mary Poppins, the angels take a firm but kind stance when it comes to how we raise our children (who are really God's children, in their eyes). The angels are blunt and direct but always loving. They love to be called upon for child-rearing questions and assistance!

Janet: I have two beautiful daughters, and I am pregnant with another child. I want to know if the angels can tell me how can I be a better mother spiritually to my children?

I was very sensitive as a child and talked to people on the ceiling until my own fears sent them away. My brother, who died when I was eight, came to me in my dreams. My oldest daughter is scared of the dark, talks in her sleep, and has nightmares that she never remembers in the morning. Is she afraid of spirits, angels, or some past-life memories? How can I encourage her to not be fearful? I think it is because she knows that there are always spirits and angels around, and maybe she can't see them but senses or hears them.

When I was her age, I was afraid of the voices I heard and blocked them out, and now I want them to come back because I am ready for them. My youngest daughter is just a light. She is happy, and I have a terrible fear periodically that she will be taken away from me. Can you please tell me how I can be a better mother to them?

Doreen: The angels say that you are a *wonderful* mom! They remind you that your intentions are the most important thing, and that you have very sincere intentions to be a great mom. That is all that counts—your sincere intentions!

Your children are definitely seeing and interacting with angels, and yes, that can be frightening for them at times. Just holding them, talking to them, and being there for them, plus always telling them your true feelings, is what is needed from you right now.

You are feeling a little drained and emotional because of your pregnancy, and this is making you feel a bit guilty. You feel as if you can't be everything to everyone right now, and it's true! This is a period of adjustment for all of you, a time to allow your children to grow up a bit so that you aren't always drained. This will help you feel more energized and cheerful, which is actually the gift your children most want from you.

Angels and Adolescent Issues

God and the angels are brilliant helpers when it comes to the challenges presented by our adolescent children. All we have to do is ask and then follow their awesome advice, as my counseling student Jackie Saunders did:

Jackie's teenage son had been having terrible problems at home and at school, and Jackie was so upset that she had become physically ill. In desperation, she turned to God for help. "I need a miracle, God," Jackie firmly said. "I need You to help me help my son right away."

A few minutes later, Jackie heard a distinct voice tell her, "Go to Danny's Family Car Wash right now." Jackie knew that Divine guidance sometimes comes in bizarre ways, but this seemed way over the top. "Danny's Family Car Wash?" she questioned. Then, in confirmation of what she had heard, the voice said, "Yes, go to Danny's Family Car Wash right now . . . and hurry!"

So Jackie hurried into her car, not quite sure why, but obediently following the voice's dictates. As soon as she pulled into the car wash, the attendant told her, "We are going to wax and detail your car for half price." Jackie argued that she didn't have enough time. The attendant said, "Yes, you do." So Jackie surrendered to the situation and allowed her car to be detailed.

As she sat waiting for her car, Jackie noticed a slumbering man in the corner with a pile of books lying on his belly. On closer look, Jackie saw that they were books on "adolescent psychology." Without thinking, Jackie woke the man up and asked him about his interest in teenage behavior.

The man shook himself awake and smiled as he explained how his own teenage son had once been a source of trouble. Then he discovered a psychologist who worked miracles with adolescent boys. Now his son was doing very well. These were books that the psychologist had recommended that the man read.

Jackie shook with excitement. "Please, please let me have the name of the psychologist!" she implored. As the man gave Jackie the psychologist's name and number, she felt that her prayer for help had been heard and answered. She drove home feeling peaceful, and planned to call the psychologist in the next couple of days to make an appointment for her son.

The next morning, Jackie woke up close to six A.M. *She heard the inner voice that had counseled her to drive to the car wash. This time it said,* "Call the doctor right now," *referring to the adolescent psychologist.*

"But it's only six in the morning!" Jackie argued.

"Call the doctor right now," *the voice repeated.* "She is leaving town very soon, and you need to call her now."

Trusting the guidance, Jackie called the psychologist and apologized for calling so early. Jackie could tell that she'd woken the doctor up, and feared alienating her. Then Jackie explained the reason for her call, "Please, I need to make an appointment for my son to see you."

"But I'm leaving to go out of town this afternoon," the doctor said. "Besides, I only work with five teenagers at a time, and I already have six in my case load."

Jackie knew that her Divine guidance wouldn't have led her to this doctor without reason, so she per-

sisted. "I can't explain it," Jackie said, "but I know that it's very important that my son see you right away."

Something in Jackie's voice must have impressed the doctor, or perhaps the angels intervened. Regardless, Jackie breathed a sigh of relief when the doctor said, "Okay, I'll see your son this morning at 8:30. It's the only time I have before I leave for my one-week trip."

The doctor ended up taking Jackie's son as a client, and he thrived under the psychologist's care. Today, Jackie's son is happy and well adjusted, and she is grateful that God and the angels led her to Danny's Family Car Wash as an answer to her prayers!

Angelic Healings

More than 300 well-documented studies show that prayer has a statistically significant effect on healing our physical bodies. Researchers know that a placebo effect and wishful thinking don't explain this phenomenon. After all, many of the studies involve subjects who don't know they are being prayed for. This includes studies in which prayers showed positive effects on plants and infant babies, who may feel, but don't consciously know, when they are being prayed for.

Many of the prayer studies are "double-blind," meaning that the researchers and physicians—as well as the patients—don't know if they're being prayed for or not. Nevertheless, those who are prayed for generally live longer, heal faster, and require fewer medications than those who aren't prayed for.

I've received dozens of unsolicited testimonials from those who say that they, or their family members, have been healed because they prayed to have healing angels sent to them. In the following case study, my counseling student Karen Montano reported that her daughter Jourdan even saw the angel involved with her healing!

I'll let Karen tell you her story first-hand:

> My husband and I had to take our daughter Jourdan (age 6) to the hospital emergency room. She was running a fever of 104 and suffering from back and abdominal pain. Before the doctor came into the treatment room, I closed my eyes in prayer, calling Archangel Michael and all my daughter's angels to be in the room.
>
> When I opened my eyes, I saw a family friend who had passed away last year standing at the foot of the gurney toward her head! He seemed to be conducting some sort of hands-on healing work over her.
>
> I then saw my aunt, whom I loved dearly and who just passed over six weeks ago, at the doorway. She smiled at me and said, "Everything will be all right!" and then she turned her head. Then, as if she were directing traffic, I saw her waving her arms to the souls that were wandering in the hallway telling them, "Everything is all right! There is no need for you to be in this room. It's okay . . . just keep on going . . . keep on moving toward the light!" It was the most peaceful experience, and I knew everything was going to be fine.
>
> Jourdan is home now, feeling fine. She says she clearly remembers my aunt working on her body and helping her to heal.

A Child's Eternal Love

Some of my most heart-wrenching sessions involve talking to my clients' deceased children. I've conducted several sessions where children who died via suicide explained their reasons and delivered profuse apologies. I've talked to dozens of adolescents who died in tragic car accidents. And, I've helped parents of murdered children understand the sequence of events surrounding their child's death.

Often, these cases bring tears to my eyes. Here is a session that was particularly poignant, in which a deceased young man sends his love to his living mother.

Ginny: Do you see anything about my son who died?

Doreen: What is his name?

Ginny: Robert.

Doreen: Okay, Robert, Robert. [I say a person's name repeatedly to call them from the afterlife plane. After about two minutes of calling Robert, I saw a tall young man appear next to Ginny's side.] Was he tall?

Ginny: Yes.

Doreen: I'm seeing a tall young man step next to you right now. He's very gangly, with a youthful face. He also dresses kind of old-fashioned. His face is so youthful that it's tough to know how old he was. He could have been anywhere in the 18 to 25 bracket.

Ginny: Yes, that's him. He was 22 and mentally handicapped.

Doreen: He's next to your left side, although he's not always with you. Robert is very quiet and has a serene energy. He makes a motion that he's having a lot of fun on the other side. He's showing me an image of himself running. I don't know if you know much about the afterlife plane, but there are many different levels and layers. In some of the afterlife areas, it looks just like the most beautiful parts of Earth.

People in the afterlife plane create these images of Earthlike life from their mental images. Robert lives in a very rural type of area, and he's showing me himself running through a wheat field with his arms outstretched as if he's flying.

Ginny: He loved the farm.

Doreen: Well, he lives in a farmlike area in the afterlife plane, and he says that he feels very free. He says, "Mommy, don't be sad." He prints out a letter *J,* or is it *I?* Did Robert know how to write?

Ginny: He could write his name and a few simple words.

Doreen: Oh, okay, it is an *I,* and he's writing out, "I love you."

ॐ ॐ ॐ

Changing Relationships and the Spiritual Path

Obviously, the study of spirituality can change your life in many different ways. It opens you to new possibilities, miraculous interventions, and healings. It also shifts your relationships considerably.

The issue of relationships is probably the greatest concern of those on the spiritual path. You may worry, "Will my friends and family still relate to me, with my newfound interests and different perspectives on life?" You may find yourself losing interest in old friends and craving new friendships with like-minded people.

You might also be concerned with how your family will react to your spiritual path. Those raised in traditional religions may receive flack from family members who view metaphysics and nontraditional spirituality through fearful eyes.

Changes are inevitable when you open your mind, heart, and life to Spirit. These changes can be wondrous, beautiful experiences if you allow yourself to trust the process. They can also be frightening and painful if you grip tightly to attachments of how you think things *should* be, or if you fear losing people. Such fears often prove self-fulfilling.

Fortunately, the angels are available to guide you through these changes and to smooth the way.

Changing Mind-Sets, Changing Friendships

"Through my spiritual studies, I made some decisions to change how I lived," an audience member named Celia explained to me. "First, I decided to stop gossiping and talking down about people. My spiritual studies made me aware that I was actually hurting myself every time I gossiped or put down someone else."

Celia was initially uncomfortable with this decision because she and her best friends regularly engaged in gossip as a group pastime. How would her friends react if she didn't join in? So, Celia asked for Divine guidance about how to handle the situation. What she received, through intuitive emotional feelings, was a true answer to her prayers.

"I knew that I was to help my friends learn that it's more fun *not* to gossip than it is *to* gossip!" Celia explained. "After all, we only did this because we thought it was the best way to have fun. So, I leveled with my friends one night and said, 'Look, this type of talk is really holding us all back. Let's stop it, and make a pact to say something if we ever hear one of us start to gossip.'

"So, whenever anyone in our group starts to talk negatively about someone or something, someone else in the group will speak up and say, 'Oops!' or something like that to call attention to the gossip. What we found is that gossip was a habit we'd all gotten into, and it took us some time to break that habit. All of us feel so much better now that we're sharing more positive things when we talk."

As Celia pointed out, when we go through behavioral transitions as a result of our spiritual path, it's an opportunity for us to be a way-shower or teacher to our friends and family. This is a tricky balancing act, however. Nobody—especially our friends and family—wants to receive sermons or lectures. The best way to teach peace is to demonstrate it through our actions. If we scream at our friends or family, "Why can't you be as spiritual as I am?" they pay attention to our demeanor and discount our words.

Ask the angels to guide your actions and words so that you can be a truly effective teacher to others.

Chakras and the Law of Attraction

True Divine guidance never speaks in terms of blame, guilt, or whether someone is right, wrong, good, or bad. So, your angels always seek out a win-win resolution to conflict. However, they may occasionally guide you away from relationships and help you close the door on a friendship whose purpose has been served.

Ending a relationship can feel frightening to anyone, but for those on the spiritual path, this process can elicit extra guilt. "I'm supposed to help people and be a loving person," you may worry. "Am I abandoning my friend if I choose to spend less time with her?"

The truth is that you may choose to spend less time with old friends, and more time with new people in your life. This does not mean that you are judging, criticizing, or abandoning anyone. You are not being a snob or isolating yourself. You are simply allowing yourself to be guided according to the spiritual law of attraction.

We are attracted to people whose mind-sets mirror our own. It's a matter of common interests creating friendships. As your lifestyle shifts, you will naturally look for people with whom you have things in common. On an even deeper and metaphysical level, your mind-set affects the energy centers in your body, which are called "chakras." Each chakra corresponds to a different life issue. Whatever issue we spend the most time thinking about determines which of our chakras are stimulated. Then, as if by radar, we attract and are attracted to people with similar mind-sets.

The angels explain that the chakras send out energy waves that bounce back like a sonar system. When we meet someone with a similar energy pattern, their chakra energy bounces back to us in a feel-good way. We are then attracted to them and are pleasantly surprised to find that we share mutual interests.

For instance, if you think about money and security most of the time, your first chakra will be affected. This is called the "root chakra," which is located at the base of the spine. Like a magnet, you will pull other people into your friendship circle who also have money and security concerns.

The second chakra, called the "sacral chakra," is concerned with body issues. This chakra is located midway between your navel and tailbone. People with physical challenges or obsessions surrounding weight, physical appetites, health, or addictions will have out-of-balance sacral chakras. You will tend to attract and be attracted to other people with body issues.

Issues that affect the third chakra, or "solar plexus," include fears or obsessions about power and control. This chakra is housed in our midsection, behind our navel. If these issues are on our mind a lot, we draw people to us with similar mind-sets.

The three lower chakras are concerned with Earthly matters. The fourth, or "heart chakra," is the first of a set of chakras concerned with higher issues. Not coincidentally, the spiritually centered chakras are located higher up in the body. The heart chakra, located in the chest, concerns itself with love. Those who are working on love issues, such as forgiveness, compassion, and soulmate relationships, are called "heart-centered." They tend to attract other loving people into their lives.

The fifth chakra, located in the Adam's apple area and called the "throat chakra," is concerned with creative expression and communication. Those involved with artistic or teaching projects—particularly of a spiritual nature—invoke the energy of their throat chakra. This chakra is especially stimulated by an integrity lifestyle, where you strive to always have your words and actions match your inner truth. By concentrating on these issues, you pull like-minded souls to you.

"The third eye" is the sixth chakra, which centers around spiritual sight and visions. If you have been visualizing and meditating, or if you are naturally clairvoyant, this chakra is opened. You will draw people of similar spiritual interests and abilities into your life.

"The ear chakras," located just above the eyebrows on the left and right side, deal with listening to Spirit. Those who silently meditate and tune in to the messages of heaven have stimulated their ear chakras and tend to attract other listeners.

On the inside of the top of the head is the "crown chakra," which is activated when a person realizes we are all one with God and each other. A person with this mind-set will naturally attract like-minded souls who share the spiritual path.

So, let's say that in the past, most of your thoughts were centered around Earthly matters such as money worries or sexual obsessions. Your circle of friends shared similar beliefs. Then you had a spiritual awakening that led you to read and meditate about Divine topics. In doing so, your primary chakra energy moved upward. So, instead of operating out of your first (money-related) or second (sex-related) chakra, you began living from the fourth (love-related) or fifth (truth-related) chakra.

As soon as this shift occurred, you would naturally lose the "pull" you once felt for people who live from your former chakra mind-set. You will either begin to desire, or start to attract, people who share your focus. Through the law of attraction—as long as you hold a positive expectation—new, like-minded friends will enter your life.

CHAKRA CHART

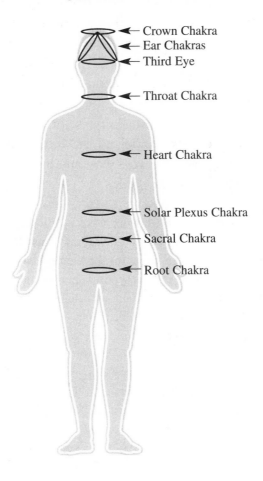

The Law of Attraction and Running into Friends

A man named Charles related this story of synchronicity:

> I was Christmas shopping in a mall near Boston when my friend and I walked into a department store at the exact moment as a young woman who had attended college with us several years before. I was just talking about her earlier that morning, saying that I hadn't seen her in years and wouldn't it be nice if I could see her again soon?

Events such as the one above are validation that this is a Divinely ordered universe. Instead of worrying about how things will work out, we need to put our time and energy into holding positive thoughts about what we desire. Through the law of attraction, we will draw those situations and experiences into our lives.

Maria Stephenson, a spiritual counselor from Arizona, said that the following experience helped her know that she and her friends were being watched over—not only by the law of attraction, but by helpful angels as well.

> A group of us from Phoenix were meeting at a hotel in Newport Beach for a conference. Several of us were sharing rooms to cut down on the expenses. Late on Friday, I arrived at the hotel and assumed that everyone in our group had already checked in, since the others were scheduled to arrive several hours before me. I checked to see if they were registered, and they weren't. So, I registered and went to the room to wait for the others to arrive. Time went by, and somewhere around 8:30, I fell asleep waiting.
>
> At about 10:40, I heard a voice in my sleep telling me to *"wake up."* I sat up and looked around. No one was there. I laid my head back on the pillow and wondered where my friends were. I again had a strong feeling, and a voice in my head said,

"Get up, get on your shoes, and go out the door." I attempted to dismiss it again, but the feeling got stronger. So, I got up, put on my shoes, and went to the door. As soon as I opened the door, there were my friends walking down the hall!

The hotel had made a mistake and had failed to put the room in my name, instead, putting it in a completely different name. So here were my friends, getting another room and having to pay for it separately since they could not find me! They were literally about to put the key in the door! If I had not walked out right then, they would have gone into their new room, and I would have never seen them. We would have been paying for two rooms. We all could not believe what had just happened. Not only had I just caught them, but the chance of them being on the exact same floor. . . . Of course, then we laughed and knew exactly what happened—thanks to my persistent angels waking me up and getting me out the door!

Angelic Healings for Family Members

A woman named Cheryl Anne shares this story of how the angels healed her sister and her dog:

> I woke up early one morning to pray for my sister who was going through horrible trials in her personal life. Even her dog was sick. I prayed for her, then blew the flame of my prayer candle out. It would not go out. I repeatedly tried to extinguish it, then realized what was happening.
>
> I closed my eyes and sat quietly there in the candle's glow. Then they came to me, the guardian angels of my niece, nephew, and sister—and yes, even the dog! They were so clear and announced their names and purposes. My sister had two angels, one on each side of her, one male, one female. Their names were Michael Edward and Ruth Ann.
>
> I wrote an e-mail to my sister to tell her what I had been shown. She was not a person of faith, so I was concerned that

she would laugh at me or be angry, and yet I knew I had to tell her. She gasped as I told her their names. She told me of a dream she had the night before: She was being pursued by a man and a woman. She ran from them, but they kept calling to her, saying, "Don't run. You need us!" When she began to wake up, she heard herself calling out what she thought was a name or strange word. She decided to write it down so she'd remember. The word she was yelling in her sleep, the word she had written down at her bedside, was "MERA."

She asked me to repeat the angels' names. When I told her, "Michael Edward, Ruth Ann," which MERA stands for, I'm not sure who was more startled! Most of my previous encounters have been very personal, and other people haven't received any sort of signs relating to them. It's always just been me and my weirdness! (By the way, her dog, who was close to death and was surrounded by tiny birdlike angelic creatures that morning, is doing just fine!)

My sister is now doing very well. She had considered herself an atheist for many years and is now in the midst of a spiritual awakening. Her dear little dog is completely healed as well. It has been an amazing time for her family. Although they have dealt with tremendous difficulty this past year, their lives are now being flooded with love and light from God and their guardian angels.

Prayers to Heal Family Relationships

Here are some examples of powerful prayers that you can say (either mentally, aloud, or in writing) to ask God and the angels to intervene in your family life. Please add or rewrite the messages in the prayers to fit your specific circumstances.

PRAYER TO CONCEIVE A BABY

Dear God,

We have so much love to give, and my spouse and I want to share our love with a baby. We ask that You and the angels help us conceive. Please send one of your brightest and happiest souls into our life, and let this being become our baby child. Thank You.

PRAYER TO HEAL PARENT-CHILD RELATIONSHIPS

Dearest God,

Please help my child and me have a harmonious relationship. I ask Your help in healing any fears that interfere with my child and me expressing love to one another. Please help my child to focus and feel happy. Please help my child accept me and my circumstances. I ask that You and the angels help my child and me release our unforgiveness and resentment. Please help us have a loving and close relationship. Amen.

PRAYER FOR CHILDHOOD BEHAVIORAL ISSUES

Dear God,

Please help me understand my child. I ask that You surround my child with love, wisdom, and intelligence. Please help my child understand and accept responsibility for his/her behavior. I ask that You guide my child to make intelligent choices based upon love, not fear. I ask that You and Archangel Michael please clear my child of any attachments or blocks that could be interfering with his/her happiness. Thank You.

PRAYER TO HEAL FAMILY RELATIONSHIPS

Dear God,

I know that my family member and I both have guardian angels. I ask that these guardian angels help us heal our issues and misunderstandings. Please help us release any anger or unforgiveness. I ask that all effects of our mistakes be lifted and forgotten by everyone involved. Please help me release any judgment I may be carrying toward myself or others. I ask that our guardian angels clearly give us Your direction, knowing that Your will for us is peace. Thank You.

PRAYER FOR A FAMILY MEMBER

Dearest God,

Please help my family member feel peace and happiness at this time. I ask that You send my family member extra angels to comfort him/her. Please surround our entire family with an extra cushion of Your Divine love. Help us to relax and to have faith and trust. Please give us a sign of Your love so that we may release our fears. Thank You for all of Your healing love.

PRAYER FOR A FRIENDSHIP THAT IS ENDING

Beloved Creator,

I know, deep down, that my friendship with _____is ending. I ask Your help to accept this transition with grace and peace. I ask that You and the angels help me be honest in a loving way, with myself, and with my friend. Please help me be true to myself so that my actions stem from love instead of from fear, guilt, or obli-

gation. Please comfort my friend so that we can both accept this change in a positive way.

PRAYER TO ATTRACT NEW FRIENDS

Dearest God,

I now see myself surrounded by loving friends with whom I share much in common. I can feel the presence of new friendships with like-minded souls, and I ask Your help in manifesting this vision. Please guide me to meet new people who are positive, spiritually minded, health conscious, and fun. Please help me to know that I deserve the love and attention of these new friends. Thank You so much.

CHAPTER FOUR

Your Ascending Body

The angels help us heal from physical challenges. They also want to help us have more energy and vitality, so they offer us guidance on how to take good care of our physical selves. As with all aspects of working with angels, we must ask the angels to help us before they are allowed to intervene. The only exception is a life-endangering situation that occurs before it's "our time" to go.

The Angels and Sleep

During an angel reading session, the angels taught me that it's important for us to have a good night's sleep so that they can better help us. This is a transcript of a session (related to sleep issues) between myself and a first-time client I'll call Rhonda. Please keep in mind when reading this that this is my first session with Rhonda, and I don't know anything about her.

I purposely only write people's names down when they make an appointment with me to avoid being influenced by advance information. Also, I work with the angels in three ways: Either I'll relay what I hear them say in my right ear, like a translator; or I'll describe the clairvoyant images that the angels show me; or the angels speak directly *through* me, indicated by the use of pronouns such as *we* or *our*.

Doreen: Your angels say they are working with you in your sleep. *On* your sleep and *in* your sleep, they say. There's a message that you need deeper sleep. [The angels show me a light coming into her bedroom and waking her up.]. Is there some sort of interruption coming during your sleep from a light?

Rhonda: Yes, I work the graveyard shift right now, and I sleep during daytime hours, and the sunlight comes into my bedroom while I'm trying to sleep.

Doreen: Oh, okay, that's what the angels mean. Can you close the curtains more, or the blinds?

Rhonda: I've got the blinds closed, but they still let sunlight peak through. I've got to put something additional up on the windows.

Doreen: Most definitely, because your angels say that this light wakes you up, and they say it's not letting you go into a deep enough sleep. Without the deep sleep, the angels can't go into your dream state and interact with you. They're very concerned about your sleep.

Rhonda: Okay, I have these other curtains to put up over the other blinds, but I've been procrastinating putting them up.

Doreen: Yes, your angels *really, really* want you to have deeper sleep, and they say to block out that light.

Rhonda [later in the session]: My mind has been chattering a lot lately. Is there any type of meditation, sound, or mantra I could do that would help quiet my mind?

Doreen: The angels say, *"We feel that the main thing you could do to help your mind is to get a better night's sleep by blocking out that light. You'll see the inner light if you block out the outer light! You don't need any other tools but to have a good night's sleep. We angels are seeking to work with you. We knock on your door each night, but you have to be in a deep level of sleep for us to access you. You're not reaching that deep level, and it's affecting your concentration."*

ぬ ぬ ぬ

Not only do the angels give advice about the importance of sound sleeping, but they also help us sleep well. All we need to do is ask them for assistance. A friend of my husband's named Terry explained his positive experience in working with the angels in this regard: "I had been working really hard and was due to have another difficult time the following day. I was feeling exhausted and needed to have a solid night's sleep. So I asked my angels to help me. It worked! I had an excellent night's sleep and awoke refreshed."

Soul Traveling and Dreams

During this angel reading session, my client Katherine and I discussed the phenomenon of having out-of-body experiences during sleep. Very often, our angels escort us to other-worldly places where we attend school and learn deep spiritual lessons. Other times, we may actually be involved in teaching others during these experiences of soul traveling.

> **Doreen:** I see that you do a lot of soul traveling in your sleep and that you sort of remember these travels as dreams, but you don't quite remember the dreams in the morning.

> **Katherine:** I ask my angels to help me remember my dreams, but I still can't remember them!

> **Doreen:** When you do soul traveling, you go into a fourth-dimensional world where things are not based on time or space. Those are beliefs of this third-dimensional world, beliefs that limit our ability to understand basics of life. So, you are learning about truths that don't translate, or don't make sense, when you wake up with a third-dimensional mind-set. However, all of your dreamtime learning and experiences are incorporated into your unconscious and *do* influence you in a positive way. So it's not necessary to remember these soul travels and dreamtime lessons in order to benefit from them.

Angel Energy

Now you know that the angels will help us sleep well if we ask for, and follow, their guidance. By doing so, we awaken refreshed and energized. There's no reason for us to feel tired, as the angels say that we have an unlimited source of energy in and around us. That source is omnipresent God, who is within you right now.

If you feel tired for no apparent reason, mentally ask the Archangel Michael to come to you by saying a prayer such as this one:

PRAYER FOR INCREASED ENERGY

Archangel Michael, I ask you and your helpers to come to me now. Please cut away and release anything that is draining me. Help to lift my energy to its natural state of vitality now. Thank you.

ↄ ↄ ↄ

You will feel the presence of this mighty angel soon after saying such a prayer. Using his "sword," Michael removes attachments that are draining you, as well as the negative energy that is weighing you down. Within minutes, you feel refreshed and revitalized. I find that this method works ten times better than drinking coffee.

A woman named Pam also discovered that the angels could help her stay awake during a long, late-night drive:

One day, my friend and I were driving home from Las Vegas. As he was driving, his eyes started to get heavy, almost closing. We were both tired, but he seemed to be worse off than I was. I took over driving, but after a while, my eyes started getting heavy and kept closing, too.

Suddenly, out of nowhere, I got a burst of energy. Less than a minute later, a car went from the far right lane and darted across three lanes. The car missed the center divider as it then spun around and stopped blocking the lane we were traveling in. I was able to stop safely and just missed hitting the car by a matter of inches. Had this occurred only minutes earlier, I would have plowed into the other car while dozing off.

Needless to say, the adrenaline pumped through my body from the incident, and there was no longer a hint of drowsiness. We arrived home safely.

Prior to this incident, my friend had often spoken of angels, but I was not sure that I believed in them. I did not disbelieve; I was just skeptical with an open mind. This was the proof for me that there are guardian angels. While back on the road after the close call with the collision, I said, "Okay, I believe!" and thanked my angels for watching over me and my friend.

Detoxifying Your Body

The angels urge us to detoxify our bodies, and you may have received some intuitive feelings that compel you to make changes in your diet and lifestyle. These are very real messages that you are receiving from your guardian angels. You are not imagining them.

The angels ask us to stop consuming toxins in the things we eat, drink, and use on our bodies. Toxins pull down our energy levels and make us feel sluggish. They also block our ability to clearly receive messages from heaven. Toxins also interfere with our spiritual growth.

The main toxins that the angels ask us to avoid are:

— *Meats, fowl, and fish, contaminated with hormones and pesticides.* Since virtually all animal flesh and by-products (milk, eggs, cheese, etc.) currently have residues of hormones and pesticides, you may consider adopting a vegetarian lifestyle or a near-vegetarian lifestyle (where you eliminate animal products once or twice a week). If you feel you must consume animal products, purchase "organic" dairy products (such as Horizon brand milk), and free-range chickens, hormone-free meat, and eggs from free-range chickens. These products are available at health food stores, as are wonderful meat and fowl substitutes, such as seitan, glutan, tempah, and baked tofu. Vegetarianism has come a long, long way in the past five years. If you haven't tried vegetarian meals in a while, give them another try—they're now delicious and difficult to distinguish from meat products.

— *Pesticides on fruits and vegetables.* Try to eat an all-organic diet. Ask your grocer to carry organic produce, or find a health food store or fruit stand in your area that sells organic fruits and vegetables.

— *Toxins in beverages.* The angels ask us to eliminate or significantly reduce alcohol, caffeine, and carbonation from our diet. Drink spring water, not "drinking water," as the angels urge us to drink water in as natural a form as possible. Drink fresh fruit juice, as the life force in fruits leaves 20 minutes after it is squeezed. Concentrated or refrigerated fruit juice has healthful vitamins, but it is not as life-giving as freshly squeezed juice.

— *Nitrates.* Avoid cured meats, such as lunch meats, sausage, and bacon. There are wonderful substitutes made from soy products that look, taste, and smell like the real thing. Many supermarkets carry these deli-substitute products, as do most health food stores.

— *Toxins in toiletry items.* Avoid laurel sodium sulphate, a nitrate catalyst, and Propylene Glycol, an industrial anti-freeze. Read the labels of your lotions, toothpastes, makeup, and shampoos. Weleda makes one of the only toothpastes that doesn't have laurel sodium sulphate as an ingredient (their "Plant Gel" and "Calendula" toothpastes are wonderful and can be ordered at 1-800-241-1030), and Aubrey makes great lotions (1-800-AUBREYH). Health food stores carry a wide variety of nontoxic products, but be sure to read the ingredient labels, because some so-called natural products have laurel sodium sulphate and other toxins in them.

— *Toxins in household products.* Avoid Cocamide DEA, DEA, Sodium Laurel Sulfate, Sodium Laureth Sulfate, Tallow, and Synthetic Fragrance. Health food stores carry natural and effective cleaners and detergents. Avoid bleach and bleached paper products, such as napkins and paper towels.

You can accelerate the detoxification process by drinking plenty of fluids and by getting adequate sleep, exercise, and fresh air. Drinking "wheat grass juice," which most juice bars and health food stores offer, can also pull metals and pollutants out of your body rapidly.

The angels say that they are working with us to increase the "vibrational frequency" of our bodies. Like a violin string that vibrates at a higher rate according to the note that is played, we are beginning to move up the scale ourselves. We are doing this to keep pace with Earth's accelerated vibrational frequency.

This doesn't mean that we move faster during the day, or that we become busier or more rushed. Vibrational frequency means that we are less dense and more sensitive to the higher, finer frequencies of the angelic realm. It means that we are more intuitive, creative, and naturally energized.

Many lightworkers feel guided to adopt a vegetarian diet. They then gradually get guidance to become a complete vegan (no animal products). After that, they are guided to eat only raw and unprocessed fruits, vegetables, nuts, and grains. Eventually, we are collectively moving toward a lifestyle of "breatharianism," where we'll receive all of our nourishment from the *prana* that is in the air. This will dramatically increase our life expectancies and ability to communicate telepathically.

If you feel compelled to delete certain foods or beverages from your diet, mentally ask your guardian angels to heal your cravings so that you won't miss the product. You'll be amazed at how easily you can give up toxic foods and drinks, if you'll ask the angels to assist you. Every week, I meet people who tell me that the angels eliminated or significantly reduced their cravings for alcohol, sugar, white bread, chocolate, colas, and other toxins. I had the same experience myself, where my cravings for junk food and coffee were completely removed.

Here's a wonderful prayer to say:

Dear Angels,

Please surround me with your healing energy, and help me to heal my cravings for unhealthful foods and drinks. Please remove my desire for toxic substances, and help me to have the motivation to live and eat healthfully. Please guide me while shopping, preparing, and eating food, and give me guidance about how to live without polluting myself or my world. With great love and gratitude, I thank you.

Angel Healers, Angel Helpers

I also talk to many people who have been healed through prayer, conversations with God, and asking the angels for help. Fred Rothlisberger, a reader of my books, sent me the following story:

I was going to go in to have my third back surgery February 16, 1998. It had been several years since my last back surgery for a congenital problem. I was worried about being put out again, as I have a hard time coming out of anesthesia.

I was out in the back yard, cleaning up after our dogs, when a voice came to me. It simply stated, *"Don't worry about the surgery; it will be fine, God has more work for you to do."* I felt very peaceful from that point on. I had the surgery, and they found a cyst growing in my spine, which was putting pressure on the spinal cord, thus causing me my pain. I was released the day following the surgery to go home.

My recovery was very fast. I have had seven surgeries in my life, and never have I felt the peace and the speed of recovery I had with this surgery.

ॐ ॐ ॐ

A woman named Shelly Long "just happened" to turn on the radio the day I was on a local Phoenix, Arizona, station. Shelly was on her way to visit her doctor for a biopsy on a lump that had been discovered in her breast. She heard me emphasizing, "You must ask your angels to help you. Unless there's a life-endangering situation before your time, the angels can't intervene without your permission."

Shelly had always been a woman of faith, but she had forgotten to ask the angels to help her to heal. So she said a prayer, requesting the angels to intervene, and then pulled into the doctor's office. During the examination, the doctor was unable to find the lump. It had disappeared since her previous visit, one week earlier!

The angels love to assist us because they have complete faith, they retain a joyful attitude while helping us. The angels have taught me that a somber attitude often makes bad situations worse. Joy is the key to manifesting desired outcomes, including healing. In fact, the angels often display a wonderful sense of humor during their work with us, as Tina Needham's story illustrates:

> I've read a lot of books that have been profound and meaningful to me. But it wasn't until I read *Divine Guidance* that I felt I had an actual tool to help me reach a different and more "active" level. I was using Doreen's advice to clear blocks and meditate, when halfway through the book I had my first angelic experience. It was so "everyday" that it still makes me laugh. I didn't hear harps or see glowing visions.
>
> I was in bed next to my sleeping husband one night, wide

awake because of the cutting pain of a strep throat infection. I heard a woman's voice in my left ear. It said: *"Master, the throat lozenge is in the bottom drawer."* Definitely, not the profound message I was looking for!

I was numb. I laid there for a moment, trying to collect my thoughts, I even woke up my husband to see if he had said anything to me (even though it was a woman's voice). I tried to explain it away. I was a skeptic at heart, which is why I was trying to remove the blocks from seeing my angels in the first place.

You see I never, ever use throat lozenges, as I can't stand how they taste and feel. I sat up with my feet on the floor, took a deep breath, and pulled open the third and bottom drawer of my bedside table. It was dark, and I rummaged around the cluttered drawer until I felt it—old and sticky, but a Hall's Mentholatum lozenge. I got goose bumps all down my arm. I got up immediately and wrote the entire experience down. It was three A.M. I will never forget it. I still don't really understand the reference to "Master."

Healing Effects of the Past

The angels aren't limited by time or space constrictions. Neither are we, but we don't sufficiently believe this yet, so we appear to be trapped in limited access to time and space.

If you have any regrets for past actions that are impacting your present-day health, the angels can help. For instance, if you abused your body with cigarettes, alcohol, or drugs in the past, your angels can help you undo the negative effects of these behaviors. The undoing will positively affect everyone involved, so, for example, any negative consequences that other people experienced because of your smoking (such as secondhand smoke) or intoxication will be healed.

Here is an angel prayer to help undo the effects of the past:

PRAYER TO UNDO THE EFFECTS OF THE PAST

Dearest Angels,
I have made mistakes in how I have treated my body,
and I ask that all effects of these mistakes be undone and
forgotten in all directions of time by everyone involved.

Life Expectancy

Part of the life plan that we develop before we incarnate is the length of time that we'll live. Together with our guides and angels, we decide if we'll live 40, 60, or 100 years. Most people opt to live long lives because they want to be with their children and other loved ones for a long time. However, other people decide to live shorter lives, either because they're reluctant to live on Earth for a century, or because they only have a brief lesson to learn before returning to heaven.

The new "Indigo Children" who were discussed earlier have higher life expectancies than previous generations. Many of these children will grow up in the new energy following the millennium shift and will live to extremely old ages. This will be because many of the conditions that are detrimental to health, such as ingesting a poor diet, bearing stress, and breathing in pollutants, won't be a factor. Humans will live in a fresh, clean world; we will consume a much more nutritious diet; and we won't compete or engage in other unhealthful activities.

The angels can tell you what your life expectancy is, if you'd like to know. When people find out their time frame for living, several positive results occur. I've watched certain individuals instantly heal from phobias after they learned that they were going to live many more years. Suddenly, they're able to release their fears of dying once they know that the end is not near. Of course, this isn't an invitation to "tempt fate" and begin jumping out of airplanes without a parachute. However, this knowledge can help people relax quite a bit.

Second, those who receive their life expectancy information become motivated to fulfill their goals now, instead of waiting for the future. They get going on the careers, hobbies, and ambitions because they know that they have a finite number of years in which to accomplish and enjoy them.

To find out your life expectancy, simply close your eyes and take a deep breath. Then, ask your guardian angels, "How old will I be when I leave the physical plane and return to the after-life plane? How old will I be in this lifetime when I pass on?"

You will either hear, see, feel, or know a set of numbers. Most people hear two or three numbers because you've selected these various ages as "outs." The first number you hear is an age when you could "go home" to heaven if you finish your mission and elect to leave. You can stay on and live to the second or third age if you like.

If you received an age that has already passed by, think for a moment about what happened to you at that age. Were you depressed, ill, suicidal, or in any accidents? If so, you chose to stay on Earth longer and live to the older ages that you original-ly chose.

If you are one of the souls who elected to be here for the mil-lennium shift and beyond, you may find that you will live to an extremely old age, in the hundreds or even the thousands. As I wrote earlier, the life expectancy in the coming energy shift will dramatically increase.

You have free will, and I believe that you can elect to go home or stay here for longer or shorter periods than you origi-nally designed. So if you don't like the life expectancy informa-tion you received, decide on a different number. In *A Course in Miracles*, it says that no one dies without their own consent. So, you are in charge, and your angels will help you fulfill these wishes.

PRAYER FOR HEALTH AND HEALING

Dear God,

I know that You created me in the perfect image and likeness of Yourself. I ask that You, Holy Spirit, and the archangel Raphael help me know and experience this health in my physical body. I am willing to release all thoughts and behaviors that create the illusion of illness and pain. I know that You are omnipresent, so therefore, You exist in every cell in my body. Please help me feel Your love in my physical body so that I can know that You cradle me in Your arms right now. Amen.

PRAYER FOR A LOVED ONE'S HEALTH

Beloved God,

Thank You for sending the Archangel Raphael and the healing angels to my loved one's bedside. I now see that You, Holy Spirit, Raphael, and the angels are embracing my loved one. I picture my loved one smiling and feeling well. I know that, in truth, my loved one is well right now, and I ask for Your continued help so that we may realize this peace and health in our daily experience. Thy will be done.

PRAYER FOR WEIGHT AND APPETITE

Dearest God,

Today, I have set my intention that my appetite for food be solely for healthful and light foods and beverages. I am willing to release any fears that would make me want to overeat. I know that You are guiding me in every moment of my life, including the times when I eat and drink. I ask that You continue to bless me with Divine wisdom and peace so that all of my decisions about consuming food and beverages will come from my higher self. Thank You, and amen.

PRAYER FOR SLEEP ISSUES

To My Creator,

Please help me to have a restful and sound sleep tonight. I ask for a guardian angel to be posted on the north, south, east, and west sides of my home during the night. I visualize my home surrounded by the Divine white light of Your protective love. I am willing to release all of my cares and worries to You and the angels so that the pockets of my soul are emptied for the night. Please send some comforting angels to my side so that I may enjoy a wonderful night's sleep.

PRAYER FOR FITNESS MOTIVATION

Dear God,

Please help me to be motivated to take good care of my body. I ask Your help in carrying through in my commitment to exercise, eat healthfully, and get sufficient rest. Please help me have faith in my ability to attain and maintain physical fitness. Please guide me to know the best ways to take care of myself. If my motivation slackens or I am tempted to procrastinate, please help me reaffirm my resolve. Thank You, and amen.

PRAYER FOR HEALING AN ADDICTION

Beloved God, Holy Spirit, and the Angels,
I know that addictive cravings are actually a craving for Divine love. Please help me feel that I am filled with Your ever-present love. I am willing to release any fears that would block me from the awareness of Your love. I ask you to clear away from me the beliefs, patterns, feelings, and thoughts that trigger my cravings. Please guide me to people, situations, and experiences that support my desire to live free of addictions. I surrender all my cravings to You, and ask for extra angels to surround me with the light of health and peace. Please help me now and always. Amen.

So much of our health and life is affected by our careers, and the angels also want to help us heal our professional and financial lives. In the next chapter, you'll see how the angels guide us to remember our life's purpose and to find meaningful vocations and avocations.

CHAPTER FIVE

Life Purpose and Your Career Path

The angels help us heal our career path, and they are very empathetic to people who feel they are in the wrong job. The angels see our hidden talents, and they know that we can help others—while enjoying ourselves—by working in a profession that incorporates our natural interests.

Many people come to me searching for their life purpose. The angels are happy to help us remember the mission for which we volunteered before incarnation. Sometimes their help comes as psychological guidance, as in the case of my client Amy.

Amy: Is there a message my angels want to give me about my life's path and direction?

Doreen: I hear your angels say in unison, *"Be true to you!"* It seems that you are following your career path somewhat, but you are still compromising the true desire of your heart. They tell me that you rationalize your feelings about your career and that you are praying for help. The answer to your prayers has already been given to you, and you are aware of it: Be honest with yourself, and take steps based upon that self-honesty. God and the angels will guide you step by step in what to say and do, in a loving way, and be assured that they will never ask you to do anything that would bring harm to you or others.

Finding Your Life Purpose

"What is my purpose?" is one of the most common questions that my clients pose. They ask this question because they desire meaningful work that makes a difference in the world. We each have a "Divine life purpose," which is an assignment we agreed to fulfill during our lifetime. God, our guides, and our angels helped us devise this purpose before our incarnation. They ensured that the purpose would mesh with our natural talents and interests. The plan also came with enough time, money, intelligence, creativity and other resources to fulfill it completely.

Annette was a retired widow who wanted to know about her life purpose and who felt a desire to contribute to the world. As the angels explained, we don't necessarily need to turn our life purpose into a paid vocation.

Annette: I wanted to find out about my life purpose because I want to do something that helps the world.

Doreen: Your angels say that you already are. They say, *"Not every purpose involves a nine-to-five job with a paycheck. Many purposes involve you merely being centered and peaceful when you're in town shopping. You are a messenger of Divine light and love. You are a role model to many, which is a subtle, but important, purpose. To be a role model, you don't necessarily have to be someone who is up on stage or in the newspapers. It can be someone, like yourself, who is a role model of peace, compassion, and gentleness."* They're showing me that these are your qualities and that other people do notice. The angels also show me that your gardening is a form of therapy for you.

Annette: Oh, I do like to garden!

Doreen: They give you the thumbs-up and say, *"Anytime you garden, you are contributing to the world through your peace of mind. Every time you have a peaceful thought, it goes out into the world and affects others, just as, conversely, angry thoughts affect others in the way that secondhand smoke does. When you are gardening, your thoughts play beautiful music that resonate throughout the spheres."* Your angels bless you for your contributions.

The angels say that you don't need to punch a time clock to make a contribution to the world. However, they also mention that if you *wanted* to do some volunteer work, you would be happy in an institutional setting such as a hospice. In your volunteer work, you would simply visit with the residents and put a hand on their shoulder and give them a kind word. Bring them tea. And while you're doing this, your loving and healing energy is going to them.

Annette: Yes, I *had* thought of doing hospice work!

Doreen: Well, that's one thing that the angels say you would enjoy and be very effective at, if you wanted to do some formal work outside the house. I see you going into the hospice residents' bedrooms and comforting them in a real simple, quiet, and loving way. Not so much what you say, but your countenance is healing to them.

Annette: That's my style, definitely.

Doreen: But your angels don't urge you to do this, Annette. Your angels say,"*This is a time in your life for you to slow down a bit, relax, and enjoy. Keep your pace under control.*"

Annette: Oh, that makes sense. I was so busy for so many years.

Doreen: They don't want you to push yourself or feel guilty. They want you to know that you are making a contribution to the world every time you have a peaceful thought.

ॐ ॐ ॐ

As Annette's angels explained, our main mission is to be at peace with ourselves. So our task involves "being" more than "doing." Yet, the desire to be of service to others is very strong in many people. There is a human fear of dying without having lived a life that has mattered. In the following session with my client Stella, we discuss how the drive to fulfill our purpose is practically instinctual:

Stella: I feel very compelled inside to achieve what I came here to do.

Doreen: Yes, of course.

Stella: And it's not the kind of feeling that just goes away over the years.

Doreen: No, nor can it. The urge that we each have to fulfill our purpose is an extremely strong instinct.

Stella: As I get older—I'm in my early '40s—I start to feel that I don't have that much time left. I've got to get started and do "it," whatever "it" is.

Doreen: Exactly. Purposes don't always have to be a paid profession. It's nice when that happens, but please don't discount how much you already help people when you talk to them, listen to them, and teach them. We'll talk with your angels during our session tonight and see what they say about your life's purpose. Deep down, you already know what your mission in life is. You've just forgotten it, and the angels will remind you if you ask for their help.

Spiritually Meaningful Careers

Sometimes, my clients tell me that they long to help the world via a spiritually related profession. Many people are making significant contributions to the world in ways that seem quite subtle. For example, some people's life purpose is to "anchor light" to the world. This means that they are sent as radiant Earth angels who send healing thoughts and energy into Earth's body and atmosphere to undo the harmful effects of pollutants and negativity. In the following session, my client Belinda and I discuss the role that her upward vibrational frequency shift is having on the world:

Belinda: Can you give me some idea about my mission in this life? I had thought for a long time that my mission was to be in a really great relationship, and from that, to raise our vibrational frequency as a couple. But lately, because I can't find that type of a permanent relationship, I'm begin-ning to wonder if my mission involves something else.

Doreen: Yes, your mission does involve raising your vibra-tional frequency. By raising your frequency, you lift the whole world and provide a service. But you also learn the balance between humility and humbleness and really love yourself as you love your neighbor. You have some priva-cy and intimacy issues, and you're learning to balance this so you know how to deal with other people. You are also learning how to express yourself for therapeutic reasons.

You also have the path of the teacher, so art, writing, and creative expression are really important to your growth. I see newspapers all around you. When we began our session, I saw you writing, so this is an avenue for you to check out—journal writing, initially, and then see where it takes you.

Belinda: Well, I do love to write.

Doreen: The angels also show me that it would be a great idea for you to have pink roses around you.

Belinda: Oh, wow! That opens my heart just thinking about it!

Doreen: Exactly, pink roses are correlated with opening the heart chakra.

The Artist's Soul

I find that people are happiest when they are in careers that match their true interests. Artistic people, such as my client

Eileen, need to be in creative careers. Some people think that they can't make much money in artistic ventures, but if we use our creative resources, we discover many practical and wonderful ways to make money artistically:

Eileen: At this age, I cannot afford to make many more career mistakes, and I ask that my angels guide me. Am I doing the right thing by marketing this computer product, or am I meant to do something else? I am tired and confused and do not want to get a real job.

Doreen: Your angels thank you for consulting them in this matter. They remind you that you are part of a team, and they love your team approach to your career. They also suggest that you come to them for other aspects of your life, including your relationships.

Your angels say that you have true artistic talents and not to let those go. You can have a job that you enjoy while you pursue your real passion simultaneously. Don't confuse the two and think that you have to suffer to make money until your real ship comes in. The computer marketing position, as you know, isn't suited to your real interests. You are just doing it for the money, and unfortunately, when we do that, we don't make as much money, *plus* we don't enjoy ourselves!

There is another job waiting for you. I see retail sales involving products for women at a boutique or some sort of store. It is low-stress, happy work, with upbeat customers. This will help your other career (it's something where you're self-employed in a creative venue) to zoom, because you'll feel happy and also financially secure.

Eileen: Thank you. I must ask who my angels are—and the other career, might it be catering?

Doreen: Catering would certainly fit the parameters of what your angels show me. Anything where you can use your artistic talents would work out very well! You have several angels around you, including Gabriel, the angel of artists and communicators. Other angels with you are Hoziel, Chamuel, and a male angel who insists that his name is Oscar.

Boosting Your Business

One evening I gave a lecture to a group of healers from all different backgrounds on how the angels could help them in their private practices. During the talk, I mentioned that the healers could ask the angels to help them attract more clients. All they needed to do was say a prayer such as, "I ask that everyone who would receive blessings by being with me, be guided to come to my practice."

One of the counselors in the audience, named Elisabeth, experienced immediate success after she said this prayer. She wrote to me, "I attended your lecture in which you gave out the affirmations about how we can get more clients. I did so immediately and every day after. Right away, I received referrals, virtually overnight."

Another one of my spiritual counseling students named Nancine asked her angels to help her begin a public speaking career. Here is her story of how the angels Divinely guided her to give speeches:

I am beginning a career in motivational speaking and have been meditating for quite some time about how to manifest an audience. By being still and quiet in meditation, I was able to hear my angels' Divine guidance. First, my angels encouraged me to look for the underlying block that surfaced if I imagined really receiving my heart's desire, and to release this belief. When I did so, I realized I had an ego concern over whether I was really qualified and had enough credentials. So I wrote out the concern, among other beliefs, and burned them in a ceremony. I wrote out positive affirmations about my qualifications and placed them all around my house.

A few weeks later, I received a speaking request on my answer machine. When I was about to return the call, I heard a gentle voice within say, *"Go to the library first, sit in quiet, and make an outline before you call."* I followed that guidance and made an outline, then returned the call. The caller asked me if I could do a workshop on business marketing. With my new outline in front of me, I was able to confidently explain what I could do— right down to the workshop title! "Wonderful," the caller said. "Will three hours be sufficient, or would you like more time?" I suddenly had my first major speaking engagement, thanks to tuning in to my Divine guidance!

During the next eight weeks prior to my speaking engagement, I took time to clear my chakras and listen for Divine guidance. Each day, the angels would take me to the keyboard and begin to write. One day, they urged me to write a biography of my career background. The very next day, the speaking organization asked me to fax over my bio and the workshop outline. A week later, she mailed out hundreds of brochures with this information. I could not have waited a minute longer, which is what the angels had told me.

One of my guardian angels suggested that I contact a local news service and create some publicity. The new service's initial response was, "No interest." A few days later, the angels said, *"Let's call them again. Be loving, but be firm."* I thought this was crazy, but I did call, acknowledging their needs and expressing the good fit of my speech in their newspaper. On the morning of the seminar, one of my neighbors excitedly told me, "I saw your name and your event in the newspaper yesterday morning!" It was the only day I had not purchased a copy, but she gladly gave me hers. There it was, on the front page of the Business section.

When I gave the workshop, I was so pleased that my audience was filled with people of the highest energy. Truly, our experience together was perfect. The organization president wrote me later, "I could see from the beaming faces throughout the room that you had truly touched an inner core." The angels continue to guide me in my speaking career.

Looking Our Best

The angels remind me of coaches, helping us to be our best at work. They prepare us in all way—intellectually, spiritually, mentally, and physically. For example, my husband, Michael, was getting ready to go to his office for the day. He knew that he wasn't going to be with clients during the morning and would be by himself at work until around noon, so he decided to skip shaving in the morning, and instead, packed his electric shaver so that he could shave in the mid-morning at the office. As he packed the shaver, he heard a voice say, *"Better pack the electric cord, too."* Michael thought this was odd, since his shaver is battery operated, and he had recently recharged the battery cell. Still, he listened to the voice and packed the cord. Three hours later, as Michael stood shaving at his office sink, the shaver's batteries suddenly died. "If I hadn't packed the electric cord, I would have been unshaven for my afternoon appointment," he said.

A Pat on the Back

A woman named Patricia told me this enchanting story: "I had worked diligently on a very complex document. When I was finished, I silently said to my angels, 'This deserves some level of praise.' Upon delivering the document to my client, he called me later and indicated that he was totally impressed and actually thanked me for my creative efforts. This from a client who has never, ever given a compliment to anyone on staff. My angels and I rejoiced!"

Stress Management

The angels continually tell me, "*All pressure is self-imposed.*" In other words, stress is of our own choosing. We may con ourselves into thinking that someone or something else is making us do something against our will, but ultimately, we always have the choice and ability to say no, even if there are heavy consequences involved in doing so. The angels say that realizing we have this option is liberating and helps us to shed the stress that accompanies feeling like an imprisoned slave.

We have so much more control over our daily lives than we realize, often because we've never tested the waters to know how much our thoughts influence everything that comes to us during the day. The angels have taught me the importance of setting our intentions for the day, first thing in the morning. Decide, "What do I want today to be like?" and it will be done.

For instance, if you want the telephone to be quiet, ask your angels to screen your calls. People who normally would call you at the drop of a hat will be guided to not call you unless the news is really important. Conversely, if we expect the day to be a crazy zoo, that is the intention that will prove self-fulfilling.

My student, Bonnie, discovered this secret one day. A salesperson, Bonnie woke up one morning and said to her angels, "I really would like to work from home today." To her amazement, every phone call she received appeared to be Divinely guided. She recalls, "Everyone who phoned was requesting appointments for next week. That gave me the time I needed to take care of some long-overdue tasks. I am now taking charge of my day, instead of allowing circumstances to dictate my schedule. Now

307

I'm completing projects that I used to carry over each day and that used to weigh me down."

Your angels can function just like wonderfully loyal office managers and assistants. Ask them to manage your phone calls, visitors, and appointments. Invite your angels to brainstorm with you so that you can develop creative new ideas. They'll help you to make your meetings on time, and as I discovered, they won't let anything get in your way.

Business Traveling

I'm on airplanes nearly every weekend, giving workshops in one or more cities. Flying this much would usually mean encountering a percentage of problems, but when you bring your angels along on trips, the statistics are more in your favor.

Because of the storms around the country, the Atlanta airport was practically shut down one Sunday night when I, and thousands of other travelers, were trying to catch planes. The only airline that was flying was Delta; all the other carriers cancelled their flights. So, everyone was pouring into the Delta terminal, struggling to get airline seats.

The Delta plane that I initially boarded for Los Angeles sat on the tarmac for 30 minutes. Then the pilot announced that because of mechanical problems, the flight was cancelled and we'd all have to leave and try to get seats on other flights.

We returned to the terminal amid a sea of people standing at a gate podium, demanding to be allowed on the only remaining flight in the airport going to California. Again, I prayed and asked the angels to help me get home. I was tired and had clients to see the next day. Somehow the crowd pushed me to the front of the line.

I began talking with a couple in front of me in line. We smiled and joked, while nervously noticing the many people who were mobbing the ticket counter. I felt that we were in the eye of a volatile hurricane. Then it was my new friends' turn to be next at the gate. The ticket agent said to them, "I've got three seats left on the plane. They're all in the rear, but they're yours if you want them."

The ticket agent looked at me, and then turned back to the couple and asked, "Is this person traveling with you, also?"

"Yes, she is," the couple replied. As I sank into my airplane seat moments later, which was miraculously an aisle seat, I thanked God, the angels, and the couple profusely for helping me.

Angel Prayers

Here are some powerful prayers to help you connect with the Divine in your work life:

PRAYER FOR HEALING JOB CONFLICTS

Dear God,

My deepest desire is to be happy while I work, and I ask Your help so that I may find peace on the job. Please help me to be understood and understanding with everyone with whom I come into contact. Please clear me of any fears that trigger relationship conflicts in the workplace. I ask that You and the angels guide me to job responsibilities and tasks that match my interests and skills. I now visualize myself feeling happy when I wake up to go to work in the morning, and I ask Your assistance in manifesting this vision. Amen.

PRAYER FOR FINDING YOUR LIFE'S PURPOSE

To Everyone Who Watches Over Me,

I seem to have forgotten my Divine life purpose, and I ask your help so that I may remember the reason I chose to come here at this time. I am willing to release all fears that keep me from remembering my life's purpose, including the fear of success and failure. I know that I am qualified to fulfill my mission, and I ask for your continued guidance in helping me to know which path makes my heart sing. Please help me to know the difference between joy and fear so that I may immerse myself in meaningful actions that serve others and bring me joy. Thank you so much.

PRAYER FOR A NEW JOB

Beloved Creator,

You have guided me to find a new job, and I ask Your help in noticing the doors that You are opening for me now. I ask for very clear and evident signs to guide me to a new job in which my talents and interests are used in meaningful ways. Please help me to know that I deserve a wonderful new job, and allay any nervousness during the interview process. I ask for extra angels to boost my confidence and courage, and to keep me centered in the sure knowledge that You are providing for me now. Amen.

PRAYER FOR HEALING STRESS

Dear God, Archangel Raphael,
and Archangel Michael,

It seems that stress is taking a toll on me, and I need your help. Please release me from the pressures that I have imposed upon myself. Raphael, I ask that you cover me with your healing energy so that my body will shed the effects of stress. Michael, I ask that you cut away the effects of negative and fearful thoughts, including cords that are draining me. I am willing to release any habits of self-punishment, time urgency, or other belief systems that create stressful situations. I know that I have sufficient time and energy, in truth, and I ask that you help me experience this sufficiency right now. Thank you, and amen.

PRAYER FOR INCREASED BUSINESS OPPORTUNITIES

Dear God, Holy Spirit, Ascended
Masters, and the Angels,

I ask that everyone who would receive blessings from my business products and services be guided to contact me today. I welcome new people and opportunities into my life with open arms. I am willing to release any negative thoughts, patterns, or beliefs that would lead me to sabotage new opportunities. Please help me know that I deserve good now. Thank you.

PRAYER FOR FINANCIAL PEACE

Dearest God,

I know that You are the source of all my good and that You provide for me in all ways. Please help me release the fears that block me from receiving Your gifts. Please help me feel the emotions of peace, gratitude, and financial security and to know that I am Your child upon whom You bestow great blessings. I now stay open to Divine guidance, which perfectly leads me to situations, people, and opportunities that are part of Your plan for my financial peace. I now see and feel myself and everyone else as completely financially secure, and my heart overflows with gratitude and joy at the abundant universe that You created. Thank You, and amen.

Angel Affirmations

I work with clients to increase their self-confidence, both by sending angels to release their self-doubts and by asking them to repeat "angel affirmations" on a daily basis. I've listed many of the angel affirmations that I use in my counseling practice in the Appendix of this book. You can use affirmations to heal issues related to your career, or to increase your self-confidence in social relationships, your love life, and in your relationship with yourself.

In working with people who feel frustrated in their jobs, or who have been unsuccessful in attaining their desired career, I usually find that a lack of self-confidence is the culprit. For instance, I had a client who was an actor. He hadn't landed a role in ten months at the time of our session. The angels told me that my client didn't expect to be hired, and that very negative expectation was affecting his performance. My client instantly realized the truth of this angel reading, and soon after, he worked with affirmations and his angels so that he would *expect* to be hired. He became a working actor again right away.

The angels want to become involved with every area of our work life. In the following chapter, you'll meet a special group of angels who can help boost your mood and energy levels.

CHAPTER SIX

Nature and Animal Angels

Did you ever notice how wonderful you feel when you walk outside? The nature angels, who live among plants and animals, are largely responsible for this therapeutic effect related to the great outdoors. One of the reasons why we feel wonderful when we're around plants, flowers, and animals is because nature is filled with powerful healing angels. Often referred to as "the elemental kingdom," nature angels are a realm of the angelic kingdom that can rapidly heal you of any challenge.

Nature Angels—The Elementals

Every living creature has guardian angels, including flowers, plants, trees, birds, and animals. There are many different types of beings in the "elemental" or nature angel kingdom. These include creatures who are considered mythical, such as leprechauns, elves, tree people, and brownies.

When we open up to our clairvoyance, we find that these beings actually exist and that they aren't that difficult to see. All you need to do is walk in wilderness and mentally call out to them. It's important to have a polite attitude, as elementals are wary of humans who have aggressive, manipulative, drunken, or cocky outlooks. They love humans who are interested in ecological preservation, which is the primary purpose of the elemental kingdom.

The fairies are the elementals who are primarily involved in healing humans. They look like Tinkerbell, diminutive humanlike beings with dragonfly or butterfly wings. They flit from flower to flower, looking like fireflies with their whitish glow.

I meet many people who have fairies as guardian angels. These are always people who have a life purpose involving nature, ecology, or animals. In the chapter on incarnated angels, you'll read about humans who actually *originated* from the elemental kingdom.

The fairies help us release negative thoughts, thought-forms, and energies that we may have absorbed from others or from our own worries. When you walk in nature, mentally ask the fairies to surround you with their love and light. They will swarm around you and will pluck negativity from you like a bee collects pollen. The fairies also instill a sense of playfulness that will inspire you to laugh and have fun, which are certainly therapeutic activities.

You can find fairies wherever there are plants or animals. The greatest number of fairies are around flowers and areas of wilderness. Your potted houseplants have fairies with them, as well. This is one reason why having a potted plant next to your bedside is healthful: The fairies can work with you while you are sleeping and help you have a wonderful night's rest.

Animal Angels

In many ways, our pets are our Earth angels. They provide us with companionship, unconditional love, and entertainment. What's wonderful is that each animal has guardian angels. So, when you are with your pet, you are not only interacting with your animal; you are also having close contact with your pet's guardian angels.

I was once asked by a talk show host if dogs' angels look like little dogs with wings. He then asked me if flies had angels (they do!). Animals have fairies as their guardian angels. Animals and birds who live in or upon water have "sylphs" as guardian angels. Sylphs are water fairies who are long, thin, and transparent, with an opalescent coloring. They do not have wings, as they swim instead of fly.

We can talk to our pets' guardian angels and ask for their help whenever there is a concern about our animal. Your pets' angels will help with challenges of all types, such as health challenges, behavioral problems, or in locating a lost animal.

Romeo, my cat, is a fluffy Himalayan with huge blue eyes and cream-colored fur. He has the strongest personality of any animal I have ever known, and everyone who meets him falls in love with him—hence, his name. In fact, if you put your face close to Romeo, he will put his tiny mouth close to yours as if he's kissing you.

Most of the time, Romeo is well behaved. Sure, he bosses my husband and me around by insisting that his plate be constantly overflowing with fresh food. Of course, it has to be the most expensive brand of cat food or he won't touch it. But beyond this idiosyncracy, Romeo has never given us any trouble . . . except for that one day when he climbed onto the roof of our two-story home. Since the roof is made of tiles and sits at a steep angle, I feared that Romeo would slip and hurt himself. I know that cats are resilient in falls, yet I also worried that Romeo—a lifelong declawed housecat—might also run away from home in the panic of falling from the roof.

I ran to a window that adjoins the roof and pried off the screen, hoping to reach my beloved boy, but he stood about two feet from my outstretched arms. Too frightened to step out onto the slippery roof, I loudly pleaded with Romeo to come to me. He looked at me and blinked sleepily, but he made no motion to walk in my direction.

I looked at my watch. My husband and I were scheduled to leave the house for an important meeting. Yet, how could we leave the house with Romeo stranded on the roof? Finally, I realized I'd neglected to pray about the situation. Always, my past prayers had resulted in speedy action from the universe. But sometimes, in the midst of crises, I would "forget" to ask for spiritual help until I'd realize that my solo human efforts were ineffective.

It occurred to me to ask Romeo's guardian angels for help. Although I had never consciously thought about my cat having angels, at that moment, it seemed like a perfect solution. After all, doesn't everyone have guardian angels? Why would animals be excluded from this gift from God?

I closed my eyes and directed my prayers to my cat's guardian angels: "Please tell Romeo to come to me at the window and allow me to pick him up off of the roof." I felt a wave of peacefulness wash over me as I opened my eyes. I felt compelled to say, "Romeo, come here," and this time, it worked!

Romeo immediately walked over to me and allowed me to lift him into the house. My cat was safely in my arms as I shed tears of gratitude for the immediate help given by his guardian angels. All of us, including animals, are surrounded by guardian angels who provide love and protection.

Angelic Protection for Our Pets

Renée, a woman who has taken several of my angel communication courses, also found that her own guardian angels provided protection for her pet cat. She related:

> I had a wonderful experience and want to share it. As always, before I go to sleep, I do as Doreen suggests, and ask God to place an angel on every corner of the house to protect us through the night. My son came home at two A.M. from work. He was tired and did not check to see if the house was locked up. He accidentally left the back door open—I mean wide open, with a two-and-a-half-foot gap.
>
> In the morning when I got up, the living room was cold, the door was open, and my cat, who would normally run outside, was pacing back and forth at the door. It was as if there was an invisible block that was preventing her from going outside. She is an indoor cat and would not know what to do on her own outside. Thank you, angels!

Humans' Best Friends—Eternally

Just like us, our pets' souls never die. Their spirits often stay right by our side following death. I frequently see dogs and cats next to my clients, and I know that they are providing the same sort of love and companionship that they did while alive. The owner may not be consciously aware of their deceased pet's presence, but on a soul level, we know when our dog or cat is there. We benefit by having the pet with us because it adds an extra layer of "love energy" around us—like a moat around a castle or a bumper on a car.

Once after I'd appeared on an East Coast morning show, I walked into the "green room" and saw a 40ish man sitting on a couch. There was a full-color, three-dimensional springer spaniel dog over his right shoulder, reclining in a crescentlike position similar to that old image of the cow jumping over the moon. Normally, I keep my spiritual visions to myself unless someone asks. For some reason, I was impertinent and asked the man, "Did you just recently lose a dog?" His wife, who was also in the green room, rushed to my side in response to my question.

It turned out that their beloved dog had recently died, and we had a beautiful family reunion right there in the green room. The dog showed me scenes of playing with his owners and jumping in piles of colorful autumn leaves with the man. The man and his wife enjoyed reminiscing over these sentimental memories. "I told my dog that we'd always be together," the man shared with me. *They are together,* I thought. *They truly are.*

The Crystal Elements and Angels

In addition to elementals and animals, the nature kingdom provides us with the "mineral realm" to help us heal. This includes crystals, which have the ability to amplify angelic energy, just as the crystals in watches and radios amplify other forms of energy.

I've found that crystals are a wonderful tool for connecting with the angelic realm. They act like megaphones by increasing the signal strength of communications and healing energies that our angels are sending us. Many of the crystals have properties that are particularly aligned with the angelic realm, including:

Clear quartz—Try wearing a clear quartz crystal on a necklace, or holding one up to the area between your two physical eyes ("the third eye"). You'll feel a sensation similar to chills or an air pressure change, which means that the crystal is directing the angelic energy to you like a prism.

Rose quartz—A wonderful crystal for opening the heart chakra, which is the center from which we feel love. The more your heart chakra opens, the more you will be open to receiving the outpouring of Divine love that God and the angels bestow upon you.

Sugalite—This beautiful purple stone is often called "The Love Crystal" because it elicits a wonderful feeling of high-level love. I find that it is completely aligned with Archangel Michael's energy. The first time I wore a sugalite necklace pendant, I was giving a speech in Colorado Springs. During the speech, I channeled a powerful message from Archangel Michael even though I hadn't planned to do so. Sugalite is wonderful for opening the throat chakra so that you can communicate more clearly and powerfully.

Amethyst—This beautiful purple crystal has an extremely high vibration, and some people find that amethysts give them a "buzz" similar to caffeine (so, not everyone can work with amethysts). However, it is a powerful crystal for opening the crown chakra, which is the energy base for "claircognizance," or "clear knowing." It will help you to more clearly receive information from the Universal mind of God, or the collective unconscious.

Moonstone—A beautiful opal-like stone that helps you increase your spiritual frequency and vibratory rate. It can also help you better connect with the high energy level of the angelic realm. Its color looks like the transparent beauty of angels.

Lapis—A royal-blue stone that is useful in awakening clairvoyance, or the ability to see the nonphysical world and higher dimensions.

Spectrolite (AKA **Labradorite**)—This beautiful greenish-blue stone reminds me of the richest colors in mother-of-pearl. It is wonderful in raising the frequency of your intuition and giving an angel's-eye view of all situations. In this way, you can rise above lower-self beliefs and see things from a higher perspective.

Angelic Prayers for Animals

Here are some prayers that you can use with animals. Please rewrite the prayers to fit your particular circumstance and to include your pet's name.

PRAYER FOR HEALING A PET

Dear God,
*   I ask that You, Archangel Raphael, and the healing angels surround my pet with Your healing love energy. Please help my pet and me to feel peace so that healing may occur. Please send us a miracle, knowing that everything is already healed in Your eyes. I ask that You help me have faith and trust so that I may experience Your love within my pet and within myself right now. Thank You.*

Prayer for a Lost Pet

Dearest God,

I know that no one and nothing can truly ever be lost, since You are omnipresent and can see everything and everyone. I affirm that nothing is lost in the eyes of God. I ask that You, Archangel Michael, Archangel Raphael, the nature angels, and my guardian angels help me reunite with my pet right now. I call upon the guardian angels of my pet to send a signal so that I may find my pet. I now relax, knowing that God, the angels, and my higher self are already communing with my pet. Thank You.

CHAPTER SEVEN

Angels, Afterlife, and Healing from Grief

Even though the angels know that nobody truly dies, they still empathize with the grief that we endure when a loved one passes away. The angels are here to help us heal from grief, sometimes by showing us signs such as butterflies, birds, or angel-shaped clouds. Other times, our deceased loved ones will deliver a message to us, letting us know that they are okay. As with any life challenge, it's important that we invite our angels to help us heal from painful losses. After all, as mentioned previously, our angels can only intervene when we give them permission.

Our deceased loved ones often function as guardian angels. Those who are recently deceased are with us off and on while they go through experiences similar to school in the afterlife plane. They are always within earshot, so if you mentally call to specific deceased loved ones, they will come to your side right away. Deceased loved ones help us during crises, and they attend holiday and family gatherings. They love to be acknowledged, so even if you're not sure whether that really is the presence of your loved one that you're sensing, say, "Hello, I love you" to them anyway.

Deceased loved ones often enter our dreams to give us angelic healing messages. These dreams are larger than life, with vivid colors and strong emotions. You *know* that they are real experiences, but your lower self may try to convince you that it was your imagination. It wasn't. The angels and our deceased loved ones enter our dreams with healing messages because they know we are wide open to guidance at that time.

Saying Good-bye

Michelle Mordoh Gross, who lives in Spain, related this touching story to me of how an angel helped her say "good-bye" to her dying mother:

> I sat there by my mother's bedside, desperately trying to comfort her, talking to her about life after death and telling her how much I loved her. Doctors could not understand why and how she was holding on to life so long. But *I* did. She wanted to hold on while I was there, until the end of her strength, wanting to spend as much time with me as possible.
>
> So it occurred to me that I was no longer of any help. On the contrary, I was involuntarily forbidding her to leave. It was a brutal revelation; still, I made the hardest decision in my life. I had to leave her so she would feel free to pass on.
>
> I visualized that I was leaving her under the care of an angel. I knew we were spending our last moments together as I held her weakened hand in mine. With a broken heart yet still talking sweetly, I told her about the angel who would be sitting where I was the moment I left. I described the most beautiful angel anyone had ever seen. I told her the angel would come to keep her company, a light in the dark. It would protect, guide, and hold her. I asked her to not be afraid, but to trust.

Tears streamed down my face as she, not able to speak anymore, squeezed my hand in acceptance. I kissed her hand, thanking her for being the bond God chose for me between heaven and earth. And so I left.

It was five P.M., a few hours later, and I was on an airplane headed home. I suddenly opened my eyes from a nap and looked out the window. The sky was bright and blue, cloudless except for a single yellow-and-orange cloud right before my eyes. It had the shape of the beautiful angel I had imagined for my mother, with wings and all! Its arms, extended before it, were holding another cloud in the shape of a person, like a mother holding a sleeping child. And more, under the person-shaped cloud, stood yet another cloud, shaped like a bed. I then knew that my mother was safely on her way home to heaven.

Two hours later, I reached my home, certain that the phone would ring—and it did! Hospital nurse told me the news I already knew. My mom had passed away at five P.M. that day. My mother is now safe—without fear, sickness, or suffering.

During our last conversation, my mother had asked me, "When will *they* come and get me?"

"When you are ready, that is the best time," was my reply. She then promised to send me a rainbow if what I believed was also true for her. And, believe it or not, eight months later, there is not a single day I haven't seen a rainbow, shining bright, and bringing color into my life.

Family Members on the Other Side

Many of the angels who help us are actually deceased loved ones. They are either permanently assigned to us as "spirit guides" or are with us temporarily during crossroads or crises in our lives. One of the joys of my sessions are the family reunions, where my clients realize that a beloved deceased relative is still with them.

Doreen: Your loving and giving nature has attracted many beings on the other side who are ready to help you. You have two deceased female loved ones with you. One of the women with you looks like she colored her hair, she's heavier-set, her face is rounder, and she wasn't elderly when she passed on—perhaps in her '60s. This woman looks like she is of an ethnic descent with darker skin.

Abby: Oh, that would be my grandmother on my dad's side! She *did* color her hair, she did have a round face, and was semi-voluptuous. You're describing her exactly.

Doreen: Yes, she's with you.

Abby: Oh, that's wonderful! We were very close when she was living, and I've missed her so much after her death.

Doreen: You've also got a man with you who appears to be a grandfather. He looks like he was a blue-collar dresser. He's tall and big, and he's on your mother's side of the family.

Abby: Maybe that's my grandfather who I actually did know, my mother's dad?

Doreen: He's handsome, with white hair, like a Bob Barker type.

Abby: Yes! Oh, I've got shivers. I've forgotten about him, but I'm so glad that he's there with me!

Doreen: He's with you right now. Did you lose a little brown dog, because there's one hanging around you?

Abby: Yes, that's my dog, Figi, whom I lost two months ago! Oh, she's with me!

Doreen: Yes, she's with you right now, acting as an angel.

ᘒ ᘒ ᘒ

Abby was thrilled to know that her favorite people and dog surrounded her. Once she understood that they were her angels, she began having mental conversations with them regularly. Abby frequently asks her grandma and grandpa to help her, and she reports that she is very grateful for their assistance.

Healing Conversations from Beyond

It's also very meaningful to me when my clients' deceased loved ones send messages to try and heal or improve their post-death relationships. This is one of the ways our deceased loved ones function in angelic ways to help ease our souls of grief or guilt. In the following case, you'll read how my client's deceased sister came through to complete some unfinished business. When we have conversations with our deceased loved ones, we help them ease their souls and bring peace to ourselves in the process.

Doreen: There's a woman with you who wasn't that old when she passed.

Ruth: Could be my sister.

Doreen: Did she have darker hair?

Ruth: Yes.

Doreen: Okay, then, that's her. There's a sisterly look and feel to her. She looks as if she was in her 50s when she passed.

Ruth: She was 52.

Doreen: Okay, so that's definitely her. She's very healthy now, I can assure you. Her face is very full, and she's not in any pain. She apologizes because she feels that she was almost sponging off you at the very end of her life.

Ruth: Oh, that's so sweet of her, but really, I didn't mind caring for her at all.

Doreen: Well, she says that she needs to get this off her chest because it's bothered her since her death. Your sister says that she felt very useless and powerless and that you know she wouldn't have imposed on you unless she absolutely had to.

Ruth: Please tell her that it was my pleasure to be with her during her final months.

Doreen: She can hear you, Ruth, and she's nodding appreciatively at your words.

Ruth: I love you, Sis! I'll always love you.

ౡ   ౡ   ౡ

My client Karla also received a message from the other side that lifted the guilt she'd carried for five years:

Karla: My mother passed away five years ago. At the time, I was heavily into drugs. As she was dying, she asked me if I still used drugs and I said no. I lied. I have felt guilty ever since the day she died because of this lie. I only did it because I didn't want to put any more on her than her illness already had. My question is: Does she know I lied? If she does, does she forgive me for it? I am in recovery now, and I have four years, eight months, and eighteen days clean and sober. However, this really bothers me *a lot*.

Doreen: Please rest your conscious, dear one. Your mother knows that you told her this because of your love for her and that you were trying to save her from additional stress and pain. She does not judge you in any way—quite the opposite! She blesses you for your caring nature.

Soon after she passed over, she helped you to become clean and sober. She still watches over you with unconditional love, as does your grandmother and two guardian angels.

Healthy Relationships with Deceased Loved Ones

Our relationships with our loved ones don't end with their death. The relationship merely changes form. As a psychotherapist and clairvoyant medium, I help my clients maintain healthy relationships with their loved ones on the other side. Healthy post-death relationships are important for the sakes of souls on both sides of the veil of death.

Grieving survivors have mixed emotions that they must sort through following the death of a loved one. The survivor probably feels a great deal of sadness, loneliness, and confusion. These are feelings that we expect of someone who has just lost a friend or family member. However, survivors sometimes feel anger or a sense of betrayal toward their deceased loved one. These feelings are difficult to work through since most survivors don't like to admit they are angry with someone who has passed away. It doesn't feel "correct" to hold resentment toward someone who is gone.

Yet, admitting these perfectly normal feelings is an important part of healing from a loss. After all, our deceased loved ones are completely aware of how we feel and think about them. We can't hide anything from a person on the other side! We can only hide feelings from ourselves—but at the expense of our peace of mind. When we deny our true feelings, we block our own happiness and also the spiritual progress of our deceased loved one.

My client Laura, for example, was very angry with her father for not taking better care of himself. Laura's dad had passed away after a lengthy illness, and she was furious at him for his unhealthy lifestyle of smoking and drinking, which had contributed to his death. Simultaneously, Laura felt guilty for being angry with her father. She felt she should "have more respect for the dead."

During our first session, Laura's father came through from the other side and asked for Laura to please forgive him. He explained that his deep concern for Laura's emotional welfare was keeping him earthbound. This is a very common occurrence: When we are extremely upset about a loved one's death, he or she stays near us to ensure that we are okay. However, unless our deceased loved one has an assignment to be our spirit guide, spending so much time with us thwarts their own progress. Laura's father wanted to move on to the spirit world so he could participate in growth-producing activities, but he first wanted her permission to leave her side.

Another client, Maryann, held very deep resentment toward her deceased father for the childhood abuse he had inflicted upon her. During our session, Maryann's father came through and expressed his deep regret for hurting her. He also asked for her forgiveness.

As Maryann sobbed tears of grief connected to both her childhood abuse and to her father's death, Maryann's deceased paternal grandfather suddenly appeared. Her grandfather explained that he had been responsible for much of Maryann's childhood abuse. He explained how he had severely beaten Maryann's father when he was a boy. This childhood abuse had spurred Maryann's father into becoming a child abuser when he grew up. The grandfather begged Maryann to forgive him and her father. He explained that by forgiving both of them, Maryann would release herself from the snares of unhealed anger and resentment.

Both Laura and Maryann wanted to forgive their deceased fathers. But wanting to forgive, and honestly forgiving are two separate processes. Both of my clients had several counseling sessions with me before they were ready to release their anger and resentment completely.

Laura was finally able to see her father's unhealthy habits as his way of dealing with his unsatisfying career. She could feel compassion for him for being stuck in a job he didn't like, and this mind-set helped her release her unforgiveness toward him. My other client, Maryann, forgave her father and grandfather after she told me, "I'll forgive my dad and my grandpa, but I won't forgive their acts." This is one way to let go of old anger. After all, it's most important to forgive the person, if not their actions.

We do ourselves and our deceased loved ones a world of good when we openly admit and work through all of our grief-related emotions. One productive method is to write a very honest letter to your deceased loved one. As you write your letter, don't edit or censor your feelings in any way. Remember, your loved one already knows everything you feel about him or her. Your loved one doesn't judge you for holding any negative feelings; he or she simply wants you to feel the peace of mind and happiness that stem from self-honesty and forgiveness.

Your relationships with your loved ones on the other side can be wonderfully fulfilling. Many of my clients tell me that their post-death relationships with their loved ones are even closer and more honest than before their death. Death doesn't mean an end to the love you have shared. Remember: Love never dies!

ॐ ॐ ॐ

Here is a prayer to help you heal from grief and to feel the comfort that your deceased loved one and God want for you. Please edit this prayer so that it comes from your heart and fits your particular situation.

ANGELIC PRAYER FOR HEALING GRIEF

Dear God,

I know that my deceased loved one is home in heaven with You. I ask that You watch over him/her so that he/she is uplifted by Your love. Please send extra angels to my loved one and help him/her feel wonderful and happy in adjusting to being in heaven. Please send extra angels to my side, and help me release my sadness and grief. Help me heal from my feelings of heaviness so that I may return to the life that I know my loved one wants for me. Please send me a sign from heaven so that I know my loved one is in Your hands. Amen.

CHAPTER EIGHT

How the Angels Help Us in the Material World

I'm often asked if it's okay to ask the angels for help with material issues. "Is it all right if I ask them for a great parking space?" "Am I wasting the angels' time by asking them to help me with something that I could easily do myself?" and "Maybe God will be offended if I ask Him for material items or trivial things." These are among the concerns I commonly hear, expressing fears that prevent us from asking for help.

The angels repeatedly say to me, *"Matter doesn't matter."* God and the angels don't perform in a "triage fashion" like doctors who have to judge which person has the most pressing needs. For one thing, God and the angels have no time and space limitations, so they are able to help everyone simultaneously.

It is also God's will that the angels help us fulfill our higher self's purpose. God and the angels know that if our minds and schedules are occupied with worries, concerns, and fears about material goods or supply, we won't have the time or energy to fulfill our purpose. It's not that the angels are here to help us achieve a lifestyle of the rich and famous; they just want to ease our mind so that we are free.

They also know that we sometimes use material items as a time-wasting device that I call a delay tactic. This means any activity that diverts your attention away from fulfilling your purpose.

So, the angels swoop in to alleviate our overinflated concerns with material situations and items. Please don't misunderstand. They don't rescue us from being irresponsible. We wouldn't grow and learn if that was the case. What God and the angels want us to know is this: *"If you need anything, please don't hesitate to call on us to help you. Surrender any situation to us that is causing you distress or making you lose your peace of mind. We promise that we will comfort you and affect the material world in a way that will support you in your present environment. Leave it to us to take you home."* By home, they mean heaven on earth— our natural state, where all of our material supplies are met in Divine order while we focus solely on giving to the world with our natural talents and interests.

Easing Your Way

When working with the angels, one of the first "tasks" they may assign you is to clear your home, office, or car of clutter. The angels say that our possessions weigh us down and that so much of our focus is on acquiring and then protecting them.

If you've been feeling lately that it's time to donate or discard your unused clutter, then consider this paragraph additional validation. From an energetic standpoint, your living and working environment will feel much cleaner and more efficient without excessive objects.

A good rule of thumb is to lose any item you haven't used for the past two years. Most domestic violence and homeless shelters would be happy to receive your unwanted goods. You'll feel great if you schedule a Saturday afternoon for a massive clean-out day.

By giving away items, you automatically invoke the Spiritual Law of giving and receiving. This means that new items will come to you, and then it will be up to your discernment whether you're simply replacing old clutter with new. A wonderful idea is to keep the circulation going by giving away something every day.

The Energy of Your Possessions

After you've cleared out unused possessions, you will feel considerably lighter and more organized. The angels will next help you clear the energy in the room through a process known, logically, as "clearing."

Kirlian photographs show that material objects are affected by the thoughts of humans who are in their vicinity. One series of remarkable Kirlian photographs featured a coin that was held by the same person, who deliberately held various emotions. The coin was photographed after the person holding it had angry thoughts. Then, the same coin was photographed when the person held it with loving thoughts. The next photograph captured the coin after the person holding it had fearful thoughts. Each photograph shows a significant change in the size, shape, and color of the "aura" or energy field around the coin.

Kirlian photography is controversial, and scientists cannot agree exactly "what" the camera is capturing. Nonetheless, these photos do document a significant shift occurring as a function of the thoughts of the person holding the coin.

Objects do tend to retain the fingerprint of their owner's dominant thoughts and feelings. This is one reason why I never purchase items from distress sales. I know that the objects retain the energy of the store owner's emotional pain and beliefs about finances. I'd rather pay full price for an object that retains a prosperous store owner's optimism.

Psychometry

When I teach people how to do angel readings, we'll frequently begin by having audience members pair up and face each other in chairs. I then ask the partners to exchange metal objects such as a ring or watch with each other. By holding a person's metal possession, you more easily receive impressions and messages from their guardian angels. We call this method "psychometry."

You can try this yourself by holding someone's keys, watch, or ring in the hand you normally don't write with. This is your "receiving hand," as it absorbs energy. The hand you normally write with is your "sending hand," which gives off energy. So, holding the object in your receiving hand, close your eyes and take a few deep breaths. Hold the intention of talking to your guardian angels and also the guardian angels of the other person. Ask these angels any question such as, "What would you like me to know about (fill in the person's first name)?" or "What message would you like me to deliver to (name)?" or a more specific question.

Then, take a deep breath and notice any impressions that come to you: a feeling, a mental image, a thought, or words. If the other person is with you, begin telling them what impressions you receive. As you talk, you will receive other messages. This is a basic method for giving an angel reading, one that most people can do successfully the first or second time.

Clearing Your Space

Just as objects speak volumes to us, so does the environment in which we live, work, and drive. The walls, floors, and furniture retain the energy of our dominant mind-set. So, if we or our family members are usually in a peaceful frame of mind, our house will reflect that peacefulness. It will be a sanctuary-like setting that anyone who walks in will notice and enjoy.

However, if you or the people who live with you have been involved in arguments or worries, the home's energy will retain the echoes of those problems. Just as furniture, walls, and carpeting absorb the smell of smoke, so do these objects absorb people's psychic stress.

So, your home, office, or vehicle may be retaining the energy fingerprints of everyone who has ever spent time there. For instance, your home may have absorbed negative energy from people who lived there before you did. Fortunately, you can clear your living and driving environment, and the angels will help you do so.

Here are some ways to clear any location, whether it's a home, car, store, or office:

1. Paint the walls.

2. Replace the carpeting.

3. Shampoo the carpeting.

4. Burn some sage-weed (available as incense or on a stick at any metaphysical bookstore). Hold the sage-weed incense or stick, and walk around the environment so that the smoke is distributed throughout the place.

5. Place a shallow bowl with either salt water or rubbing alcohol in the middle of each room you want cleared.

6. Place a clear quartz crystal in the middle of each room you want cleared. Make sure that the crystal is first cleared of old energy by placing it in direct sunlight or moonlight for at least four hours.

7. Ask Archangel Michael and his helpers, known as the "band of mercy," to enter and circle your environment. Michael and the angels will escort any negative energies away from your home, office, store, or vehicle.

Manifesting a Home

If you desire a new home, the angels can help you find the perfect living place. They will also open doors to smooth the way so that you can easily afford to move. One thing the angels have taught me is to release the human doubts that say, "Well, it's just not possible because it's illogical." The angels rise above human logic to an elevation where all things are possible.

A couple from Virginia named Martha and Stan discovered the miracles that are possible when we let go of doubt:

> *Martha and Stan, married ten years, dearly wanted to own a home. Martha, a woman of great faith, said prayers each evening and asked God and Jesus to help her and her husband find a residence that would be filled with love, and that would also be affordable. One evening she had a clear dream in which she toured an older house with Grandma-like charm: lace curtains; wooden floors; and in the upstairs bathroom, a beautiful basin sink with golden roses painted on the ceramic fin-*

ish. Martha remembers that in her dream she felt quite at home, and she knew that she wanted to live there.

The dream was so beautiful and vivid that Martha described it in detail to Stan the next morning. The couple took the dream as a sign that it was time to look for their house. So they contacted a Realtor and began house-hunting. Two weeks into their search, as the three of them toured a house, Martha caught her breath and loudly whispered to Stan, "I think this is the house I dreamed about!" An unexplained familiarity washed over Martha, and Stan got goose bumps at the thought.

As the couple entered the upstairs bathroom, they caught sight of the one detail that had so vividly stood out in Martha's dream: golden roses painted on the ceramic sink basin. "This is it!" they both exclaimed, and asked the Realtor to make an offer on the home for them.

The owner readily accepted their offer, and the couple excitedly filled out the home loan application. The day after they applied for the loan, however, Stan was laid off from his job. Since Martha didn't work, the couple was initially dejected. "How can we ever qualify for a loan without a source of income?" they wondered. So, they prayed for help and surrendered the whole matter to God, saying, "If it's God's will, we will have the house."

Within two days, Stan was hired as a commission-only salesman. The couple immediately informed the bank loan officer, who dourly exclaimed, "Well, since Stan has no track record as a salesperson, I doubt that this loan will go through. I've never seen the V.A. approve a loan unless there's a steady source of consistent income."

The bank officer was thinking on a human level and probably wasn't aware of the influence that prayers have on situations such as home-shopping. She was dumb-

struck when she called Stan and Martha the following day and said, "I don't believe it. They approved your loan!" The couple hugged and happily moved into their home with the golden rose sink.

ॐ ॐ ॐ

Over the years since I've been interviewing people about Divine intervention, this sort of story has become almost commonplace in my files. I've talked to dozens, perhaps hundreds, of people who have actively asked for spiritual help in selling their home, locating a new home, obtaining a loan, affording the rent or mortgage, and moving. Their stories are consistent: If you ask for help, you receive it in miraculous ways.

Shopping with the Angels

The angels intervene in our material world with great joy. We never need to be shy in asking for their assistance, or worry that our request is too trivial or unimportant. We must remember that the angels are here to smooth our path so that we are free to shine God's bright light. We all know that we shine brighter on days when things go our way. We stand taller, smile bigger, and are more optimistic when we're "on a roll." These are also the days when we inspire others to reach for their own stars. So, let's not hesitate to ask heaven to help us to have these kinds of days more often!

The angels love to open doors for us. We can ask for their guidance in locating needed items, and then "listen" for their guidance, which always follows a request for help. The guidance may come through a thought, vision, feeling, or voice.

An interior decorator told me how the angels helped her locate an item that her client wanted for her home:

One of my clients needed some accessories to finish a newly designed bedroom. I'd been searching for an alabaster lamp, one of her most desired items, for four months. On the way into an antique shop, I called on the angels to lead us to just what we needed and desired. Moments later, we found not only one alabaster lamp, but two, as well as some other elusive nightstands and accessories we required. It was easy, fun, and took hardly any time at all to shop with the angels.

A woman I know named Gail Wiggs had a similar experience. Every spring and fall, she attends a Phoenix arts-and-crafts fair. She looks forward to purchasing the fair's theme T-shirts, as they always feature a beautiful original silk-screen painting on the front. In the fall, she purchases a long-sleeved T-shirt. However, these shirts are extremely popular, and they sell out rapidly. So, Gail makes a point to go early to the fair so she is sure to find one. However, last fall, her busy schedule wouldn't allow her to go to the fair until quite late. She asked her angels to be sure to save her a long-sleeved T-shirt.

It was afternoon by the time Gail took a shuttle bus to the fair. The bus stopped at an unfamiliar entrance, and the driver announced that it was the last stop. Gail entered the fair at this place—a different one than she usually used—but as soon as she entered, there was an information booth with the theme T-shirts in front of her.

There was one long-sleeved theme T-shirt left—a large—which she promptly purchased. Gail checked every other information booth as she went through the fair and rapidly discovered that no other long-sleeved T-shirts were left. Gail thanked her angels, and for the next two months she began getting strong messages that she was supposed to start a T-shirt company featuring images of angels on the shirts. Gail is currently starting such a business, and she is filled with joy to be able to market items that have brought her so much joy in the past.

Be Careful What You Ask For!

My husband, Michael, and I were at the airport, walking to the baggage claim area to get our four big suitcases, filled with supplies for my weekend workshop. It was late on a Friday night, and we were hungry for dinner.

I said to Michael, "Let's ask Raphael, the archangel of healers and travelers, to get the luggage off the plane right away." I then hesitated, because I knew the importance of being careful about what you ask for. If you're going to specify to the angels what you want, you better make sure to fill in all the blanks of your request carefully. So I edited my request to Raphael, "I don't mean for you to get the luggage so quickly that they fall onto the tarmac. Just please have them be on the luggage carousel right away."

I thought I was covering all of my bases with this request, but the angels taught me how they take our requests literally. As I walked away from the carousel to rent a big luggage cart, I heard Michael's voice calling for help. I turned around and saw that all four of our suitcases had come down the luggage chute simultaneously. Unfortunately, since they came out together, Michael couldn't grab them all at once. So, we waited while our bags made their trip all the way around the large carousel at the international airport. We both had the same thought: "Next time we'll be more careful about what we ask for!"

The Angels Heal Mechanical Items

I used to watch my mother pray whenever our family automobile conked out. Amazingly, the engine would always reignite following her affirmative prayers. I've asked for Divine intervention for mechanical and electronic devices ever since.

In particular, Archangel Michael is wonderful at healing broken faxes, washing machines, and other mechanical items. I've called on him when I'm having computer glitches, and I've had the situation immediately resolved.

A spiritual counselor named Johanna Vandenberg had a similar happy outcome when she requested that Michael help her with some plumbing:

> My godson's mother had asked me to change her water filter since she was extremely busy with lots of chores. Alone in her apartment, I attempted to perform the task. It looked so simple: a sinktop domed filter—just unscrew the bottom, put in a new cartridge, and put the bottom back on again. However, I couldn't get the bottom off—it was stuck!
>
> After 45 minutes, I finally got it loose, put in the new cartridge, and screwed on the bottom. I then turned on the water, as it's supposed to run for 15 minutes before use. But all the water began dripping out of the bottom of the filter! I took off the bottom again, put it back on, water dripping, over and over, until I was cursing. The family was coming home soon, and I felt pressured to have it repaired before they returned.
>
> At this desperate moment, I suddenly held up my hands and yelled, "St. Michael and Raphael, please help me put in this water filter!" I took the bottom off, put it back on again, turned on the water, and it worked perfectly! Everything was fixed within 90 seconds! Later, I got a call from my godson's Mom, who thanked me profusely and said the filtered water is coming out about ten times the force it usually does, and how did I get it that way?
>
> I was about to throw the thing out the window, feeling so frustrated trying to fix it for about an hour and a half. Yet the angels helped me so easily, so quickly, and so beautifully! As a result, there is now clean water for that family.

So, calling upon archangels is a very effective way of getting yourself out of jams involving material objects. Other people, such as Sharon, a psychotherapist I know, prefer to call upon their personal guardian angels whenever they need assistance. No call for help goes unanswered, and you can't get a "wrong number" when you put out a call for help to heaven. Sharon's guardian angel recently helped her "heal" her vehicle:

> The heater on my Jeep was out. As I drove to work Monday morning I felt the strong presence of an angel in my passenger seat. I asked what her name was, and I heard an inner voice say, *"Angela."*
>
> I had asked for angels to guard my home and Jeep several months prior, and I felt her say that she was the angel who had been guarding my Jeep since I first asked for angelic protection for it. I asked her to contact whoever the angel was who repairs Jeep heaters, because mine has been out for about two weeks. I received an impression in my gut as if Angela had said she would do that. The very next evening, my heater started working again!

CHAPTER NINE

Spiritual Safety with the Angels

In truth, the world is a 100 percent safe place to live. However, it appears to be a dangerous place because of the thought-forms of fear that act like reflections of any worry or apprehension we've carried in our minds. Because we sometimes miscreate with our thoughts, the angels help to guard and protect us.

Protector Angels

God and the angels ensure that we and everything we own are safe and protected. Of course, this still means that we have to ask for their help and then listen to and follow the guidance that we receive. My friend Mary Ellen discovered this rule in a dramatic—and near-tragic—way:

She and her friend Nancy, both American college students in their 20s, were on a strictly budgeted vacation in Germany. They were hitchhiking across the countryside, which was a cultural norm at the time. Two U.S. army trucks stopped to pick up the two women, and they each got in separate trucks. I'll let Mary Ellen tell the rest of the story in her own words:

> The driver of the truck I was in had rather unethical intentions. He started to attack me. I was thinking as fast as I could and praying for help to thwart his advances. I told this young New York soldier that I was not that kind of woman. And he said he didn't care. Just then, an invisible male voice out side of my left ear, very audibly to me said, *"Tell him you will tell."*
>
> I didn't think that would work, so I said, "How would you like your sister to come to Europe and make love to a stranger?" I figured he would see that she would not do that and neither would I.
>
> The invisible male voice out side of my left ear repeated, *"Tell him you will tell."* I thought that would be a nutty thing to say and that it would not possibly deter any attacker.
>
> The funny part now is that I never thought it odd to hear the voice. Maybe if I had said, "Do you hear that little voice?" the soldier would have thought I was crazy and left me alone!
>
> So, I said, "If you don't get off of me, I will pull my knife on you." Now, this sounded tough, but I had a knife for my bread-and-cheese picnic. "That won't bother me." He then pulled up his shirtsleeves and showed knife marks all up and down his arms from New York street fights.
>
> I thought, *Uh-oh.*
>
> The male voice outside my left ear screamed, *"TELL HIM YOU WILL TELL!"* I thought, *Sheesh, if a knife won't work, why would that statement?*
>
> But I had nothing left to say, so I said, "I'll tell."
>
> Well, this guy leaped off of me. I was so stunned. He said, "You wouldn't!"
>
> And my brain is thinking, *Here I am in a country where I don't speak the language, I don't have anyone to call or tell, and I did not even know where we were.*

So I said, "Yes, I will tell."

He started the truck and in silence drove me to the depot where the other truck was with Nancy. She was worried about me and glad to see me drive up. I never told her about the voice, but I know that I was saved by God, the angels, and my prayers for protection.

I had a similar experience, also with a happy outcome. I was exercising on a rooftop area that had a treadmill. About halfway into my workout, I noticed a man sitting in a car across the street. It appeared that he was staring up at me, and I felt a creepy feeling, as if I were his prey.

At first I tried to ignore or rationalize the situation. After all, why would someone stare at me? I was dressed very conservatively, with a baggy sweatshirt, loose sweatpants, and no make-up. Yet, my intuition said that this man was staring at me with dishonorable intentions.

I had two choices: I could stop exercising and leave, or I could try a spiritual approach. I opted for the latter. Mentally, I held the intention of talking with this man's guardian angels. I told them that this man was frightening me, and would they please ask him to leave? I felt a sense of peace, and about three minutes later, I heard his engine ignite and gratefully watched him drive away.

One week later, a woman approached me and said that she had noticed this man staring at me on three different occasions. She gave me his license plate number since his behavior had alerted her. However, after that day when I had a discussion with his angels, no one ever saw him again!

Road Protection

The angels protect us in many ways. Sometimes the slow driver ahead of us is an angel in disguise. A woman I'll call Rebecca related this story to me about just such an angel:

> I once had a guy pull out in front of me from a parking space while I was driving through a small city where I once worked. His car was driving a little slower than I would have driven. Then, as we approached an intersection, a car zoomed right through a red light (we still had a green light). If I hadn't been cut off by the guy pulling out from the parking space, I would have been in the middle of that intersection when the car ran its red light, and I don't think I'd be here today!

Heaven also protects us in ways that defy Earthly laws. For example, if your car is running low on fuel, the angels will make sure that you reach your destination safely. For instance, they'll help you keep driving until you reach a gas station, even if you're out of fuel. Or, if you *do* run out of gas, the angels will send a rescuer to your aid quickly.

Miriam, an elderly woman I interviewed, told me that she was stuck on the side of a desolate road with a flat tire one afternoon. Unsure of how to change a tire, she prayed for assistance. Within moments, a man and woman walked up to her and offered to help. As the couple changed Miriam's tire, she noticed that they had simply "appeared" without a car. There were no buildings from which the couple could have emerged. After the new tire was on the car, the couple vanished as mysteriously as they had appeared. As a psychologist, I knew that Miriam was a lucid and intelligent adult who wasn't hallucinating or exaggerating as she told me this story.

Acting like superheroes, the angels are also able to affect physical matter to avert accidents. Karen Noe, a spiritual counselor from New Jersey, tells the following remarkable story of how the angels saved the day:

> My eight-year-old son, Timmy, and I were in a supermarket parking lot on an extremely steep hill. A very busy street with four lanes of traffic is at the bottom of this hill. As we headed for my car, I saw a shopping cart rolling very fast down the hill, heading straight for the busy road. If it had continued at this rate, it would have gone into the street and would have definitely caused an accident!
>
> As I saw it going down the hill, I immediately said, "God, please stop that cart . . . now!" The cart stopped right then and there, *in the middle of the hill, on an incline*! There was no one in the section of the parking lot where the cart stopped! Then, a man came out of nowhere and moved the cart in the other direction on top of a parking bump so that it couldn't roll anymore, and as I turned my head to tell my son to look what was happening, the "man" literally disappeared!
>
> My son is so accustomed to us calling on the angels for everything that he just said, "It's an angel again," as though he has seen this kind of thing every day (which he does).

Karen's request for help, coupled with the unwavering faith that she and her son held, created this miracle. All we need to do is ask, and then have some inkling of faith—even if the faith is fleeting. Still, I want to say that when people do experience tragic losses, it doesn't mean that God or the angels has abandoned them. Losses occur for many reasons, including the fact that it may be someone's time to go. Yet, I always believe that when we ask for help and listen to it when it comes, the angels help us to either escape danger or considerably lessen its effects.

White Light

A wonderful way to ensure the safety and stability of your home and possessions is to surround them with "white light." White light is an angel energy that has a life force and intelligence all its own. When you surround yourself or your possessions with white light, you've put up a shield that ensures its protection.

So, if someone with harmful intentions comes near you or the item surrounded with white light, that person won't be able to cause harm. They will be compelled to leave you and your possessions alone without understanding why they were repelled. In some cases, the person may not even *see* you or your items, almost as if the white light makes objects invisible to people with negative intentions.

It's easy to surround yourself, your loved ones, or your items with white light. Simply close your eyes and visualize white light surrounding the entire outline of the person or object. Imagine what the person or item would look like with an eggshell of white light completely covering them. Once you've been able to see this in your mind's eye, the task is complete!

If fears about burglars or fires keep you awake at night, you'll sleep soundly when you ask the angels to help you. Simply visualize your home surrounded by white light. Next, visualize a large guardian angel posted next to each door, and even each window if you like. With the light and the guardian angels watching over you and your home, you will sleep safe and sound.

You can also surround your children and other loved ones with white light for spiritual insulation. I also like to surround the car or plane that I'm traveling in with white light. I often ask for extra angels to escort and buffer my vehicle as well.

In addition, whenever you walk into a location where any kind of negativity or earthbound mentality exists, surround yourself with white light. If you tend to be clairsentient (also known as empathic, intuitive, or sensitive), you may be prone to absorbing negative energy from these environments. Clairsentient people tend to be acutely aware of other people's feelings, and they can easily soak up others' negativity. The result is that the clairsentient may often feel drained or discouraged.

To prevent these negative emotions, clairsentients might visualize a triple seal of light around themselves: first a layer of white light, followed by a second layer of emerald-green light for healing, and then a layer of purple light. The third layer acts like a bumper that deflects any negative influences.

The angels also say that clairsentients need to spend regular time outdoors. According to the angels, nature acts like a "smoke absorber" and removes negative energies that the clairsentient has taken in. The angels strongly recommend that clairsentients keep potted plants next to their beds, especially broad-leafed plants such as pothos and philodendrons. The plants absorb residue or negativity from the body while one is asleep, much like they remove carbon monoxide from our air.

Finding Lost Items

When I was a young girl, I lost my little coin purse while walking home from school. That night, I cried about my loss, but my mother reassured me by asking me to affirm, "Nothing is lost in the mind of God." She explained that although I didn't know where my purse was, God could see it right at that very moment.

I fell asleep, affirming repeatedly, "Nothing is lost in the mind of God," feeling full faith that God would bring my purse back to me. When I opened my eyes the next morning, there was my little red coin purse, sitting right next to my bed. My mother swore that she had nothing to do with its recovery. To this day, she says the same thing, and I believe it truly was a miracle brought about by my complete faith in God's power.

I've taught that affirmation to many people, and have since

received many letters from people who say they've also experienced miraculous recoveries of lost items by repeatedly affirming, "Nothing is lost in the mind of God."

You can also ask your angels to help you locate lost items. I had just moved into a new home, and my office supplies were in disarray in various boxes. I couldn't find my checks and needed them to pay some bills. I implored my angels, "Please, where are my checks?"

I heard a voice say, *"Check the closet!"*

As I opened the cluttered closet, I felt my attention and hands guided immediately to a large bag. There was my checkbook, exactly where my angel's voice said it would be.

A woman named Jenny had lost her keys, which included the ones to her car, home, and post office box. She and her husband searched everywhere, with no luck. Two days after losing her keys, Jenny and her husband were in their garage talking. She was getting ready to drive to the grocery store, using her husband's car since she had no key to drive her own. She was really upset that she couldn't find her keys, and said aloud to God, "Please help me find my car keys now!" As soon as she'd finished the sentence, Jenny looked at an inverted empty coffee can in the garage. It seemed to glow from within, and she was irresistibly drawn to it. Her husband didn't notice, distracted by his project.

As she picked up the coffee can, Jenny saw the unmistakable glimmer of her car keys beneath it. "How could that be?" she wondered. "I remember looking under the coffee can twice for the keys, and they weren't there before." A woman of great faith, though, Jenny didn't question the miracle that had occurred immediately after she'd asked God for help. Instead, she decided to surprise her husband, who was still preoccupied with his project.

Jenny got into her car and lightly tapped the horn. "Bye, honey, I'm going to the store now!" He absentmindedly waved at her, and as Jenny pulled out of the driveway, he suddenly realized that his wife was driving a car for which she had no keys. He ran after her, and they both laughed as Jenny explained about the Divine guidance that had led her to find them

Heaven also helps us replace ruined items, as spiritual counselor Maria Stephanson, whom you met earlier, discovered:

> I was invited to a black tie event and purchased a stunning blouse for $155 at a very exclusive shop. This was a big thing for me. I am the original "shop for the bargain" person and have never spent more than about $25 for a blouse. It was something I knew I could wear during the holidays and special occasions.
>
> About a month after the event, a very close friend of mine had a formal affair, and, trusting her completely, I let her borrow my blouse. After wearing it, she took it to the cleaners, and it was completely ruined. She was devastated, cried her eyes out, and didn't sleep all night prior to telling me. She had called the cleaners and the shop where I'd purchased it, and they both requested the receipt before they would even attempt to refund the money. She wanted to replace it, but at the shop where I purchased the blouse, it was the only one they had. I felt a little bad, but I actually felt worse for my friend.
>
> Now, my problem was that I could not find the receipt anywhere. I searched high and low for a full day, ripping everything apart and finally had resolved in my mind that this was one more thing I could just say good-bye to. However, I had just attended a one-day workshop with Dr. Virtue and started thinking about how she had given me some ways to communicate with our angels. I also listened to the *Divine Guidance* tapes.
>
> So, I decided to ask my angels, "If, in fact, I do still have this receipt somewhere, could you just show me where?" I immediately got the feeling to check a drawer in my kitchen. The message was so powerful that I spun around on my heels and walked straight to the drawer and opened it, absolutely *knowing* that the receipt would be there. And I was right!
>
> I laughed, gave thanks, and brought the receipt to my

friend. She told me she would take it to the cleaners and get a refund. The next day, she surprised me with the blouse! She had taken a chance and had gone to the shop. They had just gotten one in, and it "just happened" to be my size. They were very kind and replaced it with no questions. So not only did my angels help me find the receipt, but there was a blouse just sitting there waiting for me!

Lost and Found Money

Of the Divine intervention stories that I receive, some of the more heartwarming ones involve people who lose their purses or wallets and then recover them through miraculous means. These stories not only reaffirm my faith in God and the angels watching over us, but also bolster my faith in the essential goodness of humankind. A counselor named Gayle Earle told the following uplifting story about how her angels and good people helped her find her wallet:

> I accidentally left my wallet in the shopping cart at the grocery store. I went home, unpacked my groceries, and was back in my car on my way to the next store. I asked my angels, "Okay, which store should I go to today for the rest of the stuff I need?" I did not get a clear response, so I felt frustrated. Then I received the message, *"Do you know where your wallet is?"* I realized that I could not find it.
>
> Something compelled me to go back to the grocery store. Sure enough, someone had brought it into the store, and it was waiting there for me, cash and all. Our world is full of loving and honest people, and I am blessed to be a part of it.

In another story of lost and found money, two healers named Rachelle and Mary Lynn asked the Archangel Michael to watch over their missing purse:

Rachelle and Mary Lynn were driving from Pittsburgh to Cleveland and stopped at a restaurant for dinner. One hour later, they pulled into a gas station. Mary Lynn reached for her purse to pay for the gas, but to her horror, she realized that she'd left it at the restaurant.

Since both women have great faith in the power of angels, particularly Archangel Michael, they immediately asked him to watch over Mary Lynn's purse. Then they affirmed, "Everything is in Divine and perfect order" to help anchor their faith.

Driving back to the restaurant, they asked their angels for directions to the restaurant since they couldn't remember where it was located. They felt the presence of angels guiding and calming them, and they got off at the right exit, went to the restaurant, and the manager handed Mary Lynn her purse. Everything, including her credit cards and $200 in cash, was intact.

One month later, Mary Lynn had to call Archangel Michael in on another case of missing items! Since she is a cardiac nurse, Mary Lynn "floats" through the hospital and doesn't have a permanent desk or locker. She keeps all of her belongings, including keys, money, and day planner, in a briefcase.

One night, Mary Lynn was very busy with an emergency, and her briefcase was left unattended. After the surgery, she discovered that it was missing! So, she immediately asked Michael to locate her belongings, plus she sent blessings and Divine love to the person who had taken it. Within one hour, Mary Lynn received a phone call from security, saying that they had her briefcase. As before, all of her belongings were recovered without anything missing.

357

Whenever we lose any item, it's important to ask for spiritual help. So often I talk to folks who tell me stories of how they searched for hours for an item. Then, they finally ask God and the angels to help them and—boom!—the item is found minutes later. This is what a woman named Maggie discovered as well.

A part-time waitress and student, Maggie had carefully placed her $65 cash payment from the previous evening's work inside an envelope in her purse. Then she ran some errands during which she took out $5 from the envelope to buy food at a Taco Bell.

The next morning, she searched everywhere for the envelope full of money, but it was gone. Maggie searched all through her trash cans and under every paper in the house, spending several hours searching to no avail. Finally, in desperation, she turned to God and the angels for help.

The instant she made this request, Maggie received a mental image of the Taco Bell bag from her dinner the night before. She went to the trash can, opened the bag, and there was her envelope full of money!

Angelic Reminders

The angels take care of us and our homes as well. A participant in one of my Divine Guidance workshops related this story to me:

As I drove to work the other day, I heard a voice inside my head telling me that the coffeepot was left on. I would normally not think about this at all, as my husband frequently works out of our house, and he's the one who primarily makes and drinks coffee. Yet, the voice sounded imperative.

So I called my husband and got him on his cell phone as

he was driving. I asked him if he'd remembered to turn off the coffeepot before leaving the house. "Oops, I forgot!" he exclaimed. He returned home and turned it off, grateful that the angels were watching over our precious home.

Angels on the Road

The majority of angel stories that I receive concern automobiles. Our angels closely monitor us when we're in cars because they don't want anything to happen to us before our time. Of course, they can only do so much, such as scream warnings at us. Our free will gives us the option to ignore the angels' pleas to slow down, change lanes, and so forth.

A caller on a radio show asked me about the angels surrounding her. "There's a large female angel standing next to your right shoulder," I said. "She's wiping her brow and showing me that she helps you while driving and has kept you from a number of near misses. She acts like you keep her busy nonstop, saving you while driving. Let me ask you, do you drive like a maniac or something?"

"Well, not exactly," was her demure reply, "but I do put my makeup on while I'm driving to work." I saw an image of this woman driving with her visor mirror in front of her, applying her lipstick while her angel frantically grabbed the steering wheel.

The angels love us, but they want us to pay attention while we're driving!

The following story, told to me by a woman named Lynette, is the most typical type of Divine intervention I hear:

> I was driving in the fast lane when I heard a voice inside my head saying, *"Slow down, now!"* I slowed down a bit, and as soon as I did, a car came out of nowhere. I had to slam on the brakes to avoid hitting the car broadside. I literally stopped six inches from her car! The incredible thing was that I wasn't even

scared or shaking—startled a little, but my knees weren't knocking like I would have expected in a sudden situation such as this.

Many of the stories I hear about Divine intervention are hair-raising tales, such as David's experience.

David was driving on a busy Southern California freeway when he suddenly noticed his gas gauge needle dropping rapidly from F *to* E. Hmm, I just filled the car up with gas, *David thought.* I wonder if I left the gas cap off of the car at the gas station. *As the gas gauge fell below* E *with the reserve light on, David pulled to the side of the freeway to investigate.*

A moment after he pulled off the side of the road, David heard a huge crash. He looked up, and in the lane he had just exited from was a three-car pile-up. If he hadn't pulled off the road, David surely would have been in the collision!

He said a prayer of thanks and also prayed for the people involved in the accident. Then he cautiously stepped out of his car to confirm that his gas cap was on—which it was. David then turned his key in the ignition and was amazed to watch the gas gauge climb immediately to F. *His reliable car had never had a problem with the gas gauge before, and hasn't since. David knows that God and the angels rescued him from a serious accident by manipulating his gas gauge. They obviously knew David well enough to know that he'd immediately investigate such an occurrence!*

As David's story illustrates, the angels can affect the physical world and create miracles when needed. Madison, a healer from Utah, experienced how angels can defy physics:

> I was driving in the right-hand lane of a four-lane road. There was a car in front of me and one to the left. All of a sudden, the driver in front of me hit his brakes! I had to swerve into the left lane to avoid hitting the car. By all rights, I should have hit the car to my left side. But I looked up in the rear-view mirror and the car that had been on my left was about six car lengths in back of me. There is no doubt in my mind that I was saved by my angels.

Angelic Time Warps

Many people, myself included, have also discovered that angels can help us reach our destinations on time. One woman said that she was running late in picking a friend up at the airport:

> There was no physical way for me to reach the plane on time, so I asked my angels to help me get there. Somehow, I got to the airport, parked, and was at the gate to meet her with five minutes to spare, and her plane was on time! It was as if the angels helped me to go into a time warp, because the drive to the airport always took one hour, and I made it in 30 minutes. I wasn't speeding or driving any differently than I normally do.

Another woman told me a similar story:

> I was running late and left the house 20 minutes later than I normally do. I asked my angels to get me to work quickly, safely, and without stress. Usually, it takes me between 30 and 40 minutes to get there. Today, I arrived in 15 minutes! There was virtually no traffic, I made all but two stop lights, and at

those, I waited only seconds. I did not exceed the speed limit at all, and I actually arrived at work early! Thank you, angels.

If I hadn't experienced similar miracles of angelic "time warps," I wouldn't believe these stories. But I've had similar things happen to me and have heard so many of these stories that I now accept these events as normal options available to anyone who asks the angels for help in time traveling.

On a less mystical but related note, a woman named Patti told me this story:

> Driving home from a friend's house this evening, I took a route unknown to me. I simply affirmed, "I am Divinely guid-ed," and I felt myself led by an unseen force to take many streets that I'd never before driven on. I actually ended up shaving 15 minutes off my normal commute time from her house to mine!

Safety at Work

One day I was on a Midwest radio show doing angel readings by phone from my home. I find that I can easily see someone's angels, whether I'm talking with them face-to-face, over the phone, on the radio, or even just by thinking about the person. Our spiritual sight, or clairvoyance, is not limited in the way that our physical sight is.

The caller on the radio show said that he was a firefighter who had narrowly escaped death the previous evening. "Someone helped me to get out of that burning house," he said breathlessly. "I know it! I could feel the presence and hands of someone help-ing me escape, yet there were no other firefighters in the house with me. I was totally alone, and I know this was an angel who saved my life. I have an idea who it was who saved me, but I just want to make sure. Could you tell me who my guardian angel is?

Who saved my life last night?"

"Yes, it's your grandfather," I said. I had watched the elderly gentleman next to the caller's right side the entire time he was talking. The grandfather showed me how much he adored his grandson and wouldn't let him come into harm's way.

The caller was amazed by the instant validation. "I knew it!" he exclaimed. "My granddad passed away just three months ago. I'm holding his death certificate and photo in my hands right now. I knew he was the one who saved my life! Please tell him I said thank you, okay?"

"He can hear you right now," I replied. "He knows that you are grateful, and he also knows that you love him very much. He loves you, too."

Our angels help us stay safe at work. They'll intervene if we're faced with a life-endangering situation before it's our time to go. The fireman experienced this type of heroics from his granddad, the guardian angel.

However, for day-to-day safety issues, we must give God and the angels permission to intervene. Because of the law of free will, they can only help us if we—or someone who loves us, such as a parent, friend, or spouse—ask for their help.

Police officers consider Archangel Michael their patron saint because he watches over and protects them. Many law enforcement officers wear pins or carry images of Archangel Michael as reminders to ask for his help. Michael's protection is not limited to police officers, however. Like a living Superman, Michael is able to be with everyone simultaneously who asks for his help and protection.

Mentally ask Archangel Michael to stay next to you and guide you. He'll tell you, very loudly and clearly, if you need to get out of harm's way. Michael helps everyone, regardless of their religious or nonreligious orientation. All he asks is that you request his assistance. He'll take care of everything else.

I also find it helpful to visualize work equipment and facilities surrounded with white light. As discussed earlier, white light is a form of angelic energy that has intelligence, power, and life force. When you imagine a piece of work equipment surrounded by white light, it becomes insulated against damage or theft. Use your intuition to know if you need to regularly continue to re-seal it in light, or if the item will stay permanently sealed. If in doubt, re-seal it in white light for extra protection and insulation.

If you are worried about a loved one's safety at work, mentally call for additional angels to surround the person. Visualize your loved one encapsulated in white light. Know that the angels and light will never violate the other person's free will. However, they will create a "moat effect" which will prevent untoward energies from coming into contact with your loved one.

Peace and Quiet

The angels know that noise is a major stressor that can rattle our nerves, interrupt our sleep, and erode our peace of mind. Fortunately, when we ask for their assistance, the angels are able to intervene and bring heavenly quiet to any situation.

A radio talk show host told me that his guardian angel helped him have a peaceful morning. It was Saturday about seven A.M., and he was trying to sleep late on his day off. However, the neighbor's dog was barking furiously. *How am I ever going to sleep with this racket?* he thought, annoyed. Then he remembered that I had given him an angel reading on his show the week before. I'd told him that his main guardian angel's name was Horatio, and that he could call upon this angel for help with *anything*. "I figured I'd put Horatio to work helping me," he recalled. "So I mentally said to Horatio, 'Please get that dog to stop barking, right now!' The second I finished making the request, the dog became completely silent and stayed that way all morning long. Count me in as a believer!"

I'm very sensitive to noise because my ears are attuned to hearing angels' voices. So, when I arrived at a seminar location recently and found that the fire alarm was going off (a false alarm), I was determined to heal the situation rapidly. Their fire alarm system consisted of flashing strobe lights on the four corners of the seminar room's walls, accompanied by a very loud, shrill alarm that would sound every two minutes. You could talk at a normal pitch for a couple of minutes and then—oops!—the fire alarm would go off, and everyone would have to yell to be heard. The strobe lights were flashing continuously, creating a weird disco effect.

A few of my students were at the seminar with me, and we all huddled in a circle moments before I was scheduled to begin my lecture. Together, we asked for Archangel Michael and Raphael to fix the fire alarm. I asked for deceased firefighters and engineers to come to our aid and alleviate the situation. Then we turned the entire matter over to God. I felt assured that somehow the fire alarms would be fixed by the time my speech began.

As I was being introduced moments later, the strobe lights suddenly stopped flashing. Everyone looked around as they realized that the fire alarms had been fixed at just the moment I walked onto the stage. Ask and you shall receive!

This worked so well that the following week when I was again accosted by noise, I decided to try this technique once more. I was at the beach, relaxing after an extended period of very hard work. I had maybe two hours to enjoy myself when two young men sat right next to me and turned on their boom box, which was playing loud rap music.

I mentally conversed with the young men's guardian angels, saying, "Please let them know that their music is bothering me, and would they please turn it down?" I knew that the angels would try to help me, but I wasn't so sure whether the young men would listen to their angels or ignore their conscience! Yet, moments later, they turned off their boom box. Asking for angels' help always works.

My manager, Steve Allen, discovered the proof of this when we were filming a segment for a national television show at my home. During the interview, my refrigerator was making a lot of noise. Steve mentally asked his angels to quiet the refrigerator, and the motor shut off the instant he asked! Although Steve is a man of great faith, even he was surprised by how rapidly his request was granted.

CHAPTER TEN

Healing Our Past-Life Issues with the Angels

As a therapist, I've always been intrigued by the topic of past lives. For years, however, even though I could see the therapeutic value of conducting cathartic past-life regression sessions, I believed the whole subject was founded in fantasy. Of course, I also didn't believe in angels or life after death for a long time either! I was a left-brained skeptic about all things esoteric. It took a few miracles before I was sufficiently open to the idea of a spirit world.

Still, even when I thought that the idea of past lives was nonsense, I saw its therapeutic value. Many clients with phobias didn't heal until they underwent past-life regressions—for example, a woman who compulsively overate and didn't respond to traditional therapy. Yet, when she underwent hypnosis with the intention of finding the original trauma connected with her compulsion, she saw in her mind's eye a scenario where she had starved to death in a previous life. Immediately following the session, her appetite normalized and she dropped weight.

Now, does it really matter whether the woman actually had the past life or not? No! The only practical consideration is the here-and-now, since healing can only occur in the present moment.

In my book *Divine Guidance: How to Have a Dialogue with God and Your Guardian Angels*, I discuss practical ways to clearly receive advice and suggestions from heaven. Yet, hearing the advice isn't enough. We've got to follow it, to put Divine guidance into action. If you're feeling stuck, paralyzed in your ability to apply Divine guidance to your everyday life, it could be because of a past-life issue. For instance, many people I've worked with have received Divine guidance to become intuitive counselors or spiritual/alternative medicine healers. Yet, as much as they desire these goals, they feel an equal or greater amount of fear.

In many cases, these present-day healers had past lives where they were killed because of their intuitive or healing skills. I've worked with people who've had numerous lives of being beheaded, burned at the stake, or some other horrible form of death because their intuitive skills threatened local church or government institutions. They died in the Inquisition and during the witch-hunting eras. So, in this life, when they are Divinely guided to begin a counseling or a healing practice, is it any wonder that they feel profound fear? Actually, it's an intelligent decision if you think about it: "Let's see, I've been killed for being an intuitive before. I think I'll decide to *not* be openly intuitive in this life."

So, whether you believe in past lives or not, you can still benefit from the role that they play in applying Divine guidance to our *present* life. As I've said, Divine guidance has practical applications in helping us lead a happier, more harmonious life. However, many people unconsciously block the awareness of their Divine guidance. Or, they don't follow their guidance. The result is unanswered prayers—not because God and the angels are ignoring them, but because the Divine guidance is in limbo like a letter from heaven that the recipient refuses to open and read.

Here are some of the blocks related to past lives that prevent us from enjoying the benefits of applied Divine guidance:

Past-life vows—Ever get the feeling that you can't get ahead financially? Do your relationships seem chronically problem-ridden? Vows of poverty, celibacy, or suffering that you made in past lives may be the culprit. Again, regardless of whether you believe in past lives, it cannot hurt you—and it may just help—to sever vows that you may have made.

Here are some powerful affirmations to release the effects of such vows. I use this method with my clients who are blocked because of past-life interference, and the results are outstanding. The key to the efficacy of these affirmations hinges upon your saying them with conviction. In other words, you must *mean* what you are verbalizing instead of merely voicing the words. Say each of the following affirmations twice, either mentally or aloud, with great intent:

- *I hereby sever all vows of poverty I may have made in any lifetime, and I ask that all effects of those vows be undone in all directions of time.*

- *I hereby sever all vows of suffering I may have made in any lifetime, and I ask that all effects of those vows be undone in all directions of time.*

(**Note:** Do not say the following affirmation if you are currently following a purposely celibate lifestyle):

- *I hereby sever all vows of celibacy I may have made in any lifetime, and I ask that all effects of those vows be undone in all directions of time.*

The fear of being powerful—This particular fear often stems from past lives in which we *did* misuse our power. In particular, if we lived in the ancient civilization known as "Atlantis," the fear of misusing our power is prevalent.

Atlantis was a thriving society that used cutting-edge technology based upon crystal-driven and solar-powered energy. Atlanteans had many advanced methods for healing and transportation. Many of them also had an insatiable hunger for power. The Atlanteans used their technological know-how to develop weapons used for conquering other civilizations. One by one, Atlantis acquired power over many land masses in the world.

Ultimately, however, they misused their weaponry power and ended up destroying their own land mass. It sank in an explosion caused by weapons that were being deployed to overtake land on the other side of the world. To this day, souls who lived in Atlantis fear annihilating themselves and their loved ones through their abuse of power.

Past-Life Issues, Present-Life Challenges

If you suspect, or know, that you had a traumatic past life that led you to close down your intuitive abilities, your angels can help you release this pain. Your angels can also help you heal any health challenges related to your past lives. I've worked with many clients and students who were born with injuries or other body issues that were directly related to the way they died in past lives.

For instance, a woman named Suzanne who was impaled by a sword during battle had chronic pain in her left hip—in the exact spot where she had received her past-life fatal injury. Another woman who was hanged in a past life suffered chronic neck pain in this life and was phobic about wearing tight-necked shirts. Both of these clients are among those who have successfully eradicated pain from their lives by inviting their angels to heal them.

It's not necessary to remember or recall your past life in order for your angels to heal you. However, sometimes the angels will let you know the association between present-life issues and unhealed pain from your past life. Almost always, the healing occurs when you release the pent-up emotions from your past life.

For instance, your angels may guide you to forgive those who killed you in a past life. They may help you release centuries-old feelings of horror that you've held in response to witnessing a wartime massacre. In those instances where it is helpful and therapeutic, your angels and your own unconscious mind will allow you to remember the past-life scenes. They will never show you any information for which you are emotionally unprepared.

My client Grace finally understood why she was so drawn to Celtic countries when she received an angel reading that helped her understand how her current self-esteem issues were tied to her past life:

Grace: Why do I feel so unworthy and inadequate, and what can I do about it?

Doreen: The angels tell me that you are healing from this, but it's going slower than you like. So, you are making progress with this issue. It's interesting. You have humility as one of your spiritual qualities and part of your purpose. Apparently, part of your life purpose was to come and learn about humility in this lifetime, because in a previous lifetime you did not have much humility at all.

Your angels show me a past life in which you were a privileged daughter of upper-class parents, and you were raised with a silver spoon. I have to be blunt about what they show me: You were really snotty and kind of looked down your nose at other people. But it was because you just didn't understand; that's all you knew. You had a won-

371

derful life, and it wasn't a wasted life. But the way that you looked at people in general was colored by never having to go through any kind of challenges, and so you set up this life to balance that life and to learn humility.

But the trouble is that in many cases, you substituted humility for self-worth issues, when they are two separate things. And that's the lesson for you right now: How do you balance humility without going into shame or guilt? So the spiritual lesson, which is where you are headed on your learning path right now, is truly knowing the oneness of all of us. To know that the grandness of God is within each of us, including you. No one is more or less special than anyone else.

You still have that regalness from your past life with you. This looks like it was in a Celtic country, such as Wales or Ireland. You still have a little bit of standoffishness from that life, and that puts you into your ego state and makes you feel afraid. You're almost afraid of your natural reactions to other people, and so it's really about noticing and guarding your thoughts about other people.

As you see others, so you see yourself. If you can learn to see the bliss and beauty within others, then you'll more easily see it within yourself. Your angels say that you need to monitor your thoughts, and when you go into judgment about yourself or others, forgive yourself and let those thoughts go. Don't fight them or they'll increase in size and strength. Just notice the thoughts, and then let them go. But you're so close. Please let's not discount the progress that you've made! Your angels show me that you've just grown and grown in this issue. It's just learning to balance and not going to other extremes of self-judgment or other types of judgment. Both extremes always feel painful.

Grace: You're right, I have come a long way, and I need to give myself more credit for that.

Doreen: Well, we all have our moments of harshness about ourselves. The angels are here to help us heal this tendency because it really gets in our way more than it motivates us.

ॐ ॐ ॐ

Several of my clients have come to understand why they've had contentious relationships in this life. For example, a client named Bridgette realized that she'd had two problematic relationships in past lives with her mother. Those relationship issues had carried over into this life, where Bridgette and her mother constantly fought. Bridgette's angels helped her to realize that if she didn't heal her mother-daughter relationship in *this* life, she would probably have another lifetime battling with her mother in a *future* life. That was enough to motivate Bridgette to heal the relationship, with the help of her angels.

Karma Releasing

Karma is a long-held belief system that says that everything we do is a "cause" of "effects" that we later experience. The belief in karma is one way of looking at the Universal law of cause and effect, but it is *not* the only way. Cause and effect is an untransmutable law, but this law does not hold that we should be "punished" or "blocked" because of our past experiences. On the contrary, the Law of Cause and Effect is a law of love, and it seeks to release us from our past.

For one thing, the idea of "past" is based on a belief in linear time. We know that time is actually simultaneous, not linear. In other words, everything you have ever experienced and *will* ever experience is happening now, right at this moment. That is because there *is* no other moment but now. Humans on Earth created the belief in past, present, and future time as a way of measuring their growth and accomplishments. However, the spiritual truth is that we all are already as accomplished as we could ever want to be. We're already home, perfect in all ways, since we are in union with God. The only "path" or "goal," if any, is to realize that we've already got everything we desire. As soon as we realize this fact, we experience it.

Let's put it another way, because it's very important that this concept be explained in clear and simple terms: There are several realities co-existing right now. A good analogy is to think of these realities as several movies that are each in a VCR on top of your television set. You can choose to watch any movie you like. You don't need permission from anyone else; you are the authority figure here. One movie is a really beautiful masterpiece, a magnificent film that inspires and empowers you. Another movie is a low-budget, mediocre film. Still another movie is a "comedy of errors," in which the characters get in and out of one jam after another. Then there's the tragedy, which is filled with heavy drama, heartaches, and problems of every imaginable type.

All of these movies co-exist simultaneously, each waiting to be played and experienced right now. Which movie will *you* play and experience? You decide based upon the thoughts that you choose to think. It's important for all of us to understand that we truly do choose our thoughts, and therefore, choose the movie—or type of life—that we experience. Everyone is equally qualified to choose and experience every movie. You don't have to earn your right to experience the beautiful, harmonious movie. A powerfully peaceful and meaningful life *is* your birthright. Although going through pain and obstacles is one way to achieve spiritual growth, it's not the only way. You truly can achieve enlightenment with a peaceful life, because you are already enlightened right now.

If you are experiencing lack, limitation, or pain of any kind, it simply means that somewhere within you, you are choosing thoughts of fear. Sometimes we're not even aware of these thoughts, or we believe that we have no control over them—as if the thoughts choose *us!* With practice, you can become aware of what type of thought is in your mind each moment. Whenever you feel pain of any kind, you'll know that you have held a fearful thought. As you progress on the spiritual path, you'll develop less tolerance for pain, until you reach a point of having a "zero tolerance for pain policy." At that point, you'll no longer hold fearful thoughts, and you'll instantly recognize and release any fearful thoughts that you may mistakenly choose on occasion. You can work with the angels in releasing the fearful thoughts and their effects. After all, the angels are always with you and always ready to help you. Just think, *Angels, please help me!* and they will intervene and heal.

Every loving thought and every fearful thought has an effect. Loving thoughts come from your true self. Fearful thoughts come from your false self, or ego.

Effects stay connected to their causes. Whenever you choose a fearful thought, it stays tethered to your ego-self, like a hot air balloon. Therefore, painful experiences stay connected to you—one after another, in a seemingly endless pattern and cycle—as long as you hang on to the *cause* or the ego's fearful thoughts. However, if you release the cause, its effect flies away along with it.

The beautiful bottom line of all of this is that all of the fearful thoughts that you have had, or that others may have had about you, can be released. Their painful effects can be released along with them!

In *A Course in Miracles*, it says, "Acknowledge but that you have been mistaken, and all effects of your mistakes will disappear." What the *Course* is saying is that we can "collapse time" by returning our thoughts to truth—the basis of true reality.

Nothing real can be threatened; nothing unreal exists. Herein lies the peace of God.

This is very different from shirking responsibility for your actions; and it is also very different from the religious concept of "atoning for sins." Releasing karma simply means releasing false ideas, which are causing painful effects. After all, mistakes don't require punishment, they simply require correction. All of us have made mistakes—some of us have made mistakes that we may consider practically "unforgivable." Yet, God sees right past those mistakes and instead sees our created perfection. We are powerful beings, but we're not powerful enough to undo the perfection that came with us being made in the image and likeness of our Creator. Nothing you could have ever said, thought, or done could have ever changed how perfectly wonderful you truly are and always will be.

In some of the afterlife astral planes, there is a belief that if you make mistakes in a lifetime—such as being cruel to another person—that you must reincarnate with some physical or emotional problems to "atone" for those mistakes. When you incarnate from this framework of thinking, you elect to have a lifetime of punishing pain and problems. However, you can escape from this mistake in thinking any time you choose.

The angels will help you release the effects of mistakes in thinking made in this lifetime or any lifetime. And it doesn't matter whether you believe in reincarnation or not.

How the Angels Can Heal Past-Life Issues

Just by holding the intention to heal your past-life issues, your angels will be able to help you. In addition to having a formal session with a trained past-life regressionist, your angels can help you remember and release your past-life issues. You can accomplish this goal either in your sleep or during a meditative state:

In your sleep—Before you go to bed at night, mentally ask your angels to enter your dreams and show you any significant past lives that are related to your current-life issues. You will have dreams about other times in which you lived, and you may or may not remember these dreams, depending upon your unconscious mind's preparedness in handling the emotions.

It doesn't matter if you remember the dreams, from a healing standpoint. What matters is that, during these nighttime episodes, your angels have your permission to enter and heal your pent-up emotions. You should awaken feeling like you've done a lot of clearing-out work during your sleep. You may even feel a bit drained. Nonetheless, you'll know that you have engaged in important work in your sleep that will have a strong healing effect overall.

In your meditations—While in a meditative state, ask your angels to show you visions of your past lives. Then allow yourself to be focused, with an open mind. Don't strain to make anything happen. Instead, be like a passive movie screen that receives projections from the angels.

Your ego-mind may try to convince you that you're making up the pictures that you see in your mind's eye. Release these fears and concerns to your angels so that you don't interrupt the flow of information being sent to you.

As you watch or relive the past-life memories, be sure to maintain an awareness of your angels. Know that they were there with you in your past lives, and are with you now as you relive the old memories. Your angels will guide you so that you can heal and cleanse any past-life pain.

For example, they may ask you to imagine a different "ending" to your past-life movie, almost as if you are rewriting the script of that past life. So, instead of being traumatically killed, you invent a scene in which you die peacefully in your sleep. Your unconscious mind will override the old emotions with the new, more peaceful emotions.

Or, your angels may guide you to forgive yourself or other people in your past life. Be sure to ask your angels to help you accomplish this releasement, as you may find it difficult to forgive completely on your own. The angels will enter your cellular and emotional memory and clean away any residue of past-life negative emotions.

Here is a transcript of an angel therapy session with a client whose past-life issues were interfering with his present-life work and finances. Read how the angels helped him lift away his previous poverty patterns so that he could enjoy more prosperity and meaning in his profession:

Sam: I'm just getting ready to launch my own creatively based company. What do the angels say about this?

Doreen: You *must* do this type of work; the angels say you have no choice, because it is what and who you are.

Sam: Oh, yes, I definitely have a burning passion!

Doreen: Well, the angels show me that anything you do that involves artistic work will be enjoyable, and that there is a great potential for success. However, the angels say that you have some deservingness issues involving money. These beliefs of yours keep money one step ahead of you, instead of being in your possession in the current moment.

Your angels say that you are a very talented person, so talent is not the issue.

Sam: Oh okay, it's about knowing that I deserve to make money from my talents.

Doreen: Exactly! You've got this mental energy that keeps money from coming to you. The angels say you have an expectation that you won't have enough money.

Sam: Okay, I'm aware of that. I'm still aware that at some level I don't feel that I deserve money to come to me.

Doreen: The angels ask us to do some angel therapy on this issue right now, okay? Please take a very deep breath and see a beam of light going down through the center of your head, magnetizing any kind of stress or worries and eradicating them. I'd like to ask you to affirm with me, please: *I am willing to sever any vows of poverty that I may have made in any lifetime. I sever these vows of poverty now, and they are gone.*

Sam: I am willing to sever any vows of poverty that I may have made in any lifetime. I sever these vows of poverty now, and they are gone.

Doreen: Okay, great. There is just something in your subconscious mind that is seeing money a little differently than your angels would like you to see it. It's really important that you just see money as support for the beautiful work that you've been born to do, because you truly do intend to bring a lot of joy and merriment to the world through your work.

Sam: Well, that's exactly what I intend!

Doreen: You *have* to do this work. You have no choice because of this strong drive within you that comes from your Divine life mission. The only thing that you do have a choice about are your expectations of being supported while you do this work. That you deserve to *get* so that you can *give*.

Sam: Yes, that's definitely been an issue with me, particularly when I know that there are other people who are worse off than I. Also, in my upbringing, I've been given this message that, "poverty is holy." Even though for many years I've been intellectually aware that this message isn't true for me, it's been a difficult attitude to shake.

Doreen: Exactly. Well, in your prominent past life that relates to this one, you lived in England and you dressed like a court jester, but you didn't do that. Something similar, like a vaudeville act.

Sam: I've always been kind of drawn to the idea of the traveling minstrel.

Doreen: Exactly! That's what you were! A traveling minstrel, and what you did in that life is you "made do." You would stop in one community and do your work, and then you'd find some kind farmers and they'd take you in and board you for the night. And so that's the kind of lifestyle you had—a real carefree, "it's gonna come, I'll be taken care of" attitude. But it was almost like you were accepting the scraps of life on the other hand. In this life, we want you to take your standards up a notch.

Sam: Well, I feel ready to do that. Do you think that meditation is the answer?

Doreen: I think being conscious of this underlying attitude is the key for you. Your angels ask you to put your foot down to the universe and say, "Hey! I deserve to be fully supported for my work." Once you put your foot down to the universe, it really responds quickly.

Sam: Great! Well I'm at that point where I feel that I'm ready. I'm tired of doing artistic projects for big corporations, and I'm ready to follow my heart and create artwork from my soul. Do you feel that now is the right time for me to quit my regular commercial art job and go full-time into my own business?

Doreen: You should hang on to your regular job until you're really ready to do this other work, and you're ready to soar. In other words, when you have a firm knowingness that it's time. That knowingness won't come from fear or anger. It will come from a peaceful and quiet assurance that simply knows, "Now is the time." After all, you do have a wife, and you do have bills, and you're not a traveling minstrel in *this* life. If you were a single guy, I'd say, "Just go for it now."

As soon as you're mentally ready, you'll be able to make the break. So, you decide when that is. It's not written on any stones. Do it part-time to begin with.

Sam: I know on a deep level that my work will be successful. It's just a matter of me getting over the "pre-game jitters." I don't think it's going to take too much, though, for me to gain more confidence.

Doreen: You'll become more confident soon, I agree. Your angels and I would like to have you work with two archangels to help you further with your chosen career path. One is Archangel Gabriel, who is the angel of communicators and artists and people who serve through performing arts. Gabriel is a female archangel, and she can open up many doors for you. Even if you have no sense of her talking to you, you'll feel the evidence of her presence with opportunities.

The other archangel is Michael, who stands to your right at this moment. He's the protector angel, who is there to give you the courage to move forward.

Sam: That's interesting that the issue of courage comes up, because I feel that more than anything else right now, I need courage. I feel that Gabriel's energy has certainly been with me as an artistic communicator. But the courage to believe in myself and to know that it's okay to go out there and possibly make mistakes—I feel that this is my primary objective this year.

Doreen: Yes, absolutely. Since late 1998, we have all been experiencing a new energy that calls for us to live in complete integrity, and to let go of things that aren't honoring our true self. If we don't let go of them, we feel more and more pain. You really must do this work. Then, add on top of the mix this new energy of 1999, and you have to let go of this old stuff and move forward.

Sam: Yes, I definitely sense that strongly. On the last job I was working on, making a commercial brochure, I was feeling a heaviness that I hadn't felt on previous jobs. It was as if the heaviness was telling me, "It's time to move on." Yet I'm not feeling any anxiety that's pushing me forward. It's more of a peaceful strength.

ॐ ॐ ॐ

In the next chapter, you'll read about Earth angels who help us in surprising ways. You may discover that *you* are actually an Earth angel.

CHAPTER ELEVEN

Incarnated Angels, Elementals, Walk-Ins, and Star People

I'm often asked if angels ever incarnate in human form. The answer is most definitely yes. Hebrews 13:2 makes mention of this fact when it says, *"Be careful when entertaining strangers, for by so doing, many have entertained angels unawares."* In other words, you may have interacted with angels who look like humans without being aware that they actually were these heavenly beings. In fact, *you* may be an incarnated angel and not know it.

To me, an angel is anyone who acts angelically. In this respect, then, all of us are incarnated angels from time to time. People have come from all over the universe to live on Earth during this millennium shift. In my private psychic counseling practice, I've been able to get to know many people whose origins are not of this Earth. I've learned that there are many incarnated extraterrestrials (E.T.'s), angels, elementals, and walk-ins on the planet right now.

In the ultimate sense, we are all one—one with God, with each other, with the angels, and the ascended masters. Each of us has the same Divine spark of God-light within our core. Like multiple leaves attached to the same tree, we have the same source, and we affect each other.

However, in this illusory world where we appear to be separated beings, we do have outward characteristics that distinguish us from one another. For instance, those who are born male have an energy that is distinct from those who are born female.

There are also different wavelength energy patterns, depending on your lifestyle. Someone who, for example, spends most of his time drinking alcohol in a bar will have a different countenance and energy from someone who spends most of his time praying and meditating. Your energy pattern is affected by the places where you hang out, the people with whom you associate, and the thoughts that you predominantly think.

In the same way, there are souls who have "hung out" in most of their lives in different types of incarnations or locales. Not every child of God incarnates on Earth as a human. Some beings choose lives on other planets and other dimensions. If they have had several lives in these other places, their countenance and energy patterns reflect these surroundings and experiences. Then, when they do choose to come to Earth for an incarnation, they carry the energy patterns of their previous lives in these other places and dimensions.

Many "lightworkers" (people who are compelled to help others, especially in spiritual ways) have had previous incarnations in other dimensions or planets. They chose to incarnate in human form upon Earth at this time to act as Earth angels during the millennium shift.

In order to adjust to Earth life, they "borrowed" past-life memories from the Akashic Records (the afterlife plane library that contains records of everything that has ever happened to anyone). These borrowed past-life memories serve as buffers or cushions, so the soul will know what to expect on this planet. After all, Earth is considered one of the more volatile planets on which to incarnate. The level of aggression, violence, and pessimism here is considered quite high in the galaxies. A wonderful book on the topic of borrowed past-life memories is *Keepers of the Garden* by Dolores Cannon.

Not everyone who is an incarnated angel, star person, elemental, or walk-in is here for the first time. Those who act as Earth angels may choose to come here repeatedly. They retain the energy pattern of their realm of origination, so, for example, an incarnated angel has been in that form over her many lives.

Star People

The first time I worked with an incarnated E.T.—whom I call a "star person," I was startled. She defied all of my stereotypes about extraterrestrials. She looked a lot like an ordinary person (although there are some subtle, but key physical distinctions among star people that I've listed below). Yet, until I psychically discerned that she was working with a spacecraft, I had no clue that she wasn't from Earth.

When I told my client that I was seeing her working and traveling on a large spacecraft, she readily agreed. She, unlike some of my subsequent star person clients, was very aware of her origins. Since working with this first star person, I've had the opportunity to work with a dozen more, and I found some interesting patterns among them:

- **Distinctive eyes**—Star people have eyes that are almond shaped or shaped like crescents, with the bars pointing down like on a letter *n*. Think of Bette Midler's eyes, and you've got the picture.

385

- **Petite frames**—Most incarnated star people have small bones, and they are thin and short in stature.

- **"Wallflower" looks**—They tend to have very plain facial features, and most of them dress very casually. It's as if they want to blend into the background and not call attention to themselves.

- **Unusual auras**—Star people have auras with stripes pointing away from the body, with the colorings of rainbows. Humans and beings from Earthly dimensions have auras that surround the body like an eggshell. These distinctive aura patterns show up on Kirlian and aura photographs.

- **Diffused life purposes**—Their life purposes are to "help as needed." Star people hold open doors for strangers and let people go ahead of them in long lines, without caring whether they get a thank you in response. They are here to be nice, to collectively diffuse the planet of stress and violence. Because of this diffused life purpose, star people don't usually have a specific life purpose, but instead, they've agreed to help whoever needs help. So, they frequently have ordinary jobs where they can reach a lot of people through their encouraging words and uplifting attitudes.

- **A love of peace and honesty**—They have very little tolerance for dishonesty and violence. They came from planets where these traits are nonexistent, so they do not know how to cope with humans who are inauthentic, manipulative, or violent. Because of this lack of coping skills with common Earth problems, incarnated E.T.'s are often mislabeled with psychiatric disorders, including attention deficit disorder (ADD) and schizophrenia.

- **Unusual relationships and family patterns**—Because their planets have different customs about family life, childbirth, reproduction, and sex, many star people don't contract to have Earthly marriages or children. They feel out-of-sync with Western culture's romantic images because this isn't their style. In addition, they know that family life would interfere with the lightwork that they contracted to do during their lifetime. Very often, a female star person will fall in love with a much younger man, who is a soulmate from their star group.

- **Feeling like they are different**—Star people know, deep down, that they aren't from Earth. They often spend their lives feeling like they don't fit in here. One star person said, "I've always had this sense that I was dropped off here on this planet, and I've been waiting for someone to return and take me home." They feel, deep down, that their biological family isn't their "true" family, and they wonder if they were adopted.

Incarnated Angels

Another group of people whom I've gotten to know in my private practice are the incarnated angels. They, too, have distinguishing characteristics:

- **They look like angels**—Both male and female incarnated angels have sweet facial features, usually with heart-shaped faces and childlike features. A high percentage of female incarnated angels bleach or highlight their hair blonde.

- **Relationship challenges**—Incarnated angels have a history of co-dependent relationships due to their predisposition to giving, nurturing, and rescuing others. They also can see the best in everyone, so they often stay in abusive relationships longer than the average person would tolerate. Incarnated angels often have a history of multiple marriages and divorces.

- **Compulsive behaviors and weight issues**—Incarnated angels usually have histories of compulsive behaviors, especially overeating, and they are often overweight. They turn to food or other substances to deal with their emotional issues, especially if they are disconnected from their spirituality.

- **Professional helpers**—They are natural healers and helpers and often have healing or service work professions such as nursing, massage therapy, social work, the airline industry, or teaching. Strangers pour out their hearts to them, and they often say, "I don't know why I'm telling you such private things about myself. There's just something about you that I feel I can trust."

- **Givers, not receivers**—Incarnated angels are very generous people who sometimes have difficulty receiving. Consequently, they can manifest lack in their lives by blocking the flow of money, love, energy, and other natural resources from coming into their lives. Incarnated angels are very sensitive to others' feelings, often to the point of ignoring their own needs. This can lead these angels to feel frustrated or resentful when their own needs aren't met.

Incarnated Elementals

The incarnated elementals are another group of "Earth angels" who are here to help. They are humans whose origination is the elemental kingdom, which consists of the leprechauns, fairies, brownies, and elves. Here are their distinguishing characteristics:

- **Celtic heritage or appearance**—They often have reddish hair, fair skin, and light eyes. Their ancestry is Irish or British.

- **They look like elementals**—Incarnated leprechauns *look* like the leprechauns depicted in children's books, both in their body appearance and in their facial features. The same holds true for incarnated elves and brownies. Incarnated fairies are usually slender and willowy females who are moderate to tall in height. It's rare to see an overweight or short incarnated fairy.

- **Characteristic clothing**—Incarnated elementals often dress in outfits that you might think would be characteristic of their particular elemental species. For instance, an incarnated leprechaun would dress in green outfits and prefer to wear comfortable shoes. Incarnated fairies opt for flowing, diaphanous gowns. And incarnated brownies often wear coarse, heavily woven outer garments, similar to that of a friar or monk.

- **Mischievous personalities**—They are prone to playing practical jokes, sometimes to the point of seeming passive-aggressive in their joking. It can be difficult to know if an incarnated elemental is kidding or being serious. Part of this personality aspect comes from the elemental's distrust or even dislike of humans.

- **An alignment with nature**—The elementals have a life purpose to protect Mother Earth and her animals from humans. So, elementals are best at careers that involve plants or animals, outdoor retreats; or ecological service work. They would be very happy doing volunteer work teaching humans, especially children, to respect animals and the planet. An incarnated elemental should never work in an office or anywhere where they are cooped up indoors. Most incarnated elementals relate to animals and plants better than they do to humans. As a result, many of them are reclusive or shy.

- **Manifesting skills**—Incarnated elementals are excellent at focusing their thoughts and quickly experiencing the results in reality. They can manifest massive wealth if they put their minds to it. However, incarnated elementals who focus on pessimism also can manifest problems and poverty very quickly, too.

Walk-Ins

The fourth type of Earth angel is called a "walk-in." This is a being who incarnated through mutual agreement with a "walk-out," someone who left his or her being during an accident, illness, or while sleeping.

The walk-in is a highly evolved spiritual being with a lightworker life purpose. The walk-in needed to incarnate in a hurry for his or her purpose and decided to bypass the usual method of developing as a fetus, being born, and growing up. Instead, the walk-in soul located a living human who was not happy being alive. Perhaps the walk-in found a depressed or suicidal person, or a child who had difficulty adjusting.

The walk-in soul then communicated, usually through

dreams or thought-transfer, to the depressed person and said, "I will take over your responsibilities for you, and you will be able to go home to heaven without any negative repercussions associated with suicide." If the walk-out agreed to vacate his or her body and allow the walk-in full residency, then the two began to have trial swaps in which they tried out the arrangement several times.

If everything went smoothly, the walk-out then incurred a life-changing event such as a major illness or an accident. On occasion, the switch occurs when the walk-out is sleeping instead of during a crisis situation, but this is rare. At the agreed-upon time, the walk-out left his body, and the walk-in took up permanent residency.

Unlike a possession or attachment, the body only contains one soul, that of the walk-in. As everything is done with the full permission and cooperation of the walk-out, no negative or dark energies are involved.

The walk-in takes over the memory banks of the walk-out, and may not be aware that he or she is a walk-in. There are no set physical traits of a walk-in, since beings of all varieties become walk-ins and walk-outs. However, here are the distinguishing characteristics of a walk-in's life:

- **Drastic personality change**—Immediately after the walk-in occurred during an illness or accident, the person's friends and family members begin remarking, "You're so different—I almost feel like I don't know you anymore!"

- **Lifestyle change**—Newly incarnated walk-ins often find that they don't like the walk-out's lifestyle, so they make changes after coming into the body. They may divorce their spouse, quit their job, or move away. As part of the agreement with the walk-out, however, they take care of

391

the previous person's responsibilities even during the transitions. So, lifestyle changes are handled as responsibly as possible.

• **Name change**—The walk-in may find that the previous person's name doesn't suit him or her. So, they may choose to change their first name, adopt a spiritual name, or change their full name.

If You Are an Earth Angel

All four of the Earth angel groups are highly intuitive, yet they often have difficulty trusting their intuition. Partially, this comes from years of trying to adapt to Earth life. After all, the customs here are so foreign to their natural inclinations that star people and incarnated angels eventually learn to discount their inner feelings.

If you wonder whether you belong to any of these groups, then your inner guidance can tell you more. Before you go to sleep, say this affirmation to your higher self and spiritual group: *"Please give me a dream with clear messages about my origin that I will easily remember upon awakening."* You might also write this phrase on a piece of paper and place it under your pillow. When your subconscious is emotionally prepared, you will have a vivid lucid dream that will help you understand more about yourself.

Earth has many gifts to give to the world, including love, light, and lessons. My prayer is that, if you are among the above groups, you will open your heart and allow yourself to enjoy your time on this magnificent planet.

CHAPTER TWELVE

Number Sequences from the Angels

The angels do their best to get our attention and to communicate with us. In this way, they help us heal our own lives. However, we often discount the signs that they give us, writing them off as mere coincidences or our imagination.

The angels say:

"We can't write our messages to you in the sky.
You've got to pay attention and believe when you see
any patterns forming in your life—especially in
response to any questions or prayers that you've posed.
When you hear the same song repeatedly or see the
same number sequence, who do you think is behind
this? Your angels, of course!"

Number Sequences

Your angels often communicate messages to you by showing you sequences of numbers. They do this in two ways. First, they subtly whisper in your ear so that you'll look up in time to notice the clock's time or a phone number on a billboard. The angels hope you'll be aware that you're seeing this same number sequence repeatedly. For instance, you may frequently see the number sequence 111, and it seems that every time you look at a clock the time reads 1:11 or 11:11.

The second way in which the angels show you meaningful number sequences is by physically arranging for, say, a car to drive in front of you that has a specific license plate number they want you to see. Those who are aware of this phenomenon become adept at reading the meaning of various license plates. In this way, the angels will actually give you detailed messages (remember the Steve Martin character in the movie *L.A. Story,* where billboards kept giving him meaningful information?).

Here are the basic meanings of various number sequences. However, your own angels will tell you if your situation holds a different meaning for you. Ask your angels, "What are you trying to tell me?" and they'll happily give you additional information to help you decode their numeric meanings.

111—Monitor your thoughts carefully, and be sure to only think about what you want, not what you don't want. This sequence is a sign that there is a gate of opportunity opening up, and your thoughts are manifesting into form at record speeds. The 111 is like the bright light of a flashbulb. It means that the universe has just taken a snapshot of your thoughts and is manifesting them into form. Are you pleased with what thoughts the universe has captured? If not, correct your thoughts (ask your angels to help you with this if you have difficulty controlling or monitoring your thoughts).

222—Your newly planted ideas are beginning to grow into reality. Keep watering and nurturing them, and soon they will push through the soil so you can see evidence of your manifestation. In other words, don't quit five minutes before the miracle. Your manifestation is soon going to be evident to you, so keep up the good work! Keep holding positive thoughts, keep affirming, and continue visualizing.

333—The ascended masters are near you, desiring you to know that you have their help, love, and companionship. Call upon the ascended masters often, especially when you see the number 3 patterns around you. Some of the more famous ascended masters include Jesus, Moses, Mary, Quan Yin, and Yogananda.

444—The angels are surrounding you now, reassuring you of their love and help. Don't worry because the angels' help is nearby.

555—Buckle your seatbelts, because a major life change is upon you. This change should not be viewed as being "positive" or "negative," since all change is but a natural part of life's flow. Perhaps this change is an answer to your prayers, so continue seeing and feeling yourself being at peace.

666—Your thoughts are out of balance right now, focused too much on the material world. This number sequence asks you to balance your thoughts between heaven and earth. Like the famous "Sermon on the Mount," the angels ask you to focus on spirit and service, and know that your material and emotional needs will automatically be met as a result.

777—The angels applaud you—congratulations, you're on a roll! Keep up the good work and know that your wish is coming true. This is an extremely positive sign and means that you should also expect more miracles to occur.

888—A phase of your life is about to end, and this is a sign to give you forewarning so you can prepare. This number sequence may mean that you are winding up an emotional, career, or relationship phase. It also means that there is light at the end of the tunnel. In addition, it means, "The crops are ripe. Don't wait to pick and enjoy them." In other words, don't procrastinate making your move or enjoying the fruits of your labor.

999—Completion. This is the end of a big phase in your personal or global life. Also, it is a message to lightworkers involved in Earth healing and means, "Get to work because Mother Earth needs you right now."

000— A reminder that you are one with God, and to feel the presence of your Creator's love within you. Also, it is a sign that a situation has gone full circle.

Number Combinations

The angels will often give you a message that involves a combination of two or more numbers. Here are the basic meanings of triple-digit, two-number combinations. If your messages contain three or more numbers, blend the answers from the different number combinations. For instance, if you continually notice the sequence 312, use the meaning of the 3 and 1 number combination, plus the 1 and 2 combination.

Or, if you feel guided, add the numbers together. Keep adding the subsequent digits together until you have a single-digit number. Then, look at the meaning for that particular number from the previously outlined list of number sequences that contain three identical numbers.

Combinations of 1's

1's and 2's, such as 121 or 112—Our thoughts are like seeds that are beginning to sprout. You may have already seen some evidence of the fruition of your desires. These are signs that things will and are growing in your aspired direction. Keep the faith!

1's and 3's, such as 133 or 113—The ascended masters are working with you on your thought processes. In many ways, they are acting as mentors, teaching you the ancient wisdom involved in manifestation. They are sending you energy to keep you from feeling discouraged, and encouragement to stay focused on the true goals of your soul. Additionally, the ascended masters may be offering you advice, guidance, and suggestions on your life purpose. Always, however, they teach that every creation begins at the level of thought and idea. Ask them to help you choose wisely that which you want.

1's and 4's, such as 114 or 144—The angels are emphasizing strongly that you watch your thoughts right now. They counsel you to make a wish, as you are in a gateway that will manifest your thoughts right at this moment. (**Note:** 411 means "Ask the angels for some vital information that you need right now.")

1's and 5's, such as 115, or 551—Your thoughts are creating the changes in your life. Keep steering your thoughts in your desired direction. If the changes that you see forthcoming are not desired, you can stop or alter them by modifying your thoughts.

1's and 6's, such as 116 or 661—Keep your thoughts heavenward, and let go of materially minded worries. (**Note:** 611 means "Ask for help in repairing something in the material world that is irritating or bothering you right now.")

1's and 7's, such as 117 or 771—This is confirmation that you are doing great. You are on the right path, so keep going! This is a sign that you have chosen your thoughts well and that you should focus even more steadily on your objectives. Be sure to add appropriate emotions to your thoughts; for instance, feeling grateful for the gifts you have in life. Gratitude will speed the process of your manifestations.

1's and 8's, such as 181 or 818—You are nearing the end of a significant phase of your life. If you are tired of some part of your life, be glad that it will soon be healed or replaced with something better. Surrender and release those parts of your life that aren't working, as your thoughts of a better life are coming to pass.

1's and 9's, such as 119 or 199—A new door has opened for you as a product of your thoughts. You now have the opportunity to stare your thoughts in the face and come eye-to-eye with your own creations. Let the old fall away, as it is replaced with the new in accordance with your desires.

1's and 0's, such as 100 or 110—Powerful Divine guidance from God and the angels asks you to alter your thoughts. Perhaps you have been praying to be happier and healthier. If so, this is an answer to your prayers. God knows that the solution you seek is born within your thoughts. Ask God to guide the direction of your thoughts and support you during your time of transition.

Combinations of 2's

2's and 1's, such as 221 or 112—Your thoughts are like seeds that are beginning to sprout. You may have already seen some evidence of the fruition of your desires. These are signs that things will and are growing in your aspired direction. Keep the faith!

2's and 3's, such as 223 or 323—The ascended masters are working with you as co-creators of your new project. They are telling you that they share your excitement and know that everything is working out well for you. The masters can see that your future is already guaranteed to be filled with the happiness you seek. Enjoy this new phase of your life!

2's and 4's, such as 224 or 244—As it says in the spiritual text, *A Course in Miracles*, "The angels nurse your newborn purpose." This is a sign that you have help from above in making your desired transitions. This is a time when you especially need to know that you're not alone. The 2 and 4 number sequences are a signal from your angels to tell you that they're working very closely with you right now.

2's and 5's, such as 255 or 225—Your prayers and intentions have been clear, strong, and without reservations; therefore, expect a change to come about faster than you may have foreseen. Don't let it throw you when your wishes come true. They may come about in unexpected ways, so hold on to your faith. Talk to God often, and ask for reassurance.

2's and 6's, such as 266 or 226— A new purchase or acquisition is coming your way.

2's and 7's, such as 277 or 272—Have you recently applied for a new job, admission to a school, or a loan? These numbers signal good news. They ask you to hang tight and to not allow your faith to waver.

2's and 8's, such as 288 or 282—One door is beginning to open, and another door is beginning to close. Be sure to listen to your intuition very closely right now, as it will guide you to take steps that will ensure your steady abundance during these transitions.

2's and 9's, such as 299 or 292—If you've recently suffered a loss (job, lover, etc.), expect it to be replaced in the very near future. Everything is working in your favor, although there may be so much behind-the-scenes activity involved that you wonder if God has forgotten about you. Worry not! Feel the energy of your life, which *is* moving forward right now. You are not being punished by your recent loss. The universe is, instead, preparing you for newness.

2's and 0's, such as 200 or 202—God wants you to know that He has not forgotten or abandoned you. He loves you very, very much! In fact, God is orchestrating a wonderful new phase of your life. Talk to God often, and you'll feel this forthcoming miracle. God also reminds you of the importance of "Divine timing." Sometimes, certain factors need to fall into place *first* before your desired outcome can be reached. As long as you hold strong in your thoughts and faith, there is nothing blocking you from attaining your desire.

Combinations of 3's

3's and 1's, such as 311 or 313—The ascended masters are working with you on your thought processes. In many ways, they are acting as mentors, teaching you the ancient wisdom involved in manifestation. They are sending you energy to keep you from feeling discouraged, and encouragement to stay focused on the true goals of your soul. Additionally, the ascended masters may be offering you advice, guidance, and suggestions on your life purpose. Always, however, they teach that every creation begins at the level of thought and idea. Ask them to help you choose wisely that which you want.

3's and 2's, such as 322 or 332—The ascended masters are working with you as co-creators of your new project. They are telling you that they share your excitement and know that everything is working out well for you. The masters can see that your future is already guaranteed to be filled with the happiness you seek. Enjoy this new phase of your life!

3's and 4's, such as 334 or 344—You have *a lot* of help around you right now! Both the ascended masters *and* the angels are here to assist, guide, and love you. Reach out to them, as they are reaching out to you.

3's and 5's, such as 353 or 335—The ascended masters want to prepare you for a big life change that is imminent. They want you to know that they are holding your hand through this change and that everything will be all right. Embrace the change, and look for the blessings within it.

3's and 6's, such as 363 or 336—Your ascended masters are helping you manifest the material items you need for your Divine life purpose. Whether that means money for tuition or outlets for you to conduct your teaching or healing work, the masters are working to bring it to you. They want you to know that you deserve to receive this help, as it will better enable you to give to others.

3's and 7's, such as 377 or 373—The ascended masters are joyful. Not only do they see your true inner Divinity, but they also agree with the path that you have chosen. They want you to know that you deserve happiness, and to allow the flow of holy bliss that comes with your Divine heritage and chosen path.

3's and 8's, such as 338 or 383—"Keep going," the masters say to you. Boost the energy and focus of your thoughts and feelings. Realign your outlook with the knowledge of your oneness with God, everyone, and all of life.

3's and 9's, such as 393 or 339—This is a strong message to let go of situations in your life that aren't in integrity or that have served their purpose. Do not artificially hang on to situations because of fear. Know that each and every moment you are taken care of. It is vital that you hold a positive viewpoint about yourself and your future. This viewpoint actually *creates* what you will experience, so ask the masters to help you choose your thoughts from the high point of love.

3's and 0's, such as 300 or 330—God and the ascended masters are trying to get your attention, most likely with respect to a matter related to your Divine life purpose. Is there any guidance that you've been ignoring lately? If so, you may be feeling stuck right now. This number sequence is heaven's way of alerting you to the fact that you must do your part in the co-creation process. This means listening to and following your Divine guidance to take certain actions.

Combinations of 4's

4's and 1's, such as 441 or 411—The angels are recommending that you watch your thoughts right now. They counsel you to make a wish, as you are in a gateway that will manifest your thoughts right at this moment. (**Note:** 411 means "Ask the angels for some vital information that you need right now.")

4's and 2's, such as 422 or 442—As it says in the spiritual text *A Course in Miracles*, "The angels nurse your newborn purpose." This is a sign that you have help from above in making your desired transitions. This is a time when you especially need to know that you're not alone. The 2 and 4 number sequences are a signal from your angels to tell you that they're working very closely with you right now.

4's and 3's, such as 443 or 433—You have *a lot* of help around you right now! Both the ascended masters *and* the angels are here to assist, guide, and love you. Reach out to them, as they are reaching out to you.

4's and 5's, such as 455 or 445—Your angels are involved in one of your significant life changes right now.

4's and 6's, such as 446 or 466—Your angels caution you that your focus is too much on the material world. They ask you to surrender your worries to them so that they can intervene. Balance your focus between heaven and earth, and know that your supply is truly unlimited, especially when you work hand-in-hand with the Divine.

4's and 7's, such as 477 or 447—The angels congratulate you and say, *"Keep up the great work! You are on a roll. Keep your thoughts focused, because it's having a big and positive effect."*

4's and 8's, such as 488 or 448—This is a message from your angels that a phase of your life is about to end. They want you to know that as things slow down, they are with you and will be helping to guide you to a new situation better suited to your needs, desires, and purpose.

4's and 9's, such as 494 or 449—The angels say to you that it's time to let go of a situation that has ended. They remind you that, as one door closes, another one opens. The angels are certainly helping you to open new doors and to heal from any pain that accompanies the transition that you are now undergoing. Please ask your angels to help you have faith that these endings and beginnings are answers to your prayers.

4's and 0's, such as 440 or 400—God and the angels want you to know that you are very, very loved. They ask you to take a moment to feel this love, as it will answer many of your questions and resolve any challenge.

Combinations of 5's

5's and 1's, such as 511 or 515—Your thoughts are creating the changes in your life. Keep steering your thoughts in your desired direction. If the changes that you see forthcoming are not desired, you can stop or alter them by modifying your thoughts.

5's and 2's, such as 522 or 552—Your prayers and intentions have been clear, strong, and without reservations. Therefore, expect a change to come about faster than you may have foreseen. Don't let it throw you when your wishes come true. They may come about in unexpected ways, so hold on to your faith. Talk to God often, and ask for reassurance.

5's and 3's, such as 533 or 553—The ascended masters want to prepare you for a big life change that is imminent. They want you to know that they are holding your hand through this change and that everything will be all right. Embrace the change, and look for the blessings within it.

5's and 4's, such as 554 or 544—Your angels are involved in one of your significant life changes right now.

5's and 6's, such as 556 or 566—Your material life is changing significantly, such as a new home, car, or other possession.

5's and 7's, such as 577 or 575—This is a validation that you are "on target" with an impending change that will enrich you either physically, emotionally, or intellectually—or a combination of all three. Stay on course and you will soon see the evidence of how the changes add to your own life and to that of those around you.

5's and 8's, such as 588 or 558—This number sequence signifies that you are at the 11th hour, right before the change. Do not fear it, as you will be supported and loved throughout this change, which is now imminent.

5's and 9's, such as 599 or 595—In order for the new change to manifest, it's important to release the past. This number sequence asks you to let go of the old and know that it served a vital function during its time. However, life is fluid and change is inevitable. Know that the new is standing at your doorway, waiting for you to let it in. You invite the new in as you detach with love from the old.

5's and 0's, such as 500 or 550—An important message that lets you know that your life changes are in Divine and perfect order. They are a gift from God and in alignment with God's will for your higher self.

Combinations of 6's

6's and 1's, such as 611 or 661—Keep your thoughts heavenward, and let go of materially minded worries. (**Note:** 611 means "Ask for help in repairing something in the material world that is irritating or bothering you right now.")

6's and 2's, such as 622 or 662—A new purchase or acquisition is coming your way.

6's and 3's, such as 663 or 633—Your ascended masters are helping you manifest the material items you need for your Divine life purpose. Whether that means money for tuition, or outlets for you to conduct your teaching or healing work, the masters are working to bring it to you. They want you to know that you deserve to receive this help, as it will better enable you to give to others.

6's and 4's, such as 644 or 664—Your angels caution you that your focus is too much on the material world. They ask you to surrender your worries to them so that they can intervene. Balance your focus between heaven and earth, and know that your supply is truly unlimited, especially when you work hand-in-hand with the Divine.

6's and 5's, such as 665 or 655—Your material life is changing significantly, such as a new home, car, or other possession.

6's and 7's, such as 667 or 677—A validation that your thoughts and work with the material world are right on the mark. You have successfully balanced your thoughts and activities so that you are taking care of the mind, body, and spirit. Keep up the great work!

6's and 8's, such as 668 or 688—You are about to part ways with something in your material world, such as selling a possession. If you do not intend to lose or sell anything in your material life, you can change your thoughts and alter this direction. However, if you are intent on selling or detaching from something material in your life, consider this a sign that your wish is about to come true.

6's and 9's, such as 669 or 699—Detach from your material items, especially if you have had any obsession with any particular type of material possession. This number sequence asks you to let go and detach. Also, this is a message that something in your life that you have sold or lost is about to be replaced with something better. Be open to receiving new possessions that exceed your expectations, as you are ready to be upgraded. You deserve the best!

6's and 0's, such as 600 or 660—This is a message from your Creator about your material life. Divine guidance from God asks you to focus less on Earthly desires. It's not that God is asking you to live an impoverished life, but rather, that your Creator asks you to try a more spiritual approach to having your needs met. Know that God is within you and is your source for everything you need. Simply hold faith and gratitude, and be open to signs or new opportunities that will bring your material needs to you. *"Seek ye first the kingdom of God, and all the rest will be added unto you"* is the heart of this number sequence's message. You can get more information on this process by reading *The Abundance Book* by John Randolph Price (published by Hay House) or by reading "The Sermon on the Mount" in the Gospel of Matthew.

Combinations of 7's

7's and 1's, such as 711 or 771—This is confirmation that you are doing great. You are on the right path, so keep going! This is a sign that you have chosen your thoughts well, and it should inspire you to focus even more steadily on your objectives. Be sure to add appropriate emotions to your thoughts—for instance, feeling grateful for the gifts you have in life. Gratitude will speed the process of your manifestations.

7's and 2's, such as 722 or 772—Have you recently applied for a new job, admission to a school, or a loan? These numbers signal good news. They ask you to hang tight and not to allow your faith to waver.

7's and 3's, such as 773 or 733—The ascended masters are joyful. Not only do they see your true inner Divinity, but they also agree with the path that you have chosen. They want you to know that you deserve happiness, and to allow the flow of holy bliss that comes with your Divine heritage and chosen path.

7's and 4's, such as 774 or 774—The angels congratulate you and say, *"Keep up the great work! You are on a roll. Keep your thoughts focused, because it's having a big and positive effect."*

7's and 5's, such as 775 or 755—This is a validation that you are "on target" with an impending change that will enrich you either physically, emotionally, or intellectually—or a combination of all three. Stay on course and you will soon see the evidence of how the changes add to your own life, and to that of those around you.

7's and 6's, such as 776 or 766—A validation that your thoughts and work with the material world are right on the mark. You have successfully balanced your thoughts and activities so that you are taking care of the mind, body, and spirit. Keep up the great work!

7's and 8's, such as 778 or 788—Have you been feeling that some part of your life, such as a job or a relationship, is ending? This is a validation that your feelings are correct. The end could mean a significant positive change in the situation, or it could mean that some part of your life is nearing completion. Regardless, this number sequence heralds good news about a forthcoming positive change involving the completion of an intense situation. Hang tight, because your life is about to get easier.

7's and 9's, such as 779 or 799—Congratulations! You are shedding old parts of your life that no longer fit who you are. You are living a more authentic life that is in integrity with your highest view of yourself. This number sequence applauds your decisions to live honestly.

7's and 0's, such as 700 or 770—An "atta boy" or "atta girl" directly from God, giving you accolades for the mental, spiritual, and physical work you've been doing. You are helping yourself and many other people with your current path, and God asks you to continue with your great work.

Combinations of 8's

8's and 1's, such as 811 or 881—You are nearing the end of a significant phase of your life. If you are tired of some part of your life, be glad that it will soon be healed or replaced with something better. Surrender and release those parts of your life that aren't working, as your thoughts of a better life are coming to pass.

8's and 2's, such as 822 or 882—One door is beginning to open, and another door is beginning to close. Be sure to listen to your intuition very closely right now, as it will guide you to take steps that will ensure your steady abundance during these transitions.

8's and 3's, such as 883 or 833—*"Keep going,"* the masters say to you. Boost the energy and focus of your thoughts and feelings. Realign your outlook with the knowledge of your oneness with God, everyone, and all of life.

8's and 4's, such as 884 or 844—This is a message from your angels that a phase of your life is about to end. They want you to know that as things slow down, they are with you and will be helping to guide you to a new situation better suited to your needs, desires, and purpose.

8's and 5's, such as 885 or 855—This number sequence signifies that you are at the 11th hour, right before the change. Do not fear this change, as you will be supported and loved throughout this change, which is now imminent.

8's and 6's, such as 886 or 866—You are about to part ways with something in your material world, such as selling a possession. If you do not intend to lose or sell anything in your material life, you can change your thoughts and alter this direction. However, if you are intent on selling or detaching from something material in your life, consider this a sign that your wish is about to come true.

8's and 7's, such as 887 or 877—Have you been feeling that some part of your life, such as a job or a relationship, is ending? This is a validation that your feelings are correct. The end could mean a significant positive change in the situation, or it could mean that some part of your life is nearing completion. Regardless, this number sequence heralds good news about a forthcoming positive change involving the completion of an intense situation. Hang tight, because your life is about to get easier.

8's and 9's, such as 889 or 899—Some significant phase in your life has come to an end, bringing with it other events that will also end in a domino effect. Like a train coming to the end of the line, one car will stop while the following train cars will take a moment to slow down before stopping. This number sequence is a message that you are going through a chain of event, where many parts of your life are slowing and stopping. Worry not, though, because these changes are necessary for new sequences and circumstances to begin for you.

8's and 0's, such as 800 or 808—A message from your Divine Creator, signifying that the impending endings are part of your overall Divine plan. They are answers to your prayers, and are in alignment with God's will for you. Ask God to help you allay any fears or worries you may have about these upcoming changes.

Combinations of 9's

9's and 1's, such as 991 or 919—A new door has opened for you as a product of your thoughts. You now have the opportunity to stare your thoughts in the face and come eye-to-eye with your own creations. Let the old fall away, as it is replaced with the new in accordance with your desires.

9's and 2's, such as 992 or 922—If you've recently suffered a loss (job, lover, etc.), expect it to be replaced in the very near future. Everything is working in your favor, although there may be so much behind-the-scenes" activity involved that you wonder if God has forgotten about you. Worry not! Feel the energy of your life, which *is* moving forward right now. You are not being punished by your recent loss. The universe is, instead, preparing you for newness.

9's and 3's, such as 993 or 939—A strong message to let go of situations in your life that aren't in integrity or that have served their purpose. Do not artificially hang on to situations because of fears. Know that each and every moment you are taken care of. It is vital that you hold a positive viewpoint about yourself and your future. This viewpoint actually *creates* what you will experience, so ask the masters to help you choose your thoughts from the high point of love.

9's and 4's, such as 994 or 944—The angels say to you that it's time to let go of a situation that has ended. They remind you that as one door closes, another one opens. The angels are certainly helping you open new doors and to heal from any pain that accompanies the transition that you are now undergoing. Please ask your angels to help you to have faith that these endings and beginnings are answers to your prayers.

9's and 5's, such as 959 or 995—In order for the new change to manifest, it's important to release the past. This number sequence asks you to let go of the old and know that it served a vital function during its time. However, life is fluid and change is inevitable. Know that the new is standing at your doorway, waiting for you to let it in. You invite the new in as you detach with love from the old.

9's and 6's, such as 966 or 996—Detach from your material items, especially if you have had any obsession with any particular type of material possession. This number sequence asks you to let go and detach. Also, it is a message that something in your life that you have sold or lost is about to be replaced with something better. Be open to receiving new possessions that exceed your expectations, as you are ready to be upgraded. You deserve the best!

9's and 7's, such as 977 or 997—Congratulations! You are shedding old parts of your life that no longer fit who you are. You are living a more authentic life that is in integrity with your highest view of yourself. This number sequence applauds your decisions to live honestly.

9's and 8's, such as 998 or 988—Some significant phase in your life has come to an end, bringing with it other events that will also end in a domino effect. Like a train coming to the end of the line, one car will stop while the following train cars will take a moment to slow down before stopping. This number sequence is a message that you are going through a chain of events where a lot of parts of your life are slowing and stopping. Worry not, though, because these changes are necessary for new sequences and circumstances to begin for you.

9's and 0's, such as 900 or 909—This is a message from your Creator signifying that the part of your life that has just ended is Divinely guided. Nothing is ever truly lost. There is no death, and there are no accidents. Your recent life change, in which a significant part of your life has been halted or altered, is actually an answer to your prayer. God is letting you know that He is not taking anything away from you or "causing" your loss. Rather, your life plan or prayers called this life change to you, through your own God-given power. Be willing to forgive everyone involved so that you can be light and free as you enter into a beautiful new phase of life.

Combinations of 0's

0's and 1's, such as 001 or 010—Powerful Divine guidance from God and the angels asks you to alter your thoughts. Perhaps you have been praying to be happier and healthier. If so, this is an answer to your prayers. God knows that the solution for which you seek is born within your thoughts. Ask God to guide the direction of your thoughts, and support you during your time of transition.

0's and 2's, such as 002 or 020—God wants you to know that He has not forgotten or abandoned you. He loves you very, very much! In fact, God is orchestrating a wonderful new phase of your life for you. Talk to God often, and you'll feel this forthcoming miracle. God also reminds you about the importance of "Divine timing." Sometimes certain factors need to fall into place *first* before your desired outcome can be reached. As long as you hold strong in your thoughts and faith, there is nothing blocking you from attaining your desire.

0's and 3's, such as 003 or 300—God and the ascended masters are trying to get your attention, most likely related to your Divine life purpose. Is there any guidance that you've been ignoring lately? If so, you may be feeling stuck right now. This number sequence is heaven's way of alerting you to the fact that you must do your part in the co-creation process. This means listening to and following your Divine guidance to take certain actions.

0's and 4's, such as 040 or 400—God and the angels want you to know that you are very, very loved. They ask you to take a moment to feel this love, as it will answer many of your questions and resolve any challenge.

0's and 5's, such as 050 or 500—An important message that lets you know that your life changes are in Divine and perfect order. They are a gift from God, and in alignment with God's will for your higher self.

0's and 6's, such as 006 or 066—A message from your Creator about your material life. Divine guidance from God asks you to let go of being overly focused on Earthly desires. It's not that God is asking you to live an impoverished life, but that your Creator asks you to have a more spiritual approach to having your needs met. Know that God is within you and is your source for everything you need. Simply hold faith and gratitude, and be open to intuition or new opportunities that will bring your material needs to you. *"Seek ye first the kingdom of God, and all the rest will be added unto you"* is the heart of this number sequence's message. You can get more information on this process by reading *The Abundance Book* by John Randolph Price (published by Hay House) or by reading "The Sermon on the Mount" in the Gospel of Matthew.

0's and 7's, such as 007 or 070—A pat on the back from God, giving you accolades for the mental, spiritual, and physical work you've been doing. You are helping yourself and many other people with your current path, and God asks you to continue with your great work.

0's and 8's, such as 088 or 080—A message from your Divine Creator signifying that the impending endings are part of your overall Divine plan. They are answers to your prayers, and are in alignment with God's will for you. Ask God to help you allay any fears or worries you may have about these upcoming changes.

0's and 9's, such as 099 or 090—A message from your Creator signifying that the part of your life that has just ended is Divinely guided. Nothing is ever truly lost. There is no death and there are no accidents. Your recent life change, in which a significant part of your life has been halted or altered, is actually an answer to your prayer. God is letting you know that He is not taking anything away from you or "causing" your loss. Rather, your life plan or prayers called this life change to you through your own God-given power. Be willing to forgive everyone involved so that you can be light and free as you enter into a beautiful new phase of life.

APPENDIX

"Forgiveness, Free Yourself Now" Exercise

Anyone can feel more at peace and more energized through the process of forgiveness. This process reminds me of throwing off weights when riding in a hot air balloon so you can go higher up. Old anger, fear, and resentment are dead weights that slow us and drain our vitality. Perhaps you have some weight you can throw over the side of your hot air balloon right now. When you forgive the world—including yourself—you become lighter and much less fearful.

This process takes between 30 and 60 minutes to complete, and believe me, it is a worthwhile time investment. Many clients report that this single exercise immediately transforms their lives in powerfully positive ways. Here are some steps to freedom through forgiveness:

1. **Know the benefits of forgiveness**—Forgiveness is different from saying, "I lose," or "I was wrong, and you were right." It is different from letting someone off the hook for a perceived wrong deed. Forgiveness is simply a way of freeing your spirit and becoming an unlimited being. Peacefulness and increased energy are the prizes, and forgiveness is the price. To me, it's a bargain.

2. **Take a forgiveness inventory**—(This exercise is partially based on the work of author John Randolph Price.) Write the name of *every* person, living or deceased, who has ever irritated you. Most people find they have a three- or four-page list and are able suddenly to remember names of people they hadn't thought about in years. Some people put down names of pets who irritated them, and almost everyone writes their own name somewhere on the list.

3. **Release and forgive**—In a solitary room where no interruptions are possible, go down the list one name at a time. Hold the image of each person in your mind and tell him or her, "I forgive you and I release you. I hold no unforgiveness back. My forgiveness for you is total. I am free and you are free." This process may take 30 minutes or longer. However, it's important to stick with it until the entire list is complete.

4. **Do nightly releasements**—Every evening before retiring, do a mental review of the day. Is there anyone you need to forgive? Just as you probably wash your face every night, it's also important to cleanse your consciousness nightly so resentment won't accumulate.

The Corral Visualization

After relaxing with several slow, deep breaths, close your eyes and get into a comfortable position.

Imagine that you are standing in a country field. A road is leading to you—one that brings all your material, emotional, and spiritual supplies. The road passes through a corral to get to you. The corral has two gates: one facing the road, and one facing you. If both gates are open, supplies readily flow to you, and your gifts to the world flow from you.

Whenever we hold unforgiveness toward someone, we imprison that person in our minds where we mentally flog them with our pronouncements of guilt and blame. The image of the person we resent is "corralled" in our consciousness, and the gates to the corral slam shut like prison doors. You necessarily go into the corral along with the person you've judged in order to monitor their imprisonment. So, both gates are shut, and your locked corral blocks your flow and supply.

Look inside your corral right now and see who's there. See the high price you pay for corralling these people. If you are ready to forgive, imagine the gates of your corral automatically opening. Visualize whoever is in the corral walking out, free, happy, and forgiven. Wish them well. If this seems difficult, try forgiving the person instead of their deeds. As you forgive, feel the release, the relief, and the renewed energy as your resentment lifts. Check to make sure that you're not in the corral alone out of an ego judgment you hold against yourself.

Recheck your corral often, especially when you feel tired, ill, or afraid. You'll find that these are the times when you have the most people (including yourself) locked into your corral. Once you open the gates and clear the corral, your emotions and energy level will improve.

Angel Affirmations

Say these affirmations daily to increase your self-confidence and self-love. You can record them in your own voice, which will give you a powerful affirmations tape, or photocopy this page and post them in a prominent place. Add your own personal affirmations related to your goals and desires.

- *I am now surrounded by angels.*
- *The angels shine the love of God upon me and through me.*
- *I accept this love from God and the angels.*
- *I deserve love.*
- *I deserve happiness.*
- *I deserve health.*
- *I deserve help from heaven, and I accept it now.*
- *I call upon God and the angels to help and guide me.*
- *I listen to my inner voice and feelings.*
- *My inner voice and feelings is guidance from God and the angels.*
- *This guidance is everything I need.*
- *I follow my guidance in full faith.*
- *I know that God and the angels love me and are guiding me right now.*
- *I accept the angels' love.*
- *I accept love.*
- *I love.*
- *I am love.*
- *I am loving.*

- *I am very loved.*
- *Everyone loves me.*
- *I love everyone.*
- *I forgive everyone.*
- *I forgive myself.*
- *I send God's love to everyone I meet.*
- *I guard my thoughts carefully and only allow positive and loving thoughts to come through.*
- *There is an abundance of love in the world.*
- *There is enough for everyone.*
- *There is plenty to go around.*
- *I have an abundance of everything.*
- *I attract wonderful, loving people into my life.*
- *My angels and I enjoy new opportunities to give service to the world.*
- *I am rewarded constantly.*
- *My life is harmonious and peaceful.*
- *I am peaceful.*
- *I am radiant.*
- *I am joyful.*

ARCHANGELS & ASCENDED MASTERS

To God, the archangels,
and the ascended masters . . .
with eternal gratitude and
appreciation for their
Divine love, lessons, and support.

Gratitude

So many wonderful beings, on Earth and Heaven, collectively helped to create this book. I first want to thank Steven Farmer, my twin flame and amazing husband. My deepest appreciation to Louise L. Hay, Reid Tracy, Jill Kramer, Christy Salinas, Leon Nacson, and all of the Hay House angels. Many blessings to Bill Christy for his help with researching two of the more elusive fellows in the spirit world! Thank you to my family for being so loving, supportive, and open-minded, including Bill and Joan Hannan, Ada Montgomery, Charles Schenk, Grant Schenk, Nicole Farmer, Catherine Farmer, Susan Clark, and Nancy Fine.

Thank you to Mary Kay and John Hayden, Mairead Conlon, and Marie and Ted Doyle for bringing Steven and me to Ireland, and for providing us with the beautiful home in the midst of Marie's magical fairy glen. Thank you to Bronny Daniels, Lynnette Brown, Kevin Buck, Johnna Michelle, and Carol Michaels for your support (and the Reiki) during the writing of this book. Many blessings to Sharon George for the beautiful artwork that graces the cover.

I also want to thank those who submitted stories about their interactions with the ascended masters. And a huge bouquet of gratitude to those who read my books, use my oracle cards, listen to my audio programs, and attend my seminars. I am honored to work with you, and I appreciate your support very much.

And, as to my heavenly friends, there are no words to express my love and appreciation for the constant care and companionship you provide for me . . . for all of *us*. Thank you for guiding my words and research throughout the writing of this book.

I couldn't have done it without you all!

"There are those who have reached God directly, retaining no trace of worldly limits and remembering their own Identity perfectly. These might be called the Teachers of teachers because, although they're no longer visible, their image can yet be called upon. And they will appear when and where it's helpful for them to do so. To those to whom such appearances would be frightening, they give their ideas. No one can call on them in vain. Nor is there anyone of whom they're unaware. All needs are known to them, and all mistakes are recognized and overlooked by them. The time will come when this is understood. And meanwhile, they give all their gifts to the teachers of God who look to them for help. . . ."

— from *A Course in Miracles* Manual for Teachers

Introduction
From Old Age to New Age

An ascended master is a great healer, teacher, or prophet who previously walked upon the earth, and who is now in the spirit world, helping us from beyond. Ascended masters come from all cultures, religions, and civilizations, both ancient and modern. They include legendary figures such as Jesus, Moses, and Buddha; saints; goddesses and gods; and *bodhisattvas*, devas, and deities.

I've consciously worked with several specific archangels (extremely powerful angels who help us and who oversee the guardian angels) and ascended masters for many years, such as Archangel Michael, Jesus, and Mary. I've written about ascended masters and archangels in many of my books, and I've presented information about them at my workshops.

During my readings, I frequently help people understand which deities are with them as spirit guides. In fact, I first met many of the divinities (another term for "Divine beings") listed in this book during my readings. Sometimes I'll call on audience members at my workshops and ask them to stand up because I can see that they have so many ascended masters around them. I always ask people the same questions, and consistently receive the same answers:

Q: "Did you know that you have many ascended masters with you?"
A: "Yes" (or "I was hoping that I did").
Q: "Did you call these beings to your side?"
A: "Yes. I asked God to send me anyone who could help."

Even though I'd met and heard about these great beings, I wanted to acquire additional knowledge about the ancient Eastern divinities, as well as the New Age ascended masters. I wanted to get to know them firsthand, develop a personal relationship with each one, and know about each being's history and unique traits . . . instead of accepting secondhand reports about their personalities, characteristics, and functions from others.

So, in effect, I've written this book to function as a "Who's Who in the Spirit World," since, like many people I've met, I was confused about the identities, functions, and trustworthiness of the divinities I'd heard of up till now and had received conflicting reports about some of them. For example, I'd heard that some goddesses were friendly, while others were considered not-so-amicable. I'd also received mixed reports about various ascended masters associated with the New Age, and gods and goddesses of ancient cultures and Eastern religions. And then there were all of those saints and archangels!

Personal Choices

I've never felt comfortable telling people who they "should" talk to in the spirit world. Although I work closely with Jesus, I don't feel compelled to push him onto others. My role has been akin to helping people set their radio dial to whatever station they feel comfortable listening to. In my books and workshops, I teach people how to open the channels of Divine communication so they can more clearly see, hear, feel, and know the messengers of Heaven.

As such, I consider this book to be more of an *introduction* to various ascended masters. I recommend that you create your own experience with each deity to see if you feel happier, healthier, and more peaceful as a result. That is, act like a scientist: Try working with these Divine beings, and then notice the results.

Calling on ascended masters isn't the same as worshiping them—far from it! It's more like the "Phone-a-Friend" segment on the TV game show *Who Wants to Be a Millionaire*. If you're not familiar with it, on this program, contestants can call any one of five friends to help them answer a difficult question. For example, if they're asked a question about algebra, they could phone their college math professor (while simultaneously praying to God for help).

On that show, just like in life, there may be *several* people you know who are available to help you. As far as I'm concerned, the more friends who can help you, the better!

In other words, you can work with Jesus as your primary guide, yet still develop a benevolent relationship with other wonderful beings. You don't have to align yourself with a particular religious group or engage in impeccable behavior to attract the guidance and assistance of ascended masters. You only need to call upon them with a sincere heart, which you'll read more about later on.

In ancient times, many of the deities listed in this book were worshiped in the same way that many of us currently worship our Creator. Today, we don't *worship* deities—we appreciate them. They have small *g*'s in front of their *god* and *goddess* titles to show that they're aspects of *the* God with a capital *G*. The deities represent the various faces, aspects, personality variables, and unique traits that God presents to us. And ultimately, since God is omnipresent, then God is within the deities and also within us. In other words, all of the deities and all of us are *one* with God.

Just so there's no misunderstanding, this isn't a book promoting *polytheism,* which is the belief in, and worship of, many gods. As mentioned above, the deities in this book are aspects or creations of *the* God, with a capital *G*. The point that needs to be emphasized is that I'm not encouraging you to engage in the *worship* of divinities, but to *appreciate* them as gifts that our Creator has given us to help us love more, heal in all ways, and evolve on our spiritual path. When we accept their help, we're saying *thank you* to God.

The world's three major religions are *monotheistic,* a term derived from the Greek words *monos,* meaning "only," and *theos,* meaning "God." Judaism, Christianity, and Islam are monotheistic because people affiliated with these faiths believe that there's only one God. Christianity divides God into three aspects: the Father, the Son, and the Holy Spirit; however, it emphasizes that these are all aspects of the one single Creator. In the same way, the angels, archangels, and ascended masters are one with God and fit into a monotheistic system.

Monotheism is in contrast to:

- **Agnosticism:** The lack of certainty about God, gods, spirituality, or religion. Someone who practices this is unsure or uncertain about God.

- **Atheism:** Denying the existence of God or spirituality.

- **Deism:** The belief and certainty in natural religion, emphasizing morality.

- **Henotheism:** The worship of just one God, while acknowledging that other gods exist (or at least, being open to the possibility).

- **Pantheism:** The belief that everything is God, and that God is in everything and everyone.

- **Polytheism:** The belief in, and worship of, many gods, instead of a single Creator.

A Treasure Chest of History

While conducting research for this book, I consulted dozens of books; encyclopedias about saints, gods, goddesses, divinities, and archangels; and experts in the field. I also reviewed pages and pages of channeled information, using my background as a psychic psychotherapist to access helpful and authentic material about ascended masters.

Some of the New Age material I came across seemed authentic, but was so filled with esoteric lingo that I felt that it would seem unfathomable to those not familiar with such terms. For instance, who but a seasoned New Ager would know what a "Chohan of the Sixth Ray" is? Yes, this was typical of the material I found during my research of New Age ascended masters.

I wanted to create a book filled with down-to-earth explanations of the who, what, and where of each ascended master. I also wanted to provide a simple way for people to discern which divinity to call upon for specific issues. For example, I wanted to explain whom to call upon for healing, for help with abundance issues, and for relationship and family matters.

It seemed simple enough, but the task was daunting, as there are thousands of deities. This undertaking was complicated by my desire to also research ascended masters popularized by Madame Blavatsky, co-founder of the Theosophical Society, and her successors, Alice Bailey and Elizabeth Clare Prophet. Blavatsky began channeling beings whom she called "Brothers and Mahatmas" in the late 1870s and early 1880s. Blavatsky made names such as Kathumi, Serapis Bey, El Morya, and Saint-Germain famous in New Age circles.

During her stage shows, Blavatsky would "call up" disembodied voices and ghostly male figures who materialized handwritten messages. The critics of her day charged that the letters were in Blavatsky's and her staff members' handwriting and that she paid people to appear onstage in the guise of ascended masters.

In 1915, Alice Bailey, the daughter of a wealthy British aristocratic family, met Blavatsky and immersed herself in Theosophy. Alice began receiving channeled messages from Kathumi, and also a Tibetan Master named Djwhal Khul. She published 24 books stemming from these channeled messages, which are filled with profound, extremely advanced spiritual concepts.

From the 1950s to the present day, Elizabeth Clare Prophet and her late husband, Mark, repopularized interest in these beings, and added a few of their own.

Blavatsky, Bailey, and Elizabeth Clare Prophet all used exotic-sounding language such as: "The threefold flame of life," and "Elohim of the third ray," which isn't clearly defined. However, my background in psychology, philosophy, and channeling taught me to keep an open mind. I'd heard about Kathumi, El Morya, and Master Hillarion for years, and I'd listened to Elizabeth Clare Prophet's taped lectures. I'd even had my own profound experiences with Serapis Bey and Saint-Germain.

But I wondered, *Who were these figures, really?* Being a consummate researcher, I wasn't satisfied to rely solely upon the channelings of others. I wanted to know more about these masters' historical backgrounds myself, and hear about other people's experiences with them.

While researching the "new" ascended masters, I came across thousands of references from different sources—many of whom quoted Blavatsky's, Bailey's, and Elizabeth Clare Prophet's channeled words verbatim. In other words, there weren't many other sources of information about the masters. I did learn, though, that several of the ascended masters' current personas were apparently based on real people who had actually lived, and that their names were pseudonymous to protect the real person's identity. In addition, Blavatsky, Bailey, and Prophet contended that the ascended masters often had past lives as famous personas such as Pythagorus, Christopher Columbus, and Saint Francis.

I continued to look into these new ascended masters, but in some cases, I hit a brick wall. It seems that there is little information known about the history of some of the New Age ascended masters—other than what Blavatsky, Bailey, and Prophet have written about them.

However, I knew from experience that channeling is multidimensional, and even a person who is channeling her own ego may also pick up authentic and ultimately helpful material. So I tried contacting the beings myself. I figured that if they answered, there might be some cause for further investigation, which perhaps a researcher even more tenacious than myself might be willing to tackle.

So, when I contacted some of the New Age deities and was greeted with profoundly loving experiences and amazing information, I was pleasantly surprised. I've included the various "new" or New Age ascended masters primarily as a reference tool to know who's who in the spirit world. In cases where their origins are dubious, I've noted so within the pages of this book.

The New Age ascended masters aren't so different from the "Old-Age" divinities, however. Many ancient deities were based on legend and tradition rather than living humans. The Greeks and Romans, for instance, never stated that their gods and goddesses were actual people who crossed over. To them, these deities started out in the spirit world and remained there.

As I contacted each Old Age and New Age deity, I was struck by the completeness and distinctiveness of each being's personality and energy. Talking with each one was akin to having unique conversations with a wide variety of powerful men and women.

Often, I'd forestall doing the research on a deity until after I'd first contacted him or her. I was amazed by how closely my personal experiences matched the written descriptions of that deity's unique traits and characteristics. For instance, when I contacted Artemis, a powerful pixielike woman appeared to me. I later saw paintings of her that perfectly matched the way I saw her.

I was also struck by how similar the birth stories of the male deities were. Repeatedly, I read tales telling of a patriarchal figure who would issue sweeping orders to execute all the male babies in his kingdom because he was threatened by potential competition. The mother of the infant would hide her son, and the child would grow up in powerful circumstances that encouraged his spiritual knowledge and encouraged him to become a great hero.

I also read many accounts of a male deity being born to a rich or royal family, and then denying his heritage in favor of spiritual teaching and leadership. I started to realize that these stories were archetypal legends that may or may not be based upon historical fact.

Perhaps these stories—and even the deities themselves—provide a way to teach people about some aspect of God, such as the potential for His healing ability to be encased within the persona of a healing god. Or, maybe if we focus our prayers and thoughts on a concept over time—such as a goddess or god—the collective thought-forms gel into a living spiritual organism that behaves in the way we've come to expect. All of our human thought power is encapsulated into this deity, and comes back to us like principal and interest in a spiritual bank account. It's possible that we humans tap in to divinities that already exist. Or it's possible that our collective beliefs and legends "create" these beings, who then come to have a real life force of their own.

Surrounded by Love

My job with this book was clear: I was to select a few ascended masters, get to know them personally, do research on each one, channel messages from them, and then write down my experiences and recommendations. You hold the result in your hands. I apologize if I've left out your favorite ascended master. I needed to keep my list somewhat concise so as to not overwhelm you, the reader, with a multitude of deities. Through prayer and hard work, my intent was to create a book covering a wide range of divinities that would offer something for everyone.

While researching and writing this book, I had the wonderful opportunity to "hang out" with these amazingly wonderful, loving, and powerful divinities. I would often work late into the night after teaching a workshop all day long. So, my last thoughts before hitting the pillow would be about the goddess or *bodhisattva* I'd just finished writing about. During the night, I'd feel that I was surrounded by loving energy, as I would often be contacted by the divinities. I'd awaken feeling refreshed, utterly filled with Divine love!

Most of the channelings recorded in this book occurred outdoors, in fantastic natural settings. I was fortunate enough to spend time leaning against the magical rocks of Stonehenge and Avesbury in England; gazing at the mystical Irish Sea; climbing up the craggy volcanic coast of Kona, Hawaii; walking across the verdant hills of New Zealand; and stepping among the towering boulders of Joshua Tree, California, while channeling these messages.

One remarkable experience occurred during the channelings. I'd discovered that each ascended master delivered completely unique messages to me, and that each one had a distinct personality and style. Yet I was amazed that two ascended masters, Maitreya and Hotei, gave me virtually the same message word for word—both talked about the importance of joy and laughter. I'd channeled them several days apart, yet their messages seemed to be a continuation of the other, so I asked them to tell me what was going on.

A few hours later, I found myself in a shop that carried Buddhist materials. The first book that I selected opened almost automatically to a page about Hotei. Imagine my amazement when the material explained that Maitreya and Hotei *were the same beings!* I continued my investigation and found that this was correct. No wonder they'd told me the same thing!

❦ ❦ ❦ ❦

As a result of writing this book, I've discovered some ascended masters whom I didn't realize I was already working with. I've also consciously developed close relationships with some deities who are new to me. As you read along, you'll see that these relationships have been joyful and miraculous. My prayer is that you'll experience these beings as the loving friends that they are, and enjoy the powerful assistance that they offer us.

Within these pages, I also describe the ascended masters whom I consider to be highly trustworthy. These beings work closely with the Creator, our guardian angels, and all lightworkers on Earth to steer us in the direction of peace. They donate their afterlife time toward this cause, when they could be relaxing in the spirit world instead.

The divinities can also assist us with situations that may come up in the future, inspired by Earth and societal changes. They can help us avert "natural disasters," avoid or contain wars, ensure adequate food and water supplies, and heal our bodies. No matter what happens, the archangels and ascended masters will be with us. No one can take them away from us! And that's one more reason why it's wise for lightworkers to become familiar with the various divinities, and to be aware of the special gifts they offer. In the future, these Divinities will prove to be valuable allies (just as they are in the present).

The Newer Masters

There are some very powerful beings who have recently departed their physical bodies who are helping planet Earth from their home in the spirit world. A few of them are well known, while many are obscure personalities whose names you wouldn't recognize. I've come into contact with many of these "New Masters" during my readings, including Dr. Martin Luther King, Jr., Walt Disney, John Denver, and Mother Teresa.

However, I didn't include them in the body of this book because they're more along the lines of "famous spirit guides," rather than seasoned ascended masters. We can definitely call upon these great beings for help, and they will also offer assistance without our conscious realization. Several decades from now, these beings will likely move to the higher frequencies of their ascended associates.

When I was sitting next to the stones of Stonehenge, for example, the late Princess Diana began speaking to me while I was recording messages from Celtic deities. I didn't invoke her or call upon her; she came to me on her own. She mentioned right up front that she knows she wasn't considered the greatest mother, but said that her children were always of the greatest concern to her.

She then clearly said to me, *"Now the world's children are foremost on my mind. The children of the world are at a crossroads and in great need of leadership. I'm concerned for their welfare, as are you and a great many others. There is a schism with their underlying mass, as they reach for attainment of their way. The bubbling undercurrent of dissatisfaction among them is bursting into violent rage.*

"Just as my death was considered quite violent, so do I also see many outbursts by youth on the horizon that will shock us all . . . unless intervention can be reached.

"A grassroots campaign by mothers is the only solution that will lead us out of this ditch that has been created, a ditch buried with children, their parents, and their educators. This ditch is sinking deeper by the minute, and there is no time to waste.

"Many of us here have formed a committee to oversee adult volunteers who want to do something about it. Ask me to give you an assignment if you're hard-pressed to know what's expected of you in this campaign."

It's interesting that people whom I meet in North America readily see Princess Di as a benevolent spiritual helper, but the idea isn't so acceptable in Great Britain, where she was often vilified when she was alive. Regardless, I found her message quite compelling, which is why I included it here.

Ask from Love

The divinities described in this book are quite real. If you're new to working with spirit guides, or you're skeptical about their existence, you'll soon find that just *reading* this book is an invocation to the great divinities by your side. They will all come rapidly to whoever calls, without exception.

I had many powerful experiences with the divinities while writing this book. For instance, I still had about half of the deities to record invocations for after I'd finished the bulk of the book, so over a period of two days, I wrote invocations nonstop. I finished writing them the morning before a flight from Chicago's O'Hare airport into Phoenix's Sky Harbor airport—two very large, crowded places.

All that day, my husband and I kept marveling at how smoothly everything was going. For instance, the airport personnel were exceptionally nice, I had one of the best vegan meals I'd ever had on a plane, we were upgraded to a wonderful hotel room in Phoenix, and doors kept opening for us throughout the balance of the day. Steven and I noticed that we each felt wonderful, both physically and emotionally.

"What a great day this is," we kept saying to each other. "Everything's going so well!" Then we realized why: I'd invoked so many deities prior to the flight that we were being helped and guided by Heaven's cream of the crop!

%‰℣℣

Some advice I'd like to impart to you is this: Be sure to only ask the deities to help you with tasks associated with Divine love. If you ask them to fulfill a request involving revenge or acrimony, the negative energy will bounce back to you magnified. If you're in a situation where you're angry with someone, it's best to ask the divinities to create a peaceful solution instead of extracting a pound of flesh from the other person. After all, your true goal is always peace, and the ascended masters are very happy to manifest this for you. In fact, ascended masters help anyone who asks—regardless of that person's spiritual, religious, or lifestyle background—because they're here to enact God's plan of worldwide peace, one person at a time. Please don't worry that you're wasting the deities' time by asking for so-called small favors. If those favors bring you peace, then it's these beings' sacred honor to help you.

Besides, they're not limited to just helping one person at a time. The ascended masters can help an infinite number of people simultaneously, while having a uniquely personal experience with each individual.

The Format and Layout of This Book

This is not an all-inclusive book about deities by any means. Instead, as I mentioned earlier, I've limited my selection of ascended masters to those I've had positive experiences with. I've also whittled down the background material concerning these beings. This book doesn't tackle the entire mythological history of, for instance, the sun god Apollo. Instead, it offers enough information so that you can understand how Apollo and the other deities can become part of your spiritual team. Should you desire more background information on a particular ascended master, you can consult one of the exhaustive encyclopedias available on the subject—several of which are listed in the Bibliography.

In Part I, you'll find the most commonly used name of the divinity, alternate names, and his or her country, religion, or affiliation of origin. Then, you'll read a brief history and background about the being, followed by a current story or channeling (I've put the deities' words in *italics* to make them stand out from the rest of the text). Next, there's a list called "Helps with," outlining the specific life areas that the divinity offers assistance with.

After that, I've presented an invocation that will help you contact that particular deity. The invocations provided in this book are suggestions, not hard-and-fast rules. In fact, I like to think of them as "invitations" rather than "invocations." If you're new to working with invocations, then this book will give you a great starting point. However, in much the same way that you add your own variations to recipes while cooking, you're encouraged to use your own wording to invoke the deities. After all, the specific words that you use don't matter to the ascended masters. It's the fact that you called upon them, and that you've opened your heart in an effort to receive spiritual help.

Part II lists prayers you can use when working with multiple divinities, applicable to specific problems or situations. Just as with the invocations in Part I, these prayers are merely templates and not rigid directives. Use the words that come into your heart and mind as your guide. Then you can't go wrong when calling upon divinities. They're loving and entirely forgiving, so don't worry that eloquence is required to elicit their help!

In Part III, you'll find desired goals and life areas of all types, such as "Increasing Faith" or "Finding Soulmate Relationships." Beneath each heading are all the ascended masters and archangels who specialize in that particular area. This is a list that I've always wanted to use in my own life, and it's one of the reasons why I was guided to write this book. You'll find that it's a handy reference guide to keep nearby so you'll know whom to consult during times of need.

Part IV lists various reference materials that you may find useful, such as a Glossary of Terms, and a Bibliography for further information.

This book can also function as an oracle device. Just ask any question and allow the pages to fall open. Whatever page it opens to is the one that can provide an answer to your question.

My prayer is that this work will serve as an introduction to the Divine beings who will become your close, loving companions. May this be the beginning of many beautiful relationships with the archangels and ascended masters!

PART I

The Archangels & Ascended Masters

Abundantia
(Roman; Teutonic)

Also known as *Abundia, Habone, Fulla.*

A beautiful goddess of success, prosperity, abundance, and good fortune, Abundantia is also considered to be a protector of savings, investments, and wealth. Her image graced Roman coins in centuries past.

In Roman mythology, Abundantia brought money and grain to people while they were sleeping, shaking her gifts from the cornucopia she continuously carried.

In Norse mythology, she was called Fulla, the first and favorite attendant of Frigg (the Norse goddess of the atmosphere and clouds). Fulla carried Frigg's valuables for her, and also acted as her intermediary, performing favors for mortals who called upon the goddess for help.

Every time I see Abundantia, gold coins magically spill from her, from no particular container. The coins just seem to pour out of her, and even trail behind her, accompanied by a musical jangling sound similar to belly dancers who jingle their coin-laden outfits.

She's a vision of great beauty and angelic purity, very patient and extremely loving. *"I'm a way-shower to the mighty Source of all,"* she says. *"It's my greatest pleasure to reward your efforts, and I become ecstatic at the sound of gratitude and joy when someone is rescued through my interventions. I'm here to serve, to help you plan for uninterrupted financial bliss, and to uncover hidden treasures that you do not yet know of."*

Abundantia is like a gracious hostess, constantly asking if you need anything, and then lovingly fulfilling your every wish. She says, *"I also easily come into your dreams to answer any questions you may have about high finance, investments, and such. Never forget that finances can fuel healing projects and afford you freedom where time is concerned. But money can also be a trap if you allow worry and concern to rule over you. That's where I come in: to alleviate these lower thoughts and take you to the high road of prosperity."*

Helps with:

- Abundance, attracting all kinds of
- Financial investments, guidance about and protection of
- Good fortune
- Valuables, protecting

INVOCATION

As a show of your faith in Heaven's readiness to help you, hold one or more coins in the hand you don't write with (this is your receptive hand), and say:

"Beautiful Abundantia, I desire to be like you—carefree and filled with faith that my supply is already met in all ways. Help me replace any money worries with joy and gratitude. Help me open my arms so that Heaven may easily help me. Thank you for all of your guidance, gifts, and protection. I'm truly grateful, and I'm abundantly joyful and fulfilled. I let go, and relax in the sure knowledge that I'm completely taken care of, immediately and in the future."

Aengus
(Ireland)

Also known as *Angus, Oenghus, Angus McOg, Angus of the Brugh*.

Aengus is a Celtic god of soulmate love. His name means "young son." Aengus plays a magical golden harp that mesmerizes all who hear its sweet melodies. Like Cupid, he draws soulmates together. Whenever romance is threatened by quarrels or outside interference, Aengus weaves a net of his golden harp music around the lovers and draws them back together. It's said that when he blows a kiss, it turns into a beautiful bird who carries his romantic messages to lovers who ask for his help. Aengus lives among the fairies in a *brugh* (a fairy glen). He's the half-brother of the goddess Brigit.

Aengus's help with love relationships is legendary, beginning with his introduction to his own soulmate, Caer. Aengus first saw Caer in a dream, and his heart immediately swelled with the deepest of love for her. Upon awakening, Aengus went on a search for his beloved, although he didn't yet know who or where she was. But the determined Aengus eventually found Caer, who was bound by silver chains to beautiful swans. Aengus shape-shifted into a swan in order to successfully rescue her, and they were united in love forever.

The two soulmates sang and played romantic music to lovers everywhere. He also escorted two young lovers named Diarmuid and Grainne out of harm's way. Once they were safely ensconced, Aengus confronted their persecutor until he agreed to stop pursuing the two lovers.

It was very fitting that I first met Aengus when I called to him from my bench overlooking the Irish sea, south of Dublin. A very handsome, princely, and regal-looking man in his late 20s to mid-30s appeared to me. *"Let your servant be your master,"* he told me in a warm accent. What did this koan mean? He used it in the context of romantic love, like a key to establishing and maintaining a great relationship. He seemed to imply that this was particularly a secret for romantic dealings with men. But I still didn't know what he meant. So I sat back and meditated on the phrase.

Then, Aengus told me more: *"Never become a slave or captive to any person, substance, or situation. Be a willing servant. Give freely from a willing heart. In this way, you ensure freedom from the ensnarement of resentment, which builds up like plaque around the fond heart and extinguishes rapture. Give freely to your love, without regard for reward or consequences, but simply motivated by the pure pleasure that comes from giving . . . and that is its own reward."*

Helps with:

- Music, the romantic use of
- Passion and romance—rekindling it and keeping it alive
- Soulmate relationships—finding, creating, and protecting

INVOCATION

Wear or hold something red or pink to symbolize romance, play some soft music (preferably with harps), and call to Aengus:

"Princely Aengus, I ask for your help with my love life [describe your specific desires]. I ask for your intervention, that you may bring harmony, passion, and romance into my heart and life. I have so much love to share, and I need your help. If I'm blocking great love in some way, please help me release this block now. Thank you, Aengus."

Aeracura
(Ireland)

Aeracura is a Celtic Earth mother and Earth deity who carries a basket of fruit, or horn-of-plenty.

When I called upon her while sitting by the Irish sea, my heart immediately felt uplifted with the most lighthearted and playful type of love! I saw a beautiful fairy woman with porcelain skin and flowing light brown hair, wearing a creamy body-skimming gown that glowed. She had love in her eyes, but with a glimmer of one who enjoys a good laugh and a bit of harmless mischief in the most innocent way. She let me know that playfulness and a carefree spirit are at the heart of abundant manifestation. She emphasized this point, and I felt it in my body and heart chakra: The key to rapid and efficient manifestation is enjoyment of the process.

She said, *"I will always bring a basket of goodies to those who are receptive, mindful, and willing to receive. Think of my bountiful gifts as children who share toys with each other. It's more fun to play when you share with your friends! Call upon me for emergency money, and I shall rush to your rescue. I'm especially fond of supporting artists and nonconformists. Be not bashful in saying what you desire as you approach me. Notice how my name has a derivative of the word* cure *in it. Let's play! I love you!"*

Helps with:

- Artists and inventors, guiding and supporting
- Emergency money
- Manifestations

INVOCATION

Go outside to call upon Aeracura. Take off your shoes and socks and connect to Mother Earth with bare feet. Say to her:

"Dearest Aeracura, please come to me now. Please fill my heart with your great Divine love. Please clear my heart and mind of cares and worries. I ask that you bring your basket of bountiful gifts to me, and help me receive these gifts with love and gratitude. Help me tap in to my creativity and unleash my inner artist, to help express my love in a way that benefits the world. Please help me accept support for my artistic and creative projects."

Aine
(Ireland)

Also known as *Aine of Knockaine,* because her spirit is said to
live in a castle in Knockainy, Ireland.

Aine is an Irish moon goddess of love, fertility, protection, and environmental concerns. Her name means "bright." She's aligned with the fairies, and is often thought of as a Fairy Queen (the equivalent of an archangel in the elemental kingdom). There are many conflicting stories about Aine's beginnings and heritage as a goddess.

She was worshiped on Midsummer Eve with rituals where people would hold torches over farm fields to ask Aine for help with productivity. She protects women, especially those who respect the planet's sanctity and revere Mother Earth and her plight. She's a strong environmentalist and also keenly involved in animal rights. She can clear away curses and negative energies.

Looking like an Erté painting from a *Harper's Bazaar* magazine cover, Aine is a lithe goddess with a distinctive art-deco look to her long, silvery gown and pageboy hairstyle. When I spoke with her, she was poised next to a crescent moon, surrounded by musical instruments such as harps and pianos. Using the energy of light and musical tones, she oversees and assists Earth and other planets in this and other solar systems.

Aine isn't here so much to help us with individual concerns, but she says we can drape ourselves in her cloak of silver light anytime we seek to regain our strength, and summon up the courage to speak up, especially when performing leadership roles that will help the environment (including anything related to air and water quality, plants, and animals). Aine can help you be more playful and passionate in love relationships, as well as in your entire life. She's analogous to an archangel for the fairy and deva kingdoms—their goddess. She's especially accessible during full moons and lunar eclipses.

She says, *"I radiate Divine pure love energy like a satellite beam, positioned from the moon to divert any poisonous intentions, deeds, words, thoughts, or actions."*

Helps with:

- Animal rights and healing
- Environmental concerns
- Faith and passion, increasing
- Fertility and child conception
- Healing animals, people, and relationships
- Full-moon meditations and ceremonies
- Playfulness and enjoyment of life
- Protection, especially for women

INVOCATION

On the evening of a full moon, go outside near plants or a body of water and say aloud or mentally:

"Beloved Aine, I call upon you now. Please help me grow stronger, more powerful, and more filled with faith. Please ignite the passions of my soul, and help me relax enough to have fun and be playful while I fulfill my mission and responsibilities. Please guide me as to how I can best help the world's environment, and please surround me with loving people."

Aphrodite
(Greece)

Also known as *Cytherea, Cypris, Aphrodite Pandemos,*
Aphrodite Urania, Venus.

A phrodite is the goddess of love, beauty, and passion, associated with
the planet Venus.

Her name means "water born" or "foam born," because it's been said
that she was conceived when her father, the sky god Uranus, impreg-
nated the ocean. Her multiple love affairs with gods such as Adonis and
Ares are legendary, and that's also why Aphrodite is closely associated
with passionate sexuality.

She's known as both Aphrodite Urania, representing soulmate love
with commitment and spirituality; and Aphrodite Pandemos, representing purely physical lust. One of her many children is Eros, a god of
romantic love who in Cupid-like fashion sends arrows to those on his
matchmaking list.

I spoke with Aphrodite one evening in Kona, Hawaii, when the
planet Venus was high in the sky. As she came to me, I felt her before I
could see her. Then I saw a woman's face enclosed in a Valentine's heart.

*"I'm here to help strengthen long-term relationships, built on a dual
foundation of passion and understanding,"* she said.

*"One without the other is useless. One is for intertwining lives and bod-
ies; the other, for talks and discussions. Even still, there is much overlap, for*

a lover who understands your needs and desires is a great lover indeed. And a partner who holds passion in the heart toward you will be motivated to heal occasional hurts and wounds, and be captivated long enough to attain an understanding.

"The nature of the ever-growing, ever-living relationship is one that always thirsts after more passion and more knowledge within the context of commitment."

Helps with:

- Commitment, engagements, and marriage
- Femininity, gracefulness, beauty, and attraction/attractiveness
- Sexuality, including increasing desire and romantic passion

INVOCATION

Put yourself in a receptive mood, perhaps by listening to romantic music, watching a movie about lovers, dressing seductively, or holding a rose. Then, focus on your heart and say aloud or mentally:

"Aphrodite, I'm open to being loved deeply and completely in a romantic relationship. Please help me release any remaining blocks that could delay this manifestation. I ask that you help me radiate my inner light, and attract great love now. Please help me fully enjoy this love, and to know that I deserve it."

Apollo
(Greece)

A pollo is a sun god who oversees prophecy, light, music, and healing.

Apollo is one of the original 12 Olympian gods and goddesses. He's the son of Zeus and twin brother of the goddess Artemis. Apollo had many lovers and dozens of offspring. Legends abound about Apollo's birth family and life. One of his most famous children is Asclepius, the legendary god of healing and medicine, for whom hospitals are named after.

Apollo has always willingly offered his help to humans who need it, and he continues to intervene where needed today. He spent much time in ancient Delphi, helping oracles and prophets with their divinations. Today he helps psychics and spiritual mediums elevate their gifts to the highest of spiritual frequencies. In New Age circles, Apollo is known as an *Elohim* (which in Hebrew means "divinities"), who bestows Divine wisdom and spiritual understanding upon Earth and her inhabitants.

Apollo heals physical and emotional wounds and awakens psychic gifts by helping to replace unforgiveness with compassion and understanding. He's extremely handsome, with a lean and golden muscular form that radiates youthful beauty. Apollo motivates us to take excellent care of our bodies, and to make physical fitness an intricate part of our lifestyle.

He says, *"I am the sun god—invoke me for light of any type: Divine, mechanical, radiant, healing, or a sunshiny day. I now exist in all dimensions, so I'm available to respond to all levels of concerns. I infuse your planet with light, even on the dreariest of days."*

Helps with:

- Exercise and healthful eating; increasing motivation
- Happy endings to stressful situations
- Mechanical problems, fixing
- Psychic, clairvoyant, and prophetic abilities—opening and polishing
- Weather—banishing clouds in favor of sunshine, both literally and metaphorically

INVOCATION

Wear or hold something golden or yellow (like the sunlight associated with Apollo), and play lively music. Apollo can be contacted anytime you need assistance; however, you may have the best connection at high noon when the sun is at its peak. Say to Apollo:

"Brightest of the bright, Apollo, please come to me now. Please shine light upon me so that I may see it clearly. Help me gain a deeper understanding of my situation so that I and everyone involved may be healed. Help me feel compassion for myself and others, and to release any anger or unforgiveness now. Please help me lose all heaviness in my body, mind, and heart so that I may soar high like you."

Archangel Ariel
(Cabalistic)

Also known as *Arael, Ariael.*

Ariel's name means "lion or lioness of God," and this archangel, predictably, is often associated with lions. When Ariel is near, you might begin seeing references to, or visions of, lions around you. In fact, some artwork portrays Ariel as having a lion's head. This archangel is also associated with the wind, so when Ariel is around, you may feel or hear the wind as a sign.

Archangel Ariel is described in books of Judaic mysticism and cabalistic magic, such as *The Testament of Solomon, The Greater Key of Solomon, Ezra,* and *The Hierarchy of the Blessed Angels.* Ariel works closely with King Solomon in conducting manifestation, spirit releasement (similar to exorcism), and Divine magic.

Ariel also oversees the sprites, the nature angels associated with water. Sprites are similar to fairies, and their purpose is to maintain healthy environments near oceans, lakes, rivers, streams, and ponds. Archangel Ariel may contact you to help with this mission of purifying and protecting these water bodies and their inhabitants. If you help with Ariel's environmental mission, you may be rewarded with wonderful manifestations and increased magical power.

Ariel is very involved with healing and protecting nature—and that definitely includes animals, fish, and birds—especially wild ones. If you find an injured bird or other nondomesticated animal who needs healing, call upon Ariel for help. Ariel works with Archangel Raphael to heal animals in need.

Archangel Ariel says, *"I'm deeply concerned about the world's environmental systems, which are always in delicate balance and are now in need of reform and restoration. I have plenty of assignments available for those willing to assist in this endeavor. I promise to only give out assignments that are related to your interests and time schedules. Your reward will be the joy that stretches out from your heart, extending into the very environment you're blessing with your dedicated efforts. I thank you very much for coming to the planet's rescue!"*

Helps with:

- Divine magic
- Environmentalism, especially concerning water bodies
- Manifestation
- Wild animals, fish, and birds—healing and protecting

INVOCATION

Call upon Archangel Ariel anytime, anywhere. However, you'll be most likely to feel, hear, see, and know her presence if you conduct this invocation outside in nature (especially near a body of water):

"Archangel Ariel, I call upon your presence now. I desire to help heal the world's environment, and I ask you to give me a Divine assignment for this important mission. I ask that you open the way and support me in this endeavor. Thank you for the joy that this mission brings to me and the world."

Archangel Azrael
(Hebrew, Muslim)

Also known as *Azrail, Ashriel, Azriel, Azaril, The Angel of Death.*

Azrael's name means "whom God helps." His role is primarily to help people cross over to Heaven at the time of physical death. Azrael comforts people prior to their physical passing, makes sure they don't suffer during death, and helps them assimilate on the other side. He also surrounds grieving family members with healing energy and Divine light to help them cope and thrive. Azrael lends support to surviving friends and family members, easing their journey in material, spiritual, and emotional ways. If you've lost someone, call upon Azrael for support and comfort.

Azrael also works with grief counselors to shield them from absorbing their clients' pain, and to guide their words and actions for maximum effectiveness. Call upon Azrael to bring comfort to a dying loved one, and to help during the time of crossing over. Azrael will be there for everyone concerned. You can also ask Azrael to help your departed loved one, and to meet with him or her in Heaven.

Archangel Azrael is very quiet and composed. He has great respect for the grieving process, and he doesn't impose upon those who are going through it. Moreover, Azrael stands by as a source of quiet strength and comfort.

He says, *"During sleepless nights of anxious grieving, where you toss and turn, I can ease your restless mind and help you sleep. A rested mind and body is stronger and more able to withstand the grieving process. So, do not hesitate to call on me for my prayers, assistance, or intercession during times of need. I will invoke other angels alongside you and your loved ones, and we will do everything within God's power to support you with dynamic love."*

Helps with:

- Comforting the dying and the grieving
- Crossing over the newly deceased person's soul
- Grief counseling
- Support for the grieving—material, spiritual, and emotional

INVOCATION

No special attire or behavior is necessary to call upon Archangel Azrael—just a sincere desire to help in a situation involving grief or death. Just think the thought, and Azrael is there. A sample invocation is:

"Archangel Azrael, please comfort me now. Please help me to heal. Please lift my heart above heaviness and help me realize the blessings that this situation holds. Please help me release my tears and connect to my beloved in Heaven. I ask that you infuse this connection with energy so that I may clearly communicate with [him or her]. I know that my loved one is nearby and that you watch over both of us. [If there is any situation related to the grief that you need help with, tell Azrael about it now.] Thank you, Azrael."

Archangel Chamuel
(Judeo-Christian)

Also known as *Camael, Camiel, Camiul, Camniel, Cancel,*
Jahoel, Kemuel, Khamael, Seraphiel, Shemuel.

Chamuel's name means "he who sees God," or "he who seeks God."
Chamuel is usually on the list of the seven core archangels, and he's
considered a powerful leader in the angelic hierarchy known as the
"Powers." The Powers are angels who oversee protection of the world
from fearful and lower energies. They act like bouncers who turn away
anyone who would attempt to overtake the world in a negative way. If
you're fearful about world events, call upon Chamuel for comfort, protection, and intervention.

Chamuel also protects our personal world, too. He helps us seek out
important parts of our lives, such as love relationships, friends, careers,
lost items, and our life purpose. Chamuel works with us to build strong
foundations for our relationships and careers so that they're long-lasting,
meaningful, and healthy.

Archangel Chamuel is very kind, loving, and sweet. You'll know he's
with you when you feel butterflies in your stomach and a pleasant tingling in your body. He says, *"Allow me to escort you through life's travers-*
es, and to make your journey smooth and successful. It's my greatest pleasure
to bring in peacefulness to replace any energy of pain."

461

Helps with:

- Career, life purpose, and lost items—finding
- Relationships, building and strengthening
- Soulmates, seeking out
- World peace

INVOCATION

Call upon Chamuel to recover anything that seems to be lost. He hears your thoughts, so you can mentally call him, even in when you're in a panic:

> "Archangel Chamuel, I seem to have lost [name of object or situation]. I know that nothing is truly lost, since God is every-where, and therefore, can see where everything is. Please guide me to find what I'm looking for. Thank you, Chamuel."

Archangel Gabriel
(Judeo-Christian, Muslim)

Also known as *Abruel, Jibril, Jiburili, Serafili.*

Gabriel's name means "God is my strength." Gabriel (who is female) is the famous angel who told Elizabeth and Mary of the impending births of their sons, John the Baptist and Jesus of Nazareth, respectively. The Archangel Gabriel also dictated the spiritual text of Islam, The Koran, to Mohammed. As a result, Gabriel became known as the "messenger" angel. Gabriel's role continues in the world, helping both parents and human messengers.

In the first role, Gabriel guides hopeful parents toward child conception or through the process of adopting a child. Gabriel gives strength and courage to these parents, and helps moms-to-be stay centered in blissful faith to create the best atmosphere for their baby.

In the second role, the archangel helps anyone whose life purpose involves art or communication. Call upon Gabriel for help, guidance, and agenting if you're an actor, artist, author, dancer, journalist, model, musician, reporter, singer, songwriter, teacher, or do anything involving delivering spiritual messages. Gabriel will open doors to help you express your talent in a big way. The archangel also acts as a coach, inspiring and motivating artists and communicators, and helping them to overcome fear and procrastination.

Gabriel has long been known as a powerful and strong archangel, and those who call upon her will find themselves pushed into action that leads to beneficial results. Gabriel is definitely an archangel of action! She says, *"I'm here to manage those who speak up and speak out on behalf of societal needs. This process of advocacy is an ancient one, and few things have changed over the course of time, save for some technological advances. In other arenas, though, art and speech have maintained a constant and steady force, lending power to people who desire change and helpfulness. Allow me to open the doors of opportunity for those among you hearing your heart's call to perform, play, and create on a wider scale."*

Helps with:

- Adopting a child
- Artists and art-related projects
- Child conception and fertility
- Journalism and writing
- Television and radio work

INVOCATION

Before beginning any artistic or communication project, ask Gabriel to guide and oversee your activities by saying aloud or mentally:

"Archangel Gabriel, I ask for your presence as I [describe the project]. Please open my creative channels so that I may be truly inspired. Help me open my mind so that I may give birth to unique ideas. And please help me to sustain the energy and motivation to follow through on this inspiration. Thank you, Gabriel."

Archangel Haniel
(Babylonian, Cabalistic)

Also known as *Anael, Aniel, Hamiel, Onoel.*

Haniel's name means "glory of God," or "grace of God." In ancient Babylon, a group of men known as "priests-astronomers" worked with astrology, astronomy, moon energy, and various deities for their divination and spiritual healing work. One of the archangels with whom they worked was Haniel, who was associated with the planet Venus.

Some Cabalistic texts credit Haniel as escorting Enoch to the spirit world. Enoch was one of only two humans to ever be transformed into archangels—in his case, into the Archangel Metatron. (The other case was the prophet Elijah ascending into the Archangel Sandalphon, as you'll read about later on.)

Haniel helps us recover the lost secrets of natural healing remedies, especially involving the harnessing of the moon's energy in potions, powders, and crystals. Haniel also helps us enjoy more grace in our lives. To add beauty, harmony, and the company of wonderful friends to your life, call upon Haniel. This archangel will also help you stay poised and centered before and during any important event, such as a speech, performance, first date, or job interview.

Archangel Haniel has a moon goddess energy: etheric, quiet, patient, and mystical. Haniel's wisdom comes from many eons of experience in working with humans. She says, *"Yes, I'm patient with humanity because I can see all the good they've created. For every moment of intolerance, there are hundreds of deep kindnesses to overshadow the darkness. The light of humanity shines brighter today than ever. If you could see humanity from my point of view, you'd know why I have such deep regard and love for you all. I'm happy to help in whatever cause advances humanity above the din of clashing egos, and elevates you to the level from which you have come: God's grace and eternal beauty."*

Helps with:

- Grace, bringing it into our lives
- Healing abilities
- Moon energy
- Poise
- Psychic abilities, especially clairvoyance

INVOCATION

If you've got an important function coming up that demands an excellent performance or refined social graces, ask Haniel to accompany you. You can call upon Haniel by thinking her name and describing your need, or by stating a formal invocation such as:

> "Archangel Haniel, overseer of grace, poise, and charm, please bring your Divine energy of loving wisdom to [describe the situation]. Thank you for guiding my words, actions, and mannerisms and helping me to enjoy myself, while bringing blessings to everyone who sees or hears me. I ask that your Divine magnetism draw only positive energies to me. O thank you, glorious Haniel, thank you."

Archangel Jeremiel
(Judaic)

Also known as *Ramiel, Remiel.*

Jeremiel's name means "mercy of God." In ancient Judaic texts, Jeremiel is listed as one of the seven core archangels.

He's also associated with helping Baruch, a prolific author of apocryphal Judaic texts in the first century A.D., with his prophetic visions. One vision, catalyzed by Jeremiel, was of the coming Messiah. In another vision, Jeremiel took Baruch for a tour of the different levels of Heaven.

In addition to being an Archangel of prophetic visions, Jeremiel helps newly crossed-over souls review their lives. This is a service he helps the still-living with, too. If you'd like to take an inventory of your life up till now so that you can make positive adjustments, call upon Jeremiel. He will help you fearlessly assess your history and learn from prior experiences so that you're even stronger and more centered in love in the future.

Jeremiel says, *"A life review today, held at regular intervals, will prove to be of great benefit to you in determining your next station and steps. By reviewing your life along the way, you make your duty that much more enjoyable when you get to the other side. You'll already have reviewed the major crossroads, and won't suffer or have regrets when you admit to yourself that you could have done better.*

"A life review is far more comprehensive on the other side, of course, but you can compose one while you're still in physicality. Carve out some quiet time and ask me to enter your thoughts or dreams at night. I shall display pictures of major events within your life that will spark your memory of smaller occurrences. It's often in those seemingly minor interactions with other people that your greatest realizations occur. This is where life lessons often spring from. Then, you can easily base your philosophies and decisions upon what you've realized, which will always be for the benefit of everyone involved."

Helps with:

- Clairvoyance and prophetic visions
- Life reviews and making life changes
- Psychic dreams, including their interpretations

INVOCATION

If you're concerned about the future, call upon Jeremiel for additional insight and information:

"Archangel Jeremiel, please help me release fears, worries, and tension about my future . . . and the future of the world. [Tell Jeremiel about any situation that is weighing particularly on your mind.] I ask for your prophetic insights about the future. Please clearly give me guidance about anything that I may do or change to create the highest and best future for myself and all concerned. Thank you."

Archangel Jophiel
(Judeo-Christian)

Also known as *Iofiel, Iophiel, Jofiel, Zophiel.*

Jophiel's name means "beauty of God." This archangel is known as "the Patron of Artists." She was present in the Garden of Eden, and later, she watched over Noah's sons.

As the archangel of art and beauty, Jophiel helps us metaphysically and physically. First, Jophiel helps us think beautiful thoughts; to see and appreciate beauty around us; and to, therefore, create, manifest, and attract more beauty into our lives. After all, beautiful thoughts lead to beautiful outcomes.

In the physical world, Jophiel helps with artistic projects and illuminates our creative spark. She gives us ideas and the energy to carry out artistic ventures. Jophiel also helps us create beauty at home, at work, and in our relationships. She helps us to slow down and smell the roses.

Archangel Jophiel has an uplifting energy that's fun and pleasant to be around. She's friendly and positive, like an ideal best friend. She says, *"Worry never helped anything, so why turn to it during times of need? It won't nurture or heal you—quite the opposite, actually. It's so much better to put the effort into something creative as a way to quietly meditate through positive action. Create, create, create! In this way, you mirror God's own creativity. That's why you feel closest to God when you're fully engaged in writing, speaking, and other artistic projects."*

Helps with:

- Artistic projects and artists
- Beautiful thoughts
- Interior decorating
- Slowing down from a hectic pace

INVOCATION

If you find yourself in an ugly situation, chances are good that ugly thoughts helped to manifest it. Call upon Jophiel to turn things around:

"Archangel Jophiel, please help me with [describe the situation]. Thank you for helping me see the inner Divine beauty within myself and everyone involved. Thank you for your intervention in creating a beautiful outcome. In gratitude, and in the name of all that is beautiful, I thank you, Jophiel."

Archangel Metatron
(Judaic, Cabalistic)

Also known as *Metatetron, Merraton, Metaraon, Mittron.*

The meaning of Metatron's name isn't clear, since his name doesn't end in the "el" suffix of all the other archangels (with the exception of Metatron's twin brother, Sandalphon). "El" stands for "El Elyah," the Hebrew name of the all-loving God of Abraham—as opposed to the jealous, vengeful God of Moses, who is called Jehovah. So, archangel names describe their function, and then end in "el" to mean "of God." The term *angel* itself means "messenger of God."

Metatron's unusual name probably stems from his uncommon origins, as one of only two archangels who were once mortal men who walked upon the earth (the other one being Sandalphon, who was the prophet Elijah). There is various speculation among texts and experts that the name Metatron means "he who occupies the throne next to the Divine throne," or that his name is a derivation of the name *Yahweh,* the Jewish term for the unspoken sacred name of God. He has also been called "the Angel of the Presence."

Metatron is the youngest of the archangels, since his creation occurred after the other archangels. The prophet and scribe Enoch, who is said to have "walked with God" (in the book of Genesis), retained his God-given purity during his mortal life. Enoch was also a scholar on heavenly secrets, having received *The Book of the Angel Raziel* (also

471

known as *Sefer Raziel*), a textbook about God's workings penned by Archangel Raziel, and given to Adam, Noah, Enoch, and Solomon. As a result, God escorted Enoch directly to the seventh Heaven—the highest level—to reside and work. Enoch was given wings and transformed into a great archangel named Metatron.

Since Enoch was a skilled and honest scribe upon Earth, he was given a similar job in Heaven: to record everything that happened on Earth and keep it in the Akashic records (also known as *The Book of Life*). Enoch is in charge of recording and organizing this material.

Metatron is a fiery, energetic angel who works tirelessly to help Earth's inhabitants. He acts as an intermediary between Heaven and Earth, since he's had extensive experience as both a human and an angel. As such, he helps us understand Heaven's perspective, and to learn how to work with the angelic realm.

Metatron also has a special place in his heart for children, especially those who are spiritually gifted. After the Exodus, Metatron led the children of Israel through the wilderness and into safety. He continues to lead children today, both on Earth and in Heaven. Metatron is very concerned about children who are labeled as having Attention Deficit Disorder (ADD) or Attention Deficit Hyperactivity Disorder (ADHD), and he helps parents, educators, scientists, and health-care professionals find natural alternatives to Ritalin and other psychoactive medications.

Metatron helps newly crossed-over children adjust to Heaven, and helps living children love themselves and be more focused. Metatron also helps children become spiritually aware and to accept and polish their spiritual gifts.

Metatron's energy is strong and highly focused, like a laser beam. He's very motivational, and will encourage you to overcome procrastination and to take bold steps forward. He's also philosophical and can help you understand things like other people's motivations for action, and why different situations occur.

He says: *"My human life gave me the ability to grasp human concepts of life and death, which are abstract concepts to those who've always existed in the ethers. I do understand the gripping fear of death that underlies many human emotions. Having crossed that divide, though, I want to underscore the sentiment that you've so often heard: that there truly is nothing to fear in coming here. The time is planned according to your soul's calendar, and death cannot occur one moment before that time is reached.*

"There is no such thing as a premature or unplanned death, and unpleasantries associated with death are largely of the human imagination. Even those who die violently are spared from heinous suffering mainly due to God's intervention. Their souls are cast out of their bodies at the time of inevitability, long before any suffering could set in. Their disassociation with the event occurs because they're already focused upon the realization of that which follows after the physical existence. The fascination they have in experiencing their newfound life, following death, removes all concentration from the suffering that the human seems to undergo at the moment of death. We assure you that all of this comes from the compassion of the Great Creator, who is with us all, always."

Helps with:

- Attention Deficit Disorder (ADD) or Attention Deficit Hyperactivity Disorder (ADHD)
- Children's issues
- Recordkeeping and organization
- Spiritual understanding
- Writing

INVOCATION

If a child you care about has been labeled as having ADD or ADHD, and medication has been recommended or prescribed, call upon Archangel Metatron to see if alternative treatments are viable:

"Archangel Metatron, I ask for your powerfully loving intervention in helping [name of child], who has been labeled as 'disordered.' Please help us to know God's will for this child,

and guide all of the adults involved to do what's best for the child. Please help us stand strong among authority figures, and to do what we know is right. Please help all of the adults involved in making decisions on behalf of this child engage in harmonious discussions, even if there are differing opinions. Metatron, please protect this child from any harm, now and in the future. Thank you."

Archangel Michael
(Judeo-Christian, Islamic)

Also known as *Beshter, Mika'il, Sabbathiel, Saint Michael.*

Michael's name means "he who is like God" or "he who looks like God." Archangel Michael is a leader among archangels. He's in charge of the order of angels known as "the Virtues," and he oversees the lightworker's life purpose. His chief function is to rid the earth and its inhabitants of the toxins associated with fear. The humans whom he enlists and works with are called "lightworkers," and Michael asks them to perform spiritual teaching and healing work on a professional or casual basis.

Michael has inspired leaders and lightworkers since his time in the Garden of Eden, where he taught Adam how to farm and care for his family. Joan of Arc told her inquisitors that it was the Archangel Michael who gave her the impetus and courage to lead France during the Hundred Years' War. In 1950, he was canonized as Saint Michael, "the Patron of Police Officers," because he helps with heroic deeds and bravery.

Archangel Michael is extremely tall and handsome, and he usually carries a sword, which he uses to release us from the snare of fear. When he's around, you may see sparkles or flashes of bright blue or purple light. Michael is a fiery energy, and his presence is enough to make you sweat. I've had a number of female students tell me that they thought they were having menopausal hot flashes until they realized they'd just invoked Michael, and it was his presence creating all the heat!

Michael also has an incredible knack for fixing electrical and mechanical devices, including computers. I've called on him a number of times to help me with errant telephones, fax machines, and types of electronics, and he always comes through. A student of mine even invoked him when she was fixing a friend's plumbing (something she knew nothing about, but offered to do because she had faith that she *could* figure it out). As soon as this woman called Michael, the plumbing seemed to fix itself, and the operation was completed in no time!

Michael guides and directs those who feel lost, or stuck with respect to their life's purpose or career path. He can stimulate the unmotivated or fearful into action. Michael also provides clear guidance about which step to take next.

Helps with:

- Commitment and dedication to one's beliefs
- Courage
- Direction
- Energy and vitality
- Life's purpose, all aspects of
- Motivation
- Protection
- Space clearing
- Spirit releasement
- Worthiness and increased self-esteem

INVOCATION

Call upon Michael whenever you feel afraid or vulnerable. He will instantly come to your side, lending you courage and ensuring your safety, both physically and emotionally. You'll feel his warrior-like presence next to you in much the same way that a loving bodyguard would protect you. Anyone who might have intended to harm you will have a change of mind or heart.

Michael doesn't require that you say a formal invocation, and he will come to anyone who calls upon him. For example, you could think the thought:

> "Archangel Michael, please come to me now. I need your help!"

Then mentally describe the situation with which you need assistance. As stated earlier, you'll know he's with you when you sense his characteristic warm energy.

Archangel Raguel
(Judeo-Christian)

Also known as *Akrasiel, Raguil, Rasuil, Rufael, Suryan.*

Raguel's name means "friend of God." His chief role in Heaven is to oversee all of the other archangels and angels. He ensures that they're all working well together in a harmonious and orderly fashion, according to Divine order and will. As a result, he's often referred to as "the Archangel of Justice and Fairness." Raguel loves to be a champion to underdogs, and he can help those who feel slighted or mistreated become more empowered and respected.

Archangel Raguel is enthusiastic and friendly, and he's a "battery"—meaning that he'll energize you when you need a boost. Think of having a best friend who's a combination attorney, spiritual counselor, therapist, and motivational coach, and you'll have an idea of Raguel's multiple talents and the extent of his helpfulness. Raguel is a loving gentleman who will never interfere with your free will. However, if you ask him for help, he'll be there in an instant.

He says: *"I so often see people who let themselves down without realizing their potential and options. My availability is unlimited, and there really aren't any reasons to attempt anything alone with so much friendship available. I often work anonymously within groups of other helpers, so you may not know that I'm there helping you at your request. But know that I am!"*

Helps with:

- Arguments, resolving
- Cooperation and harmony in groups and families
- Defending the unfairly treated
- Empowerment, especially for underdogs
- Mediation of disputes
- Orderliness

INVOCATION

Raguel is a wonderful resolver of conflicts. If you've had an argument with someone and you need closure with that person, ask Raguel to intervene:

"Archangel Raguel, thank you for intervening into my relationship with [name of other person involved], bringing both of us to a level of peace and harmony. I'm grateful for your help in resolving our differences with love and cooperation. I appreciate the forgiveness that we feel toward one another. I know that God's will is eternal peace, and as children of God, I'm aware that both of us are the embodiment of that peace. Thank you for helping us live that truth, now and forever. In peace and gratitude, I thank you."

Archangel Raphael
(Judeo-Christian)

Also known as *Labbiel.*

Raphael's name means "God heals" or "God has healed," based upon the Hebrew word *rapha,* which means "doctor" or "healer."

Raphael is a powerful healer of physical bodies, both for humans and animals. Those who call on Raphael are healed rapidly. It's said that he healed the pain that Abraham felt after being circumcised as an adult.

Raphael can be invoked on behalf of someone else. Raphael will go to wherever he's requested; however, he can't interfere with that person's free will. If an ailing person refuses spiritual treatment, it can't be forced. However, Raphael's presence will have a comforting effect, which will aid in natural healing by reducing stress and anxiety.

In the *Book of Tobit,* Raphael travels with Tobias, who is Tobit's son. During this journey, Raphael keeps Tobias safe from harm. This earned Raphael his other role as "the Patron of Travelers." Raphael is a wonderful aide when it comes to safe travel, assuring that all of the transportation, lodging, and luggage details go miraculously well. He also helps those on inward spiritual journeys, assisting them in their search for truth and guidance.

Raphael also showed Tobias how to use parts of the fish he'd caught in medicinal ways, such as for healing balms and ointments. This is an example of how Raphael not only conducts spiritual healing work directly upon the ill or injured, but also guides human healers in knowing which Earthly treatments to use on their patients. Healers can mentally call upon Raphael for guidance before or during treatment sessions. Raphael also helps would-be healers with their education (including getting the time and money for school), and then assists them in establishing their healing practices by attracting wonderful clients.

Raphael is a healer and guide for wild and domesticated animals. I've had wonderful results when asking Raphael to retrieve lost pets for myself, friends, and clients. The results are almost immediate, as animals seem to be especially open to his gentle, loving care.

Raphael ultimately helped heal Tobit's blindness, and he's worked with thousands of my students at my workshops to open their "third eye," which is a spiritual energy center (chakra) that regulates clairvoyance. Raphael is very sweet, loving, kind, and gentle, and you know that he's around when you see sparkles or flashes of emerald-green light.

Archangels Raphael and Michael often work in tandem to exorcise troublesome spirits and escort away lower energies from people and places. *The Testament of Solomon* describes how Raphael brought the magical ring to King Solomon, inscribed with the powerful six-pointed star. Solomon used the ring and its symbol to subdue demons. So, part of Raphael's healing work involves spirit releasement and space clearing.

Helps with:

- Addictions and cravings, eliminating and reducing
- Clairvoyance
- Eyesight, physical and spiritual
- Healers, guidance and support for
- Healing, for humans and animals
- Pets, retrieving lost
- Space clearing
- Spirit releasement
- Travelers—relating to protection, orderliness, and harmony

INVOCATION

Anytime that you, or another person or animal, experience physical distress, call upon Archangel Raphael for angelic treatment. He'll intervene directly into the person or animal's body, and also provide guidance about what can be done to effect a healing.

To invoke Raphael for yourself, just think to yourself:

> "Archangel Raphael, I need help with [describe the situation]. Please surround and infuse my body with your powerful healing energy of Divine love. I now surrender this situation entirely to God, and know that through this releasement, I'm open to revealing my God-given health in all ways. Thank you for the energy, wellness, and happiness, God and Raphael!"

To invoke Raphael for someone else, you can visualize him and other angels surrounding that person or animal with their healing presence and emerald green light. You can ask God to send Raphael, or you can ask Raphael directly:

> "Archangel Raphael, please pay a healing visit to [name of person or animal] and promote health and wellness for everyone concerned. Please help lift all of our thoughts to those of faith and hope, and remove all doubts and fears. Please clear the way so that Divine health is manifested now and forever. Thank you."

Archangel Raziel
(Judaic, Cabalistic)

Also known as *Ratziel, Saraqael, Suriel.*

Raziel's name means "secret of God" because he works so closely with the Creator that he knows all of the secrets of the Universe and how it operates. Raziel wrote down all of these secrets in a tome of symbols and Divine magic called *The Book of the Angel Raziel*, or *Sefer Raziel*. After Adam and Eve were expelled from Eden, Raziel gave Adam the book for guidance about manifestation and God's grace. Later, the prophet Enoch received the book prior to his ascension and transformation into Archangel Metatron. Noah was also given a copy of the book by Archangel Raphael, and Noah used the information to build his ark and help its inhabitants after the flood.

Many scholars say that the cryptical book (which is available today in bookstores) was actually penned by a Jewish scholar of the middle ages, perhaps Eleazar of Worms or Isaac the Blind. However, the book is difficult to decipher, and it's said that readers must call upon Raziel in order to make sense of it.

Raziel can help you understand esoteric material, manifestation principles, sacred geometry, quantum physics, and other high-level information. He can also open you up to higher levels of psychic abilities and increase your ability to see, hear, know, and feel Divine guidance. Like a Divine wizard, Raziel can also assist you with manifestations.

Raziel is very loving, kind, and intelligent. His presence can seem subtle, but as you invoke him over time, you'll become aware of his positive influence in your spiritual practices.

Helps with:

- Alchemy
- Clairvoyance
- Divine magic
- Esoteric information
- Manifestation
- Psychic abilities

INVOCATION

To deepen your spiritual understanding of esoteric concepts, call upon Raziel. Since his messages are profound, it's best to contact him in a quiet environment. Close your eyes, breathe deeply, quiet your mind, and mentally say:

"Archangel Raziel, please help me open my mind to the Divine secrets of the Universe. Help me release any limiting beliefs or fears so that I may have spiritual understanding at the deepest and clearest level. In particular, I would like your instruction about [describe a problem that you'd like a solution to, asking any questions one at a time and giving plenty of time between them so that Raziel has a chance to answer each one and you have a chance to absorb and digest his responses]. Thank you, Raziel, for teaching me."

Archangel Sandalphon
(Judaic)

Also known as *Sandolphon, Sandolfon.*

Sandalphon is only one of two archangels whose name doesn't end with an "el" (which means "God" in Hebrew). Sandalphon's name means "brother" in Greek, a reference to his twin brother, the Archangel Metatron. The twins are the only archangels in Heaven who were originally mortal men. Sandalphon was the prophet Elijah, and Metatron was the wise man Enoch. God gave both men their immortal assignments as archangels to reward them for their good work upon Earth, allowing them to continue their sacred service from Heaven. Elijah's ascension occurred when he was lifted up to Heaven in a fiery chariot pulled by two horses of fire, accompanied by a whirlwind, an event recorded in the second chapter of the Book of 2 Kings.

Sandalphon's chief role is to carry human prayers to God so they may be answered. He's said to be so tall that he extends from Earth to Heaven. Ancient Cabalistic lore says that Sandalphon can help expectant parents determine the gender of their forthcoming child, and many also believe that he's involved with music as well.

Archangel Sandalphon's messages and musings come as soft whispers on the wings of angels—they're so gentle that they can breeze by if you're not paying attention. When you invoke Sandalphon, stay aware of any words or music you hear in your mind, as they're most likely answers to your prayers.

Helps with:

- Music
- Prayers, delivering and answering
- Unborn babies, determining the gender of

INVOCATION

If you have a prayer that you urgently want answered, call upon Archangel Sandalphon by thinking of your prayer and saying:

"Beloved Archangel Sandalphon, deliverer and answerer of all prayers, I ask for your assistance now. Please deliver my prayer [recite the prayer] to God as soon as possible. I ask that you relay a clear message to me that I'll easily understand. Please update me as to the progress of my request, and let me know if I need to do anything. Thank you, and amen."

Archangel Uriel
(Judeo-Christian)

Uriel's name means "God is light," "God's light," or "fire of God," because he illuminates situations and gives prophetic information and warnings. For example, Uriel warned Noah of the impending flood, helped the prophet Ezra to interpret mystical predictions about the forthcoming Messiah, and delivered the Cabala to humankind. Uriel has also been credited with bringing the knowledge and practice of alchemy—the ability to turn base metal into precious metal, as well as the ability to manifest from thin air—to humankind.

Uriel is regarded as one of the wisest archangels. He's very much like an old sage whom you can call upon for intellectual information, practical solutions, and creative insight. Instead of having to climb a mountain to reach the sage, Uriel will instantly come to you. However, Uriel's personality isn't as distinctive as Archangel Michael's, for example. You may not even realize that Uriel has come to answer your prayers until you notice a brilliant new idea that's entered your mind.

Perhaps because of his connection to Noah, as well as his affinity with the weather elements of thunder and lightning, Uriel is considered to be an archangel who helps us with earthquakes, floods, fires, hurricanes, tornadoes, natural disasters, and Earth changes. Call upon Archangel Uriel to avert such events, or to heal and recover in their aftermath.

Helps with:

- Alchemy
- Divine magic
- Earth changes
- Problem solving
- Spiritual understanding
- Studies, tests, and students
- Weather
- Writing

INVOCATION

Since Uriel has so many talents and helps us in so many life areas, it's a good idea to call upon him regularly. Think of him as a mentor who can oversee life lessons. One of the greatest ways in which Uriel helps us is by giving us additional information so that we can make informed decisions. In such cases, call upon him in a way such as this:

"Archangel Uriel, I ask for your wisdom on [describe the situation you'd like illumination about]. I need as much information as possible so that I can clearly see the truth of the situation. Please help me make an informed decision by filling me in on all of the perspectives involved. Please help me clearly hear and understand this information, and to be as open-minded as possible. Thank you, Uriel."

Archangel Zadkiel
(Judaic)

Also known as *Satqiel, Tzadkiel, Zadakiel, Zidekiel.*

Zadkiel's name means "the righteousness of God." He's considered to be the archangel of mercy and benevolence, perhaps because of his role in stopping Abraham from sacrificing his son, Isaac, as an offering to God.

Zadkiel can help you feel mercy and compassion toward yourself and others, and let go of judgment and unforgiveness. In this way, he's a healing angel who works beside Archangel Michael to replace negative energies with faith and compassion. Zadkiel helps us see the Divine light within ourselves and others, instead of focusing on the surface personality, behavioral mistakes, or the ego.

If you're having difficulty forgiving yourself or someone else, ask Zadkiel to intervene. He'll act like a chimney sweep who cleans your body, mind, and heart of unforgiveness. This doesn't mean that you're sanctioning someone's abusive behavior. It just means that you're no longer willing to cart around the emotional residue of old situations.

Archangel Zadkiel is also widely known for his help with memory functions. If you need to memorize important information, you need to remember where you put your car keys, or you just want to develop your memory in general, call upon Zadkiel.

Helps with:

- Compassion
- Finding lost objects
- Forgiveness of self and others
- Healing, emotionally and physically
- Memory enhancement
- Remembering important information
- Studies, students, and tests

INVOCATION

Anytime you feel upset, ask Zadkiel to intervene:

"Archangel Zadkiel, please help me heal my heart. If I'm holding on to unforgiveness, please help me release it fully. If there's something I'm not seeing, please help me to see clearly. If I need more compassion, please fill my heart with mercy. If I'm worried or anxious, please fill my heart with faith and calmness. I now surrender this situation fully to you and God, and I trust that your God-given healing power takes care of every detail with Divine grace, harmony, and wisdom. Thank you."

Artemis
(Greece)

Also known as *Artemis Calliste, Delia, Luna, Mother Artemis, Phoebe.*

A Greek goddess of the new moon, with parallels to the Roman goddess Diana, Artemis is the daughter of Zeus and Leto. Her brother is Apollo.

Known as "the Huntress of Souls," Artemis carries a bow and arrow and spends most of her time in nature with the wood nymphs. She's a protectress of anyone who calls upon her, and particularly defends unmarried young women, children, and animals. However, she always protects nonviolently, using wisdom as her sole weapon. She's considered a nature, fertility, and moon goddess.

Artemis sets her sights on her goals, and as a result, she's a powerful manifestor. She teaches us the importance of spending time in nature, and to follow our intuition as we strive to become more natural and authentic humans.

I called upon Artemis just after the new moon.

"Power can be paralyzing," replied the pixielike woman with short-cropped hair, a beautiful large-eyed face, and ears slightly pointed on the top. She seemed to be captivated with hunting something, but I knew it wasn't an animal or a person. Artemis then told me that she was hunting metaphorical gold: *"I track down wisdom and experiences that I can later recount to children in the form of fairy tales. Today I'm mostly*

concerned with helping wisdom grow in upcoming generations. The children are unsure of their boundaries and limits. They know that they have power that can exceed that of their parents, so they hold back, unwilling to release this mighty power, for fear of overpowering their adult guardians.

"Children today feel unsafe unless their parents are more powerful than they are. That's why I work dually alongside parents of the young. I encourage them not to perpetuate a battle of wills with their offspring, but to assume their power for the sake of their children's own awareness and to balance and use their power with love."

Helps with:

- Animals and wildlife
- Camping and hiking
- Children, especially girls
- Environmentalism
- Fertility, child conception, and adoption
- Intuition, increasing and honoring
- Power, especially feminine
- Protection

INVOCATION

Go outside to call upon Artemis—preferably, stand barefoot on the earth, sand, soil, or grass. Then say:

"Artemis, I ask for your companionship and guidance in helping me open up my natural intuition and my feminine strength and power, which resides within each man and woman. I open my arms to your friendship and leadership. Help me reconnect with nature and my natural self. Help me honor my true feelings and stand up for what I know to be true, deep in my heart. Help me to be strong, wise, and beautiful in all ways. Thank you."

Ashtar
(New Age)

Also known as *Commander Ashtar.*

Ashtar is a human-looking mediator who works with extraterrestrials and humans, helping to create a peaceful Universe.

Ashtar is a member of the Great White Brotherhood [see the Glossary], and he works closely with Jesus, Archangel Michael, and Saint-Germain. Like a nightclub bouncer, Ashtar protects Earth from negative visitors or energies from other planets. He's involved with ensuring peace between planet populations through the Intergalactic Federation. He also heads a group of humans and extraterrestrials known as "the Ashtar Command."

Ashtar's mission is to avert nuclear war on Earth, which would have a negative ripple effect across many galaxies. He wants to help humans reach their highest potential (a process known as *ascension*) and be completely focused on Divine love. Ashtar guides humans away from third-dimensional thinking that believes in limits and restrictions and is focused on time measurement. He also gives personal guidance on how to stay safe and calm during the many changes occurring on Earth.

I attempted to contact Ashtar several times and was told that the best time to reach him was on a clear, starry evening, or while flying at high altitudes in an airplane. So I decided to combine the two and communicate with him while flying at 30,000 feet at night!

I've seen Ashtar and have been aware of his presence with many of my clients, especially those whom I call "Starpeople" (those who have a connection to other galaxies). He's the pale man with white hair portrayed on the "Support" card in my *Healing with the Angels* oracle deck and on the cover of my book about Starpeople, *Earth Angels*.

"I'm here," Ashtar said to me when our connection was complete. *"You felt me as warm love before you could hear me. I come from a different dimension, one that your conscious mind—while existing in third-dimensional, time-warped thinking—cannot as easily grasp as your soul can during its nightly sojourns to visit us for a higher education.*

"I won't encroach upon your missions, but I'm here if you need me. I promise to keep you safe from all outward invasions."

Helps with:

- Aliens, understanding and having peaceful interactions with
- Earth changes
- Profound thinking
- Protection
- Releasing fear
- Spiritual understanding

INVOCATION

Ashtar is easiest to connect with at night, when the stars are illuminated in the heavens. Hold your intention to contact him in your mind, and he'll come to you. If you have fears concerning aliens, Ashtar's presence with you will be subtle, as he's a loving being who doesn't want to evoke fear in any way.

Athena
(Greece)

Also known as *Pallas Athena, Athene.*

Athena's roots are ancient and multicultural; however, she's best known as the Greek warrior goddess of wisdom, household affairs, and arts and crafts.

Athena is the daughter of Zeus, and her temple was the Parthenon. Legends discuss Athena's courage and intuitive wisdom during battles. In artistic renderings, Athena is usually depicted with a breastplate, shield, and sword, and often accompanied by an owl. This bird has come to be associated with her, perhaps due to her wisdom.

When she bears the extra title "Pallas," Athena is known as a warrior goddess who protects, and who inspires women to exhibit their inner strength and have the courage to stand their ground. She encourages humans to use intuitive wisdom, rather than anger or violence, to heal arguments. In New Age teachings, Pallas Athena is regarded as an ascended master of the fifth ray of light, which is the ray concerning truthfulness and integrity.

When I called upon Athena, I saw a beautiful woman standing in a single-person chariot with metal wrist cuffs and a metallic headdress. Her energy was very intense, and she was panting, as if she'd just completed a sizable task.

"No job is too big for me," she said bluntly. *"I'm a taskmaster who gets*

the job before me done to full completion. Often I delegate to star beings."

Athena pointed out the stars in the sky, referring to them as sweet, living beings bearing the souls of innocent, loving children who are devoted to helping Athena. *"The whole universe breathes,"* she said in response to my unspoken questions about the stars. *"It reverberates with life, and there's no place where life is not—it is a continuous pattern of ever-moving energy that is everywhere, without exception. And that is how I handle my tasks at hand: by commanding the energy with the firm, loving touch of a determined parent. You can do the same."*

Helps with:

- Arguments, resolving
- Arts and artists
- Crafts and craftspeople
- Justice, attaining
- Protection, physical and psychical
- War, avoiding and resolving
- Writers and writing

INVOCATION

One way to invoke Athena is to say:

"Athena, I need your assistance, and request your powerful presence, please. Beloved sister, I ask for your intervention in my life. Please infuse every part of my existence with graceful strength: my thoughts, movements, relationships, and all situations with which I'm involved. I ask that you help my friends and family to accept and honor my new-found power. Please help me harness and use this strength in peaceful and loving ways. I thank you!"

Babaji
(Himalaya)

Also known as *Mahavatar Babaji, Shri Babaji.*

Made famous by Paramahansa Yogananda's book *Autobiography of a Yogi,* Babaji is known as "the deathless avatar" because he overcame physical limitations regarding the human life span. It's said that he didn't die, but ascended with his physical body. Many accounts of him appearing physically to spiritual seekers have been written. However, he usually comes to those who invoke him on the spiritual plane, and they "hear" Babaji through thoughts, feelings, or visions.

Babaji's mission is to bring humanity closer to God, and to follow God's will. He encourages people to follow their own spiritual path, and says that all religions lead to God. He encouraged Yogananda to bring Kriya Yoga (which involves 18 yoga postures—also known as *asanas* or *mudras*) to the West. Kriya is known as a tool of enlightenment and may have helped spark the current popularity in yoga.

Helps with:

- Addictions and cravings, overcoming or reducing
- Breathwork
- Clear communication with God

- Manifestation
- Materiality, detaching from
- Protection from religious persecution
- Simplifying your life
- Spiritual growth
- Yoga practice

INVOCATION

Say the name Babaji repeatedly, feeling the energy of his name in your heart. In his autobiography, Yogananda said that if you say Babaji's name with reverence, he directly blesses you. He told me that we can best contact him while we're engaged in breathwork and yoga. Babaji said that he's one with all breath, and when we consciously breathe in and out deeply, we're consciously connecting with him.

Brigit
(Ireland, Spain, France, and Wales)

Also known as *Brid, Brighid, St. Brigid, Brigantia,*
Mary of the Gaels, Bride, Brigid.

B rigit is a warrior goddess who has struck a perfect balance of
femininity and no-apologies power. Depending upon whom you
ask, her name either means "the bright one," "the bright arrow," or "the
powerful one." All of these names describe Brigit perfectly.

Originally a highly respected Celtic Goddess afforded much acclaim
in ancient Ireland, Brigit had a shrine erected in her honor in the town
of Kildare, where women tended to a flame that burned continually. In
the fifth century, Brigit was adopted by the Catholic church and was
deemed "Saint Brigid."

Brigit is the female equivalent of Archangel Michael, fiercely protecting and lovingly clearing those who call upon her. Like Michael,
Brigit also inspires Divine guidance and prophetic information. She's the
half-sister of the Celtic love god, Aengus, sharing the same mother with
him. Brigit is known as a triple goddess of the flame who uses her flames
to help purify us; and increase fertility, creativity, and promote healing.
"Triple goddess" means that Brigit has three different personas or aspects,
as if she's three different people, each with distinct duties and specialties.

Brigit is a sun goddess, associated with fire. When she's in your presence, you may feel hot and actually begin to perspire. Brigit is celebrated

499

each February 1 during an event originally known as "Imbolc," the rite to usher in springtime and welcome the birth of new livestock.

I invoked Brigit while sitting by the Irish sea on a hot summer afternoon. Brigit appeared as a fiery redhead with beautiful, long, wavy hair. Her intensity surprised me at first, yet it was accompanied by loving confidence, like the sun that merely burns without any hint of anger, fear, or urgency. Brigit reminds me of a combination of Mother Mary, with her graceful feminine love, and Archangel Michael, with his no-nonsense commitment to purpose and protection. She's a "super-mother," one who's simultaneously accessible and loving, yet fiercely protective without fail. I get the feeling that nothing can get past Brigit's impeccable protective power and energy.

She says: *"I'm the embodiment of fiery devotion to the good people of the planet Earth. At one time, I walked upon Earth, and my heart was broken in many ways by careless and thoughtless actions against myself, my people, and the land. The rest of my time I devoted to trying to understand human nature. I now have insight into the 'nature of the beast,' if you will, of the human heart. I see that its frailty lies in indecision and worry. Cast, therefore, your cares onto me, and I shall carry them away.*

"Humanity is heavy with grief now over the loss of innocence [**Author's note:** To me, this sentence seemed like a post-September 11 reference] *and the many rivalries that have been invented and imposed. These are artificial boundaries, and the committee with which I work seeks to blur the lines of these boundaries to build unity and salvation. Devotion to oneness at this time is essential, a single-pointed focus upon the One. Inside of each of us is a savior. Learn to invoke your internal savior as a counterbalance to cares and worries. Watch how this inner deity quietly and discreetly intervenes.*

"It's with these workings that we all come together—we who oversee the Mission on a grand scale, and all of those upon the planet who hold great desires to bring goodness home. This teamwork is built upon the framework and understanding of our oneness. It isn't difficult to understand the mechanics of these workings, as they're orchestrated for your higher good. I call it the workings of 'inner salvation'—instead of simply focusing upon

improving outward situations and other people's lives, try this instead: Go inward and explore the inner mission, the inner territory, the inner deities."

Helps with:

- Courage, increasing (especially for women)
- Life purpose and finding direction
- Protection
- Warmth—in relationships, body, and environment

INVOCATION

You can contact Brigit at any time; however, it's especially effective to light a candle and stare at its flame as you say:

"Great Brigit, I know that you hear me the moment that I think of you. I ask for your presence and assistance. Please lend me your courage and power so that I may rise to the level of my highest capabilities. Please warm my heart and mind with your brightness, and burn away any thoughts, feelings, or behaviors that stand in the way of my Divine potential. Help me to have the courage to be my very best, and to lose all fear of being powerful."

Buddha
(Asia)

Also known as *Siddhartha Buddha, Buddha Goutama, Lord Goutama.*
The name Buddha means "the Enlightened or Awakened One."

Born on the full moon, May 8 (the exact year isn't agreed upon, but it's believed to be in the 500 B.C. era), Prince Goutama Siddhartha grew up wealthy behind palace walls, with every need taken care of. As he grew older and walked beyond the palace, he noticed poverty-stricken, diseased and elderly people, individuals that he had not previously been aware of. Determined to help alleviate the suffering that he witnessed, the prince renounced his royal title and wealth and left the palace.

However, Siddhartha's ascetic life didn't bring him the full enlightenment he desired. So he sat beneath a bodhi tree and vowed not to rise until he'd become fully enlightened. He breathed in and out deeply during the evening of a full moon, dispelling bodily cravings and fearful thoughts. Once he overcame these lower energies, he began recalling his past lives. This helped him see the endlessness of life, and he was filled with understanding as to how to overcome unhappiness, pain, and death. When he arose from sitting, he was a Buddha.

Buddha's teachings about detachment from suffering through inner peace became the basis for Buddhism. Because he had lived both extremes of living—as a rich prince and as an ascetic—Buddha proposed that the key to happy living was "the Middle Way," or moderation in all things.

You may find that Buddha is easier felt than heard. When you call upon him, you'll probably feel a swelling of warm love in your heart. That's his calling card, a sign that you've truly connected with his loving presence.

Helps with:

- Balance and moderation in all things
- Joy
- Peace, inner and world
- Spiritual growth and understanding

INVOCATION

Sit quietly, and focus upon the sound of your breath. Notice it slowing down as you listen. Feel and hear your heart beating in conjunction with your breath. Imagine that there's a magical door deep inside your being. It's a beautiful opening, decorated with powerful symbols and crystals.

From your heart, ask to connect with Buddha. Then imagine opening the door and seeing him there inside of you. Keep breathing deeply, feeling your connection through breath to beloved Buddha.

Fill your heart with his sweet kindness, his gentle power, and his surety. Feel the safety and peace that comes from being in his presence. Ask him any question that you like, feel the answer in your heart and body, and hear the answer whispered into your mind. Notice that all of Buddha's words are couched in utmost respect for you and everyone involved. Thank him after your meeting is concluded.

Cordelia
(England, Wales, Ireland)

Also known as *Creiddylad, Creudylad.*

Cordelia is the beautiful goddess of spring and summer flowers, and of flower fairies. Shakespeare portrayed Cordelia as the daughter of King Lear in his play of the same name. However, she's actually the daughter of the sea god, Lir, so she was born a sea goddess.

Cordelia is celebrated on May 1 during Beltane, an ancient celebration marking the beginning of summer, when the weather is warm enough to allow ranchers to let cattle out of their pens and into the fields.

Cordelia came to me while I sat on the grounds of Stonehenge, leaning against one of the ancient stones. She gave me this message: *"Merriment intertwined with ancient Celtic wisdom—I weave the stellar wisdom of astral energies with an infusion of pixie dust from the Earthly pollen of nature's wise ones. I'm an instrument of contradiction: the earth and the sky; the sunrise and the sunset; the cold and the heat. Extremes without compromise are a powerful combination. Feel them deep inside your ancient bones, connected with Mother Ground (what you call the Earth Mother). Your bones are borne of her, and in a continual loop will return to her once again.*

"Feel the freedom of releasing yourself from Earthly concerns and walking in the middle between Earth and her stars, unconcerned for anything

but joy, mirth, and playfulness as I help to teach you how to provide for all of your Earthly needs."

Helps with:

- Celebration
- Courage
- Gardening and flowers
- Joy
- Life changes
- Stress management

INVOCATION

Call upon Cordelia whenever you feel stressed or trapped indoors. You can "escape" from office routines by closing your eyes and imagining yourself standing in a field of flowers with her during a perfect springtime afternoon. Mentally say to her:

"Beautiful Cordelia, I come to you as a friend in need of some time off from duties and responsibilities. Please take my hand and bring me fresh air, freedom, and the fragrance of flowers. Carry me away for a much-needed respite. Renew my spirit and fill my heart with joy, laughter, and playfulness. Help me carry this high energy in my heart and mind for the rest of the day. Help me approach my responsibilities with joy. Thank you!"

Coventina
(United Kingdom)

Coventina is a Celtic goddess who oversees the sprites and water nymphs. She's a goddess of rain, rivers, lakes, streams, ponds, oceans, and water-based creatures. Coventina loves the cattails and lily pads by riverbanks. She heals those who swim in the water while invoking her. Coventina also helps with the growth of vegetation near beaches, rivers, lake fronts, and islands.

Because of her relationship to water, Coventina can swim into psychic domains and help with inspiration, psychic abilities, dreams, and prophecies. She's also associated with purification and cleanliness, and you can call upon her for a spiritual baptism to relieve you of worries and judgments, and to help you abstain from unhealthful and addictive substances.

In ancient times, people would throw coins into a well associated with Coventina to request her assistance. (This is believed to be the origin of the "wishing well.") Because of the bounty of coins, Coventina represents abundance in all ways. Legend also associates Coventina with flying fish, and today she can be invoked to fly in airplanes safely and fearlessly.

Since Coventina is primarily considered a British divinity (although she helps out worldwide), it was fitting that I talked with her while at the ancient stone circle temple, Stonehenge, in southern England. She told me, *"I will help anyone who is involved with ecological welfare, especially concerning water cleanliness, the preservation of water and its inhabitants, and water run-off issues. I'm dedicated to the whales, dolphins, and cetaceans."*

Helps with:

- Abundance
- Dolphins and cetaceans
- Environmentalism
- Healing with water
- Psychic abilities and prophecy
- Purification and cleanliness
- Swimming
- Water cleanliness and supply

INVOCATION

Coventina works with us in our dreams, if we call to her before going to sleep. She'll bring the higher selves of dolphins and whales alongside her. Together, they will give you high-level messages that you may not remember the next morning, but whose information will be incorporated into your subconscious mind, where it will help you with answers and guidance. So, before going to sleep, say to her:

"Coventina, I ask that you and your dolphin and whale companions enter my dreams tonight and take me above the third-dimensional plane to the place of answers and wisdom. [Ask her any questions that you would like answered during the night.] Thank you for your help and strong support."

Damara
(United Kingdom)

D amara's name means "gentle." She's a sweet and docile goddess of home and hearth who helps with family harmony—that is, maintaining peaceful energy within the domestic realm. Damara also assists with the manifestation of money to help pay for family expenses.

She says, *"I'm happy to heal, guide, and help you feel the heat of love, passion, and deep caring unadulterated by fear or worry. I'm also glad to help heal children's cuts, bruises, and hurt feelings. I'm especially available to help families with young children. I will gladly guide a mother in decision-making for her family's welfare. And if the woman is considering decisions about whether to divorce or leave her children's father, she can call upon me for input and assistance."*

Helps with:

- Abundance—especially for household needs
- Children, guiding and healing
- Home, peace within the
- Manifestation—especially for family and household needs

Invocation

Call upon Damara whenever you need help with household relationships, including those with your spouse, live-in partner, roommate, parents, or children—in other words, if you need intervention with anyone with whom you're living. Here's an example of how to contact her. Close your eyes and think:

> "Damara, I need your help right away, please! I ask that you go to [name of person in household you need help with] and discuss my desire for peace and harmony. Please let [name] know that I'm a loving person with good intentions. Please help [name] to drop all judgments about me, and for me to do the same, in turn. Damara, I ask that you fill our home with so much energy of love that nothing else can exist. When anyone enters this home, they're healed. I'm so grateful for this intervention, Damara."

Dana
(Ireland)

Also known as *Danu, Danann.*

D ana's name is rooted in the Old Irish word *Dan,* which means "knowledge." She is a powerful Celtic creator goddess, believed to be a Great Mother aspect of the Divine Creator. Historians say that she has the most ancient roots of any Celtic deity, esteemed by the pre-Gaelic Tuatha Dé Danaans, a group of alchemists in Ireland. When the Gaelics overtook Ireland, legend says that the Tuatha Dé Danaans became the leprechauns who today inhabit Ireland.

When I invoked Dana while sitting on a bluff overlooking the Irish sea, I first saw a coat similar to one that a king might sport—regal and bejeweled. Next, I saw a king's crown. "But Dana is a female deity!" I mentally protested. Then I saw her—not as I expected her to look (my mental image was that she'd look like someone's eccentric aunt). Instead, I saw a rational, young-looking woman who emanated wisdom and intelligence.

Dana placed the crown on my head and the coat over my shoulders. I started to argue, but she stopped me. *"You're all royalty,"* Dana explained, meaning all of humanity, *"and you need to allow me the honor of dignifying you all with my services."*

I could tell that Dana didn't mean that she'd perform every feat of manifestation for us, but she assured me that her energy was *"magically intertwined with each act of magical manifestation."* She said, *"Remember that I'm just another aspect of God, and that your Western master teacher Jesus taught you that you are all gods."*

Dana showed me wavelengths of energy, all intertwined like parallel lines of rope, and said that each of us was part of those wavelengths. Her wavelength was often the foundation, bottom, or supporting line of energy that we could rest upon. *"Let nature do its course as you perform miracles,"* she added. And again she emphasized that we're all kings, queens, gods, and goddesses . . . deities in our own right: *"You're deities in the making, as you test out your own skills with chaperones like me by your side."*

Helps with:

- Abundance
- Alchemy and Divine magic
- Animals, healing
- Children, fertility, and mothering
- Elemental kingdom, meeting and working with the (particularly leprechauns)
- Worthiness, self-esteem, and deservingness issues

INVOCATION

Wear, look at, or hold something that makes you feel abundant—or even better—that makes you feel like royalty. This could mean going to a jewelry store and trying on a beautiful ring, or looking at a photograph of an opulent estate. Imagine yourself with unlimited resources, and feel a sense of total financial security. Even if you can imagine and experience this sensation for just a brief time, that's enough. Then mentally say to Dana:

"Dana, thank you for lending me your magical abilities, which I now use in the service of joy, fun, and support of my Divine mission. Thank you for your generosity in showing me how to accept these resources, and how to enjoy them. Thank you for helping me receive without guilt, and to know that I deserve this attention and support and that it will ultimately allow me to help the planet."

Devi
(India)

Also known as *Ambika, Ghagavati, Devee, Ida, Shakti.*

Devi is a Hindu or Vedic goddess who is known as the "Universal" or "Great" mother. The "Mother" in the term *Mother-Father God,* she's the female energy of God. Devi, therefore, is the embodiment of God-power: absolute, creative, and supportive. She's one of India's most important and powerful goddesses.

The term *Devi* is sometimes used generically to describe any goddess. All goddesses are considered to be aspects of the One Devi, who is the female energy of the One Creator.

As I called upon Devi while sitting on a bluff overlooking the Pacific off the Kona coast in Hawaii, I first felt a motherly energy feed me a sweet-tasting substance. It felt like Mom was giving me a treat.

Devi said, *"Let me sweeten your palate* [similar to cleansing your palate] *so that you can fully taste, hear, and understand my joyful message. Cleansing is a vital first step, allowing even greater messages of love to come through.*

"Drop all thoughts of worldly possessions as you hear my call. The world needs you to minister to the grief that permeates the very essence of others' souls. I'm pushing you toward compassion in action—taking steps to heal the world's aching grief.

"My heart swells with love and gratitude for those who reach out in service and kindness for people in need. You cannot be devastated by loss when your heart is fixed upon helping others. It takes you out of self-consciousness

513

when you're attuned to ministering to others.

"I'm here to minister alongside you so that you can feed the populace's hungry hearts and bodies. I want to protect young children from growing wary of love and becoming frozen in their hearts. Hell is literally when people's hearts freeze over, rendering them cold and useless and preventing them from participating in the planet's heart song.

"Many individuals are growing restless at this juncture, and they need shepherding into the new atmosphere that embraces love and love's manifestations."

Helps with:

- Addictions, releasing and detoxification from
- Meaningfulness—finding more in life and career
- Purification of body and mind
- Relationships, all aspects of

INVOCATION

Devi is best contacted while sitting alone in nature, either in a comfortable chair or on the sand, grass, or ground. Wrap your arms around yourself in an embrace, and imagine that Devi is joining you, giving you a hug. Feel her love in your heart and body, and breathe it in even deeper with a long inhalation and slow exhalation. Mentally ask her to come into your heart, mind, and body and purify away any toxins, staleness, darkness, or hardening of your feelings. Feel her beams of loving energy directed throughout your body, and know that she's carefully purifying you in the most thorough yet gentle way. You may find that you twitch as she releases lower energies. When your body feels still, stay in mental communion with her as long as you feel comfortable. Ask her to help you stand up, and feel the renewal of energy in your body. Give thanks to Devi, and make plans to be with her often.

Diana
(Rome)

Also known as *Diana of Ephesus.*

Sharing attributes similar to that of the Greek goddess Artemis, Diana is a moon goddess who helps with fertility and abundance.

The daughter of the chief god, Jupiter, Diana is called the goddess of childbirth because her mother bore her painlessly. Immediately after Diana was born, she helped with the birth of her twin brother, Apollo.

Diana is associated with bathing and purification. At the Temple of Diana in Ephesus, Turkey (one of the largest temples in the ancient world, and one that is noted in Acts 19 in the Bible), female followers would engage in ritual hair-washing at Diana's shrine.

Diana spends time with elementals, and forest and wood nymphs. She is particularly fond of women, and also helps lesbians with relationship and societal issues. She's usually depicted with the bow and arrow that her father gave to her as a young girl, symbolizing female strength and power.

One night as the moon was waxing, Diana said to me, *"I help you* [meaning everyone] *rise above all Earthly concerns, in the same way that the moon hovers above the earth. Be like the moon, shining light gaily upon others, and then like the new moon, regularly withdrawing for personal respite.*

"The moon isn't afraid to shine, nor does it fear attention, ridicule, or rejection. These lower fears sink Earthlings into despair and depression because the soul knows that it's capable of so much more! The soul doesn't like

515

to be harnessed or restrained—oh, no! Unleash yourself completely, so that I may shine upon you as a reflection of your outwardly manifested holiness."

Helps with:

- Animals—breeding, pregnancy, and birthing
- Childbirth, painless
- Elementals, connecting with
- Lesbian concerns
- Twins

INVOCATION

Diana's connection is especially strong on moonlit nights. However, you can always contact her at any time.

"Diana, please help me shine brightly like you. Assist me in releasing anxieties about ridicule or rejection so that I may enjoy being my true self fully. Take me to a higher place, where I may best serve humanity as a shining example of one who listens to inner wisdom, love, and guidance. Help my life to be full, very full, of light. Thank you."

El Morya
(Theosophical Society; New Age)

El Morya is a new ascended master, first recorded in the 1880s by
Madame Blavatsky, founder of the Theosophical Society, and
repopularized in the 1960s by Mark and Elizabeth Clare Prophet and
other authors of the "I AM Teachings."

El Morya appears to be based upon an actual man named Ranbir
Singh, son of Raja Gulab Singh, who was the ruler of Kashmir in the
1840s. Kashmir was threatened with takeover by the British in 1845,
but Raja Singh paid a ransom to convince the British to leave the country alone. When the Raja died in 1858, Ranbir became Maharaj of
Kashmir.

Historians hail Ranbir for unifying the states of Nagar and Hunza,
and for creating humane and fair civil and criminal laws. Ranbir was
quite popular among his constituents. He passed away in 1885, the
same time that Madame Blavatsky was writing her channeled books
about the ascended masters. Blavatsky claimed to have spent time with
El Morya in India, and she may have been protecting a friendship with
Ranbir by giving him a pseudonym.

Blavatsky's Theosophical Society defines the term *Morya* as "the
name of a Rajpoot tribe, so-called because of its being almost altogether
composed of the descendants of the famous Moryan sovereign of Marya-
Nagara. The Moryan Dynasty began with certain Kshatriyas of the Sakya
line closely related to Goutama Buddha, who founded the town of

Morya-Nagara in the Himalayas." Blavatsky, and later, Elizabeth Clare Prophet, did make reference to El Morya being a "Rajput prince" and a "Tibetan Mahatma," both apt descriptions of Ranbir.

When I invoked El Morya, he came to me rapidly in a most extraordinary way. The man that I saw closely matched the paintings that Blavatsky had made of El Morya, although I purposely didn't look at her artwork until after my channeling of El Morya.

"Put aside your cares, concerns, and worries, and come to me," I was told. A brown-skinned man, slightly heavyset with a glowing smile of love and arms outstretched, faced me. *"Let me embrace you and perform an energy transfusion, replacing faithlessness with faith."* I melted into his young-grandpa-like embrace, felt my breath become deeper, and experienced a tingling sensation throughout my hands, wrists, calves, and feet.

El Morya explained that he was surmounting my inner obstacles, which he said were walls of defenses that I'd built up as misguided shields. *"So much better to use these instead,"* he said, holding up two beautifully ornate shields. *"This is a heart protector, and this one is for the small of your back—two vulnerable areas for lightbearers like you. Through a form of psychic surgery, I shall permanently install these shields deep into the chasm of your being, protecting you from harm of any sort.*

"These shields will allow problems to roll off of you like butter on a heated surface." He explained that these shields were a buffer to tone down impulsiveness based on emotionally based decisions not tempered by wisdom.

"I'm so glad that you called upon me, and I invite all who read these words to do the same. I shall install shields at their request, individually attuned to each person's energy field. The shields can always be removed at the blink of an eye, should you say the word. However, I'm certain that you'll feel much better and more grounded as a result, and will be comforted by their placement."

Helps with:

- Decision-making
- Faith
- Groundedness
- Protection—especially energy and psychic

INVOCATION

"Beloved El Morya, who serves the Divine light, please come to me now. Escort me to the place of selfless service where Divine assignments are made. Shield me from the negative thoughts of my own mind, as well as negative energy in general. Help me stay centered in my commitment to learn, grow, heal, and teach with a positive intent and positive energy. Thank you."

Forseti
(Norse)

Also known as *Forete.*

The Norse god of justice, fairness, arbitration, and reconciliation, Forseti, whose name means "presiding one," stills all strife; in other words, he's the ultimate peacemaker. He's an arbitrator in Heaven, listening to both points of view in arguments, and creating win-win solutions. He resolves differences with love so that everyone involved in the original dispute is persuaded to reconcile.

I spoke with him at twilight atop the monolithic stones of the Joshua Tree National Park in California, where he said, *"I'm here, guiding your trail at every turn. The wheels of justice seem to move slowly, but I'm behind the scenes, working tirelessly on your behalf. Whatever legal ties or angles seem to be thrown at you, I'm here to bounce them straightaway. Think of me as the ultimate lawyer of legal peace and justice—I'm free of cost, I make house calls, and I respond to your entreaties immediately."*

Helps with:

- Arguments, resolving
- Fairness
- Legal matters, resolving

- Peace
- Protection—especially legal in nature
- Truth issues

INVOCATION

Call upon Forseti when legal matters arise, or are threatened. He goes to work on your behalf immediately:

"Dear Forseti, I ask for your intervention into this situation, to promote an awareness of kindness and fairness. Thank you for the peaceful resolution of this dispute, which is now being completely resolved."

Ganesh
(Hindu; India)

Also known as *Ganesha*.

Ganesh is an elephant-headed deity who removes obstacles for anyone who asks for his help. He is the Hindu god of prosperity and wisdom, who also assists with writing and art projects. Many different stories abound that explain why Ganesh has an elephant's head. In most stories, Ganesh lost his head (perhaps because of his father's anger), and Ganesh's mother took the first head that she could find—a baby elephant's—and placed it on her son's neck.

In Hinduism, Ganesh is the first deity contacted during prayers. It's recommended that you invoke Ganesh prior to conducting a ceremony, engaging in writing, or before any endeavor in which you want to succeed.

Ganesh is extremely loving, sweet, polite, and gentle, yet also very strong. He's large enough to blaze trails ahead of you so that your path is clear, but he's also so filled with love and sweetness that you don't have to worry that his brute strength could turn against you. He's analogous to Archangel Michael, in that he's a loving and loyal protective force.

Ganesh is called "the Remover of Obstacles" because he mows down any blocks that could stand in his path. Think of a tame elephant walking ahead of you on a trail, trampling brush so that your way is clear. That is Ganesh.

I was having difficulty at airports at one time because security guards kept stopping me to open and search my carry-on bags. Since my husband and I travel nearly every weekend, I quickly grew weary of these frequent suitcase searches. I wanted the security personnel to ignore me and just let me through without stopping me. So, I placed a small statue of Ganesh in my carry-on bag. From that moment on, my bags were never again searched.

Ganesh immediately comes to those who call upon him. For example, I was on the telephone talking with my friend Johnna following the death of her mother. I was consoling her when I suddenly saw a clairvoyant image of Ganesh next to her. I said, "Johnna, did you call on Ganesh?" And she answered, "Yes! I'm wearing a necklace with a medallion of Ganesh on it. I've been rubbing the picture all day, calling for Ganesh to be with me."

Ganesh says, *"I see all obstacles as being surmountable; in fact, I don't see obstacles at all, and that's the point: All barriers in your path are self-imposed. They represent your decision to be afraid of moving forward. You cast your fear outward by projecting thoughts into the future, worried that either this or that may occur. Your worries about the future have created blocks and boogeymen that you will meet on your future path. But don't worry—since they're your own creation, you can will them away.*

"Ask me to assist, and I puncture the balloons of dark illusions. Even if you've managed to manifest a worst-case scenario, call upon me to heal and guide you. All thought-forms are on a level playing field, and no matter how dire the appearance, they're all equally surmountable. I plow through them all quite easily with my unwavering faith in 'all good, all love.' That's the only power that exists. The rest are all unreal illusions. Let them go and know the truth of all situations: God and love always prevail."

Helps with:

- Abundance
- Artistic projects
- Household peace and harmony
- Obstacles, removing and avoiding

- Wisdom issues
- Writing

INVOCATION

If you're unfamiliar with how Ganesh looks, find a picture of him in a book or on the Internet. Once you're familiar with his visage, it's easy to call upon him by visualizing him in your mind and saying:

"Beloved Ganesh, thank you for smoothing my path today, with harmony and peacefulness reigning supreme. I appreciate your walking before me, clearing all obstructions that could impede my progress. Help me see the blessings within everything today. Thank you."

Guinevere
(United Kingdom)

Also known as *Gwenhwyfar.*

Guinevere, whose name means "white one," is a goddess of love rela-tionships, fertility, and motherhood—and she also works with the flower fairies. Her painting graces the cover of this book.

She's the Celtic triple goddess behind the story of King Arthur, Camelot, and the Round Table. At Glastonbury Abbey in southern England, two graves are marked with placards indicating that King Arthur and Guinevere may be buried there. The Abbey is magical, sacred, and filled with white doves—one of my favorite places on Earth. It's not hard to imagine that Arthur and Guinevere would rest in such an enchanting place.

I invoked Guinevere at Avebury, which is an ancient magical stone circle (similar to Stonehenge, but much larger) in southern England. I asked her, "What do you most want to help us with?"

Guinevere replied, *"Romantic entanglement is my specialty, for I have empathetic resonance with every woman who has suffered the fate of feeling unloved or unlovable in quest of romance. Any woman who feels she's on the wrong foot 'in a man's world'—walking on uncharted territory—should explore this world with me as her steady companion."*

Helps with:

- Romantic love, enhancing and finding
- Women's issues

INVOCATION

Draw a heart and stare at it while you call on Guinevere for help with romantic concerns:

> "Sister Guinevere, you appreciate the depth of love within my heart, and my capacity to give to another. You understand my desires completely. I now give you permission to intervene as my romantic intermediary, preparing me for a wonderful relationship, and opening my heart and mind to profound love infused with spirituality, honor, trust, and commitment. Thank you for helping me be with my One True Love without delay."

Then kiss the drawing of the heart, and hold it to your chest. Imagine that it's your Beloved Soulmate, and send loving energy to this person (even if you're not yet aware of who it might be). Ask Guinevere to help you maintain faith in romantic love.

Hathor
(Egypt)

Also known as *Athor, Athyr, Hat-hor, Hat-Mehit, Hawthor, Tanetu, The Celestial Cow, Queen of the Earth, Mother of Light, The Eye of Ra.*

Hathor is the ancient and beloved Egyptian goddess of the sun, sky, newborns, and the dead. Her celebrations were marked with a lot of drinking, music, and dancing, so Hathor is considered to be a patron of music, dance, and mirth. She's also associated with feminine beauty, cosmetics, fashionable clothing, and romantic relationships.

Hathor is a love and fertility goddess who helps bring soulmates together, oversees conception, protects pregnant mothers, acts as a midwife, and helps with raising children. As a multipurpose goddess responsible for nurturing all newborns, as well as helping the dead cross peacefully to the underworld, Hathor divided herself into seven goddesses to get everything done. She was then referred to as "the Hathors."

She says, *"When it comes to fairness, the heart already knows what the truth is. So, I do not judge—I simply lead the person inward quietly so that they can hear the decision of their heart.*

"I'm not here to chase down or interrogate anyone—that's not my role at all. I'm more like a guide along the most vital trek of all, that which entails making decisions regarding 'How shall I live my life?' Each and every moment affords us ample opportunities to seek and grow. Rest is a part of the operation, too, to be sure.

"But indecision leads us away from ourselves, and ultimately, then, from our Creator-Source. Indecision rests upon the inability to hear and trust the voice of one's own heart. My role, then, is to send my magical energy outward to those who request my assistance through prayer, worry, or even casual conversation.

"Those who are prepared, absorb my rays, which tip the scales of indecision in the direction of the true heart's desires. In this way, I'm a truth detector; however, it's up to each individual to summon courage to see and live their own truth."

Helps with:

- Artistic projects
- Beauty, attractiveness, and cosmetics
- Celebrations, music, parties, and dancing
- Children, conceiving, pregnancy, and parenting
- Decision-making
- Soulmate, finding one's

INVOCATION

Hathor loves dance and music, so play music and sway or dance as you contact her:

"Dear Hathor, I now surrender my decision to you, my higher self, and the Creator, and I get out of the way. Thank you for helping me make the best possible decision for the highest good for everyone concerned. Please help me clearly hear the decision within my mind and heart, and give me the courage and energy to follow that guidance."

Horus
(Egypt, Greece)

Also known as *Har, Harendotes, Harmakhet, Haroeris, Har-pa-Neb-Taui, Harseisis, Harpokrates, Hor, Horos, Ra-Harakhte.*

Horus is a powerful falcon-headed sky and sun god representing strength and victory. His father, Osiris, was killed by his uncle, Seth. His mother, Isis, magically brought Osiris back to life just long enough to conceive Horus. Then Seth killed Osiris again and dismembered his body so that he couldn't be revived. To avoid Seth's murderous actions, Isis bore and raised Horus in the papyrus marshes of Buto. Isis used the magical skills she'd learned from Ra and Thoth to keep Horus safe.

When Horus was a young man, he fought Seth to avenge his father's death. During the battle, one of Horus's eyes was injured. Eventually, Horus won the throne of both upper and lower Egypt. After that, Horus represented strength, victory, and justice. Every pharaoh in ancient Egypt was considered a living incarnation of Horus.

Horus appears as a falcon head with a large eye (the uninjured one) representing the third eye of clairvoyance. This all-seeing eye also helps us see the truth in all situations.

My experience with Horus (who has been one of my guides for some time) is that he doesn't talk much, but is more of a man of action. He puts his falcon eye up to your third eye, like a lens that gives you clearer psychic vision and insights into any situation on your mind. He helps you see the current truth about issues and how to heal the situation.

Horus's magical healing formula is: to see all people in the situation through the eyes of love. See them as being sweet, loving, and pure . . . which they are in spiritual truth.

Helps with:

- Clairvoyance
- Courage
- Mother-son relationships
- Standing your ground
- Strength
- Vision, physical and psychic

INVOCATION

You can call upon Horus to help you with spiritual or physical vision. The invocation can be done with your eyes either open or shut. You'll probably feel a tingling in your head, especially around the eyes and between the eyebrows when you say this invocation:

"Dear Horus, please lend me your eye so that I may see clearly. I ask for your intervention into my vision in all ways. Open my third eye fully so that I may see spiritually like you! Open my physical vision so that I may see clearly like you! Open my mind's eye completely so that I may see the inner plane like you! Thank you for clear sight. Thank you for releasing me from fear completely. Thank you for opening my eyes fully, that I may drink in the delicious sight of truth and beauty."

Ida-Ten
(Japan)

Also known as *Idaten*.

Ida-Ten is the Japanese god of law, truth, purity, legal victory, and justice.

A protector of monasteries, he has miraculous speed. As a mortal, he was a handsome young general in charge of protecting Buddhist monks, and Buddhism itself. Ida-Ten can guard against religious persecution or help you avert ridicule with respect to your spiritual beliefs.

As quiet as a church mouse, this mild-mannered deity whispers powerful, provocative advice into your ear regarding legal moves and maneuvers. Highly ethical, Ida-Ten nonetheless says, *"I consider lawsuits a form of sport wherein the champion exhibits superior wit, outsmarting the other like in a game of chess."*

Helps with:

- Justice
- Lawsuits, winning
- Protection against religious or spiritual persecution
- Protection of spiritual centers
- Truth issues

INVOCATION

Ida-Ten can be contacted as you're coming out of meditation to seal your practice with positive energy. Mentally say to him:

"Precious Ida-Ten, all-loving and protective force from above, please surround my spiritual project now. Insulate me from all forms of fear so that I may be spared any harsh treatment or words. Prevent me from making judgments of any kind, and help me walk in truth while avoiding controversy. Peace is my true desire, Ida-Ten. Thank you."

Ishtar
(Assyria, Babylonia, Mesopotamia)

Also known as *Absus, Inanna.*

A Babylonian mother and warrior goddess with multiple unique traits ranging from gentleness to motherly protection, Ishtar is also invoked for healing physical pain and maladies.

She's associated with Venus, and some even believe her to be the embodiment of the planet itself. Ishtar openly displays her sensuality, and this may be why some fundamentalists have judged and rejected her.

As I invoked Ishtar, I clairvoyantly saw a picture of me standing with lots of ants crawling near my feet. Ishtar showed me that lower energies or thought-forms were similar to a herd of ants and other insects crawling on the ground—distracting and irritating if they crawled on one's feet, but ultimately not dangerous.

She then shined a beam of light from above my head, downward, which formed a circle around me, as if I were standing in a shower of bright light. The ants couldn't penetrate the light, nor did they want to. They would crawl right up to the light and then bounce back as if they'd just run into a wall of glass.

Ishtar said, *"Allow me the pleasure and honor of draping you in this robe of light, darling. I'm at your service, and know that this doesn't diminish my ability to perform humble service. I know that the noblest of professions is to shine beams of light to cast away shadows and to illuminate the highest of Divine wisdom. Make no mistake about it: I'm here to ease and eliminate pain, suffering, and sorrow through my protective stance.*

"Allow me to shield you with my barriers of light that only allow love to come shining through, and filter out negativity in all forms. A positive new day shines for you, as you are draped in my robe of loving light. Drink it in, Dear One. Quench your thirsty soul away from all fear."

Helps with:

- Child conception and parenting
- Compassion
- Healing, all kinds of
- Gentleness
- Love relationships and marriage
- Protection against lower energies
- Sexuality
- War, prevention or resolution of
- Weather

INVOCATION

Burn a white candle and stare at the flame, or stare at any light source as you speak to Ishtar. This is an especially effective invocation if you've just experienced a negative situation and wish to shake off its effects:

"Divine Ishtar, I stand in the midst of pure light with you now. Thank you for draping me in this light and showering me with the energy of love. I thirst for this love, so please quench me now. Wash away all effects of fear, and unleash me from others' fearful thoughts completely. Release me, release me, release me. Intervene with the others involved in this situation and rinse away any remaining ill feelings. I'm now free, and everyone involved is free as well. This is the truth. Thank you, Ishtar."

Isis
(Egypt)

Also known as *Divine Mother, Goddess of the Mysteries, Goddess of Nature, Isis Myrionymos, Lady of Magic, Lady of Sacred Sexuality, Mistress of Hermetic Wisdom.*

Isis is a multifunctional Egyptian moon goddess who embodies femininity, motherhood, magic, healing, and power. She married her brother Osiris and launched on a career teaching women across Egypt about home-life skills. While she was away, her other brother Seth murdered Osiris. Upon discovering the murder, Isis helped revive her husband from the dead, and they conceived a son, Horus.

Egyptian scholars regard Isis as the original high-priestess of magic. Legend says that Isis convinced Ra to reveal his secret name to her. Once she heard the name, Isis was automatically privileged to receive a complete understanding of high magic. (Thoth, the god of high magic, helped her refine and direct her knowledge.) It's said that Isis used a magical rod for her healings and manifestations, and used rattles to remove negative energies and lower spirits.

Isis is considered an Underworld Queen due to her resuscitation of her dying (and then dead) husband, and also due to her work escorting the dead in general. Her protective wings are engraved around Egyptian sarcophaguses, as they symbolize Isis's ability to renew the souls of the dead.

When I called upon Isis, I heard her say, *"I am Isis, Egyptian queen of the Nile!"* And there she was: a beautiful woman wearing a shawl of large bird wings outstretched like the largest eagle's wing span. She was very feminine, thin, and elegant—the epitome of classiness. She was constantly observing, watching everything like a hawk. I could tell that she had a blunt, to-the-point side to her, expressing her powerful leadership qualities.

She said, *"Have patience with yourself* [she meant everyone, in a universal sense] *while you're still growing and learning. Give countless thanks to yourself for your baby steps along the way. Although they may seem insignificant to you, they're major milestones for your inward self.*

"Celebrate each step," Isis repeated. *"As you appreciate every task that you complete, every kindness that you exhibit, everything—no matter how seemingly small—very soon life takes on the quality of a grand celebration. This is the antithesis of separation from the Divine, and it's your magic elixir for the ages."*

A beautiful friend of mine, Insiah Beckman, had a powerful experience with Isis when she traveled to Egypt in 1999. She's been actively working with Isis ever since. She told me:

"In Egypt, I became one with all life near the Temple of Isis. I could hear the ground, the pebbles, the grass, the Nile, the trees, and everything around me speak. I heard these beautiful voices say to me: 'Welcome home! Welcome home! You have come home again. This is where you lived many, many lifetimes ago!'

"A message was then channeled to me to reclaim who I am and begin my work. I knew then that I incorporated the energy of the goddess Isis that I had left behind in my last lifetime on Earth. The Isis energy is the energy of the Divine Mother—it's the loving and nurturing energy that all the Divine Mothers carry. I believe that they are one and the same, and that they're reincarnations in different forms and cultures to meet the times.

"My experience is this expansiveness that I feel at times, when my heart and energy field totally open up and incorporate all life with love and compassion. My prayer every day is for love, peace, understanding, and respect among all cultures, races, religions, and all life. I abhor any form of disharmony that puts my energy field totally out of sync."

Helps with:

- Divine magic
- Feminine strength, power, and beauty
- Joy
- Self-esteem

INVOCATION

Picture Isis standing behind you with her eagle wings extended, as if you have wings yourself. As you breathe, feel her power infused within you. Notice the loving and graceful energy of her strength. Be aware of the blissful feelings of peace as you say:

"Beautiful Isis, goddess of peaceful power, please infuse me with your graceful strength and your loving confidence. Help me be like you: refined, poised, confident, and loving. Help me soar like an eagle in all ways, inspiring and helping others as I fly high. Thank you."

Isolt
(Celtic)

Also known as *Esyllt, Iseult, Isolde, Ysolt, Ysonde.*

Isolt is the goddess of love and passion in relationships, who helps enhance sexual satisfaction, and offers assistance in finding a soulmate. Princess Isolt was the daughter of an Irish king during the reign of Arthur of Camelot. The various and conflicting legends about her passionate and tragic romantic entanglements with Tristan, prince of Cornwall, have earmarked Isolt as a goddess to the lovelorn.

I invoked her while sitting in an inverted boat that had been made into a temple, high above the Irish sea on a misty morning. Before any spirits would agree to talk with me on this day, the fairies first asked me to remove trash that someone had left on the sand. Once I did so, they opened the way for my transmissions.

I then called upon Isolt, the goddess of passion and sex. I was told that she was out of range "at a very high frequency." Finally, as I invoked further, I was clairvoyantly shown a rainbow with lightning bolts radiating from its underside. *"Isolt is a ray,"* I was told, a heavenly energy of deep, genuine, playful, and all-consuming love. *"Sprinkle it on any occasion like sugar,"* I was told playfully. Far more than a heroic goddess entity, Isolt is an energy beam that spreads when we tap in to it. I was told that we can use it for our love lives whenever and as often as possible. It's healing, and also aphrodisiac-like in its attracting power.

Helps with:

- Breakups, separations, and divorces—healing from
- Passion, reigniting
- Romantic love, attracting

INVOCATION

Put your hand on your chest and feel your heart beating. Imagine rainbow-colored rays of energy emanating from your hand, encircling your heart. Then call on Isolt:

"Loving Isolt, please send passionate energy filled with healthy and romantic love through my hand and into my heart. Thank you for healing anything that could block me from enjoying passion and romance completely. Thank you for opening my heart to true love."

Jesus
(Judeo-Christian)

Also known as *Jeshua, Lord and Savior, Lord Jesus, Christ, Sananda.*

What we know about Jesus of Nazareth comes from the four Gospels and the letters of Paul in the New Testament. Since the Gospels were written 70 or more years after the physical passing of Jesus, it's obvious that none of the authors met Jesus during his human lifetime. Their accounts, then, are based upon secondhand (or more) information passed down through time. No historian who lived during the time of Jesus' human life mentioned him in written accounts of that time period. Yet, there's no arguing the impact that this man has made on humanity up to the present day. Everything from the Gregorian calendar to religious institutions, from wars to spiritual healings, are based on his life in some way.

Many people report seeing apparitions of Jesus, and they often experience miraculous healings as a result. My books *Angel Visions* and *Angel Visions II* contain several stories about Jesus' miraculous powers. Testimony also comes from those who pray for Jesus' intervention . . . who then witness a miracle that they *know* was a result of those prayers. Other people report feeling deep love and comfort when they sense Jesus' presence near, or within, them.

Many have studied Jesus' approach to healing sickness, and they've applied those principles to garner impressive results. Many Christian and New Thought churches emphasize Jesus' teachings about love and forgiveness, and promote these methods as ways to cure personal and worldly ills.

There's a widespread belief that Jesus is watching over the world and its inhabitants, ensuring that harm doesn't befall us. In New Age circles, Jesus is believed to be the head of the Great White Brotherhood, a committee of great spiritual teachers and healers overseeing the spiritual renaissance on the planet.

My own experiences with Jesus are lifelong and extensive. I call upon him before every healing session, and have always found him to be the greatest healer among my friends in the spirit world. He is equally powerful with people and divinities of all religious and nonreligious backgrounds, and emanates unconditional love that can heal someone plagued by guilt, fear, and unforgiveness.

Helps with:

- Clear communication with God
- Divine guidance and direction
- Faith issues
- Forgiveness
- Healing of all kinds
- Manifestation
- Miracles

INVOCATION

Picture Jesus standing in front of you. From your heart, send him as much love as you can feel and imagine. Notice what happens next: The love is returned to you, magnified manyfold. Keep sending and receiving this love, monitoring your breath to make sure that you're breathing in this healing energy.

At the same time, mentally tell Jesus anything that's bothering you, minor or major. Pour your heart out to him, and reveal your deepest secrets—he's absolutely trustworthy and will always use this information in a positive way. Then, ask him to intervene and give you direction as to how to heal the situation. Don't tell him *how* to heal it; just know that it's in his loving hands, and that he will work directly with God to create a peaceful resolution for everyone involved. Give thanks in your heart, and let go.

Kali

(Hindu; India)

ᏒᎯᏇ

Also known as *Black Mother, Kali-Ma, Raksha-Kali.*

Kali is a Hindu aspect of Devi, who is the ultimate goddess. Kali is the goddess of the endings of cycles, the death and transformation energy that lets go of the old and brings in the new. Some are threatened by Kali's seemingly destructive power; however, Kali is actually a loving energy that helps free us of fear. She only destroys that which could keep us in bondage, or which could slow or divert our Divine mission, in the same way that a loving mother would take away dangerous items from her children.

Kali has the personality of a high-energy, supercharged woman on a clear mission. She has an impatient artist's temperament, like a stage mom who knows what needs to be done and doesn't have time to argue. She says, *"My passions have overwhelmed many who have likened me to a silver storm of fury. They've called me fickle, temperamental, and wrathful. Yes, my passion does have an edge, as it is forthrightness unleashed.*

"I say, 'If you aren't willing to help me, or let me help you, then at least get out of my way.' When you invoke me, get ready for unbridled action. It may feel like I push you along too fast, and it may feel unsafe. But I assure you that I'm simply helping you through doors that open so that we can proceed as light-beings. We have much catching up [with the mission] to do, and dilly-dallying only further thwarts our efforts.

543

"Do not procrastinate, delay, or fear the change that always accompanies action and moving forward. Do not be afraid of making the wrong decision; rather, fear living in indecision. I am Kali, single-minded focus mixed with fiery passion and deep caring about many causes."

Kali told me that she, like a lot of women, has been called a "bitch," when she's simply being powerful and unwavering.

Helps with:

- Courage
- Determination
- Direction
- Focus
- Motivation
- Protection
- Tenacity

INVOCATION

Kali comes immediately if you think of her name: "Kali, Kali, Kali." She arrives like a sudden and powerful rainstorm, with purpose and determination. She's excellent at extracting the heart of the problem from any situation presented to her. So, if you tell her that you want help with your love life, for example, Kali will see the true underlying issues. She'll give you very clear, forceful direction, without mincing any words.

Krishna
(Hindu; India)

Also known as *The Divine One.*

The Hindu Trinity includes Brahma, Shiva, and Vishnu, the three gods who create, protect, and oversee the life cycles on Earth. The god Vishnu incarnates whenever he's needed in physical form to overcome inhumane practices. Krishna is the eighth incarnation (also called an *avatar*) of Vishnu.

Krishna incarnated at midnight on the eighth day of the season of *Bhadrapada* (the Hindu word for "late summer") sometime between 3200 and 3100 B.C. He delivered the Hindu spiritual text, the Bhagavad Gita. Today, Krishna is one of India's most popular deities.

Krishna's legends portray him as a romantic figure, and many paintings show him and his partner, Radha (one of the goddess Lakshmi's incarnations) exhibiting beautiful romantic love. Some Feng Shui experts recommend placing a picture of Krishna and Radha in the romance corner* of your home to manifest a soulmate relationship.

Krishna is a deliverer of joy and happiness. When you call upon him, you'll likely feel a swelling of warm, loving energy in your heart and belly. He says, *"Never underestimate the healing power of love. Its depths are further than the reaches of any ocean, and there is no barrier that it cannot overcome. Use this power within your mind that is everlasting, with no need to hold back, as it's a constantly renewable resource to use again and again. Pour love over every situation, and watch the rewards you will reap!"*

Helps with:

- Blessings
- Food, purifying and spiritualizing
- Gardening, crops, and flowers
- Joy
- Relationships
- Romantic love
- Spiritual awakening
- Vegetarianism

INVOCATION

Krishna loves to connect with people through the offering of, and blessing of, food. Prior to eating something, look at the food and mentally call upon Krishna. Tell him that the food is your offering to him. As he accepts your gift, he will bless and purify the food with his highly spiritualized energy. Thank him, and then completely ingest his blessings by eating the food slowly, enjoying each bite completely. Have a mental conversation with him while you're eating this food. You'll notice that the experience is like being with a very wise dining companion who offers you stellar wisdom and sage advice.

* For those of you unfamiliar with Feng Shui, it is the ancient Chinese art of placement. As part of Feng Shui practice, one is directed to situate certain items in specific areas of one's domicile in order to effect a certain goal. For example, if you wish to find a soulmate, you would place objects that symbolize love in the "romance corner"—usually the far right quadrant of one's home. For more information, please consult Terah Kathryn Collins's book *The Western Guide to Feng Shui* (Hay House, 1996).

Kuan Ti
(China)

Also known as *Kuan Jung, Kuan Yu.*

Kuan Ti is the Chinese warrior god who acts to prevent war. He's a prophet who predicts the future, and he protects people from lower spirits.

In his human incarnation, Kuan Ti was a Chinese war hero and Han dynasty general, well known for his warriorlike skills and intelligent decisions. When he passed away, he was elevated to the status of god. He works arm-in-arm with Archangel Michael on matters of justice within government systems.

He says, *"The men who are in positions of power are playing a dangerous game with their saber-rattling. It will backfire and explode into wars of dangerous proportions if this high drama isn't curtailed. It's all a game of power that they play, but of the most explosive kind. The populace must intervene and demand peaceful methods, rather than these dangerous ploys to capture control and coin. I will intervene along with you, as we replace our fear-based leaders with those who act from wisdom and understanding. It's the only way."*

While I was sitting in a bird aviary in China, I mentally asked Kuan Ti advice on avoiding wars and manifesting world peace. He replied with powerful energy: *"Inner soldiers are needed at this time—those who will march to their inner commander in spiritual terms. Those who will carry out their inner commander's marching orders and who do not worry about reprimands from the outside world. The only authority figure requiring your obedience is the mighty General within. In this respect, truth shall prevail, and peace upon this planet is possible once again."*

Helps with:

- Justice and freedom for falsely accused prisoners and prisoners-of-war
- Legal matters
- Prophecies about world events
- Psychic abilities, increasing accuracy and details of
- Space clearing
- Spirit releasement
- War, preventing and ending

INVOCATION

Call upon Kuan Ti if you're concerned about world events, especially those involving warfare. Mentally say:

"Kuan Ti, I ask for your intervention, wisdom, and council about [describe the situation to him]. Thank you for intervening and bringing about a peaceful resolution through wisdom and understanding. Thank you for assisting and counseling the leaders involved, and helping them use their power in wise ways for the benefit of all."

Kuan Yin
(Asia)

Also known as *Kwan Yin, Quan Yin, Guanyin, Quan'Am, Kannon, Kanin, Kwannon.*

Kuan Yin is one of the most beloved and popular Eastern divinities. A physically and spiritually beautiful Chinese goddess of mercy, compassion, and protection, her name means "she who hears prayers." Kuan Yin does, in fact, hear and answer every prayer sent her way.

Kuan Yin is both a goddess and a *bodhisattva,* which means "enlightened being." Bodhisattvas can become Buddhas; however, Kuan Yin has such a deep love for humanity that after she attained enlightenment, instead of ascending to Buddhahood, she chose to remain in human form until every one of us becomes enlightened. She's devoted to helping us fully open up to our spiritual gifts, attain profound knowledge and enlightenment, and reduce world suffering. It's said that the mere uttering of her name affords guaranteed protection from harm.

Kuan Yin is often called "the Mother Mary of the East," because she represents feminine divinity and goddess energy in the Buddhist religion, in the same way that Mary radiates sweet loving femininity within Christianity. Kuan Yin teaches us to practice a life of harmlessness, using great care to ease suffering in the world and not add to it in any way. You may see the color red when she's around, such as red sparkles of light or a red mist that appears from out of nowhere.

A woman named Mary Urssing told me this beautiful story of her interactions with Kuan Yin:

"I was in Hawaii and had just purchased a crystal pendant depicting Kuan Yin. Right after donning the necklace, I started to hear her talk to me in a soft, soothing Asian voice. On the last morning of my vacation, I was awakened by Kuan Yin telling me to go outside for a walk. I sat on our porch but was urged to walk. I did just that, carrying a portable cassette recorder with headphones, through which I heard beautiful Hawaiian music. I noticed a plumeria flower on the ground that was pink, to me a sign of love. I would normally pick these flowers and immediately put them in my hair, but things were different today. I just held the flower.

"As I neared a waterfall, I heard Kuan Yin tell me that I was to have an initiation of self-passion, far beyond self-love. The moment was very sacred, as I knew that I was taking a vow that was more intense than anything I'd ever done. I accepted, and was told to stand inside the waterfall in a cove, a cocoon of sorts. I was to really be, feel, and know self-love. I felt this with all of me and grounded this moment into my complete being. Trying now to put it into words doesn't seem to do justice to this personal ceremony.

"As I took in this energy, I was asked to seal it with the symbol that I unknowingly had chosen for this time—the plumeria. As I threw my flower into the waterfall to ritualize my ceremony, I saw it sink, and as it did, the water in its place turned the most beautiful color of deep, passionate red. I actually saw the water turn red! All of this instantly changed me, and I knew that it was time to honor myself and my power.

"Later that day, I told my friend Marlies that I'd had the most amazing experience at a waterfall. She asked, 'Was it at Kuan Yin's waterfall?' I was surprised by her question and asked her for more information. She explained that Kuan Yin's statue was in one of the waterfalls on the island. Sure enough, as I scouted around later that day, there it was—a beautiful statue of Kuan Yin tucked away on a stone shelf in the cove of the waterfall. She had called me to her sanctuary!"

In Kona, Hawaii, there are many beautiful statues of Kuan Yin. Near one statue that depicts her holding a lotus flower, she said this to me: *"Here are my sacred instructions: First, have mercy upon yourselves. You have endured much in your land, and you have eons of lessons yet before you. Only through a gentle touch is Nirvana revealed. Stretch and reach for greatness, but always with a gentle approach. Seek not opportunities, but allow them to gently come to you as a lotus flower floats upon the currents of water amidst a gentle breeze. Strive, but not with hurry—enjoy the process upon which you embark. Know that each step along the way is akin to a party—a celebration of movement, which is itself a miracle.*

"Appreciate the godliness within yourself, within each of you. Do not chide yourself for your errors and mistakes, but laugh, grow, and learn from them instead. You, my gentle child, are doing just fine—in fact, very well indeed.

"If I were to give you any word of wisdom, it would be the word that best embodies love upon this Earth plane to me: compassion. Growing past all shame and embarrassment, and moving toward appreciation, not just for the 'good' parts of yourself and others, but for all along the way—it's all good, believe me. And if you can know that as the eternal truth sooner rather than later, your happiness will come galloping toward you at the speed of mustangs with winged hooves. Believe that as the truth. Now.

"Wisdom comes from sitting still and listening, not from rushing to get ahead. A still heart receives love and information more readily than one that is harried. Do something simple today: Pick a flower and simply study it with no intent. Be blank. Be open. And know that whatever comes to you is good, and a lesson in the making—always and forever."

Helps with:

- Clairvoyance
- Compassion
- Feminine grace, beauty, and power
- Kindness, gentleness, and sweetness, toward self and others
- Love, receiving and giving
- Mercy
- Musical abilities, developing (especially singing)
- Protection—especially for women and children
- Spiritual enlightenment and gifts

INVOCATION

Kuan Yin always hears and answers our prayers, and no special ritual is necessary to contact her. However, you may feel a more heart-centered connection with her through the use of flowers. For instance, hold a blossom, gaze at a budding plant or bouquet, or draw or look at a picture of flowers. Those who work closely with Kuan Yin often chant the mantra: *Om Mani Padme Hum,* which means "Hail to the jewel in the lotus flower."

One prayer that will help you invoke Kuan Yin is:

"Beloved Kuan Yin, please hear the prayers within my heart. Please uncover and understand what my true needs are. I ask for your intervention into the areas of my life that are triggering pain. Please come to my aid and assistance, guiding me to see my situation in a new light of love and compassion. Please help me to be like you and live peacefully and purposefully."

Kuthumi
(Sikh; Theosophy; New Age)

Also known as *Mahatma Kuthumi mal Singh, Koot Hoomi, Sirdar Thakar Singh Sadhanwalia, K.H.*

Kuthumi is a pseudonym for a Sikh spiritual leader who lived in the 1800s named Sirdar Thakar Singh Sadhanwali, according to Theosophical researchers (including author K. Paul Johnson).

Madame Blavatsky met Singh during her extensive travels in India. This is also when she met and studied under the Eastern Indian spiritual teachers who would be the basis for Djwhal Khul, Master Hillarion, and El Morya, whom she referred to as "the Mahatmas." Blavatsky promoted these men's spiritual teachings in North America, protecting their true identities with pseudonyms. She would produce letters from Singh and the other Mahatmas, sometimes claiming that the letters materialized from the ethers.

When the men passed over, Blavatsky and her followers (most notably Alice Bailey and Elizabeth Clare Prophet) began channeling messages from them. This was the first usage of the term "ascended masters." According to the "new" Theosophists, Kuthumi's past lives include Saint Francis and Pythagoras.

When I called upon Kuthumi, he came to me dressed as a circus clown! He said, *"Life is a three-ring circus, and the key is to not let yourself get distracted by events around you. Steady focus and a willingness to search for higher truth will move your consciousness away from anxiety and instill it with peace.*

"Refuse to be distracted or thwarted. Use your stubbornness rightly by concentrating only upon that which is good—in that way, you truly overcome evil in every sense of the word. Allow me to show you ways to access the reaches of the higher dimensions where peace is accessible to all. Above the din of the Earth plane, we reach Nirvana together, singly, yet side-by-side. The holiest prospect is teaching peace through self-attainment."

Helps with:

- Dedication to life purpose
- Focus

INVOCATION

If you find yourself distracted from your major goals and life purpose, ask Kuthumi to help you maintain diligence when it comes to your priorities. He'll help you organize your schedule in a balanced way. Ask him for help anytime you feel overwhelmed by multiple tasks:

> "Dearest Kuthumi, I ask for your intervention. Please remove all distractions from my mind and schedule, allowing me to focus completely on my true life's purpose. Please let any life changes occur gently and peacefully, and help me notice my spiritual guidance and Divine will. I now release to you any ego-based fears that would deter me from my path. Help me recognize when I procrastinate with respect to my purpose so that I may be fully immersed in the joy of spiritual service."

Lakshmi
(Buddhist, Hindu, India, Jain)

Also known as *Haripriya, Jaganmatri, Laxmi, Matrirupa, Vriddhi.*

Lakshmi's name is derived from the Sanskrit word *Laksya,* which means "goal" or "aim."

Lakshmi is a beautiful, golden-skinned moon goddess of prosperity and good fortune who brings blessings of abundance to everyone. Lakshmi also represents beauty, purity, generosity, and true happiness. It's said that she sprang forth from the churning ocean bearing gifts and lotus flowers, looking so beautiful that all of the gods immediately wanted her as their wife. She chose to be with the sun god, Vishnu. She was thereafter reborn as Vishnu's companion in each of his lives.

Because Lakshmi's true mission is to bring eternal happiness to Earth, she helps us find meaningful careers that bring about handsome rewards, including personal fulfillment. She knows that wealth, in and of itself, isn't enough to create lasting happiness—it must be accompanied by spirituality and a feeling of accomplishment. So Lakshmi may lead us to our life's work, which will create joy and abundance for ourselves and others.

Lakshmi is associated with lotus flowers. Some legends say that she was born from, and lives in, one of these blossoms. In artwork, she's usually depicted carrying, or standing upon, a lotus, which is a symbol of spiritual awakening and peace.

Lakshmi brings grace, beauty, and love into homes, and ensures that all household needs are met. She's adored by Ganesh, and they often work together to help people meet their goals.

Lakshmi speaks in a sweet, melodious voice and says, *"The attainment of wealth is one of life's greatest mysteries and challenges. Most spiritual aspirants abhor the pursuit of money, yet they long for the freedom and services that it affords. Many of your spiritual teachers and healers are conflicted about accepting money for their work, yet they long for the day when they can quit other forms of employment and devote themselves fully to the service of spirituality.*

"This dilemma must be dealt with, for we here in the strata you call 'Heaven' see many solutions at hand, most of which we can help you with, without your needing to strain or think so much. This, I will tell you: Pressing with your mind to try to make things happen is your greatest barrier and blockage, which can only be overcome when you become convinced that all riches worth having are already manifested within. When you relax with this knowledge and know with certainty that all is taken care of, then all restrictions are lifted completely."

Helps with:

- Abundance
- Beauty and aesthetics
- Happiness, lasting
- Home supplies and food, manifesting
- Space clearing for the home

INVOCATION

Lakshmi loves a grateful and appreciative heart. So as you call upon her, imagine that all of your wishes have been granted in a Divine way. Feel grateful that this is so. Know that the power of your Creator, combined with your faith and Lakshmi's loving help, manifests into form miraculously. Her manifestations are the physical embodiment of the love and gratitude that you now feel.

Stay focused on your desires, seeing and feeling them as being already manifested. Then give thanks to Lakshmi by mentally chanting: *"Om Nameh Lakshmi Namah,"* which is a prayer of thanks and reverence.

Lugh
(Celtic)

Also known as *Lug, Lugus, Lleu.*

Lugh is a youthful sun god with a magical hound, helmet, and spear that completely protect him and all who call upon him. Lugh helps humans develop their inner sorcerer or sorceress with Divine love. He's also associated with fertility and yielding a bountiful summer harvest.

Legends say that Lugh was a master craftsman, poet, healer, and jack-of-all-trades, and that there was no skill that he couldn't perform.

When I called upon Lugh to provide me with a message for this book, a breathtakingly handsome man with a helmet and shield appeared before me, with a Roman look to his dress. He said, *"You called? What can I help you with?"* When I described a particular situation that I could use his assistance with, Lugh said, *"Just a minute—something is brewing here. I'll check into it and be right back."*

He then returned a fraction of a moment later, carrying some sort of potion. It looked like a blue powder glistening with a liquidlike sheen. Lugh said, *"This is based upon my assessment of your inner yearnings, leanings, and tendencies."* He very politely asked if he could anoint me with the healing potion that he explained was custom-made for the situation. He added that he tailor-made all of his magical recipes for each individual and their particular situation.

I lay back, and Lugh swept the hair off my forehead. He seemed to brush my aura there as well. He asked me to remove my sunglasses so that he could freely anoint me. He pinched some of the powder and drizzled it on my forehead, then spread generous portions all over the top of my head and face, covering me like a skullcap.

He asked me to breathe in the essence very deeply, and then he said, *"This potion is infused with magical properties that will help support the resolution of this problem, in much the same way that vitamins infuse you with energy and help you have a strong workout at the gym. The vitamins lift you up, but it's still up to you to go to the gym and do the work. In the same vein, allow my apothecary potion to support your efforts, boost your faith and confidence, and bring you all the way back home centered in peace and joy."* Then he closed his healing ceremony with me by saying, *"All my love!"* and disappeared.

Helps with:

- Alchemy
- Artistic projects—including art, crafts, poetry, and music
- Divine magic
- Healing from painful situations
- Protection of all kinds
- Solutions to any problem

INVOCATION

Lugh is a powerful force who will come quickly when called. Think of his name and feel the strength, power, and magnitude of his energy. Then, tell him about your needs and the issues that you request help with. As described above, he may leave for a moment to retrieve a healing balm or potion. Give him as much time as he needs to address your situation fully. You'll know when he's finished with his treatment because his energy will withdraw until you next call upon him.

Send him your thank-yous, and know that he receives them gratefully. Lugh will watch over the progress of your situation, all the way to completion, so feel free to call upon him anytime during the process of resolution.

Lu-Hsing
(China)

Also known as *Pinyin Lu Xing.*

Lu-Hsing is the god of salaries, pay, success, career progress, investments, steady accumulation, wealth, and employees. He's one of three Chinese stellar deities known collectively as "the Fu Lu Shou San Hsing," the gods who bring about happiness, fortune, wealth, and longevity.

Lu-Hsing was a mortal man named Shih Fen who was a high-ranking royal court official in the 2nd-century B.C. He was deified following his death. Lu-Hsing takes note of, and rewards, those who are committed and dedicated to their careers. He warns against engaging in corrupt behavior to get ahead. Lu-Hsing suggests healing unpleasant or dishonest situations through prayer, and by seeking Divine guidance first, before taking more drastic action such as calling the corruption to the attention of others.

Invoke Lu-Hsing before a job search so that doors will open to you easily, leading to the high road of your chosen profession. But be aware that Lu-Hsing's signs telling you which doors to walk through can be quite subtle. It takes an agile mind and much alertness to properly heed his guidance. Those who receive his counseling will appreciate the dry wit that he exhibits and the twists and turns he orchestrates, which seem to be part of his modus operandi. Always invoke Lu-Hsing before asking your boss for a raise or promotion.

"Do not rest on your laurels," he cautions. If you want to enjoy your current success instead of worrying about how to climb the next mountain, you'll need to tell Lu-Hsing that you want to pause for a regrouping.

I invoked Lu-Hsing during a visit to China, and I asked him to address the topic of attaining financial security and success. He said, *"The secret of financial success is the willingness to adopt a warrior spirit in attitude, grace, and presence. This does not mean adopting an air of aggressiveness, but rather, a spirit of making treaties and pacts with oneself and others.*

"Warriors have an outlook of expecting a positive outcome, and a willingness to do whatever is needed to incur that outcome. It means not giving up, but allowing for flexibility, and to flow with the energy or chi as it moves along. Be strong, be vigilant for success, and be sensitive to the energy undercurrents, and you shan't go wrong."

Helps with:

- Employment, all aspects of
- Job interviews
- Raises and promotions

INVOCATION

Call upon Lu-Hsing before any major event involving employment. Imagine that you're having a mental meeting with him and that Lu-Hsing is the ultimate executive who will clear the way for whatever you request. Visualize him taking notes during your discussion, and know that he'll take care of everything. Ask him to give you very clear guidance that you'll easily understand. Then, write, "Thank you, Lu-Hsing" on a piece of paper, fold it, and hold it in your palm during the applicable situation—whether it's asking your boss for a raise, getting through a job interview, or taking part in an important meeting.

Maat
(Egypt)

Also known as *Ma'at, Maa, Maet, Maht, Mat, Maut.*

The Egyptian goddess of truth, fairness, and justice, Maat is the daughter of the sun god, Ra, and consort/wife of the magical scribe god, Thoth. Legend says that when Ra created the world, he created his daughter to be the embodiment of integrity.

Maat is the goddess of fairness, integrity, promises, truth, and justice. Her symbol is the feather, which she uses with a scale of justice to weigh the heaviness of guilt or deceit within a newly deceased soul's heart.

She has impeccable abilities to discern true character, honesty, and motives in people. Invoke Maat to keep dishonest individuals and situations away from you, and for protection against dark or lower energies. If Maat deems your motives to be pure, she'll treat you with the warmest love. If not, then she may put you through trials of purification—or you can engage in rituals, lifestyle changes, affirmations, and ceremonies to avert her trials and bring you her comradeship. She doesn't judge; she's truth itself. Maat also oversees legal matters to ensure harmony and honesty.

She says, *"Everyone possesses magical abilities, and for a younger woman, the key lies in being very attuned to her menstrual cycle. As she practices building greater harmony with the cycles of the moon and realizes their connection to her flow, she will become 'moon-struck' and open herself to a shift that unleashes practical and esoteric abilities—both of which will create in her a beautiful confidence only seen in great displays of feminine energy. The big cats, for instance, are unapologetic about their power. They're enchanting because they put their full force in each step.*

"For men and women who are not of childbearing age, the cycles of the moon do not have such obvious marks, yet we're all still affected. Anyone— even spirits—within the gravitational pull of this planet will feel the sway that the moon creates."

"Pay exquisitely close attention to your relationship with the moon, this great source of light. Visit her often. You will find her to be a source of magical abilities that will give you important messages."

Helps with:

- Addictions and cravings, overcoming
- Clarification in confusing situations
- Discerning the truth, and integrity in others
- Divine magic
- Integrity and commitments—for oneself and others
- Orderliness
- Protection against deceit and manipulation
- Purifying the body

INVOCATION

If you're confused or undecided about a situation, ask Maat to help you clarify your true feelings and intentions. She'll give you insight into the other people involved in the situation as well. Before you call upon her, though, be absolutely certain that you're willing to face the truth and possibly receive information that you don't want to know (such as being told about someone's lack of integrity, for example).

When you're ready to work with Maat, show her respect by sitting upright. Then say:

"Beloved and Powerful Maat, please come to me now. You are the shower of truth and integrity, and I need you to shine your light upon [describe the situation or name the person involved]. Please shine the light of truth onto my mind and heart, helping me feel and know its wisdom. Please help me release any narrow thinking that could blind me to the facts, and help me use the truth as the foundation for all actions. Thank you."

Maeve
(Ireland)

Also known as *Mab, Medb, Medhbh, Madb, Queen of Connacht.*

A powerful warrior goddess whose name means "intoxicated woman," Maeve is renowned for her strong will and her ability to manifest whatever and whomever she wants. She's associated with the menstrual cycle and feminine beauty. Maeve is also a fairy queen and land goddess who is loved by horses.

Call upon Maeve anytime you need guidance about natural and alternative healing methods. For instance, when you're in a health-food store, ask Maeve to guide you to vitamins, minerals, herbs, and oils to help with whatever situation you need assistance with. Like a friendly and wise shopping companion, Maeve will steer you to the right products or books to use.

I spoke with her near a river laced with fragrant flowers outside Dublin, Ireland. The area was rich with beautiful fairies who were tending to the flowers. Maeve came quickly when I called her, and she told me:

"I oversee the magical kingdom of the fae. I'm not one of the fairy folk, but I delight and am invoked in their Divine plan and mission. Therefore, when you call upon them, you likely also call upon me. My mission is to be a leader, and to untwist spells so that they can be purified and centered before their delivery to the fairy folk. You might say that I'm a mediator or

translator between them and yourselves, making sure that the wishes they grant you are of the highest value.

"Unlike the angels on-high, the fairy folk live in more of a time density and must use their time wisely. So must you! You can ask me to ferret out your material wishes, as I'm also keen to provide for you in the highest way. Yet I help you avoid possessions that would in fact 'keep' you and require such high maintenance as to distract you from your lighted pathway.

"I'm especially fond of the healers among you, and must admit a special penchant for the youth involved in healing ambitions. Ask me for advice on herbal alchemy, potions, oils, and elixirs. I infuse them with magical energies of the highest caliber!"

Helps with:

- Alchemy
- Aromatherapy
- Elementals, connecting with (especially the fairies)
- Feminine beauty, strength, and attractiveness
- Healers, beginning practitioners, students of healing, or would-be healers
- Herbology
- Horses, healing and protecting
- Menstrual cycles

INVOCATION

Maeve comes whenever or wherever she's needed; however, you may find that your initial conversations with her are clearer and easier to discern if you begin speaking with her outside in nature, especially where flowers grow freely. Look at a flower and imagine the fairies flitting in and out of the petals, tending them with joy and love. Then mentally say:

"Queen Maeve, it is I [state your name]. I'd like to get to know you, and I respectfully ask for your mentorship in my healing work and on my spiritual path. I'm sincerely dedicated to healing, and I promise to continue taking good care of the environment. I'm willing to help in your mission of world healing, and ask that you take me under your powerful wings and guide me clearly and powerfully. Thank you for opening doors to my healing work and career."

Maitreya
(Buddhist; Chinese; New Age)

Also known as *Buddha of the Future; Future Buddha; Lord Maitreya,*
Lord Maitreya Maitri, Happy Buddha, Hotei, Laughing Buddha,
Maitreya Buddha, Miroku-Bosatsu.

Historians disagree about Maitreya's history. Many scholars believe
that he was a monk named Sthiramati who showed great compassion and kindness toward others. It's said that Sthiramati was so committed to bringing about happiness that he was bestowed the name
Maitreya, which means "the loving one."

However, he's sometimes called Hotei, who was a T'ang Dynasty
monk renowned for giving candy to children. Chinese Buddhists believe
that Hotei was one of Maitreya's incarnations. Others believe that
Maitreya incarnated during the time of Krishna as the famous Rishi
written of in the Vedas, and also during the time of Goutama Buddha's
Earth life.

In some Buddhist populations, it's believed that Maitreya is the
bodhisattva (enlightened one) who is successor to Goutama Siddhartha
as the next Buddha. He's often portrayed as a smiling Buddha with a
protruding belly, called "the Laughing Buddha."

It's prophesied that between 4- and 5,000 years after Goutama
Buddha left his physical body, Maitreya will reappear on Earth in
human form when Buddhism needs reigniting. Maitreya will then teach

and lead people through example, and eventually replace Goutama Buddha as *the* Buddha.

In New Age circles, he's called Lord Maitreya, and he's viewed as a member of the Great White Brotherhood, along with Jesus, Saint-Germain, and Archangel Michael. He's said to be a master of the sixth ray of light of enlightenment and ascension.

I spoke with Maitreya while seated in front of a large Laughing Buddha statue, which seemed to become animated as soon as I mentally began talking with him. A friend of mine, Lynnette Brown, was seated next to me and also heard similar messages from him and saw him move and speak.

Maitreya said, *"Laughter is sacred. Laugh more, play more, and sing more to harmonize yourself with the natural world. Even humming moves your vibrational chord outward to mesh with the universe and all of humanity. Music is a gift bestowed upon all of us, from the Allness. Nirvana itself is a song, a dance, and a play. Delight in the unfoldment of this great musical that you call 'life.' And call upon your enlightenment, not through striving, but on the wings of laughter and song.*

"There will come a day when joy will reign once again. Nirvana is joy and carefree laughter. When you laugh, you're most connected to the Infinite, because the breath emitted through laughter is the Allness. A heart filled with gaiety, mirth, playfulness, and laughter is a heart filled with Nirvana-essence. Be childlike eternally, Beloved Being, and worry not about your ancestors or of creation—it in itself is locked in a tight chamber of safety that nothing can permeate or destroy. Life itself is eternal, and an unfoldment of joy.

"By centering your mind on the intention of enjoying yourself, you are centered in the moment, and thus you capture the full flavor of that moment as deliciously as sweet, juicy fruit. Savor its delectable sensations and all of its variety, for life is a banquet and a feast. And just as in a buffet, where you must try various platters to attain the experience that teaches you your likes and dislikes, so must you also gain knowledge through a wide range of experiences. And thus you can be selective as to that which you place on your platter and partake into your belly. Enjoy the process, and be unafraid to taste and sample new selections put before you.

"Laughter truly is the best medicine of all—you take yourselves far too

*seriously, and in so doing, you edge out the secret of harmony on your plan-
et: living in joy. Today, seek out ten people who are not smiling, and go out
of your way to put a smile on their face. In that way, you will have lit ten
candles of light amid darkness."*

Helps with:

- Joy
- Laughter and a sense of humor
- Lovingness
- Peace, global and personal

INVOCATION

Imagine, or look at, a picture of the Laughing Buddha—with his
huge smile, arms extended joyfully upward, and his large belly protruding. His whole manner exudes the complete release and bliss of a good
laugh. Imagine yourself rubbing his belly, and feel how "contagious" his
laughter and joy are! Perhaps you'll notice yourself smiling, giggling, or
even laughing out loud. Notice how your heart fills with warm love,
peace, and utter security.

Mentally tell Maitreya about any situation or relationship that troubles you, and notice how he helps you release anxiety. He vows to intervene if you promise to continually monitor yourself for worry, and
immediately give all of your concerns to him. Feel the weight lifted from
your shoulders, and know that there's nothing to fear.

After spending time with Maitreya, watch a funny movie, read a
humorous book, or swap silly stories with a friend. The point is to fully
release the situation to him through the follow-up process of engaging
in play, laughter, and comedy.

Mary, the Beloved Mother
(Judeo-Christian, Catholic)

Also known as *Mother Mary, Our Lady of Guadalupe,
Virgin Mary, Queen of the Angels.*

Mary's historical data isn't well known, as the four Gospels that describe her don't go into much detail. Other documents about Mary, such as the *Proto-Evangelion of James,* discuss her birth, childhood, and adulthood—however, scholars can't agree on the validity of such texts. And then there are the New Age books, which provide information about Mary's life based on channeled or regressed information.

The Gospels say that Mary lived her life in Nazareth, which was a small working-class village. She lived with her husband, Joseph; her son, Jesus; and—according to historians—Joseph's four sons and one daughter from his first marriage. Because Joseph worked outside the home as a carpenter or furniture maker, Mary likely spent most of her time tending to family and household needs. Most women in Mary's time didn't receive any education or literacy training. Historians and religious scholars speculate that Mary led a difficult life, struggling to raise enough money for food and taxes, and trying to avoid the dangers of ongoing military and political uprisings.

New Age authors speculate that Mary may have taken baby Jesus to Qumran and temporarily lived among the Essenes, where they both learned the mystical secrets of the Dead Sea Scrolls. They also hypothesize that the brothers and sisters in the household were also offspring of Mary and Joseph.

Many modern-day people, especially children, have seen visions of Mother Mary in places such as Fatima, Lourdes, and Guadalupe. Mary's apparitions and the messages that she delivers to those who see her help us recognize the presence of miraculous masters among us.

Mary has been called "the Queen of the Angels," and her famous interactions with Archangel Gabriel during the annunciation certainly herald this title. Her present persona, too, is definitively angelic: She's among the most loving, patient, and kind of the ascended masters. The angels love her, and they work with her to effect miracles. Yet, behind her gentleness, there's a firm "mother bear" who lovingly warns us to shape up.

Mary is especially concerned with children, and she counsels us to use wisdom, intelligence, and love in our parenting decisions. She's especially watchful of the new "Indigo and Crystal Children," who bring gifts of salvation to the planet. Mary will assist anyone whose life purpose involves helping these young ones, and she will open doors to child advocates. She helps those whose intentions are benevolent toward children, including those who seek to abolish chemicals that harm children's psyches, including dietary pesticides and additives, and psychoactive medications such as Ritalin.

A woman named Mary Frances sent me this story explaining how Mary helped her and her children:

"I was 39, pregnant, and quite large. My daughter was seven years old. We were taking care of a friend's daughters on this day and decided to drive to the coast to gather seashells. We drove the car into a very sandy lot, parked, and enjoyed the day at the beach. Then we all got into the car, and lo and behold, we couldn't get out of the deep sand. The wheels of the car were stuck. We all got out to see if the car would move without our weight in it, but it wouldn't. Nothing seemed to work. We were stuck, and all alone in a very isolated location!

"My daughter began crying and praying aloud. She said,

'Oh, dear Virgin, you've said that we should call you anytime we need your help. We're stuck in the sand, my mother is pregnant, and I can't push the car as I'm too small. Please, please, please.' The other two girls laughed and asked me, 'Does she really believe this?' I answered, 'Of course she does!'

"It was getting dark, though, and we all began to worry—when from out of nowhere, a pickup truck with three men came into view. The men stopped and pushed us out of the sand, and we were on our way in no time. I couldn't help but look at my friend's daughters and say, 'See?!'"

I frequently call upon Mary for help with healings and guidance, and I always find that she fills my heart with the sweetest warmth and love. I recently asked Mary for a message when I visited a shrine dedicated to her at the magnificent (circa 1200) cathedral in Cologne. My lower back felt stiff and sore from traveling, so I also lit a white candle in front of her statue and asked her for a healing. My candle joined dozens of others in a beautiful ceremony of lighted prayers.

I knew that Mary was with me when I felt her familiar calling card of loving warmth in my heart. The warmth encompassed my entire chest and stomach and caused my breath to deepen.

"*Compassion,*" she repeated swiftly in one of my ears in the sweetest voice—like the music of the wind blowing through springtime leaves. "*Compassion is what the world hungers for most, which means love coupled with an understanding of the other person's point of view and feelings.*

"*So much strife stems from an aggressive desire for compassion—a desire to force the other parties involved to agree with you, because everyone is too afraid to admit that they can see and understand why the other acts in this way. Throw down your arms and come to me for a reuniting with all others. Throw your arms around me and feel my embrace! Allow me to soothe shattered nerves and hurt feelings.*

"*Come to me, those of you who are afraid. I shall help you rise above all strain and suffering so that you may see the unlimited viewpoint of all others. You will see that those whom you fear or resent are merely children who are afraid, too.*

"Lay down your arms, humanity. You are weary from constantly defending yourselves against imagined dangers that are of your own making. Be unafraid of truth, which overcomes all fear. And the hard and fast truth that never wavers is that your Father loves you eternally. Allow me to pour this love in your direction and cover you with its healing power. You may bathe in this well of Divine love at any time, simply by reconnecting your thoughts to those of God's. How to do that? Through having compassion for yourself and others. If you are unable to reach this state, allow me to assist you. For, like your Father, I shall love you always eternally."

As I stood up and walked out of the cathedral, I no longer felt any back pain.

Helps with:

- Children, adopting
- Children, all other issues related to
- Children, support for those who help
- Fertility
- Healing of all kinds
- Mercy

INVOCATION

Mary comes to anyone who calls upon her, regardless of that person's religion or past behavior. She's all-loving and all-forgiving. When she appears, you may smell fragrant flowers or see sparkles of cornflower-blue lights. You'll feel a sense of peace and safety, as if a powerful and loving mother has just entered a child's bedroom to chase away nightmares and replace them with sweet dreams.

Invoke Mary by imagining or looking at a picture or statue of her, or call upon her aloud or mentally:

"Beloved Mary, Queen of the Angels and Mother of Jesus, I ask for your help. [Describe the issue.] Thank you for showering this situation with your blessings and giving me insight, so I may learn and grow from this experience. Thank you for showing me God's will so that we all may have peace."

Melchizedek
(Judaism; New Age)

M elchizedek's name is said to mean "king of righteousness" or "genuine or rightful king." He was a Canaanite priest-king of Salem (now known as Jerusalem) and was a teacher of Abraham. Ancient mystical texts describe him as one who conducts spirit releasement on a massive scale, working in conjunction with Archangel Michael.

Descriptions of Melchizedek's history are conflicting. In the Dead Sea Scrolls, he's called Michael, and there's some allusion to Melchizedek being one and the same with Archangel Michael and Jesus. This latter speculation is echoed by Apostle Paul's letters to the Hebrews, in which Paul discusses Melchizedek and Jesus as both being great high priests, and that Melchizedek was a foreshadowing to Jesus' appearance on Earth. The Eastern spiritual text *Nag Hammadi* also discusses Melchizedek as being a past incarnation of Jesus Christ.

According to *The Book of Enoch,* Melchizedek was the child of Noah's brother, Nir. Nir's wife died before giving birth, and Melchizedek was delivered posthumously from his mother's womb. However, there's other speculation that he's actually Noah's son Shem.

It is said that Melchizedek made the first offering of bread and wine to Abraham for his military victory. He's even depicted as holding a cup or chalice in a stone sculpture from the Chartres Cathedral in France. Saint Paul spoke of Jesus Christ as a priest according to the order of (or in the succession of) Melchizedek because Jesus later instituted the use of bread and wine in the Eucharistic sacrifice at the Last Supper. The Council of Trent even discussed Melchizedek offering bread and wine, and then Jesus instituting it at the Last Supper.

In New Age circles, Melchizedek is thought of as a group of high-level spiritual beings who are custodians and teachers of ancient esoteric secrets. The group is sometimes called "the Cosmic Priesthood" or "Order of Melchizedek." This group was described in Psalms: *"The Lord has sworn and will not change his mind, you are a priest forever according to the order of Melchizedek."*

When I called upon Melchizedek, an extremely tall man with piercing blue eyes appeared before me. He showed me that he oversees a switching station into which stream various colors of the rainbow. These hues are the energies of universal vibrations, given off by everything: the planets and stars; organizations; and thoughts and emotions.

Melchizedek said: *"I am part of the regulating program that balances and harmonizes all energies. These energies are flowing continuously, and they form the basic structure of the universe. All substances are formulated from these agents. All atomic particles revolve around them, too. So, to rearrange the substance of some situation, you must call upon the internal colors to rearrange it so that differing amounts of those colors exist, and the order in which they appear is changed.*

"A reduction in red essence, for instance, reduces the pain threshold. As the tolerance for pain is reduced, the situation must become softer and gentler. The formulas for re-creating situations using the colors are a sacred science that is very complex. It's probably best for you to involve my organization in the process. We operate on the Law of Noninterference with your Earth operations. However, we do make ourselves readily available to those who direct their attention toward us and pose requests for our assistance."

Melchizedek showed me how his regulatory system could instantly rearrange and reorganize matter by remixing its energy color components. This could be used to undo a negative situation, to increase flow and supply, and to create or attract new substances or situations.

Helps with:

- Correcting an unpleasant situation
- Esoteric understanding
- Manifestation
- Purification
- Shielding against psychic attack
- Spirit releasement
- Therapy involving colors (that is, Aura-Soma, chakra clearing, crystals, Feng Shui, Reiki, etc.)

INVOCATION

"Wisdom of Melchizedek, power of Melchizedek, order of Melchizedek, I invite and invoke your presence and protection. Melchizedek, thank you for clearing away all lower energies thoroughly! Melchizedek, thank you for purifying me and this situation. Melchizedek, thank you for rearranging this situation so that it reflects only the highest spiritual laws and energies. Divine wisdom, power, and order now guide my actions, thoughts, and words; and I am safe and protected in all ways."

Merlin

(Celtic; United Kingdom)

Also known as *Merddin, Myrddin, Merlyn, Emrys.*

A controversial figure—did he really live, or was he merely a leg-end?—Merlin represents the great old sage-wizard archetype. He's known as a powerful magician, a spiritual teacher, and a psychic vision-ary who helped King Arthur during fifth-century Camelot in Wales. He's associated with the goddesses of Avalon and Glastonbury, includ-ing Viviane, Guinevere, and The Lady of the Lake.

Those who question his reality as an actual human being say that Merlin may have been based upon an ancient Druid mystic. In any event, biographical information about him is seemingly nonexistent. However, many divinities didn't lead physical lives, but they're still quite powerful and real among us in the spirit world. Merlin is one of them. Although some New Age philosophers argue that Merlin was an early incarnation of Saint-Germain, I and many of the peers whom I respect have interacted with Merlin's spirit as a personality quite distinct and apart from Saint-Germain.

Merlin is happy to give lightworkers a magical leg-up; however, he always cautions that we use our "inner wizards" in the name of spiritu-al service and not for self-gain.

I thought it was fitting to ask Merlin to speak to readers of this book while I sat at the Stonehenge circle in England. He said, *"Welcome to the*

Mystery School, where both dark and bright mysteries reside together. I'm the champion of both dark and light, recognizing the power within both forces if they're approached fearlessly, but with uncompromising respect for their force. If it's an increase in magical knowledge, spell-casting, or inner strength or power that you seek, by all means call upon me. I'm pleased to teach and guide, but be aware that I'm perceived as a powerful taskmaster, one who doesn't take lightly to gluttony or indolence. Be prepared to work hard without compromise when you invoke me."

Helps with:

- Alchemy
- Crystals
- Divine magic
- Energy work and healing
- Prophecy and divination
- Psychic abilities
- Shape-shifting
- Time-warping

INVOCATION

During his mortal lifetime, Merlin rarely spent time indoors. He frequently left Camelot to meditate by himself in the forest, and only went back when he was called upon by Arthur and others for assistance. For this reason, it's best to invoke Merlin when you're outside, especially among trees.

Before you even call on him, Merlin knows of your intentions. He knows who you are, what situation you're requesting help with, and the best solution. But he waits before approaching you, first scanning you to see if you're a student who's willing to learn over the long haul—or if you're someone who just wants a quick fix.

Merlin comes to those who have a sincere desire to learn the spiritual secrets of alchemy, Divine magic, and manifestation skills that will be used in the light and not for personal glorification. He emphasizes to his students that these skills must never be used to harm or destroy anyone or anything physically or emotionally. Merlin's knowledge is his prized possession, and he shares it willingly with those whose hearts are loving and pure.

It doesn't hurt to call upon Merlin even if you're not sure that you're ready. *He* knows. Simply think his name and mentally ask him to come and assist you. If you're ready to learn and work, you will feel his presence and mentally hear his words. If you're not ready, Merlin will guide you to an archangel or master who can prepare you for readiness. Either way, thank Merlin for his loving care.

Moses

(Judeo-Christian)

The Prophet Moses was called upon by God to lead his people out of slavery in Egypt and to the "promised land of milk and honey" in Israel. He and the 12 tribes of Israel wandered through the desert and across the vast lands. Finally, after 40 years of constant travel, Moses was compelled to climb Mount Sinai, where he received an assurance from God that his people would be led to their promised land. Moses received Commandments from God that he was asked to deliver to the Israelites. These Commandments formed the basis for monotheism—the First Commandment being not to worship any other gods.

Moses was born in 15th-century B.C. Egypt to Amram and Jochebed. The Pharoah, who was threatened by the increasing power and wealth of the Jewish people, ordered the murder of all newborn Jewish babies. Moses' mother placed her baby in a waterproof reed basket and set him to float down the Nile river, where she hoped he would attract the attention and compassion of the Pharaoh's daughter. Her plan worked, and Moses was raised in the palace of the Pharaoh as if he were born of royalty.

Biblical accounts that tell of God teaching Moses to perform miraculous feats include: Moses striking a rock that gave forth enough water to quench the thirst of an entire congregation and their animals; parting the Red Sea and walking through it; having clear conversations with God through a burning bush; making a serpent turn into a rod; and others. He was a testament to the miracle of faithfully following Divine guidance.

Moses helps spiritual aspirants and teachers of all faiths and religions, and he's one of my own guides. While I was sitting on New Zealand's western coastline, Moses gave me a profoundly stirring message. His words continue to help and intrigue me: *"Striving inherently places the intention forward into the future, with your focus and intent being centered on subsequent gains and improvement. So much better to stay with your current situation and attain enjoyment, and extract the sum of lessons gained from that scenario before moving on to a new game plan. Withdraw your future plans, and concentrate instead upon this moment. Notice where you are, how you arrived there, and the circumstances that led to your arrival.*

"Once an understanding has been met, turn to the next moment, and so forth. Future-tense focus keeps you trapped in a vacuum that obliterates your ability to draw nurturing, lessons, guidance, and sustenance from the present. The monumental lessons for all mortals is to learn an appreciation for whatever circumstances arise. Do not seek to switch to a new situation until you have fully extracted every minute enjoyment out of your present one. Life is about what's happening to you presently—that's all that matters."

Helps with:

- Authority figures, dealing and negotiating with
- Clear communication with God
- Courage
- Faith
- Leadership
- Miracle-working

INVOCATION

Moses' life story is a testament to accepting a leadership role, even if you feel unsure or unqualified to perform that function. In the same way, Moses can help you "step up to the plate" and do the best job possible. Anytime that you feel uncertain about your power or abilities, call upon Moses:

> "Beloved Moses, please lend me your courage, and help me overcome fear and cast out doubt. I ask you to fill my heart with faith in my God-given abilities. Please guide my words and actions so that I may lead and guide others according to God's will. Thank you."

Nemetona
(England)

Also known as *She of the Sacred Grove.*

Nemetona is the Celtic goddess of power places, sacred grounds and circles, labyrinths, and medicine wheels.

A shrine to Nemetona stands at the ancient healing spa, Bath, in southern England. In ancient times, Celts never held sacred ceremonies indoors—they were always held in open-air settings. Nemetona watched over these gatherings in the way that an angel or master would watch over a church or temple today.

I spoke with Nemetona, appropriately, at the sacred circle Stonehenge, not far from Bath. She struck me as being somber, stately, and stern in the most loving but no-nonsense way. Infused with ancient energy, she stands guard over power places, holding in the energy of the prayers invoked by people who visit these lands. Nemetona has overseen outdoor sacred rituals and ceremonies throughout time (she explained that they all occur simultaneously, instead of in linear time).

Nemetona said, *"When you pray in a sacred power place, you join in a simultaneous reality with ancient rituals being currently performed in a parallel dimension. Prayers for increased power, psychic abilities, and manifesting abilities join with ancient tribal dances and sacred-rite prayers."*

Helps with:

- Infusing ceremonies with guidance, overseeing wisdom, and protection
- Space clearing in your home's back and front yard

INVOCATION

When you begin a ceremony, especially one that involves having people stand or sit in a circle, or one where people walk a labyrinth, invoke Nemetona to oversee the process:

> "Sacred goddess, Nemetona, we invite your presence and participation into our circle. Please infuse it with your magically loving energy, and bless all involved with our ceremony. Nemetona, please clear the space in, around, below, and above our circle. Thank you."

Oonagh
(Ireland)

Also known as *Onaugh, Oona.*

Oonagh was married to Fionnbharr, the head of the Tuatha Dé Danaans, the inhabitants of Ireland before the Gaelics took over the land. The Tuathas became leprechauns after the invasion. Oonagh was faithful and patient with her husband even though he had many affairs with human women.

In artwork, Oonagh is portrayed as having golden hair that's long enough to touch the ground. She's a goddess of devotion in love relationships, aesthetics, and magic; and she's also a fairy queen.

I called on Oonagh while sitting in the midst of an Irish fairy garden, and I saw the most beautiful vision of opalescent, shimmering, glittering light with the brightest fairy in the middle, glowing from the inside. I could hear music like a celestial choir, and instrumental hums emanating from her, as if her every move elicited an electric rhapsody of melodies. Oonagh didn't say anything—she just beamed with joy, love, and beauty.

When I asked Oonagh what she wanted to tell the readers of this book, she simply gushed, *"Love."* After a few moments of pregnant silence, she continued: *"Be in Love. Not 'in love,' as in relationship love with just one other person, but be stationed in the midst of Love. That is what you see glowing around me. That is why your breath deepened, you smiled, and your heart rate increased when you first caught sight of me.*

"It is I who inspires ballet and other lovely dance, for the flower fairies

have taught us all to be graceful ballerina dancers in so many ways. Use movement to make your heart swell with excitement and gratitude. Being stationary too long makes your legs swell and your body feel old and tired. Call upon me for the motivation to exercise, and I shall visit you at twilight and again just before dawn. I shall sprinkle over you my magical and potent fairy dust to get you moving upon awakening. I shall act as a physical therapist and dance coach to encourage you to stretch, sway, dance to rhythms in nature and music, and enjoy the beauty and grace of your heavenly body. Live in love."

Helps with:

- Beauty and attractiveness
- Dance and movement
- Divine magic
- Exercise and motivation
- Fairies, contacting
- Love relationships, all aspects of

INVOCATION

Oonagh loves to dance and move her body, and she loves it when we engage in this activity with her. To synchronize yourself to Oonagh's presence, imagine yourself as a graceful ballerina (male or female), dancing among the flowers. Better yet, stand up and dance in an imagined or real field of flowers. As you move around (in your imagination or in reality), think the word *love* repeatedly. Then, mentally ask Oonagh to dance with you. As she moves alongside you, have a mental conversation with her about your love life. Hold nothing back—tell her everything that's on your mind: your worries, desires, past relationship issues, and current situations. Notice how she lifts heaviness out of your heart during this conversation and helps you to feel light and carefree, which is the essence of faith. Thank Oonagh for her dance and her assistance.

Pele
(Hawaii)

Also known as *Ka-'ula-o-ke-ahi: Redness of the Fire.*

Pele is the fire goddess who rules Hawaii's volcanos and takes various forms: a young, beautiful woman; a wizened crone; a dog; and a flame. In the Hawaiian islands, Pele is highly respected as a powerful deity.

Many legends surround Pele's origination. A common theme is Pele's sibling rivalry with her older sister, Hiiaka, goddess of the ocean. When Pele decided to use her firepower to bring land up from the sea to create new islands, her sister battled her. Hiiaka poured water onto Pele's beloved lava, and steam from the two warring sisters poured out of the volcanos.

Other tales are of Pele's tragic love affairs with mortals and gods. The lava is said to be Pele's hair and tears from her anguish over her love life. It's been said that taking lava rocks from the Hawaiian islands will result in Pele's wrath. Supposedly, many tourists have mailed back lava to the islands to undo bad-luck streaks that occurred after bringing the lava home.

Pele is a powerful yet trustworthy goddess who helps us tap in to our passions and true heart's desires. In Kona, she told me, *"We each have burning fire within us, fire that when properly channeled, fuels us with passion and a sense of purpose. If we deny ourselves as we follow our desires and passions, we may erupt in a volcano of fury. Even then, however, we can turn our anger and indignation into creative forms of beauty, much like when my lava flow hardens and turns to rock, allowing new soil and extensions of my islands to be formed."*

Pele also helps us be more honest in relationships, especially when we're feeling angry or hurt. She knows that if we keep our feelings buried within us, the hidden anger will smother and extinguish the flames of passion, or else explode like a volcano. Ask her for guidance when you need to tell someone that you're angry with them so that you can keep the passion in that relationship alive.

Helps with:

- Empowerment
- Energy
- Goal-setting and goal-getting
- Honest communication in relationships
- Passion
- Prioritizing

INVOCATION

As the goddess of sacred fire, Pele helps us burn a flame of passion in our careers, relationships, and lives as a whole. If you feel that your life is colorless in any way, call upon Pele for help. First, light a warm-colored candle (such as red, orange, yellow, or white), then stare at the flame and say with great reverence and respect:

"Sacred goddess Pele, I ask for your help in reigniting my inner flame. Help me be illuminated with passion for life. [If you have a special project or relationship that you'd like to get enthusiastic about, describe it to her now.] Help me temper this passion with loving kindness, and summon up the courage to speak my truth if anger arises within me."

Saint Francis
(Catholic)

Also known as *Saint Francis of Assisi, Francis Bernardone, Poverello.*

Born Francis Bernardone in 1181, in Assisi, Italy, into a rich family, Francis spent his youth getting into his share of trouble. As a young adult, he served part time as a soldier, during which time he was imprisoned. It was in that Perugia jail that Francis had a epiphany, wherein he heard Jesus tell him to put aside his worldly life. This experience profoundly changed him, and when he was released, he followed a path of spirituality and devotion.

Francis led the life of an acetic, dressing and acting like a beggar while preaching about Jesus and peace. He volunteered in hospitals, ministering to the sick, and formed a spiritual order called The Franciscans in 1212.

Francis may be best remembered for his Dr. Doolittle-like interactions with animals. Legend says that during an outing, he saw a flock of birds. As Francis stopped and began preaching to them, the birds cocked their heads and behaved like members of an enthralled audience. After Francis was done, he walked next to the birds, even brushing them with his jacket, and they didn't move. After that experience, Francis began preaching to birds, animals, and reptiles about God's love. They responded to him as tame, rather than wild, animals. For instance, the birds would become quiet as he spoke, and a wild rabbit continually jumped on his lap even after he put it on the ground several times. Similarly, a wolf accused of killing and harming both people and animals became placid under Francis's loving guidance.

He wrote many prayers and meditations, including the famous Prayer of Saint Francis:

> *Lord, make me an instrument of your peace;*
> *where there is hatred, let me sow love;*
> *when there is injury, pardon;*
> *where there is doubt, faith;*
> *where there is despair, hope;*
> *where there is darkness, light;*
> *and where there is sadness, joy.*
> *O Divine Master, grant that I may not so*
> *much seek to be consoled as to console;*
> *to be understood, as to understand,*
> *to be loved as to love;*
> *for it is in giving that we receive,*
> *it is in pardoning that we're pardoned,*
> *and it's in dying* [to ourselves] *that we're born to eternal life.*

Francis passed into the spirit world on October 4, 1226, and two years later, he was canonized as Saint Francis of Assisi.

I've seen Saint Francis in the presence of many of my clients who are animal lovers, or whose life purpose involves helping and healing these wonderful creatures. He continues to be a passionate advocate of animals, and helps us learn from these wise and gentle beings with whom we share the planet.

Helps with:

- Animal communication and healing
- Career, finding a meaningful
- Environmentalism

- Life's purpose, finding one's
- Peace, personal and global
- Spiritual devotion
- Youths trying to overcome delinquency

INVOCATION

Since Saint Francis is so closely associated with nature and animals, you'll feel the greatest connection with him in a natural setting or when you're with your pets or other animals. A kind, grandfatherly being, Saint Francis will come to anyone who calls upon him, especially if you're willing to help animals or the environment. If you're outside in nature, use all of your senses to enjoy the beauty: smell the fragrances, listen to the sounds, and feel the wind blowing past you. If you're indoors with pets, use your senses to notice details as well. The point is to slow down and appreciate nature's intricacies and loveliness.

As you're immersed in appreciation, mentally ask Saint Francis to join you (chances are that he already has before you even called upon him). When you sense his presence, take a few moments to talk to him cordially, just like you're engaging in conversation with a friend.

Saint Francis always asks us to take our time and appreciate the moment, so you needn't rush while asking Saint Francis for help or for a Divine assignment. Just enjoy the mental conversation, and allow the topics to naturally flow to the point where you request his assistance. As you develop this bond of friendship, you'll start to mutually support one another—you from your vantage point on the Earth plane, and he from his heavenly home.

Saint-Germain
(New Age)

Also known as *Comte de Saint-Germain, The Count of
Saint-Germain, der Wundermann, Saint Germaine,
Saint Germain, The Wonderman of Europe.*

Saint-Germain isn't a saint in the Catholic sense and shouldn't be confused with "Saint Germaine Cousin" or "Saint Germanus," two
actual Catholic saints. Instead, he was a real man who was a royal count
of the French region called "Saint-Germain."

His real full name is Comte de Saint-Germain, or The Count of
Saint-Germain. He was a man born of royal blood somewhere between
1690 and 1710, although reports conflict as to his parents' lineage.
Some say that his mother was Marie de Neubourg, the widow of King
Charles II of Spain, and that his father was Comte Adanero. Others
(particularly those associated with Theosophy) hold that his father was
Prince Ragoczy of Transylvania. A few reports say that *he* was Prince
Ragoczy. Still others claim that he's a Portugese Jew.

Regardless of his origin, history shows that Count Saint-Germain
rubbed elbows with high society and European royalty. He was multi-
talented, playing the violin like a virtuoso, giving psychic readings, master-
ing numerous languages, and painting exquisite artwork. He also spent
time studying and teaching occult and alchemy subjects, and he was
involved with the founding of several secret societies, including the

Freemasons. He boasted of being able to turn lead into gold, and to know of a secret technique to remove flaws from diamonds while increasing their size.

In addition, Saint-Germain gave his friends elixirs that would supposedly erase wrinkles and restore youth. This might be true, as most reports of note say that he looked like a youthful middle-aged man throughout his life. It's also said that, although he frequently dined out with friends, he never ate in public. He told many people that the only food he ever ate was a special oatmeal concoction that he made at home.

Reports say that Saint-Germain was quite wealthy, although no source of his wealth was ever established. He was enamored with gemstones—or were they crystals?—and he carried them with him, often giving them as gifts. He painted gems in his artwork in strong, bold colors.

Saint-Germain kept details about his birth and personal history private, and he was considered a fascinatingly mysterious man in his day. Occasionally he'd make references to past lives—for example, saying that he was with Nero in Rome. He also remarked that he'd return to France in 100 years. Prince Charles of Hesse-Kassel, whom Saint-Germain lived and practiced alchemy with, reported that the count died at his castle on February 27, 1784. However, many credible accounts show that Saint-Germain was seen several years later. For instance, official Freemason documents reportedly show that Saint-Germain was the French representative at their 1785 convention.

Saint-Germain was also deeply involved in French politics and worked alongside King Louis XVI on several missions. It's believed that he (Saint-Germain) was partially responsible for Catherine the Great taking the throne.

A visionary who offered his psychic visions freely, Saint-Germain gave private readings to royalty and those of social influence. For example, he told Marie Antoinette of his prophecies about the French Revolution 15 years before it occurred. Occasionally Saint-Germain's behavior and eccentricities got him into trouble, and he was arrested at least once.

Some people believe that Saint-Germain attained immortality, and that he faked his death to avoid attracting undue attention. Annie Besant, one of the original Theosophists, claimed to have met him in

1896. Guy Ballard, whose pen name is Godre Ray King, wrote about meeting Saint-Germain at Mount Shasta, California, in the 1930s. Recently, Elizabeth Clare Prophet wrote and lectured about Saint-Germain, emphasizing her belief that he carries a violet flame to transmute lower energies.

The "I AM Teachings," a New Age work related to the Great White Brotherhood [see Glossary] considers Saint-Germain's role in history highly important. In New Age circles, it's believed that his past lives include Joseph, father of Jesus; Merlin; Shakespeare; and Christopher Columbus. He's regarded as being the Lord or Chohan of the Seventh Ray, which is the high-frequency violet color in the hierarchy of color vibrations. In other words, he's a very important figure in the ascension movement for the human race and the Great White Brotherhood.

My first remarkable experience with Saint-Germain happened while teaching a beginning psychic-development class in Atlanta. Students were paired up, facing each other, giving each other readings. When the students were done, I asked them to share their experiences with me. A woman in one corner of the room raised her hand. She was a Jewish woman who was new to New Age teachings. Her partner during the reading was a Catholic priest from England who'd flown to Atlanta to take my class.

"Who is Saint-Germain?" the woman asked me. Neither she nor her partner had ever heard of this man who'd come through their reading so strongly.

"I got Saint-Germain, too!" said another student in the opposite corner of the room. "Me, too!" exclaimed two other students. What was remarkable was that the four students who'd encountered Saint-Germain during the reading had never even heard of him before, and they'd been sitting in different corners of the room. Saint-Germain was showing us that he was there, and that he was all around us. I understood that day that he would be co-instructing my students.

I've come to know Saint-Germain as a loving, benevolent ascended master who wishes to work with lightworkers—that is, people who want to help the world clean up its act. He provides guidance, protection, and courage. If those sound like qualities that Archangel Michael provides, it's no accident, since the two work hand-in-wing together.

Helps with:

- Alchemy
- Authority figures and influential people, comfortably interacting with
- Courage
- Direction
- Life purpose
- Miraculous manifestations
- Perseverance
- Psychic protection
- Space clearing

INVOCATION

In my experience, people don't call Saint-Germain—he's the one who calls first! He seems to just show up wherever lightworkers are gathered in classes, study groups, or prayer meetings. He works with spiritual teachers to encourage their outgoing nature and leadership skills.

That's not to say, however, that you can't request a special audience with him when you desire a message or some type of motivation. Simply think, *Saint-Germain, I need your help.* Wait a moment, and then mentally let him know the situation or question with which you need assistance.

You'll know that he's with you because a creative answer will come to you suddenly. You may also see violet-purple sparkles of light in the room. Or, you may start seeing violet-purple everywhere you go, on people's clothing or on flowers, for instance. You'll also begin thinking or writing profound thoughts on how to help others.

Saint John of God
(Catholic)

Also known as *João Cidade, Juan Ciudad, Father of the Poor.*

Saint John of God is the patron of the mentally and physically ill and hospital employees, and he also helps booksellers and those with heart ailments.

He was born João (which means "John" in English) Cidade, in Portugal in 1495. At age eight, he and his family moved to Spain. As a young man, he worked as a shepherd, a soldier, and a traveling book peddler. In 1538, he had an epiphany after hearing John of Avila speak on repentance. João gave away his money and belongings and was subsequently hospitalized in a psychiatric wing of the Royal Hospital.

In his opinion, the hospitalization experience was degrading and dreadful, and he decided to devote his life to upgrading hospital treatment. After his release from the hospital, he was homeless and disillusioned, which helped him develop a very strong affinity with other homeless and disenfranchised people.

João worked tirelessly to reach many people who suffered from illness (mental and physical) and deprivations of all types. In the beginning, when the weather was inclement, he would share the porch of a friend's house with those needing shelter. This began The Hospitaller Order of Saint John of God, which today, 450 years after it was founded, continues to provide shelter to people throughout the world.

He also bought a facility and cared for poor, homeless, sick, and unwanted people in his new hometown of Granada, Spain. João was known to give what he could, beg for those who couldn't, and even help carry those who could not walk. His motto was: *"Labor without stopping. Do all the good works you can while you still have the time,"* and he was known to counsel others by citing the Biblical verse: *"Whatever you do to one of the least of these, my brothers and sisters, you do to me."*

When someone was admitted to his hospital, legend says that he or his staff would wash the person, feed them, and then pray with them. Empathetic and encouraging, he listened to everyone's problems and offered his most sincere advice. People were so impressed by his dedication and honesty that they gave him money and volunteered to help him in his ministry. It was these people who gave him the title "John of God."

Using his position with the powerful, he advocated successfully for the poor to improve their condition. Due to contributions and the work of dedicated volunteers, John of God's mission continues to spread the message and the practice of "hospitality." John died of pneumonia on March 8, 1550, while immersed in prayer after saving a man who'd almost drowned.

Saint John of God is a jolly fellow who exudes joy. Just calling upon him is enough to elevate the mood and lift the spirits. He reassures those who are depressed or worried, and helps people feel physically, emotionally, and financially safe and secure. Invoke him at the first sign of sadness, or to heal a broken heart.

Helps with:

- Anxiety
- Depression
- Healing
- Heart ailments
- Hospitalizations
- Joy, increasing
- Space clearing
- Spiritual dedication

INVOCATION

Saint John of God comes to anyone of any religious or spiritual faith who calls upon him, just by thinking of his name. You can also ask him to visit your loved ones or clients who are depressed or anxious. Or, you can hold this prayer in mind to call him to your side:

"Golden-hearted Saint John of God, please bring me the joy of God, which you exude. Please surround me with your loving care and attention. Help me banish pessimistic thoughts and attitudes, and rise above the appearance of problems. Help me trust in Divine order and let go of the need to control. Please help me have a mind filled with faith, a heart filled with joy, and a voice filled with laughter. Please guide me so that I may live your legacy of helping others and serving God. Amen."

Saint Padre Pio
(Catholic)

Also known as *Francesco Forgione, Padre Pio.*

Born Francesco Forgione on May 25, 1887, in Naples, Italy, Francesco changed his name to Pio, which means "Pius," when he entered the Capuchin monastery at age 16. Padre Pio began experiencing the *stigmata*—a condition characterized by pain, open wounds, or blood appearing in the same places on the body where Jesus was impaled with nails and a thorny crown. The stigmata wounds and blood remained visible for the next 50 years.

Many have verified miraculous healings associated with Padre Pio, both during his mortal life and beyond. He's renowned for helping the blind to see and healing various injuries and seemingly incurable ailments. During his life, Padre Pio was able to bilocate, levitate, and accurately predict the future. He also founded a hospital and a series of prayer groups.

Saint Padre Pio is a very spirited divinity with a lot of enthusiasm, joy, and a persona that reveals his deep faith and optimism. He has an infectious and optimistic outlook, and just by calling him, you're likely to feel uplifted.

Helps with:

- Eyesight, including blindness
- Forgiveness
- Healers, increasing the abilities of
- Healing of all kinds
- Prophecy
- Spiritual growth

INVOCATION

During his life, Padre Pio performed many healings from his confessional booth. He asked people to admit the true underlying source of their pain aloud. You can do the same while calling upon Padre Pio for intercession. He helps people of all religions and creeds equally. An example of an invocation might be:

"Beloved Saint Padre Pio, please help me to [describe the situation]. I admit that this problem has stirred up disturbing feelings such as [name whatever emotions you can]. I'm willing to completely forgive myself and the others in this situation, and I ask that you help me do so. Please help me reveal light, love, and forgiveness. Thank you, God. Thank you, Jesus. Thank you, Saint Padre Pio. Amen."

Saint Therese
(Catholic)

Also known as *Therese of Lisieux, Therese of the Child Jesus,
The Little Flower, The Little Flower of Jesus.*

Saint Therese is a powerful and loving healing saint from France.
You'll know that she's heard your prayers when you see or smell
roses. She was born Therese Martin in 1873, and at age 15 became a
nun at a Carmelite convent. At the young age of 24, she passed away.

Many people report verified healings after praying to Saint Therese
or visiting her relics. As Therese lay dying in 1897, she said, "After my
death, I will let fall a shower of roses." Since that time, she's been associated with those beautiful flowers. For that reason, she's the patron saint
of florists; however, she helps with so much more, particularly in the
area of physical healing.

It's been said that she helped many aviators during World War II, so
she's also considered a patron saint of pilots, flight attendants, and air-
based military personnel.

In her autobiography, *The Story of a Soul,* Therese discussed how
simplicity, and also trusting and loving God, were the keys to living a
happy and sacred life. She said that what matters in life "is not great
deeds, but great love."

I first met Saint Therese when I was meditating in 1994. I loved
meditating so much that I'd spend hours sitting with my eyes shut, just

listening and enjoying the wonderful feelings of peace and Divine love. One day I heard a woman's voice talking to me. She said, *"Little Flower,"* then she said, *"Saint Therese."* Not having a Catholic background, I didn't know who she was, so I called a local Catholic church and asked the priest for information. He patiently explained Saint Therese's background to me, and told me about her connection to Little Flower.

The priest was so kind that I summoned up the courage to tell him about my experience during meditation. He was very open-minded and accepting, and told me that he thought Saint Therese was with me because of my work as a spiritual counselor and healer. He explained that she helps sincere people, regardless of faith.

Since that time, I've seen Saint Therese with other people to whom I've given readings. Sometimes she's with women who are named Therese or Theresa. It's wonderful to know that I still have her as a constant and steady companion and guide as well.

Helps with:

- Gardening—especially flowers
- Healing all forms of illness or injury
- Pilots and airline crews
- Spiritual counseling

INVOCATION

Catholics normally recite the Novena Rose Prayer to ask for Saint Therese's blessings. Non-Catholics may also request this loving saint's assistance. It's said that if you practice this devotion for 9 to 24 days, you'll see a rose as a sign that your request has been heard and granted:

"O Little Therese of the Child Jesus, please pick for me a rose from the heavenly gardens and send it to me as a message of love. O Little Flower of Jesus, ask God today to grant the favors I now place with confidence in your hands [mention specific requests]. Saint Therese, help me to always believe as you did in God's great love for me so that I might imitate your 'Little Way' each day. Amen."

Sanat Kumara
(Hindu; Vedic; New Age)

Also known as *Karttikeya, Sumara, Skanda-Karttikeya.*

Kumara is a warrior god, devoted to ridding people and the earth of negative entities and lower energies.

Legends abound explaining Kumara's creation, with the common thread being his relationship to the number six—perhaps because of his talents in banishing negative spirits. One tale recounts that Heaven was plagued with demons, so Shiva used his third-eye flame to beget six children who would specialize in slaying demons. However, their mother hugged the six children with such enthusiastic love that she squeezed their bodies into one child with six heads.

Hindus revere Kumara as a leader among gods who banishes darkness in the minds of men and spirits. His demon-slaying activities are thought to be metaphorical, symbolizing Kumara's slaying of ignorance.

In New Age circles, he's hailed as a member of the Great White Brotherhood, working alongside Jesus and Archangel Michael to help the planet and her population with the ascension process.

Sanat Kumara says, *"Power is my focus—power for one and for all . . . redelivering personal power to people everywhere, direct from the Great Source of All. Through my realization of the Great Allness, I am able to tap in to its plentitude and draw up from the power supply and distribute it to everyone. By illuminating the masses with this personal power, there's an infusion of justice and grace in the world, for no one can usurp your personal boundaries when you know that your supply of power is unlimited and completely unfettered. Lean on this knowledge, and never be afraid to exercise your rights in all situations that call upon you to be strong."*

Helps with:

- Ego, overcoming
- Fatigue, lifting
- Healing work
- Space clearing
- Spirit releasement
- Spiritual knowledge and enlightenment

INVOCATION

Kumara is a powerful spirit who has a primal, indigenous feel to him, like an intense witch doctor. When you call upon him, Kumara responds at lightning speed and with lovingly powerful energy. If you're fatigued, call upon him for help:

"Sanat Kumara, please bring me your powerful energy to uplift my spirit and vitality. Please help me rise above negative thoughts and emotions, like a bird above dark clouds. I ask your assistance in tapping me in to the true and eternal Source of all energy. Please clear away lower spirits and energies from within and around me, and infuse me with Divine healing light."

Then breathe deeply while Kumara does his work. In a few moments, you should feel revived and refreshed.

Sedna
(Inuit/Eskimo)

Also known as *Ai-willi-ay-o, Nerivik.*

Various legends say that Sedna fell (or was thrown) off her parents'
boat, and that dismembered parts of her body formed the sea lions
and other sea creatures. Sedna is considered the Creator goddess of all
inhabitants of the sea—the *ultimate* sea goddess.

Sedna will grant wishes to those who go to the sea—and who ask
her lovingly, honestly, and gently for favors. Since she's so connected
with water and dolphins, Sedna also helps with intuition and brings
messages about dolphins into one's dreamtime.

I invoked Sedna while sitting on a boat in the middle of the Pacific
ocean near Hawaii. Although she's available for help and guidance anywhere, I wanted to meet Sedna at her home to ask her for a message for
this book. She began by saying, *"I'm the mistress of the great ocean, which
brings magic to your atmosphere. Weather arises from the ocean currents,
moisture, and winds.*

*"Caution is warranted regarding the care and protection of this massive
water surface. Aside from not discarding your waste products into the sea,
your incessant use of cleaning supplies must, must, must be averted—this
very minute!*

*"Water itself is enough to engender cleanliness—it's purity, inherent
blessings, and life-giving qualities can be used instead of soapsuds to wash*

away grime. Hot water will remove germs in and of itself—no need for dis-infectants, which are polluting the waters and atmosphere of this last remaining great planet.

"Allow me to help replace your cares and worries with magical under-water adventures that I can channel to you during your dreamtime. Call upon me for wishes whenever you like, and cast your cares and worries to me now. I will swallow them into my cavernous sea and wash them until the underlying essence of your concerns is revealed . . . and then healed. Take good care of my darlings—the sea lions, dolphins, and fish—for me."

Helps with:

- Abundance—especially food supply
- Animal rights—especially relating to water-based animals, fish, and birds
- Dolphins and whales
- Dreams and intuition
- The granting of wishes when you're in the ocean
- Hands and fingers, healing
- Hurricanes, dispelling
- Ocean conservation
- Protection while swimming, sailing, or surfing

INVOCATION

It's best to connect with Sedna when you're in or around water, as this is her domain. Say to her:

"Dearest Sedna, Goddess of the waters, I desire to develop a connection with you through my intuition and dreamtime. Please bring me a clear message about [name the situation you'd like help with]. Please bring the dolphins into my dreams and help me uncover the truth about this situation. Thank you."

Serapis Bey
(Egypt, Greece, and New Age)

Also known as *Serapis, Apis, Asar-Apis, Osiris-Apis*.

Originally an Egyptian god of the underworld named Serapis who was in charge of the ascension at Luxor, Egypt; in New Age circles, he's now known as Serapis Bey. He helps people work toward ascension through spiritual enlightenment. Serapis Bey motivates people toward physical fitness and healthful lifestyles due to his interest in beauty and aesthetics; he also helps them withstand the coming changes that are prophesied. Like a spiritual fitness guru, he inspires, motivates, and provides hope for the future.

Serapis Bey also helps artists and musicians with their creative projects. An extremely loving ascended master, he's actively involved in averting war and bringing peace to Earth.

I've long had an affinity and affection for Serapis Bey, and have found him to be a wonderful coach who lovingly demands the best from us. He pushes us to take exceptional care of our bodies, and if you begin working with him, expect to be given some pointers on exercise and nutrition.

He says, *"Once again, we're reunited, as I've been with so many of you countless times before. You're here for another initiation, are you? Another rung on the ladder of ascension for you. I'm here to help you carefully and cautiously choose your next move. Many of you are rushing so much that you can no longer hear your inward guide. You __must__ create silent space for yourself.*

"Get away from the frantic pace and worldly noise at regular intervals. Even a brief break will refresh you and reconnect you to the Voice you love with all of your heart, the Voice you trust uppermost. When you allow yourself to become distant or disconnected from this Voice, you feel insecure and afraid for reasons unknown to you. You become like an infant pulled away from her mother's nursing breast: lost and confused.

"Make the Voice your uppermost priority, a valuable friend whom you vigilantly keep track of. If you cannot hear the Voice, it's simply a sign to become quiet and still momentarily until you regain awareness of this inner source of guidance and direction."

Helps with:

- Addictions and cravings, overcoming
- Artists, musicians, and creative endeavors
- Ascension
- Clear communication with God
- Exercise and weight-loss motivation
- Peace, personal and global
- Prophecy

INVOCATION

Serapis Bey can be contacted anytime you need loving care, spiritual insight, or peace and quiet. Hold the mental intention of connecting with him, then stop a moment, close your eyes, and take some deep breaths. As you inhale, think about your desires. As you exhale, imagine that you're releasing whatever is bothering you. You'll feel or sense Serapis Bey's presence alongside you, mirroring your breathing pattern. At some point, you'll either hear his voice or sense some thoughts that come from him.

Don't worry—Serapis Bey won't override your free will. However, he *will* give you clear guidance and instructions about self-improvement, along with the motivation to undertake these endeavors. As you go through any process requiring stamina and focus, call him to your side.

Solomon
(Judeo-Christian)

Also known as *King Solomon.*

Solomon was the king of Israel, following his father, King David's, reign in the 900 B.C. era. In light of King David's intensity, Solomon was viewed as a gentle and wise man who blended alchemy and Judaic mysticism with common sense and wisdom. Solomon was instrumental in many of Israel's advances in government and architecture. Most notable is Solomon's overseeing of the construction of the Temple of God, in which the Ark of the Covenant was housed.

The book of 1 Kings in the Bible makes reference to Solomon's remarkable wisdom: *"Solomon's wisdom surpassed the wisdom of all the sons of the east and all the wisdom of Egypt. For he was wiser than all men. . . . Men came from all peoples to hear the wisdom of Solomon. . . ."*

References in the Torah, Gospels, and ancient Judaic texts refer to Solomon's exorcism and magical skills. A 15th-century Greek manuscript called *The Testament of Solomon* describes him using a magical ring (known as "Solomon's Ring") that has a Star of David engraved on top. Scholars point out that the six-pointed star was originally associated with cabalism, high magic, and Pythagorean mysticism. Solomon may have been instrumental in making it a symbol of Israel and Judaism.

The Testament of Solomon also contains one of the numerous accounts of Solomon controlling demons, both to banish them and to control them as "spiritual slaves" to perform magical duties. Texts about Solomon usually discuss him banishing and controlling 72 particular demons, each with a specific name and function. Before he left Earth, Solomon contained these 72 demons so that they wouldn't disturb people.

Solomon has ascended to such a high level that you may not feel his presence when you call upon him. Instead, your higher consciousness will tap in to his collective wisdom. He's a wise, old sage similar to the God archetype who sees all and knows all, and he already knows who you are, what your Divine assignment is, and how you can do things better and more efficiently. He'll help you improve different areas of your life, which is sometimes frightening or irritating to those who misconstrue his messages as a power or control struggle. But those who are wise will be open to his assistance.

Solomon says, *"Poetry is the name of life. Poetry is artistry in motion. For it's not the accumulation of knowledge to which we're aspiring, but the ability to live life in a grander, more fluid, and more aristocratic fashion. To take charge through godliness of your inner demons and squeeze out all excess so that you may truly reign with princely power over your domain. Get control of all your faculties. Handle addictions and patterns directly, and be free—free to rule, free to live, and free to express your inward callings in boundless ways."*

Helps with:

- Cabalistic understanding
- Divine magic
- Joy
- Manifestation
- Space clearing
- Spirit releasement
- Wisdom and understanding

INVOCATION

Call upon Solomon to help you with any difficult or seemingly impossible situation. As a Divine magician, he'll direct sacred energy to support you:

"Solomon, O Solomon, I need your help and assistance, please, and I need it now. Please come to me and shine light on this situation [describe it to him], and help loosen the chains of fear and unforgiveness. I need a miracle, and I need it now. Help resolve this matter, and lift me out of the trenches of darkness. Thank you for your wisdom and courage, and for providing the perfect solution to this matter."

Sulis
(British)

Also known as *Sul, Sulla, Sulevia, Sulivia.*

An ancient goddess of healing waters whose shrine was at the Bath spa in southern England, Sulis's name means "eye" and "seeing." So it makes sense that she helps with physical and psychic vision. The eye is also associated with the sun, so Sulis is known as a sun goddess, which is rare, as male deities are usually sun gods, while female deities have moon and star connections. This solar association may stem from Sulis's relationship with hot springs.

Sulis oversees all pools of water associated with healing, especially natural hot springs. Today in Bath, people come from all over the world to drink from her well in the center of the hot spring's restaurant. The water is rich with sulphur, and is said to function as a fountain of youth.

I spoke with Sulis near Bath, and she said: *"It was I whom you saw in the rainbow over Stonehenge. I'm in the prism effect of water drops, reflecting the Divine light inherent in all water, including oxygen. Plants are precious to me, and yes, as you asked, I can help gardeners grow everything from bumper crops to healthy houseplants. Just don't expect me to rid plants of aphids—I'm a natural horticulturist who respects the balance between the Earth kingdom (which the insects truly reign over—think of their hardiness as a testament to their regalness) and the plant community."*

Helps with:

- Blessings
- Clairvoyance
- Eyesight, physical and spiritual
- Gardening
- Water used in ceremonies
- Wishes

INVOCATION

It's a good idea to invite Sulis to any ceremony involving water. You can conduct a version of a water ceremony by drawing a hot bath and filling it with sea salt, essential oils, and a few flower petals. Surround the bathtub with candles, soft music, and at least one potted plant. Dim the lights, ignite the candles, and as you get in the bathtub, say:

"Sister Sulis, I invite your loving presence. Sulis, please bring your beloved blessings, your caring nature, your spiritual vision, and your youthful beauty; and bestow it upon the waters within and around me. Please help fulfill my wish, which is [describe your wish]. Thank you, beloved Sulis. Thank you."

Tara
(Buddhist, Hindu, Jainist, Lamaist)

Also known as *Green Tara, White Tara.*

When Avalokitesvara, the *bodhisattva* (enlightened one) of compassion and protection, shed tears that formed a lake, a lotus flower rose to the top of the water. When the flower opened, a beautiful goddess stepped out of the middle, and her name was Tara. She's the female counterpart and consort of Avalokitesvara. Tara has many different sides and personalities to her, represented by different-colored Taras (Green Tara, White Tara, Red Tara, Blue Tara, and Yellow Tara). In her Yellow, Blue, and Red personas, Tara is temperamental, but as White and Green Tara, she's loving and very helpful.

Tara's name means "star," and like stars that provide navigation for sailors and travelers, Tara helps us travel smoothly and safely and find our way—whether on a trip, on our spiritual path, or just during daily life.

Green Tara is known as a "speedy" goddess who rapidly induces insight and who quickly comes to your aid. If you need emergency help physically or spiritually, call upon Green Tara.

White Tara helps increase life expectancy, and if you call upon her, she will bring you longevity. She also is a bringer of Enlightenment.

Green Tara is very intense, yet she's a very loving warrior spirit. Green Tara is a no-nonsense divinity who conducts rapid energy exchanges to help and assist those who call upon her. She says, *"I get matters settled quickly and go right to work using wisdom and action. I set my sights on an intended outcome, and bring those preferences into experience."* She attains her goals, in other words.

In contrast, White Tara is gentle, peaceful, patient, doting, nurturing, and maternal. She is the essence of purity. She approaches problems with prayer and by holding a steady focus on the beauty of Divine love. Her eyes overflow with gratitude, joy, and love. She feels and sees only love, so that's what comes forth in her presence. She says, *"I am here to shift people's hearts away from an inclination of worry. I love and I am happy, and this has a settling effect upon people whose lives I touch. It is my pleasure to spread joy far and wide."*

Both Green Tara and White Tara Help with:

- Compassion
- Protection
- Removing and avoiding obstacles

Green Tara helps with:

- Emergency aid
- Overcoming fear
- Understanding and insight

White Tara helps with:

- Enlightenment
- Longevity

Invocation

Green Tara: Sit quietly and meditate upon the color green while chanting *Om Tare, Tuttare Ture Svaha,* which means:

> "Tara, Swift Saviouress, please liberate me from all forms of suffering and imprisonment, and help me be balanced in my spirituality."

White Tara: Sit quietly, breathe deeply, and meditate upon the color sky blue. Then pray to White Tara:

> "Please let me be like you, White Tara, filled with compassion and grace. I am you, White Tara. I am Tara. I am Tara."

Feel yourself filled with overflowing warm love, joy, and compassion.

Thoth
(Egypt)

Also known as *Aah, Aah Tehuti, Djehuti, Tehuti, Thout, Zehuti.*

The Egyptian god of high magic, manifestation, symbols, geometry, writing, music, and astronomy, Thoth was the scribe of the gods, and he penned many books about Hermetic secrets of magic and manifestation. Legend says that one of his books, *The Emerald Tablets,* was written when Thoth was a priest-king in Atlantis. Thoth and the book survived Atlantis's demise, and he founded an Egyptian colony based on Atlantean wisdom.

It's said that Thoth's symbols are the basis for modern Freemasonry, and that he designed many Egyptian pyramids and temples.

Thoth was believed to materialize and heal with the use of chants, toning, and sound, along with sacred geometry, symbolism, and arithmetic. He taught the moon goddess, Isis, how to practice high magic, and he's credited with being the inventor of writing in ancient Egypt.

He says, *"You speak of Atlantis as being a peak of human knowledge, yet there are far greater cultures than these that existed on this planet and beyond. I've participated in several, and I shall continue to do so for service, sport, and adventure. The human 'race' is fast drawing to its finish line, and it's time for all of us to withdraw and go home. This is the natural cycle and evolution of every great culture—to reach its peak and then withdraw, like seasons of life itself. Expansion, withdrawal, expansion, withdrawal. Do not fear either route, for your* [he meant everyone's] *safe passage is assured. You will be applauded for your participation, which takes courage and bravery indeed.*

"*My words are not to alert you to mass destruction, but to thrust upon you an imperative: Your technology must shift to becoming air-based instead of land-based. Air-based stations can withstand the impact of your electrical currents, while your land and water suffers greatly from this assignment. Move your source of electricity to satellite components before the world goes dark with overload. You're nearing capacity right now.*

"*Reduce your dependency upon technology immediately, and return to more natural conditions. This is the only peaceful way out of the experiment. Modern conveniences have made many of you fat, lazy, and slothlike. Get up and realize your potential! Attain fitness, everyone! I do not mean to chastise you, but to motivate you with my deepest honor, love, and respect.*"

Helps with:

- Divine magic
- Life purpose
- Mathematics
- Prophecy and divination
- Psychic abilities
- Sacred geometry
- Teaching
- Writing

INVOCATION

Call upon Thoth whenever you need psychic insight, or when you seek Divine magic to help resolve a situation. His name is difficult to say without feeling like you're lisping, so when you invoke Thoth, a smile may come to your face. This mirth and joy is appealing to Thoth, so don't worry about offending him. Say aloud or mentally:

"Beloved Thoth, I call your name as your student of the Divine secrets that you so lovingly teach. Thank you for your guidance and instruction in resolving [name the situation you need help with]. Please help me be open to the power so that it may run through me as a Divine channel. Thank you, teacher. Thank you, Thoth."

Vesta

(Roman; New Age)

Also known as *Hestia, Prisca.*

Vesta is a sun and fire goddess who oversees the home and hearth. In ancient times, a sacred fire was continuously burned and tended in her honor by vestal virgins. Every fire was thought to contain part of Vesta's living spirit.

In New Age circles, Vesta works with Helios, the Roman sun god, as Solar Logos. This term denotes divinities who light the flame of the lightbody within spiritual aspirants, using the sun rays from one's solar plexus.

Vesta showed me an image of herself on a chariot with Apollo, riding among the heavenly stars each evening, and tucking in those of us on Earth each night. Blessing and protecting us, I saw her showering each of us with compassion, as she recognizes the tough job we all have to do. She's similar to Archangel Haniel, who illuminates us with stardust so that we'll remember our magical properties and qualities.

Helps with:

- Divine light—increasing its size, brightness, and visibility
- Fire control
- Home—filling it with warmth and love

- Passion, igniting and keeping
- Protection—especially for children
- Space clearing

INVOCATION

It's a good idea to invite Vesta into your home if there's been recent friction among those who live there. Vesta can clear the energy of fear and anger so that future conflict is less likely to occur. She'll bring a feeling of warmth, love, and ease to the household, which will comfort all who enter the home.

Since Vesta is the goddess of the hearth or fireplace, one way to call her is by lighting a fire or a candle. As you light the flame, say to her:

> "Beloved Vesta, please bring your flame of Divine love into this household and light the fire of kindness, compassion, and understanding within everyone who lives and visits this home. Help us to burn away any fears concerning love, and to feel warm and secure."

Vywamus
(New Age)

Vywamus is an ascended spiritual teacher and healer who helps lightworkers awaken their inner power and spiritual gifts, and discover their life's purpose. New Age teachers say that Vywamus is a holographic higher-self aspect of Sanat Kumara. In this respect, Vywamus and Sanat Kumara function as two separate individuals even though they're aspects of the same person (and in truth, we're all *one* anyway).

A very loving and compassionate guide, Vywamus assists rapidly in all aspects of emotional, mental, physical, and spiritual healing. He helps lightworkers face their shadows as a way of illuminating them with light.

A friend of mine named Morgan Ki'ilehua has had extensive experiences with Vywamus. She told me:

> "For many years in meditation I would see 'this man.' It didn't seem to matter whether I was meditating at home, following a guided-meditation CD, or in a meditation group at someone's home, 'this man' was always there. What I always found so interesting was that he always appeared the same way. He would be standing facing me, and he was very tall and slender. His pageboy-style shoulder-length hair was white. His long robe was blue and white. His face was clean-shaven, and he had a small, sharp nose with patient, gentle, small-set eyes. His age? Somewhere over 50 years old. There were never any words

spoken, never a feeling of any type of communication, yet there was a very strong sense of him being a very wise teacher. This continued for years. I now know that it was Vywamus.

"Several years ago, I met a woman named Saemmi Muth who told me that she was a channel for an entity called Vywamus and that her channelings had been appearing in the *Sedona Journal of Emergence* for about 15 years. I booked a private session with her, although I didn't quite know why, and I also felt skeptical.

"Nevertheless, I kept my appointment with Saemmi. During the session, Vywamus talked way above my head. I didn't understand what he was telling me about rays, dimensions, the spiritual hierarchy, and where my vibration was at the time. I just sat, listening in awe and still skeptical.

"Then I said to Vywamus, 'I do have two physical plane questions.' Vywamus said, *'You want to know about your father and your husband.'* 'Yes,' I replied. *'Your father is fine, he's in lesson* [my father had transitioned four years prior to this].*'* This was discussed briefly. Then Vywamus said, *'Your husband is fine, also; however he had an exit window and chose not to take it.'* (My husband, Alex, had had a brain seizure and a massive heart attack a few months before, and at that time, the doctors told me he wouldn't live through the night—yes, he's still here.) This part of the session was my proof, as Saemmi knew nothing about my father or details about my husband. I was a believer!

"A Vywamus Group started meeting in my home once a week. There were five or six of us. Once a week Saemmi would 'bring in' Vywamus, and the group would ask questions. We had some very powerful and enlightening evenings. Vywamus encouraged me to begin channeling.

"Much of my training was done by Vywamus through Saemmi. There was a particular session we had that was a major shift for me. Saemmi called prior to a 'training day' and told me that Vywamus wanted me to write down seven questions for our session. I could ask any question I wanted. My seven questions were ready when we met. As we sat at the table, Saemmi brought in Vywamus as usual. Vywamus asked me if I was ready for my questions. I said yes and began to read from my list. Vywamus stopped me and said, *'Channel me and get the answers.'*

"Trusting my abilities, I brought in Vywamus to speak through me, asked the questions, and got the answers. With the assistance of Vywamus, I now channel two meditation groups a week, have workshops on spirit communication and psychic development, and have completed three channeled, guided-meditation CDs. My journey with Vywamus has been fascinating, exciting, and informative. I could not imagine my life without him now. I'm in constant communication with this loving, wonderful cosmic being. Anyone who desires can channel Vywamus, as he's available to us all. Open your heart, use your Divine Intent, and simply listen."

Helps with:

- Direction
- Encouragement and inspiration
- Healing—spiritual, emotional, and physical
- Life purpose, all aspects of
- Motivation and overcoming procrastination
- Talents, discovering your

INVOCATION

As mentioned above, my friend Morgan Ki'ilehua teaches classes on connecting with Vywamus. On the next page is an invocation that she and her students use. She says that you can use it for channelings, private sessions of any kind, or personal connections with Vywamus. She says that this invocation is especially powerful immediately before bedtime, or when you desire a personal communication at a higher vibration.

Vywamus is electrical, and his color is blue. During this process, you may feel a tingling in your arms, hands, or legs. You may experience electricity moving through you. You may have a sense of spiraling, or see the color electrical blue. Remember, we're electromagnetic beings, so you're safe. If for any reason you feel uncomfortable, just ask that the process be made comfortable for your physical being.

First, close your eyes and focus on your breath. Bring your attention within your being. Imagine that you're bringing in from the Universe a cloud of electrical blue. Add some white, and if you like, some soft pink. Allow this blue cloud to surround you so that you can feel yourself completely within it. Take your time with this process so that you feel cocooned in the electrical blue cloud.

When you're ready, state your intent to channel Vywamus. For example:

> "Vywamus, I'm open to channel your energy and to receive your guidance."

You can ask any question you wish. Please keep in mind that Vywamus does not work as a psychic, but rather a highly evolved spiritual teacher.

Yogananda
(India, North America)

Paramahansa Yogananda was an Indian yogi born in 1893. In 1920, at his teacher Babaji's request, Yogananda traveled to America to introduce the Western world to the practice of Kriya yoga. He wrote the popular book *Autobiography of a Yogi* and opened Self-Realization Fellowship (SRF) centers worldwide. Yogananda's centers, books, and teachings blend Eastern and Western spirituality, and many of his writings quote Jesus Christ as an example of love, compassion, and forgiveness. (In fact, Jesus is one of the six gurus of SRF, the other five being Yogananda, Krishna, Babaji, Lahiri Mahasaya, and Sri Yukteswar.) Yogananda, like Babaji, teaches that all religions have an underlying unity.

Yogananda's legacy includes bringing yoga to North America and introducing Westerners to meditation and chanting. All of his teachings focused upon developing loving connections and communication with God; and living a happy, healthy life.

Yogananda passed physically from the world in 1952, but he continues to teach, heal, and guide people as one of the newer ascended masters.

My dear friend Michael Wise, lead singer for the band Angel Earth, wrote down his accounts of working with Yogananda, and sent me the story just two months before he passed away. Now Michael is with his beloved Yogananda.

"My experience with Guruji Paramahansa Yogananda began in the spring of 1992 when his book *Autobiography of a Yogi* literally fell off of the shelf of a local bookstore into my hands. I purchased the book and was enthralled with its contents. I then began studying Yogananda's Kriya Yoga meditation technique through his Self-Realization Fellowship.

"It was in the early morning, 4:30 A.M. of a winter's day in 1994, during my daily meditation routine before going to work, that I reached a very loving and sacred place. My diligent practice and trust in Yogananda's teachings brought me to a level of meditation that I'd never before known. In what seemed like an instant, I was transported to a place of serene beauty: a sun room with a huge arching window overlooking a garden rich in colorful flowers, trees, and sunlight as bright as I'd ever seen. I just stood in silence amazed at the sight, sound, and feeling of the experience.

"Then, just to the left of the window, I noticed a small table with four chairs around it. In the chair to my left and the one at the back of the table, two figures appeared. They were moving and seemed very alive, and then they came into sharper focus. I was very startled as I recognized one of them to be Yogananda himself! He looked up at me and smiled, then I heard a voice call my name—it was the other figure, who suddenly came into focus. *'Michael,'* the voice said, and then I recognized the other figure to be Jesus! Jesus called my name again and smiled and gently said to me, *'Be as a child at play.'*

"Yogananda then leaned forward and added, *'. . . and continue to study my lessons!'* Both smiled at me. I was then gently returned to my place in my basement studio in my home. The experience is still very vivid in my memory as I write this in May of 2002. Both Yogananda and Jesus have been with me every step of the way of my awakening to the Spirit within. They're with me now and always will be as we share this experience of transformation here on Earth."

Helps with:

- Clear communication with God
- Divine love
- Healing—spiritual, emotional, and physical
- Peace, personal and global
- Unity of religious beliefs
- Yoga practice

INVOCATION

Yogananda is actively and deeply involved with world affairs, and comes to anyone who desires to bring peace to the planet. The best way to reach Yogananda is through meditation. Meditate while mentally repeating the word *love* and simultaneously holding the intention of contacting him. You may then see a mental vision of Yogananda and have the experience of conversing with him. During this conversation, you could ask Yogananda for Divine direction about your spiritual path or any other question or concern you may have.

PART II

Invocations
for Specific
Needs and
Issues

Prayers to Connect with Multiple Divinities, for Specific Needs

The suggested prayers listed here are just that: suggested. They simply represent one of many ways to invoke the deities who oversee the situation with which you need help. You may wish to try out these invocations as they're printed first and then take note of the results. Then, in subsequent prayers, modify the wording as your inner guidance directs.

You don't need to use fancy or poetic verbiage to invoke the divinities. All you need to do is mentally say their names and ask them for help with whatever issue, problem, or situation you're concerned about. You can use the list in Part III to quickly research which divinities specialize in the particular area you're interested in. It's better to say a simple prayer as soon as you notice you need assistance, instead of trying to come up with the "perfect" prayer. The sooner we call for help, the easier a situation is to resolve. This is similar to calling the fire department at the first sign of smoke instead of waiting until it's turned into an uncontrollable blaze.

When you say these prayers, it's important to hold in mind the question or situation for which you're seeking help. You can either say the prayers mentally or speak them aloud. These prayers are even more effective if you can hold them in your hand, so you might want to photocopy the pages from this book that the applicable prayers are on, or handwrite them. Say each prayer three times, with full conscious awareness of each word, and then put the printed prayer in a special place such as on your altar, on an inside window ledge facing the moonlight, or beneath your pillow or bed.

When you're done saying a prayer, thank the divinities for their help. Mentally check in with them often. They're available to you while your situation is being resolved, so it's wise to seek counsel from them, talk to them about your successes or challenges, and ask them questions.

Remember, you cannot bother a divinity, and you're not pulling them off of something or someone more important. You and your situation are of vital importance to them, now and always. They're able to be with everyone who calls upon them simultaneously; and they can have a unique, personalized experience with each person. Ascended masters and archangels have no limiting beliefs, so they have no time or space restrictions. It's their great pleasure to help you, because when *you're* at peace, the world is one person closer to being peaceful as a whole.

Abundance

To increase your supply of money, food, time, opportunities, or whatever you desire more of, here's a powerful prayer. As you say this prayer, utter each name slowly, feeling the energy of each name:

> *"Beloved Abundantia . . . Damara . . . Dana . . . Ganesh . . . Lakshmi . . . and Sedna . . . thank you for the abundant supply in my life, overflowing with beautiful opportunities for me to express my Divine light so that others may benefit as well. Thank you for the peace, happiness, and love you bring me. Thank you for all of the time and energy that I have to fulfill my dreams and desires. Thank you for the abundant financial support and supply. I gratefully accept all of your gifts, and ask that you keep them coming."*

Addictions and Cravings

If you're truly ready to release a substance, craving, or addictive pattern from your life, this is a very powerful method. After saying this prayer, you'll likely find that all cravings are gone. Or, you might have one last binge-for-the-road, which leads you to give up the addiction for good.

First, imagine that the item, person, or situation that you want to release is sitting on your lap. Then imagine that it's floating in front of your navel. See or feel all of the cords, webs, and roots extending from your navel to the items you're releasing. Then say this prayer:

"Archangel Raphael, beloved angel of healing!
Babaji, teacher of overcoming the physical world!
Beloved Devi, who cares so deeply!
Shining Maat, bringer of Divine light!
Serapis Bey, overseer of ascension!
Please cut the cords of addictions and cravings from me.
I now fully release any and all patterns of addictions, and
I completely embrace my freedom and physical health."

Clairvoyance

This prayer can help you open, or increase, your ability to see psychically. For extra clairvoyant power, hold a clear quartz crystal up to your third eye (the area between your two eyebrows) while saying this prayer:

"Divine light, please enter my third eye and fill it with illumination, clarity, and the ability to clearly see across the veil. Powerful Apollo, I thank you for opening my third eye! Archangels Haniel, Jeremiel, Raphael, and Raziel, I thank you for your magical Divine energies and assistance with my spiritual sight now! Victorious Horus, thank you for stationing your eye in front of my own, so that I may see multidimensionally like you! Beloved Kuan Yin, I thank you for sending me energy from your third eye to my own so that I may see love in everything and everyone! Dearest Sulis, thank you for invoking the power of my clairvoyant energy! I thank you all for fully opening me up to see truth, beauty, light, and eternal life!"

Clear Communication with God

This powerful prayer can help you clear away blocks so that you can more clearly hear God and your Divine guidance:

"God, I deeply desire a closer relationship and clearer communication with You. I ask for Your assistance in opening me up so that I can clearly hear, see, feel, and know Your messages for me. Jesus . . . Moses . . . Babaji . . . Yogananda . . . you demonstrated the ability to clearly hear God during your lifetimes on Earth. I ask your assistance in teaching me your ways. Please work with me so that I'm fully open to hearing God's messages and that I trust what I hear. Thank you, God. Thank you, Jesus. Thank you, Moses. Thank you, Babaji. Thank you, Yogananda."

Connecting with the Fairies

If you'd like to see fairies, or at least feel a greater connection with them, try saying this prayer while outdoors. It's especially powerful to say it, mentally or aloud, while you're in an area where wildflowers grow. You'll know that you've successfully made the connection with the fairies when you feel compelled to pick up litter in the outdoors. This is one of the first communications that fairies normally make with humans. If you pick up litter, and treat animals and the environment with great respect, the fairies will show their appreciation by granting you wishes.

"Beloved Dana, goddess of the leprechauns; beautiful Diana, mistress of the wood nymphs; powerful Maeve, queen of the fairies; golden Oonagh, protector of the fairies: I ask your assistance in connecting with the elemental world. Please introduce me to the fairies, and ask them on my behalf how I can get to know them better. I would like to develop a connection to the fairies and elementals, and I ask that you show me the way. Please help my

mind and spiritual vision to be open to communications from their magical realm. Thank you."

Courage

If you feel worried, anxious, afraid, or vulnerable, this prayer can give you more courage *and* protect you and your loved ones from harm.

"Powerful protectors from Heaven. Powerful allies by my side! I need your strength, courage, and protection beside me. Please come to me now!

Thank you, Archangel Michael, for giving me the courage to move forward fearlessly.

Thank you, Ashtar, for protecting me in all ways.

Thank you, Brigit, for helping me be a loving warrior on behalf of my beliefs.

Thank you, Cordelia, for removing stress and tension from my mind and body.

Thank you, Green Tara, for bringing me rapid results to my prayers.

Thank you, Horus, for helping me clearly see the truth of this situation.

Thank you, Kali, for helping me stand my ground.

Thank you, Moses, for helping me be a fearless leader.

Thank you, Saint-Germain, for helping me stay positive, cheerful, and optimistic.

Thank you all for being with me and helping me rise up to, and rise above, all illusions of problems. Thank you for helping me grow and learn from all challenges. Thank you for reminding me to breathe and be centered in peacefulness!"

Finding Your Life's Purpose

Here's a prayer to help you discover your overall life's purpose, as well as get direction about the next step to take. Your prayer will likely be answered with a combination of Divine guidance and signs. Divine guidance includes internal messages such as feelings, thoughts, ideas, and visions that tell you what your heart truly desires. Signs are repetitious messages that you see or overhear coming from sources other than yourself, such as a phrase that you continually see on posters, in newspapers, or that you hear people say. It's best to write down these inner and outer messages and look for a constant theme that will direct you to your next step . . . and overall purpose.

"Archangel Michael . . . Jesus . . . Saint-Germain . . . and Vywamus . . . you can see what is the best next step for me to take. I need to hear, feel, and see this information clearly. I need to have faith in taking this next step. I need to feel courage and excitement about this next step. Thank you for supplying me with information, encouragement, and motivation.

"Archangel Chamuel . . . Brigit . . . Saint Francis . . . Thoth . . . and my higher self . . . beloved and Divine teammates in my life purpose, I am grateful for your clear guidance about my life purpose. I am grateful because I truly believe that I deserve happiness, success, and abundance. I am grateful to know that I am worthy of receiving your help and support. Thank you, God. Thank you, divinities. Thank you all."

Finding Your Soulmate

If you desire a spiritually based romantic relationship, then say this prayer. You can amplify the power of the prayer by first imagining the feeling of being in such a relationship. Imagine that you're with your soulmate and are completely loved and honored. Then say:

"Love gods and goddesses sent from Heaven above; Aengus and Aphrodite, male and female deities signifying beauty and loveliness; Guinevere and Isolt, bringers of magical love: I invite you to my spiritual wedding, wherein I am wed to my soulmate first in spiritual union. I feel my beloved deeply within my body and soul. I send this feeling to my soulmate, and I thank you for delivering these feelings to my beloved as my sacred Valentine message. Thank you for uniting my soulmate and me through the ethers. Thank you for clearly guiding us to find one another. Thank you for bringing us together in blissful union. Thank you for overseeing my love life."

Global Peace

These divinities are already watching over the world, keeping war at bay, and talking with world leaders about peace. Our prayers add a great deal to the momentum of global peace. Each prayer adds so much, is definitely powerful, and is very needed. On behalf of the rest of us who live on this planet, thank you for saying this prayer (or one like it) on a regular basis:

"God is peace . . . God is everywhere . . . therefore, peace is everywhere, in truth. This is the truth. And I thank You, God, for this truth. Thank You for sending your ministers of peace to watch over us now and always. Thank you, Archangel Chamuel, for helping all of us find inner peace. Thank you, Buddha, for being the embodiment of peace. Thank you, Forseti, for successfully resolving conflict peacefully. Thank you, Kuan Ti, for your wise counsel with world leaders. Thank you, Maitreya, for replacing all anger with joy. Thank you, Saint Francis, for helping us stay devoted to God's peace. Thank you, Jesus, for overseeing humanity. Thank you, Serapis Bey, for helping us all live at our highest potential. Thank you, Yogananda, for helping us feel Divinely loved."

If war is pending, or has already broken out, then say this prayer:

"Archangel Michael, I ask that you intervene in this situation to the degree that it is affecting me. Please release the spirits and lower energies in this area, and take them to the light for healing and transmutation. Ashtar, please watch over our planet and ensure its peace, balance, and intactness. Athena, please intervene to the degree that this situation involves me, and work with the world leaders toward alternatives to war. Ishtar, please help the people to show leadership and strength. Kuan Ti, please help us all have the foresight to know the effects tomorrow of our actions today. Thank you, heavenly leaders. Thank you, God. Thank you for the peace surrounding and within this world. Thank you for the peace within the hearts of everyone, everywhere."

You can add to this prayer a visualization of Archangel Michael holding a vacuum above the planet, lifting up all negative energy from any geographical areas experiencing conflict.

Healing a Child

If a child is in need of healing or relief from pain, then say this prayer. It's been said that when parents pray on behalf of their children, those prayers are answered first in Heaven.

I also recommend handwriting the prayer and placing it face up on a cabinet or shelf in the child's bedroom. If the child is old enough to say prayers, ask the child to say the prayer with you:

"Thank you, God, for my child's perfect health. Thank you for peace within my child's body. Thank you, Archangel Raphael, for your powerful healing energy, which heals everything rapidly with each breath my child takes. Thank you, Damara, for gently comforting and reassuring me and my child. Thank you, Hathor, for clearly instructing me on how I can best help my child. Thank you,

Mother Mary, for watching over all of us and sending us your Divine healing love."

Healing a Pet

If your cat, dog, or other animal has a physical challenge, then you'll want to call upon the great animal healers in Heaven to help and heal. As you say this prayer, either look at your pet in the flesh or in your mind, or gaze at a photo of your beloved furry friend:

"Healers in Heaven, I love [name of pet] *with all my heart. Please join my love with yours and send it to* [name of pet]. *Dearest Aine, I ask that you surround my pet with your bright silver energy of peace and happiness. Dearest Raphael, I ask that you encircle my pet with your emerald-green energy of health and wellness. Dearest Dana, I ask that you help my pet's system to be balanced and in its natural state of vitality. Dearest Saint Francis, I ask that you communicate with my pet and let me know what I can do to bring my pet comfort.*

"Thank you, Aine . . . Raphael . . . Dana . . . Saint Francis . . . for your healing work. Thank you for my pet's perfect health. Thank you for my pet's comfort. Thank you for lifting our spirits. I now surrender this situation to you and God with complete faith and confidence."

Healing for Oneself

If you experience a physical challenge, it's comforting to know that you have access to powerful healers. This prayer can supplement any other spiritual or medical treatment you're implementing:

"Beloved Jesus, loving healer of God . . . beloved Aine, loving healer of God . . . beloved Archangel Raphael, loving healer of God

. . . beloved Archangel Zadkiel, loving healer of God . . . beloved Saint Therese, loving healer of God. The love of God is now inside of me. I am completely filled and healed with the love of God. Jesus . . . Aine . . . Raphael . . . Zadkiel . . . Therese . . . I am so grateful for the ministering, healing, and comfort that you bring to me . . . thank you for surrounding and filling me completely with positive energy. Thank you for clearing and cleaning me completely. I am now completely well. I now feel absolutely wonderful, filled with the spirit of love in all ways. I am energized. I am happy. I am rested and refreshed. Thank You, God. Thank you, Divine healers."

Protection and Guidance for Your Child

If you're worried about your child, say this prayer of protection and guidance to ease your mind, and to help protect and guide your child:

"Dana . . . Hathor . . . Ishtar . . . Mother Mary . . . mothering goddesses and teachers of parents, I surrender my worries to you. Please nurture my child and this situation [describe your concerns] *so that we may all be joyful and feel peace. Please teach me how to best guide my child. Please direct my words and actions so that I speak my truth in a way that my child will hear. Please help me stay centered in faith and courage.*

"Archangel Michael . . . Artemis . . . Kuan Yin . . . Vesta . . . powerful protectors of children, I ask that you closely watch over my child [say your child's name]. *Thank you for closely monitoring and protecting my child. Thank you for ensuring my child's safety, happiness, and health. Thank you for guiding my child in a direction that brings about blessings, wellness, meaning, and abundance. Thank you, Dana . . . Hathor. . . Ishtar . . . Mother Mary . . . Archangel Michael . . . Artemis . . . Kuan Yin . . . Vesta . . . for protecting and guiding my child. I am truly grateful."*

Resolving Conflict

If you've had a disagreement with someone, or you're in the middle of a conflict of some kind, then it's a good idea to ask for help from the divinities. This prayer isn't to help you win or to get the other person to apologize. It's simply to create peace and forgiveness all the way around:

"Beloved helpers in Heaven, please come to me now . . . Archangel Raguel, heavenly minister of fairness . . . Athena, goddess of peaceful solutions . . . Forseti, overseer of truth and justice . . . Guardian angels of [name the person or persons involved in the conflict] *. . . I thank you for your intervention. I ask that you deliver my message to everyone involved in this situation and let them know of my desire for peace. I ask for a peaceful and rapid resolution, and I surrender this entire situation to you and God, knowing that it is already resolved. I know that only peace exists in truth, and that peace is everywhere, including within this situation and within everyone involved. Please clearly guide me as to my role in this peaceful resolution. Thank you."*

Weight Loss

Healthy weight loss involves exercise and healthful eating. This prayer can boost your motivation to exercise, and reduce your cravings for high-fat foods:

"Heaven, help me stay fit and toned, and be a healthy weight. I ask that the powerful spiritual motivators and coaches please come to me now. Apollo . . . Oonagh . . . Serapis Bey . . . I need your masterful help. Please increase my desire to exercise. Please help me find an exercise program that easily fits my schedule, budget, and interests. Please help me take the first step. Please help me get the support of my family so that I may exercise with their blessings.

Please help me see results so that I may stay encouraged.

"Archangel Raphael . . . Babaji . . . Devi . . . Maat . . . I now surrender to you my cravings for high-fat and sugary foods. . . . You know which foods and drinks are healthful and which are not for my body. I ask that you adjust my cravings so that I only desire healthful foods and drinks. Please increase my motivation to eat light, nutritious foods. Please increase my motivation to drink light, natural beverages.

"Thank you for overseeing my physical health and well-being."

PART III

A List of Whom to Call Upon for Specific Needs

Calling Upon Archangels and Ascended Masters

When a specific need arises, turn to the list on the following pages so that you'll know which archangels and ascended masters to call upon. You can use this information in many ways. For instance, you can place your hand over the divinities' names listed under your specific need. As you hold your hand there, think the thought, *Beloved Divinities, I need your help, love, and assistance with* [describe the particular situation]. *Thank you for this Divine intervention.*

You can also take the list and look up and read about each Divinity in Part I. In that way, your knowledge of the archangel or ascended master deepens. The combination of having personal experiences and interaction with a Divinity, along with reading about that being's history and background, makes for a rich relationship.

A quick way to deal with an issue is to look at the list corresponding to your situation and say each being's name as you do your prayer or even sing it. The intention of your prayer is more important than the words or method. The divinities hear your prayerful intention, and they respond with love immediately. No prayer is denied or ignored. After all, the archangels and ascended masters help us because they're enacting God's plan of peace on Earth, one person at a time. If they can help you to find peace through their Divine intervention into some Earthly situation, then it's their sacred pleasure to do so.

This list covers a broad range of human needs and situations. If you don't see a listing for your specific situation, then find one that closely matches it. You can also pray for guidance as to which Divinity would be most appropriate for your cause.

Abundance
Abundantia
Coventina
Damara
Dana
Ganesh
Lakshmi
Sedna

Emergency Supply
- Aeracura
- Green Tara

Addictions, help with
Archangel Raphael
Babaji
Devi
Maat
Serapis Bey

Aesthetics
Lakshmi

Airline Pilots and Crew
Saint Therese

Alchemy
Archangel Raziel
Archangel Uriel
Dana
Lugh
Maeve
Merlin
Saint-Germain

Animals

Breeding, Pregnancy, and Birthing
- Diana

Communication
- Saint Francis

Finding Lost Pets
- Archangel Raphael

Healing
- Aine
- Archangel Raphael
- Dana
- Saint Francis

Horses, healing and protecting
- Maeve

Protecting
- Aine
- Archangel Ariel
- Artemis
- Sedna

Answered Prayers
Archangel Sandalphon
Jesus
Kuan Yin

Arguments, resolving
Archangel Raguel
Athena
Forseti

Aromatherapy
Maeve

Artists and Artistic Projects
Aeracura
Archangel Gabriel
Archangel Jophiel
Athena
Ganesh
Hathor
Lugh
Serapis Bey

Ascension
Serapis Bey

Attractiveness
Aphrodite
Hathor
Maeve
Oonagh

Aura-Soma Therapy
Melchizedek

Authority Figures—dealing with them fearlessly
Moses
Saint-Germain

Balance
Buddha

Beautiful Thoughts
Archangel Jophiel

Beauty
Aphrodite
Archangel Jophiel
Hathor
Isis
Lakshmi
Maeve
Oonagh

Blessings
Krishna
Sulis

Blindness
Jesus
Saint Padre Pio

Breakups, healing from
Isolt

Breathwork
Babaji

Cabala, studying and understanding
Solomon

Camping
Artemis

Career
Archangel Chamuel
Lu-Hsing

Celebration
Cordelia
Hathor

Ceremonies
Nemetona

Chakra Clearing
Archangel Michael
Melchizedek

Children
Adoption
- Archangel Gabriel
- Artemis
- Mother Mary

Attention Deficit Disorder
(ADD or ADHD)
- Archangel Metatron

Childbirth, painless
- Diana

Conception and Fertility
- Aine
- Archangel Gabriel
- Artemis
- Dana
- Hathor
- Ishtar
- Mother Mary

Crystal Children
- Archangel Metatron
- Mother Mary

Custody
- Damara

Determining Gender of
Unborn Baby
- Archangel Sandalphon

Guiding
- Damara

Healing
- Archangel Raphael
- Damara
- Jesus
- Mother Mary
- Saint Therese

Indigo Children
- Archangel Metatron
- Melchizedek
- Mother Mary

In General
- Archangel Metatron
- Artemis
- Kuan Yin
- Mother Mary

Mother-Son Relationship
- Horus
- Mother Mary

Overcoming Acting-Out
Behavior
- Saint Francis

Parenting
- Dana
- Hathor
- Ishtar
- Mother Mary

Protection
- Archangel Michael
- Artemis
- Kuan Yin
- Melchizedek
- Vesta

Those Who Professionally
Help Children
- Archangel Metatron
- Mother Mary

Twins
- Diana

Clairvoyance, increasing
Apollo
Archangel Haniel
Archangel Jeremiel
Archangel Raphael
Archangel Raziel
Horus
Kuan Yin
Sulis

Clear Communication with God
Babaji
Jesus
Moses
Yogananda

Clear Thinking and Clarification
Maat

Commitment
To a Love Relationship
- Aphrodite

To One's Beliefs
- Archangel Michael
- Maat

Compassion
Archangel Zadkiel
Ishtar
Kuan Yin
Tara

Cooperation from Other People
Archangel Raguel

Cosmetics
Hathor

Courage
Archangel Michael
Ashtar
Brigit
Cordelia
Horus
Kali
Moses
Saint-Germain
Green Tara

Crafts and Craftspeople
Athena
Lugh

Cravings, eliminating or reducing
Apollo
Archangel Raphael

Crystals
Melchizedek
Merlin

Dancing
Hathor
Oonagh

Decision-Making
El Morya
Hathor

Defending the Unfairly Treated
Archangel Raguel

Determination
Kali

Detoxification
Archangel Raphael
Devi
Melchizedek

Direction
Archangel Michael
Jesus
Saint-Germain
Vywamus

Divination
Merlin
Thoth

Divine Guidance
Jesus
Moses
Oonagh

Divine Light
Vesta

Divine Love
Jesus
Yogananda

Divine Magic
Archangel Ariel
Archangel Raziel
Dana
Isis
Lugh
Maat
Merlin
Solomon
Thoth

Divorce
Healing from
• Isolt

Making Decisions about
• Damara

Dolphins
Coventina
Sedna

Dreams
Archangel Jeremiel
Sedna

Earth Changes
Archangel Uriel
Ashtar
Melchizedek

Ego, overcoming
Buddha
Jesus
Moses
Sanat Kumara

Elementals (fairies, leprechauns, etc.); seeing, hearing, and connecting with
Dana
Diana
Maeve
Oonagh

Emergency Money
Aeracura
Green Tara

Employment
Lu-Hsing

Empowerment
Archangel Raguel
Pele

Encouragement
Vywamus

Energy
Archangel Michael
Pele
Sanat Kumara

Energy Work and Healing
Melchizedek
Merlin

Engagement (in a love relationship)
Aphrodite

Environmental Concerns
Aine
Archangel Ariel
Artemis
Coventina
Saint Francis

Esoteric Information
Archangel Raziel
Ashtar
Melchizedek

Exercise
Apollo
Oonagh
Serapis Bey

Extraterrestrials
Ashtar

Eyesight
Archangel Raphael
Horus
Jesus
Saint Padre Pio
Sulis

Fairness
Forseti

Faith, increasing
Aine
Archangel Raphael
El Morya
Jesus
Moses

Family

Divorce Involving Children
- Damara

Harmony
- Archangel Raguel
- Damara

Femininity

Aphrodite

Feminine Power and Strength

Artemis
Brigit
Isis
Kali
Maeve
Pele

Feng Shui

Melchizedek

Financial Investments

Abundantia

Fingers, healing

Sedna

Fire Control

Vesta

Flowers

Cordelia
Krishna
Saint Therese

Focus

Kali
Kuthumi
Saint-Germain

Food

Abundant Supply
- Jesus
- Lakshmi
- Sedna

Purifying and Spiritualizing
- Krishna

Forgiveness

Archangel Zadkiel
Jesus
Saint Padre Pio

Freedom for Falsely Accused Prisoners and Prisoners-of-War

Kuan Ti

Gardening
Cordelia
Krishna
Saint Therese
Sulis

Gentleness
Ishtar
Kuan Yin

Goal-Setting and Achievement
Pele
Saint-Germain

Good Fortune
Abundantia

Grace
Archangel Haniel

Gracefulness
Aphrodite

Grieving, comfort and healing for
Archangel Azrael

Groundedness
El Morya

Hands, healing
Sedna

Happiness, lasting
Lakshmi

Happy Endings
Apollo
Archangel Uriel

Harmony
In Families
- Archangel Raguel
- Damara

In General
- Archangel Uriel

In Groups
- Archangel Raguel

While Traveling
- Archangel Raphael

Healers, guidance and support for
Archangel Raphael
Jesus
Melchizedek
Saint John of God
Saint Padre Pio

Healing

Abilities
- Archangel Haniel
- Archangel Raphael
- Jesus
- Maeve
- Saint Padre Pio

Addictions
- Archangel Raphael
- Babaji
- Devi
- Maat
- Serapis Bey

Animals
- Aine
- Archangel Ariel
- Archangel Raphael

Blindness
- Jesus
- Saint Padre Pio

Cardiovascular and Heart
- Saint John of God

Eyesight
- Archangel Raphael
- Jesus
- Saint Padre Pio
- Sulis

From Grief
- Archangel Azrael

From Relationship Breakup, Divorce, or Separation
- Isolt

Hands and Fingers
- Sedna

Horses
- Maeve

In General
- Archangel Raphael
- Ishtar
- Jesus
- Saint John of God
- Saint Padre Pio
- Saint Therese
- Sanat Kumara
- Vywamus
- Yogananda

Menopause
- Maeve

People Emotionally
- Archangel Zadkiel
- Jesus
- Lugh
- Saint John of God
- Vywamus

People Physically
- Aine
- Archangel Raphael
- Archangel Zadkiel
- Jesus
- Saint John of God
- Saint Therese

People Who Are Hospitalized for Mental or Physical Reasons
• Saint John of God

Premenstrual Syndrome (PMS)
• Maeve

Relationships
• Aine

With Aromatherapy
• Maeve

With Aura-Soma
• Melchizedek

With Crystals
• Merlin
• Melchizedek
• Saint-Germain

With Energy Work
• Merlin
• Melchizedek

With Water
• Coventina
• Sulis

Healthful Eating
Apollo

Hiking
Artemis

Home
Money for Household Needs
• Damara
• Lakshmi

Space Clearing the Back- and Front-Yard Area
• Nemetona

Space Clearing the Home Interior
• Archangel Michael
• Archangel Raphael
• Artemis
• Kuan Ti
• Kuan Yin
• Lakshmi
• Saint-Germain
• Saint John of God
• Sanat Kumara
• Solomon
• Vesta

Humor
• Maitreya

Hurricanes, diverting and dispelling
Sedna

Inspiration
Vywamus

Integrity
Maat

Interior Decorating
Archangel Jophiel

Intuition, increasing
Artemis
Sedna

Inventors
Aeracura

Job Interviews
Lu-Hsing

Journalism
Archangel Gabriel

Joy
Aine
Buddha
Cordelia
Isis
Maitreya
Saint John of God

Justice, attaining
Athena
Ida-Ten

Kindness
Kuan Yin
Mother Mary

Labyrinths
Archangel Raziel
Melchizedek
Nemetona
Solomon

Laughter
Maitreya

Leadership
Melchizedek
Moses

Legal Matters, resolving
Forseti
Ida-Ten
Kuan Ti

Lesbian Concerns
Diana

Life Changes
Archangel Jeremiel
Cordelia

Melchizedek
Saint-Germain
Solomon

Life Purpose
Archangel Chamuel
Archangel Michael
Brigit
Kuthumi
Saint Francis
Saint-Germain
Thoth
Vywamus

Marriage
Aphrodite
Ishtar

Mathematics
Melchizedek
Thoth

Meaning in Life, increasing
Devi
Saint Francis

Longevity
White Tara

Lost Items, finding
Archangel Chamuel
Archangel Zadkiel

Mechanical Problems, fixing
Apollo
Archangel Michael

Love, receiving and giving
Kuan Yin
Maitreya

Medicine Wheels
Nemetona

Mediation of Disputes
Archangel Raguel

Manifesting
Aeracura
Archangel Ariel
Archangel Raziel
Babaji
Damara
Jesus

Meditation
Buddha
Jesus
Yogananda

Memory Enhancement
Archangel Zadkiel
Kuthumi

Menopause
Maeve

Menstrual Cycle
Maeve

Mercy
Kuan Yin
Mother Mary

Miracles
Jesus
Moses

Money
Abundantia
Damara
Dana
Ganesh
Lakshmi
Sedna

    Emergency Supply
    • Aeracura
    • Green Tara

Moon Energy
Archangel Haniel

Motivation
    For Life Purpose
    • Archangel Michael
    • Kuthumi
    • Vywamus

    To Eat Healthfully
    • Apollo
    • Archangel Michael

    To Exercise
    • Apollo
    • Oonagh
    • Serapis Bey

Music and Musicians
Aengus
Archangel Gabriel
Archangel Sandalphon
Hathor
Kuan Yin
Lugh
Serapis Bey

Newly Deceased Loved Ones (help and comfort for their souls)
Archangel Azrael

Obstacles, avoiding and overcoming
Ganesh
Tara

Orderliness and Organization
Archangel Metatron
Archangel Raguel
Kuthumi
Maat

Parties
Hathor

Passion, increasing
Aengus
Aine
Aphrodite
Isolt
Pele
Vesta

Peace
Global
- Archangel Chamuel
- Babaji
- Buddha
- Forseti
- Kuan Ti
- Maitreya
- Saint Francis
- Serapis Bey
- Yogananda

Household
- Ganesh

Personal
- Babaji
- Buddha
- Forseti
- Kuthumi
- Lakshmi
- Maitreya
- Saint Francis
- Serapis Bey
- Yogananda

Perseverance
Kuthumi
Saint-Germain

Physical Fitness
Apollo
Oonagh
Serapis Bey

Pilots
Saint Therese

Playfulness
Aine

Poetry
Lugh

Poise
Archangel Haniel

Pregnancy
Determining Gender of
Unborn Baby
- Archangel Sandalphon

Harmonious
- Hathor

Painless Childbirth
- Diana

Twins
- Diana

Premenstrual Syndrome (PMS)
Maeve

Prioritizing
Pele

Procrastination, overcoming
Archangel Michael
Pele
Vywamus

Promotions at Work
Lu-Hsing

Prophecies about World Events
Kuan Ti

Prophetic Abilities, increasing
Apollo
Archangel Jeremiel
Merlin
Serapis Bey
Thoth

Protection
Against Deceit and
Manipulation
- Maat

Against Psychic Attack
- Athena
- El Morya
- Ishtar
- Melchizedek
- Saint-Germain

From Lower Energies
- Archangel Michael
- Ishtar

From Religious or Spiritual
Persecution
- Babaji
- Ida-Ten

In General
- Archangel Michael
- Artemis
- Ashtar
- Athena
- Brigit
- Kali
- Lugh
- Tara

Legal
- Forseti
- Ida-Ten

Of Animals
- Aine
- Archangel Ariel
- Artemis
- Maeve

Of Children in Particular
- Artemis
- Kuan Yin
- Vesta

Of Oceans and Lakes from Pollution
- Archangel Ariel
- Sedna

Of Spiritual Centers
- Ida-Ten

Of Travelers and Their Luggage
- Archangel Raphael

Of Valuables
- Abundantia

Of Women in Particular
- Aine
- Artemis
- Brigit
- Kuan Yin

Psychic Abilities, increasing
Apollo
Archangel Haniel
Archangel Raziel
Coventina
Kuan Ti
Merlin
Thoth

Purification and Cleanliness
Coventina
Maat

Radio Careers, Interviews—dealing with
Archangel Gabriel

Raises in Salary
Lu-Hsing

Recordkeeping
Archangel Metatron

Relationships
All Aspects
- Devi
- Ishtar
- Krishna
- Oonagh

Attracting
- Aengus
- Aphrodite
- Guinevere
- Isolt

Breakups, Divorce, and
Separation, healing from
- Isolt

Building and Strengthening
- Archangel Chamuel

Commitment
- Aphrodite

Healing
- Aine

Honest Communication
- Pele

Increasing Warmth Within
- Brigit
- Vesta

Lesbian
- Diana

Marriage
- Ishtar

Mother-Son
- Horus

Romance
Aengus
Aphrodite
Guinevere
Isolt
Krishna

Sacred Geometry
Thoth

Sailing
Sedna

Self-Esteem
Archangel Michael
Dana
Diana
Isis

Sexuality
Aphrodite
Ishtar
Pele

Shape-Shifting
Merlin

Simplifying Your Life
Babaji

Slowing Down from a Hectic Pace
Archangel Jophiel

Solutions to Difficulties
Apollo
Archangel Michael
Archangel Uriel
Jesus
Lugh

Soulmate Relationships, finding
Aengus
Archangel Chamuel
Hathor

Spirit Releasement
Archangel Michael
Archangel Raphael
Kuan Ti
Melchizedek
Sanat Kumara
Solomon

Spirituality
Awakening
- Krishna

Devotion
- Saint Francis

Enlightenment
- Buddha
- Kuan Yin

- Sanat Kumara
- White Tara

Growth
- Babaji
- Buddha
- Saint Padre Pio

Understanding
- Archangel Metatron
- Archangel Uriel
- Ashtar
- Buddha
- Jesus
- Sanat Kumara
- Solomon
- Green Tara

Sports
Apollo

Standing Your Ground
Horus

Strength
Horus

Stress Management
Cordelia

Students and Studying
Archangel Uriel
Archangel Zadkiel

Support
    For Those Who Are Grieving
- Archangel Azrael

Swimming
Coventina
Sedna

Talents, discovering
Archangel Michael
Vywamus

Teaching
Archangel Metatron
Archangel Michael
Mother Mary
Thoth

Television Careers, Interviews—dealing with
Archangel Gabriel

Tenacity
Kali

Time-Warping
Merlin

Travelers (protection, orderliness, and harmony)
Archangel Raphael
Ganesh

Truth
Forseti
Ida-Ten
Maat

Twins
Diana

Unity of all Religious Beliefs
Babaji
Yogananda

Valuables, protecting
Abundantia

Vegetarianism
Krishna

Vitality
Archangel Michael

War, avoiding or stopping
Archangel Michael
Ashtar
Athena
Ishtar
Kuan Ti

Warmth—in relationships, body, and environment
Brigit
Vesta

<u>**Water**</u>
<u>Abundant Supply of</u>
- Coventina

<u>Cleanliness</u>
- Coventina

<u>Protecting the Oceans and Lakes</u>
- Archangel Ariel
- Sedna

<u>**Weather**</u>
<u>In General</u>
- Archangel Uriel
- Ishtar

<u>Increasing Sunshine</u>
- Apollo

<u>**Wedding Ceremonies**</u>
Ganesh

<u>**Weight Loss**</u>
Apollo
Archangel Raphael
Oonagh
Serapis Bey

<u>**Whales**</u>
Coventina
Sedna

<u>**Wisdom**</u>
Ganesh
Solomon

<u>**Women**</u>
<u>Protecting</u>
- Aine
- Archangel Michael
- Artemis

<u>**Women's Issues**</u>
Guinevere

<u>**Worthiness**</u>
Archangel Michael
Dana

<u>**Writers and Writing Projects**</u>
Archangel Gabriel
Archangel Metatron
Archangel Uriel
Athena
Ganesh
Thoth

<u>**Yoga Practice**</u>
Babaji
Yogananda

APPENDIX

Glossary of Terms

Archangel—A powerful overseer of other angels, and a manager of specialized functions, such as clearing away fear, protecting humans, or healing. Different religions and spiritual groups talk about different numbers of archangels. Some groups claim there are only four, some say seven, and other groups say there are an infinite number.

Ascended Master—A great spiritual teacher or healer who walked upon the Earth as a human, and who continues to help . . . from his or her heavenly home.

Ascension—The process of fully remembering one's unity with God and the one Spirit that unites all people in brother and sisterhood. Those who ascend may bypass the death process, and their entire body may be lifted into Heaven along with their soul. *Ascension* is also a term used for spiritual awakening and enlightenment.

Avatar—A living human who is fully enlightened. Usually, avatars are miracle workers and spiritual teachers.

Bodhisattva—In Buddhism, this term refers to a person who has become enlightened to the point of being eligible for Buddhahood.

Cabala—An ancient Judaic mystical text that discusses secrets of divination and manifestation with symbols, numbers, and wisdom. (Also spelled *Kaballah, Kabalah.*)

Chohan—A term used among Theosophists and in New Age circles to describe an ascended master's specialty. For instance, someone might be a Chohan of love and enlightenment.

Deity—A being who is revered for their spiritual contribution while on Earth, and for their help that continues from the vantage point of Heaven.

Divinity—A being who works directly with the Creator or Universal Force to help Earth and her inhabitants. The terms *deity* and *divinity* can be used interchangeably.

God—When the term appears with a lower-case "g" (god), it means an aspect of the Creator (God)—which has a capital "G." This being has a male energy or identity.

Goddess—An aspect of God the Creator that has a female energy or identity.

Great White Brotherhood—Leaders in Heaven who oversee the safety and spiritual direction of Earth and her inhabitants, and also the light-workers who help upon Earth. The term does not refer to Caucasian males. It comes from the white light that surrounds the members of the council, which includes goddesses.

Lightworkers—A living human who feels called to help Earth and her inhabitants in a way that uses spiritual energy. For instance, a light-worker might feel called upon to engage in healing, teaching, or artistic work to help make the planet a better place.

Shape-Shifting—The ability to take on a markedly different physical appearance. Sometimes this is done at will, sometimes unconsciously.

Space Clearing—Clearing negative energy out of a specific place, such as a home, office, room, temple, backyard, or front yard.

Spirit Releasement—Clearing negative energy out of a person or animal's body and aura.

Triple Goddess—Three aspects of femininity: the virgin, mother, and crone. Triple goddesses have personality or behavior aspects of the virgin, who represents purity, sweetness and innocence. The same goddess may also have a side to her that is the mother, which means she acts matronly and nurturing. A third aspect of the same goddess that may show up is the "crone," which means that she may have a dark and angry side to her, as well as a wise teacher aspect.

Bibliography

Ann, Martha and Imel, Dorothy Myers, *Goddesses in World Mythology: A Biographical Dictionary* (Oxford University Press, 1993, Santa Barbara, CA)

Betz, Hans Dieter, *The Greek Magical Papyri in Translation* (The University of Chicago Press, 1986, Chicago)

The Bible, New King James Version

Boucher, Sandy, *Discovering Kwan Yin: Buddhist Goddess of Compassion* (Beacon Press, 1999, Boston)

Brooke, Elisabeth, *Medicine Women: A Pictorial History of Women Healers* (Quest Books, 1997, Wheaton, IL)

Bunson, Matthew, *Angels A to Z: A Who's Who of the Heavenly Host* (Three Rivers Press, 1996, New York)

Cannon, Dolores, *Jesus and the Essenes* (Ozark Mountain Publishing, 1999, Huntsville, AR)

————. *They Walked with Jesus* (Ozark Mountain Publishing, 2000, Huntsville, AR)

Charlesworth, James H. (ed.), *The Old Testament Pseudepigrapha: Apocalyptic Literature & Testaments* (Doubleday, 1983, New York)

Coulter, Charles Russell and Turner, Patricia, *Encyclopedia of Ancient Deities* (McFarland & Company, Inc., 1997, Jefferson, North Carolina)

A Course in Miracles (Foundation for Inner Peace, 1992, Mill Valley, CA)

Craughwell, Thomas J., *Saints for Every Occasion: 101 of Heaven's Most Powerful Patrons* (Stampley Enterprises, Inc., 2001, Charlotte, NC)

Davidson, Gustav, *A Dictionary of Angels: Including the Fallen Angels* (The Free Press, 1967, New York)

Doreal (Translator and Interpretor), *The Emerald Tablets of Thoth-the-Atlantean* (Source Books, Inc., 1996, Nashville, TN)

Epstein, Perle S., *Oriental Mystics and Magicians* (Doubleday, 1975, New York)

Eshelman, James, *The Mystical & Magical System of the A∴A∴ The Spiritual System of Aleister Crowley & George Cecil Jones Step-by-Step* (The College of Thelema, 2000, Los Angeles)

Forrest, M. Isidora, *Isis Magic: Cultivating a Relationship with the Goddess of 10,000 Names* (Llewellyn Publications, 2001, St. Paul, MN)

Hall, Manly P., *The Secret Teaching of All Ages: An Encyclopedic Outline of Masonic, Hermetic, Qabbalistic, and Rosicrucian Symbolical Philosophy* (The Philosophical Research Society)

James, Simon, *The World of the Celts* (Thames and Hudson, 1993, London)

Jones, Kathleen, *Women Saints: Lives of Faith and Courage* (Burns & Oates, 1999, Kent, England)

Johnson, K. Paul, *The Masters Revealed: Madame Blavatsky and the Myth of the Great White Lodge* (State University of New York Press, 1994, Albany)

Jothi, Rev. Dharma, Telephone interview, October 16, 2002

Kyokai, B. D., *The Teaching of Buddha* (Society for the Promotion of Buddhism, 1966, Tokyo)

La Plante, Alice and Clare, *Heaven Help Us: The Worrier's Guide to the Patron Saints* (Dell Publishing, 1999, New York)

Laurence, Richard (translator), *The Book of Enoch the Prophet* (Adventures Unlimited Press, 2000, Kempton, IL)

Lewis, James R., and Oliver, Evelyn Dorothy, *Angels A to Z* (Visible Ink Press, 1996, Detroit)

Lopez, Jr., Donald (ed.), *Religions of China in Practice* (Princeton University Press, 1996, Princeton, NJ)

Makarios, Hieromonk of Simonos Petra, *The Synaxarion: The Lives of Saints of the Orthodox Church*, Vol. 1 (Chalkidike, 1998)

Markale, Jean, *Merlin: Priest of Nature* (Inner Traditions, Int'l., 1995, Rochester, VT)

Mathers, S.L. MacGregor, S.L., *The Key of Solomon the King*, Translated reprint (Samuel Weiser, 1986, York Beach, ME)

Matthews, Caitlin, *The Celtic Book of Days: A Celebration of Celtic Wisdom* (Gill & Macmillan, Ltd., 1995, Dublin, Ireland)

McCoy, Edain, *Celtic Myth & Magick: Harnessing the Power of the Gods and Goddesses* (Llewellyn Publications, 2002, St. Paul, MN)

Monaghan, Patricia, *The New Book of Goddesses and Heroines* (Llewellyn Publications, 2000, St. Paul, MN)

Morgan, James C., *Jesus and Mastership: The Gospel According to Jesus of Nazareth as Dictated Through James Coyle Morgan* (Oakbridge University Press, 1989, Tacoma, WA)

Ronner, John, *Know Your Angels* (Mamre Press, 1993, Murfreesboro, TN)

Runyon, C. P., *The Book of Solomon's Magick* (Church of the Hermetic Sciences, Inc., 2001, Silverado, CA)

"Saint-Germain, comte de," Encyclopaedia Britannica.

Sakya, Jnan B., *Short Descriptions of Gods, Goddesses, and Ritual Objects of Buddhism and Hinduism in Nepal* (Handicraft Association of Nepal, 1998, Kathmandu, Nepal)

Savedow, Steve (Editor and Translator), *Sepher Razial Hemelach: The Book of the Angel Raziel* (Samuel Weiser, Inc., 2000, York Beach, ME)

Starck, Marcia, *Women's Medicine Ways: Cross-Cultural Rites of Passage* (The Crossing Press, 1993, Freedom, CA, 1993)

Stewart, R. J., *Celtic Gods, Celtic Goddesses* (Cassell & Co., 2000, London)

Telesco, Patricia, *365 Goddess: A Daily Guide to the Magic and Inspiration of the Goddess* (HarperSanFrancisco, 1998, New York)

Trobe, Kala, *Invoke the Goddess: Visualizations of Hindu, Greek & Egyptian Deities* (Llewellyn Publications, 2000, St. Paul, MN)

Vessantara, *Meeting the Buddhas: A Guide to Buddhas, Bodhisattvas, and Tantric Deities* (Birmingham, England, 1998)

Yu, Chun-fang, *Kuan-yin: The Chinese Transformation of Avalokitesvara* (Columbia University Press, 2000, New York)

SELF-HELP RESOURCES

The following list of resources can be used to access information on a variety of issues. The addresses and telephone numbers listed are for the national headquarters; look in your local yellow pages under "Community Services" for resources closer to your area.

In addition to the following groups, other self-help organizations may be available in your area to assist your healing and recovery for a particular life crisis not listed here. Consult your telephone directory, call a counseling center or help line near you, or contact:

AIDS

CBC National AIDS Hotline
(800) 342-2437

Children with AIDS (CWA) Project of America
(800) 866-AIDS
(24-hour hotline)

The Names Project— AIDS Quilt
(800) 872-6263

Project Inform
19655 Market St., Ste. 220
San Francisco, CA 94103
(415) 558-8669

PWA Coalition
50 W. 17th St.
New York, NY 10011

Spanish HIV/STD/ AIDS Hotline
(800) 344-7432

TTY (Hearing Impaired) AIDS Hotline (CDC National HIV/AIDS)
(800) 243-7889

ALCOHOL ABUSE

Al-Anon Family Headquarters
1600 Corporate Landing Parkway
Virginia Beach, VA 23454-5617
(800) 4AL-ANON

Alcoholics Anonymous (AA)
General Service Office
475 Riverside Dr.
New York, NY 10115
(212) 870-3400

Children of Alcoholics Foundation
164 W. 74th St.
New York, NY 10023
(800) 359-COAF

Meridian Council, Inc.
Administrative Offices
4 Elmcrest Terrace
Norwalk, CT 06850

Mothers Against Drunk Driving (MADD)
(254) 690-6233

National Association of Children of Alcoholics (NACOA)
11426 Rockville Pike, Ste. 100
Rockville, MD 20852
(301) 468-0985
(888) 554-2627

National Clearinghouse for Alcohol and Drug Information (NCADI)
P.O. Box 234
Rockville, MD 20852
(301) 468-2600

National Council on Alcoholism and Drug Dependence (NCADD)
12 West 21st St.
New York, NY 10010
(212) 206-6770
(800) 475-HOPE

Women for Sobriety
(800) 333-1606

ALZHEIMER'S DISEASE

Alzheimer's Association
919 N. Michigan Ave., Ste. 1100
Chicago, IL 60611
(800) 621-0379
www.alz.org

Alzheimer's Disease Education and Referral Center
P.O. Box 8250
Silver Spring, MD 20907
(800) 438-4380
adear@alzheimers.org

Eldercare Locator
927 15th St. NW, 6th Fl.
Washington, DC 20005
(800) 677-1116

CANCER

National Cancer Institute
(800) 4-CANCER

CHILDREN'S ISSUES

Child Molestation

Child Help USA/Child Abuse Hotline
232 East Gish Rd.
San Jose, CA 95112
(800) 422-4453

Prevent Child Abuse America
200 South Michigan Ave., Ste. 17
Chicago, IL 60604
(312) 663-3520

Crisis Intervention

Boy's Town National Hotline
(800) 448-3000

Children of the Night
P.O. Box 4343
Hollywood, CA 90078
(800) 551-1300

Covenant House Hotline
(800) 999-9999

Kid Save Line
(800) 543-7283

Youth Nineline
(referrals for parents/teens
about drugs, homelessness,
runaways)
(800) 999-9999

Missing Children

**Missing Children...
HELP Center**
410 Ware Blvd., Ste. 710
Tampa, FL 33619
(800) USA-KIDS

**National Center for
Missing and Exploited
Children**
699 Prince St.
Alexandria, VA 22314
(800) 843-5678

Children with Serious
Illnesses
(fulfilling wishes):

Brass Ring Society
National Headquarters
213 N. Washington St.
Snow Hill, MD 21863
(410) 632-4700
(800) 666-WISH

Make-a-Wish Foundation
(800) 332-9474

CO-DEPENDENCY

**Co-Dependents
Anonymous**
(602) 277-7991

**DEATH/GRIEVING/
SUICIDE**

Grief Recovery Institute
P.O. Box 461659
Los Angeles, CA
90046-1659
(323) 650-1234
www/grief-recovery.com

**National Hospice and
Palliative Care
Organization**
1700 Diagonal Rd.,
Ste. 300
Alexandria, VA 22314
(703) 243-5900
www.nhpco.org

**SIDS (Sudden Infant
Death Syndrome) Alliance**
1314 Bedford Ave.,
Ste. 210
Baltimore, MD 21208

**Parents of Murdered
Children**
(recovering from violent
death of friend or family
member)
100 E 8th St., Ste. B41
Cincinnati, OH 45202
(513) 721-5683

Survivors of Suicide
Call your local Mental
Health Association for the
branch nearest you.

**AARP Grief and Loss
Programs**
(202) 434-2260
(800) 424-3410 ext. 2260

DEBTS

Credit Referral
(information on local credit
counseling services)
(800) 388-CCCS

Debtors Anonymous
General Service Board
P.O. Box 888
Needham, MA 02492-0009
(781) 453-2743
www.debtorsanonymous.org

DIABETES

**American Diabetes
Association**
(800) 232-3472

**DOMESTIC VIOLENCE
National Coalition
Against Domestic
Violence**
P.O. Box 34103
Washington, DC
20043-4103
(202) 745-1211

**National Domestic
Violence Hotline**
P.O. Box 161810
Austin, TX 78716
(800) 799-SAFE

DRUG ABUSE

**Cocaine Anonymous
National Referral Line**
(800) 347-8998

**National Helpline of
Phoenix House**
(cocaine abuse hotline)
(800) 262-2463
(800) COCAINE
www.drughelp.org

**National Institute of
Drug Abuse (NIDA)**
6001 Executive Blvd.,
Rm. 5213
Bethesda, MD 20892-9561
Parklawn Building
(301) 443-6245
(for information)
(800) 662-4357 (for help)

**World Service Office,
Inc. (CA)**
3740 Overland Ave., Ste. C
Los Angeles, CA
90034-6337
(310) 559-5833
(800) 347-8998
(to leave message)

EATING DISORDERS

Overeaters Anonymous
National Office
P.O. Box 44020
Rio Rancho, NM
87174-4020
(505) 891-2664

GAMBLING

Gamblers Anonymous
New York Intergroup
P.O. Box 7
New York, NY 10116-0007
(212) 903-4400

HEALTH ISSUES

Alzheimer's Association
919 N. Michigan Ave.,
Ste. 1100
Chicago, IL 60611-1676
(800) 621-0379

**American Chronic Pain
Association**
P.O. Box 850
Rocklin, CA 95677
(916) 632-0922
www.theacpa.org

**American Foundation
of Traditional Chinese
Medicine**
P.O. Box 330267
San Francisco, CA 94133
(415) 392-7002

**American Holistic Health
Association**
P.O. Box 17400
Anaheim, CA 92817
(714) 779-6152
e-mail: ahha.org
www.ahha@healthy.net

Chopra Center for Well Being
La Costa Resort and Spa
2013 Costa Del Mar
Carlsbad, CA 92009
(760) 494-1600
www.chopra.com

The Fetzer Institute
9292 West KL Ave.
Kalamazoo, MI 49009
(616) 375-2000

Hippocrates Health Institute
1443 Palmdale Court
West Palm Beach, FL 33411

Hospicelink
190 Westbrook Rd.
Essex, CN 06426
(800) 331-1620

Institute for Noetic Sciences
P.O. Box 909
Sausalito, CA 94966
(415) 331-5650

The Mind-Body Medical Institute
Francis St., Ste. 1A
Boston, MA 02215
(617) 632-9525

National Health Information Center
P.O. Box 1133
Washington, DC 20013-1133
(800) 336-4797

Optimum Health Care Institute
6970 Central Ave.
Lemon Grove, CA 91945
(619) 464-3346

Preventive Medicine Research Institute
Dean Ornish, M.D.
900 Bridgeway, Ste. 2
Sausalito, CA 94965
(415) 332-2525

HOUSING RESOURCES

Acorn
(nonprofit network of low- and moderate-income housing)
739 8th St., S.E.
Washington, DC 20003
(202) 547-9292

IMPOTENCE

Impotence Institute of America
P.O. Box 410
Bowie, MD 20718-0410
(800) 669-1603
www.impotenceworld.org

MENTAL HEALTH

American Psychiatric Association of America
www.psych.org

Anxiety Disorders Association of America
www.adaa.org

The Help Center of the American Psychological Association
www.helping.apa.org

The International Society for Mental Health Online
www.ismho.org

Knowledge Exchange Network
www.mentalhealth.org

National Center for PTSD
www.dartmouth.edu/dms/ptsd

National Alliance for the Mentally Ill
www.nami.org

National Depressive and Manic-Depressive Association
www.ndmda.org

National Institute of Mental Health
www.nimh.nih.gov

PET BEREAVEMENT

Bide-A-Wee Foundation
410 E. 38th St.
New York, NY 10016
(212) 532-6395

Holistic Animal Consulting Centre
29 Lyman Ave.
Staten Island, NY 10305
(718) 720-5548

RAPE/SEXUAL ISSUES

Rape, Abuse, and Incest National Network
(800) 656-4673

Safe Place
P.O. Box 19454
Austin, TX 78760
(512) 440-7273

National Council on Sexual Addictions and Compulsivity
1090 S. Northchase Parkway, Ste. 200
South Marietta, GA 30067
(770) 989-9754

Sexually Transmitted Disease Referral
(800) 227-8922

SMOKING

Nicotine Anonymous
P.O. Box 126338
Harrisburg, PA 17112
(415) 750-0328
www.nicotine-anony-mous.org

STRESS REDUCTION

The Biofeedback & Psychophysiology Clinic
The Menninger Clinic
P.O. Box 829
Topeka, KS 66601-0829
(913) 350-5000

New York Open Center
(In-depth workshops to invigorate the spirit)
83 Spring St.
New York, NY 10012
(212) 219-2527

Omega Institute
(a healing, spiritual retreat community)
150 Lake Dr.
Rhinebeck, NY 12572-3212
(845) 266-4444 (info)
(800) 944-1001 (to enroll)

The Stress Reduction Clinic
Center for Mindfulness
University of Mass-achusetts Medical Center
55 Lake Ave. North
Worcester, MA 01655
(508) 856-1616
(508) 856-2656

ABOUT THE AUTHOR

Doreen Virtue holds B.A., M.A., and Ph.D. degrees in counseling psychology. She's the author of over 50 books and oracle card decks dealing with spiritual topics. Best known for her work with the angels, Doreen is frequently called "The Angel Lady."

Doreen has appeared on *Oprah, CNN, The View,* and other television and radio programs, and writes regular columns for *Woman's World* magazine. Her products are available in most languages worldwide, on Kindle and other eBook platforms, and as iTunes apps. For more information on Doreen and the workshops she presents, please visit: www.AngelTherapy.com.

You can listen to Doreen's live weekly radio show, and call her for a reading, by visiting HayHouseRadio.com®.

Hay House Titles of Related Interest

YOU CAN HEAL YOUR LIFE, the movie,
starring Louise L. Hay & Friends
(available as a 1-DVD program and an expanded 2-DVD set)
Watch the trailer at: www.LouiseHayMovie.com

THE SHIFT, the movie,
starring Dr. Wayne W. Dyer
(available as a 1-DVD program and an expanded 2-DVD set)
Watch the trailer at: www.DyerMovie.com

▲▼▲

THE ESSENTIAL LAW OF ATTRACTION COLLECTION,
by Esther and Jerry Hicks (The Teachings of Abraham®)

THE ESSENTIAL LOUISE HAY COLLECTION, by Louise Hay

THE ESSENTIAL WAYNE DYER COLLECTION, by Dr. Wayne W. Dyer

All of the above are available at your local bookstore,
or may be ordered by contacting Hay House (see next page).

▲▼▲

We hope you enjoyed this Hay House book. If you'd like to receive
our online catalog featuring additional information on Hay House books
and products, or if you'd like to find out more about the
Hay Foundation, please contact:

Hay House, Inc., P.O. Box 5100, Carlsbad, CA 92018-5100
(760) 431-7695 or (800) 654-5126
(760) 431-6948 (fax) or (800) 650-5115 (fax)
www.hayhouse.com® • www.hayfoundation.org

▲▼▲

Published and distributed in Australia by: Hay House Australia Pty. Ltd., 18/36
Ralph St., Alexandria NSW 2015 • *Phone:* 612-9669-4299
Fax: 612-9669-4144 • www.hayhouse.com.au

Published and distributed in the United Kingdom by: Hay House UK, Ltd., Astley
House, 33 Notting Hill Gate, London W11 3JQ • *Phone:* 44-20-3675-2450
Fax: 44-20-3675-2451 • www.hayhouse.co.uk

Published and distributed in the Republic of South Africa by: Hay House SA
(Pty), Ltd., P.O. Box 990, Witkoppen 2068 • *Phone/Fax:* 27-11-467-8904
www.hayhouse.co.za

Published in India by: Hay House Publishers India, Muskaan Complex, Plot No.
3, B-2, Vasant Kunj, New Delhi 110 070 • *Phone:* 91-11-4176-1620
Fax: 91-11-4176-1630 • www.hayhouse.co.in

Distributed in Canada by: Raincoast, 9050 Shaughnessy St.,
Vancouver, B.C. V6P 6E5 • *Phone:* (604) 323-7100 • *Fax:* (604) 323-2600
www.raincoast.com

▲▼▲

Take Your Soul on a Vacation

Visit www.HealYourLife.com® to regroup, recharge,
and reconnect with your own magnificence.
Featuring blogs, mind-body-spirit news, and
life-changing wisdom from Louise Hay and friends.

Visit www.HealYourLife.com today!

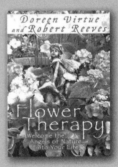